THE EIGHT ZULU KINGS

THE EIGHT ZULU KINGS

John Laband

Jonathan Ball Publishers
JOHANNESBURG & CAPE TOWN

Published in South Africa in 2018 by
JONATHAN BALL PUBLISHERS
A division of Media24 (Pty) Ltd
PO Box 33977
Jeppestown
2043

ISBN 978-1-86842-838-0
ebook ISBN 978-1-86842-839-7

*Every effort has been made to trace the copyright holders and
to obtain their permission for the use of copyright material.
The publishers apologise for any errors or omissions and would be grateful
to be notified of any corrections that should be incorporated in future editions of this book.*

Twitter: www.twitter.com/JonathanBallPub
Facebook: www.facebook.com/JonathanBallPublishers
Blog: http://jonathanball.bookslive.co.za/

Cover by MR Design
Design and typesetting by Triple M Design
Set in 11.5/15pt Van Dyck MT Std

Printed by *paarlmedia*, a division of Novus Holdings

CONTENTS

❆

ABBREVIATIONS AND ACRONYMS

ANC	African National Congress
BAA	Bantu Authorities Act
BPP	British Parliamentary Papers
CNC	Chief Native Commissioner
Codesa	Convention for a Democratic South Africa
Contralesa	Congress of Traditional Leaders of South Africa
EFF	Economic Freedom Fighters
IFP	Inkatha Freedom Party
KLA	KwaZulu Legislative Assembly
MK	Umkhonto we Sizwe
NAD	Native Affairs Department
NNC	Natal Native Congress
NPC	Natal Provincial Council
SACP	South African Communist Party
SAIC	South African Indian Congress
SANNC	South African Native National Congress
UDF	United Democratic Front
ZAR	Zuid-Afrikaansche Republiek (South African Republic/ Transvaal)
ZTA	Zululand Territorial Authority

�֎

MAPS

INTRODUCTION

❀

THE LION

Thirty-five years ago I witnessed a spectacle of potent symbolism. I was among the guests of the reigning Zulu[1] monarch, *Ingonyama* ('Lion' in an honorific sense, meaning His Majesty) Goodwill Zwelithini kaBhekuzulu.[2] We were gathered on Saturday, 20 August 1983 to attend the official opening of oNdini, the partially restored *ikhanda*, or military homestead and royal residence, of his great-great-grandfather, King Cetshwayo kaMpande.

In 1873 Cetshwayo had ordered the construction of oNdini, envisioned as his principal *ikhanda*, in the thorn-bush country of the Mahlabathini plain on the northern banks of the White Mfolozi River, right in the heart of the Zulu kingdom. The *ikhanda* was an immense, elliptical assemblage of close to 1 400 beehive-shaped thatched huts enclosing a vast parade ground. A palisade constructed of a double row of stout timbers two and a half metres high enclosed the whole complex, which had an outer circumference of some 2 169 metres.[3] ONdini was built on a gentle slope allowing for natural drainage down to the Mbilane stream, and the slight elevation of the site exposed it to cooling breezes and presented sweeping views across the level plain towards the ring of hills to the north. Nowadays, the plain in the vicinity of oNdini is criss-crossed with roads, railways and power lines and is thickly cluttered with dwellings. The ugly, sprawling modern town of Ulundi laps about its site ever more densely, and the airport is only five kilometres away to the west. But in 1873 there was little to distract the eye other than grazing herds of royal cattle and a further eight, somewhat smaller *amakhanda* erected in the vicinity of oNdini. Just southwest across the White Mfolozi eight more *amakhanda* were clustered in the emaKhosini valley, or the 'Valley of the Kings'. This was hallowed ground reserved for royal homesteads (*imizi*) and *amakhanda* because it was the sacred burial place for Zulu, Ntombela, Phunga, Mageba, Ndaba, Jama and Senzangakhona, the semi-legendary *amakhosi* (chiefs) of the petty Zulu chiefdom who were the ancestors of King Shaka, the founder of the Zulu kingdom.

The layout of oNdini was identical in almost every particular except its mammoth scale to that of the other *amakhanda* in the emaKhosini valley and the Mahlabathini plain, as well as a further ten *amakhanda* positioned across the kingdom as regional centres of royal authority and as the mobilisation points for the age-grade regiments of warriors, or *amabutho*. At the top of the *ikhanda* and directly opposite the main gate across the open parade ground was the royal enclosure, or *isigodlo*, which was divided into two sections of about 50 huts in all. In the central, 'black' section were the king's private sleeping hut and his large council hut. Exceptionally, Cetshwayo had also built a rectangular, four-roomed house of European design where he held audiences. More traditionally, the 'black' enclosure also contained the huts of his wives, or *amakhosikazi*, as well as those of his favoured *umndlunkulu*, or maids of honour, who had been given to him as tribute. They cooked for and waited on him and the *amakhosikazi*, and served him as concubines. The two 'white' sections on either side accommodated his deceased father King Mpande's widows and other miscellaneous female relations of the royal house, royal children, those *umndlunkulu* who had not drawn his fancy, and the *izigqila*. These last-mentioned were women who had been captured in war or were the wives or daughters of men the king had executed. Not only were they obliged to be at the sexual disposal of men of the royal house, but they also performed all the menial domestic chores in the *isigodlo*. Their days were filled cultivating the gardens, fetching water, gathering firewood, cooking food and waiting on the women of high status whose clay chamber pots they emptied.

Two enormous *izinhlangothi*, or wings of huts, three or more rows deep, sprung out from either side of the *isigodlo* and swept around the great parade ground. There several thousand *amabutho* (in the sense of warriors or members of age-grade regiments) were quartered when they rotated in and out to serve their king. A number of cattle enclosures were built in the parade ground against the inner palisade of reeds and grasses that fenced off the warriors' huts. Directly in front of the *isigodlo* at the top end of the parade ground was the *isibaya*, the special cattle enclosure sacred to the king. There Cetshwayo and the members of his inner royal council (*umkhandlu*) would discuss matters of state and he would pass judgment on wrongdoers. It was also the place where he would perform the religious rituals required of the monarch, sacrifice cattle to propitiate the royal *amadlozi*, or shades of the ancestors, and officiate over the great national ceremonies.

The *ikhanda*'s name, oNdini, derived from the Zulu word for a rim, as of a bowl, and was an alternative name for the mighty range of the Drakensberg – the beetling eastern escarpment of the high South African central plateau – which the Zulu also called the uKhahlamba, or 'Barrier of Spears'. The connotations were therefore an assertion of the place's impenetrability. Unfortunately, this proved to be misleading. When the British invaded the Zulu kingdom in 1879, the final battle of the Anglo-Zulu War was fought on 4 July in the Mahlabathini plain. Once they had routed the Zulu army, British mounted units set all the *amakhanda* in the plain ablaze as they moved from hut to hut with flaming torches of grass. ONdini itself made an enormous bonfire that smouldered for four days. For the Zulu looking down from the surrounding hills at the great columns of smoke, it was a clear sign that their kingdom had fallen.

The site of oNdini was abandoned, but not forgotten. In 1906 the Mahlabathini plain was thrown open to white occupation,[4] and in the course of the 20th century farmers ploughed over much of the remains of the *izinhlangothi*, the great wings of warrior huts. But agriculture left the *isigodlo* untouched. There the circular floors of the huts, made of a mixture of the earth from ant-heaps compressed with cow dung, and polished to a blackish dark-green, glossy smoothness, had been baked solid in the conflagration that consumed oNdini. So too had the hearths, circular cavities in the centre of the floors with raised, flattened edges. The burned wooden

3

posts of the huts left holes in the floors indicating where they had stood.

When archaeologists began their painstaking work on the *isigodlo* area, accurate reconstruction of the circular, domed huts was consequently feasible. In 1981 local people were engaged to exercise their traditional hut-building skills in recreating some three dozen beehive-shaped huts over the remains of the baked floors. Thousands of curved intersecting saplings and sticks were used in the construction of each hut and were tied together with grass where they crossed, rather like compact wickerwork. A neat thatch of long, tough grass covered this framework.

And so it was that we were congregated there on 20 August 1983 to celebrate their work and to wander among the huts of the *isigodlo*, as King Cetshwayo himself might have done, and to crawl through the low entrance into his very own hut. It was already late in the afternoon, though, before a spine-tingling ceremony was performed in the newly fenced *isibaya* in front of the *isigodlo*, where numbers of cattle had been driven into the enclosure.

Cattle were central to traditional Zulu culture and religious ritual. In pre-colonial Zululand they were the prime indicator of wealth in a society that had few other means of accumulating it. Through the custom of *ilobolo*, when a man married he handed cattle over to his wife's family to formalise the compact and to compensate them for the loss of the young woman's labour. The Zulu language contains hundreds of cattle terms by which to identify the distinctive shapes of horns, the presence or absence of a hump, and the numerous different colours and patterns. Favourite cattle had praise-names and were even trained to respond to whistled commands. Iron Age Bantu-speakers migrating southwards through Africa had introduced domestic cattle into southern Africa about two thousand years before, and Nguni cattle, with their spreading horns and multicoloured skins, were the favoured indigenous strain in the Zulu country. Most prized was a beast with a milky-white hide and distinctive dark muzzle, nose, ears and hooves known as *inyonikayiphumuli*, 'the bird that never rests'. Before the British conquest in 1879, all cattle born of this colour were the property of the king, but with Cetshwayo's defeat the British seized his herd of white cattle as booty. A small number survived nevertheless, and in 1983 a viable breeding herd had recently been re-established to take their place in the reconstructed *isibaya* at oNdini.

It is believed that cattle found in the realm of the *amadlozi* are white, and this association enhances their significance in rituals associated with the ancestors. While we watched respectfully from outside the *isibaya*, King Goodwill Zwelithini entered the enclosure wearing a kilt of animal tails with a leopard skin draped across his shoulders. Nowadays, rare and expensive leopard skins are reserved exclusively for royalty, but they did not have quite that special association among the first Zulu kings, who very seldom wore them, but only sat on them. A necklace of leopard or lion claws encircled the *Ingonyama*'s neck. During the 19th century Zulu kings had distributed such necklaces to their councillors and favourites, but now they adorn only members of the royal and chiefly houses. On his head was a padded band and flaps of leopard skin and the tall slate-grey tail feather of the blue crane – reserved for monarchs and distinguished warriors.[5] Grasping his great white oxhide shield and sacred spear, he began to dance among the white Nguni cattle as he invoked, informed and praised the shades of his royal ancestors. It was only correct that he should be arrayed in all his finery while he did so, for wearing gala dress has everything to do with the next world, since it shows proper respect for those who have gone before and is in itself a form of praise.

With the frisson of a historian, I was only too conscious that it was 104 years since a Zulu king had last danced in this very spot, and that in the intervening years the Zulu monarchy had suffered terrible vicissitudes and near total eclipse. This late 20th-century royal resurgence was therefore all the more remarkable, even if the 'king' I was witnessing dance for his royal ancestors was only tenuously such. In terms of the Union of South Africa's legislation of 1927, he enjoyed only the honorary status of Paramount Chief of the Zulu People,[6] first conferred on 20 March 1952 on his father, King Cyprian. Nevertheless, ever since 1972, when the apartheid government had set up the 'Bantu homeland' of KwaZulu – and then in 1977 declared it a self-governing territory within the Republic of South Africa – 'King' Goodwill Zwelithini had been the constitutional monarch of this evolving 'Bantustan'.[7]

In 1983 I could not have predicted how Goodwill Zwelithini's royal status, recognised by the apartheid regime, would fare under a post-apartheid government that was both democratic and avowedly socialist. I did not foresee that in 1994 an amendment to the Interim Constitution of South Africa would 'provide for the institution, role, authority and status' of the traditional Zulu monarch in the Province of KwaZulu-Natal.[8] Nor did I anticipate that the final South African Constitution of 1996 would provide for the recognition of the 'institution, status and role of traditional leadership',[9] let alone that the Traditional Leadership and Governance Framework Act of 2003 would define only three recognised positions of traditional leadership, namely, king, senior traditional leader and headman/woman.[10] In terms of the same Act, the Commission on Traditional Leadership Disputes and Claims (the Nhlapo Commission) would be set up to investigate all the existing paramountcies officially recognised prior to 1994 – including that of the Zulu – and to determine which qualified as kingships or queenships. President Jacob Zuma announced the Nhlapo Commission's findings in 2010, and seven kings were recognised: those of the abaThembu, amaXhosa, amaMpondo, amaZulu, Bapedi, amaNdebele wakwaManala and amaNdebele, and vhaVenda. In 2016 the president added the Rain Queen of the Balobedu, the closest exemplar of divine monarchy in southern Africa and renowned far and wide as the great rainmaker.[11]

Today, the handsome, 35-year-old Zulu king I once watched joyously dancing in the *isibaya* at oNdini is a much heavier, less supple man of close to 70 years, his face deeply crevassed by life and its vicissitudes. It must be some compensation to him, nevertheless, that his then questionable royal status has now been constitutionally recognised and is assured. Not only that, in 2017 he was among the 6 150 traditional leaders in South Africa who received in excess of R650 million paid out in government stipends. As a king, he received R1 126 057.[12] On top of this stipend, traditional leaders also receive allowances and other benefits paid at the discretion of the individual provinces. King Goodwill Zwelithini is the leading beneficiary nationally, making him better off financially than any other South African king. In the 2015/2016 financial year alone the Zulu Royal Household received the R57.6 million necessary to maintain the king's accustomed lifestyle.[13]

Besides the advantages of wealth, the respect and loyalty Goodwill Zwelithini supposedly commands among some 10 million Zulu give him a potentially far more numerous following than that of any of his fellow royals, even if it is more enthusiastic in the traditionalist countryside than in the urban areas. He also benefits from the abiding prestige of a Zulu monarchy that is widely remembered as having been more potent than any other in the pre-colonial era, and is celebrated for its outstanding military prowess and determined resistance to the forces of white imperialism. All these many strengths and advantages combine to make Goodwill Zwelithini indisputably the premier king among those recognised in modern-day South Africa.

Even so, it is not hard to conceive the incredulous derision with which Shaka, the formidable and all-powerful founder of the Zulu kingdom, would have viewed the present king's emasculated royal prerogatives, closely constrained as they are by the constitution of a democratic republic. Indeed, for all the royal protocol and privilege that lap him about, King Goodwill Zwelithini is essentially no more than a ceremonial figure embodying Zulu traditions and customs who, by his own admission, valiantly attempts to promote age-old cultural values in rapidly changing times.[14]

With this in mind, my objective in writing this book is to explain why the Zulu monarchy has followed the trajectory it has from its robust beginnings to its present politically constrained (though lavishly cushioned) circumstances. In doing so, I shall first situate it in the wider context of African kingship to show how the first four Zulu kings, namely, Shaka kaSenzangakhona (r. 1816–1828), Dingane kaSenzangakhona (r. 1828–1840), Mpande kaSenzangakhona (r. 1840–1872) and Cetshwayo kaMpande (r. 1872–1884) essentially conformed in their royal ideology, style and exercise of power to the practices of other pre-colonial rulers. More specifically, I shall describe how they enlarged the Zulu kingdom and confronted their African neighbours, and how effectively they dealt with ever-present internal threats to their rule. During their reigns, the expanding colonial world impinged ever more aggressively on the Zulu kingdom, and accordingly my focus will shift to considering with what degree of success they confronted this mortal challenge.

Next, I shall discuss how Cetshwayo and Dinuzulu kaCetshwayo (r. 1884–1913) were violently overthrown, deposed and exiled by the forces of colonialism, and will indicate that their fate was by no means unique among other formerly independent African kings. Likewise, I shall show that their exertions, and those of their successors – Solomon Nkayishana Maphumuzana kaDinuzulu (r. 1913–1933), Nyangayezizwe Cyprian Bhekuzulu kaSolomon (r. 1933–1968) and Goodwill Zwelithini kaBhekuzulu (r. 1968–present) – to retain or regain something of their royal status under white rule followed a pattern familiar elsewhere in colonial Africa, and entailed many humiliating compromises in return. Finally, I shall contemplate the Zulu monarchy in the parlous transitional phase to post-apartheid rule, and shall investigate why – unlike so many other African monarchies in the post-colonial era – it has survived to take its place in the new order, albeit with only symbolic and ceremonial prerogatives.

In probing the history of the Zulu monarchy up to the time of writing, it will be the eight kings themselves who take centre stage. How they acted was inevitably constrained by the particular historical circumstances in which they found themselves, and by the prevailing culture of the society in which they operated. Even so, despite such limitations, all adopted individual courses of action as monarchs that reflected their personalities and sharply exposed their individual strengths and flaws of character as expressed in their powers of statesmanship – or in their political ineptitude. Some were unfortunate despite their most sagacious and prudent endeavours, while others clearly reaped what they had sown. All faced extraordinary challenges in a southern Africa that has changed out of all recognition since Shaka's founding of the Zulu kingdom two centuries ago.

KING SHAKA
kaSENZANGAKHONA

❁ ❁ ❁

CHAPTER ONE

BORN OUT OF SHAKA'S SPEAR

African monarchy in one form or another is an exceptionally ancient institution. An abundant array of monarchs ruled over much of the continent before yielding to colonial conquest, their titles as romantically exotic to Western ears as the maharajas, maharaos, maharanas, nizams and nawabs of princely India. A clockwise trawl of African rulers commencing in the northeast of the continent would have netted the *negus* of Ethiopia, the *kyabazinga* of Busoga, the *mwenemutapa* of Mutapa, the *ngwenyana* of Swaziland, the *muhongo* of Matamba, the *ngola* of Ndongo, the *alafin* of Oyo, the *ahosu* of Dahomey, the *emir* of Ilorin, the *sarki* of Kano, the *sultan* of Sokoto, and the *bey* of Tunis. Rulers were predominantly male, but there were instances in principally patriarchal African societies of a woman exceptionally exercising power. The actual sway of a ruler could be extremely localised, and it is best to think of these petty potentates as 'chiefs'. A 'paramount chief' exercised a much wider, if still fairly loose, sway over a conglomeration of other chiefs and tributaries that recognised the overarching authority of his particular ruling house and him as their overlord. Most powerful of all was the person we would call a 'king'. He ruled over a sizeable territory in which conquered chiefs and tributaries were incorporated into a relatively centralised state, with its panoply of courtiers, administrators and soldiers obedient to his command.

The tradition of monarchy of this type in Africa stretches back thousands of years to Narmer, the ruler of Upper Egypt who conquered Lower Egypt around 2950 BC and united the white and red crowns in the *pschent*, the double crown of the pharaohs. After Narmer there were pharaohs in Egypt for two and a half millennia until 30 BC, when Cleopatra VII memorably committed suicide rather than adorn a Roman triumph and the conquerors executed her teenaged son and co-ruler, Ptolemy XV Caesarion. But the snuffing-out of pharaonic Egypt was far from being the end of monarchy in the Nile valley as far south as the Ethiopian highlands, or along the Mediterranean littoral north of the Sahara Desert. In Nubia, the upper Nile valley south of Egypt, the rulers of the successive kingdoms of Kerma, Kush and Meroë kept the pharaonic style of monarchy alive from 1750 BC to AD 350. When Meroë finally fell it was to the Christian kingdom of Aksum to the south, centred on the Ethiopian highlands. The ancient traditions of Aksum were preserved by the Solomonid dynasty which came to power in AD 1270 and endured until the last emperor of Ethiopia was overthrown by communist soldiers in 1974, seven hundred years later. The Arabs, who by AD 711 had wrested all of North Africa from the Red Sea to the Atlantic from the faltering Eastern Roman (Byzantine) Empire, thereafter ruled over their conquered lands as Muslim monarchs well into the 20th century, with a king still reigning in Morocco today.

Ancient African monarchies were not confined, however, to these regions. In the Sahel – the semiarid region on the southern borders of the Sahara that merges into the grazing lands of the savannah – three great empires anchored on the Niger River supplanted each other in turn between the eighth and late sixteenth centuries: Ghana, Mali and Songhai. To the east of these empires lay the kingdom of Kanem-Bornu, whose origins were as old as those of Ghana, while to their south were a number of West African forest kingdoms founded contemporaneously with the Middle Ages in Europe. South of the equator, large kingdoms also emerged more than half a millennium ago, such as Kongo and Ndongo (in what is now northern Angola), and a number arose even earlier around the Great Lakes. The highlands of south-central Africa were dominated by the 12th-century kingdom of Zimbabwe which was eventually subsumed by the Mutapa kingdom.

Further south, however, the formation of kingdoms began only in the latter half of the 18th century, considerably later than in many other parts of sub-Saharan Africa. King Goodwill Zwelithini is the eighth Zulu monarch, and the Zulu kingdom dates from 1816. Compare that to some other contemporary African kings whose status is recognised, as is Goodwill Zwelithini's, in the constitution of their countries. Otumfo Nana Osei II is the 16th Asantehene of Asante in modern-day Ghana, and his kingdom was founded in 1701. Ronald Muwenda Mutebi II is the 36th Kabaka of Buganda in Uganda. The first of his line was Kato Kinto, who reigned in the very first years of the 14th century. As for Ewuare II, the 39th Oba of Benin in Nigeria, his line goes back to Eweka I in the late 12th century. Compared to kings of such ancient pedigree, the Zulu king is very much a parvenu.

Yet we must be cautious here, since those royal lineages mentioned above are not quite what they seem. Take Benin, for example. It was Ewuare I, who reigned from about 1440 to 1473, who consolidated royal power and turned Benin into a great kingdom. The first eleven Obas before him were only minor rulers. So too were Shaka's chiefly forebears, who, by the same token, if added to the Zulu list of kings, could putatively take the royal line back into the late 16th century. And what credence can we put in the accuracy of these impressive king-lists, especially when they stretch back over multiple generations? Even when there are surviving ancient written records and inscriptions, as is the case with the Egyptian pharaohs, there is often considerable uncertainty regarding chronology and the correct ordering of the succession of rulers. How much more tentative and unreliable is the case with the lines of African kings in those sub-Saharan societies that, until the colonial period, were without writing![1]

With the arrival of missionaries and administrative officials it became possible to record in writing the memories of individuals, either of their own experiences or of those passed down directly from the older generation.[2] However, oral history such as this stretched back only so far, and for events in the deeper past it is necessary to rely on oral tradition passed down over the generations. In every African kingdom – including that of the Zulu – a tradition is preserved of the origin of the ruling dynasty that asserts the abiding claim of a single descent line to the sole right to rule. Kings, elders, praise-singers and the like are all living repositories of this sanctioned tradition. Yet just how much of this 'history' is authentic and to what extent it is mythical is a complicated, specialist business to unravel, and the answers are seldom satisfactory.

In 1832 Dr Andrew Smith visited the Zulu kingdom and from enquiries made on the spot drew up the first written attempt at Shaka's genealogy.[3] At the beginning of the 20th century the colonial magistrate James Stuart began recording the invaluable oral testimony of nearly 200 mainly Zulu informants and noted down three further versions.[4] And in 1929 a missionary and pioneer anthropologist, the Reverend AT Bryant, compiled no fewer than 11 versions of the genealogy of the early, pre-Shakan Zulu rulers drawn from the works of missionaries and officials, as well as from the testimony of five members of the Zulu royal house (including King Cetshwayo himself), and came up with his own preferred likely line of descent.[5] More recently, in 1996 the Zulu historian MZ Shamase published his own favoured royal genealogy.[6]

And where does this leave us? Only with an all but undisputed genealogy based on oral history from Shaka to his father, Senzangakhona, grandfather Jama and great-grandfather Ndaba. After those three generations, oral tradition takes over from oral history and multiple possible versions of royal genealogy begin to surface. As Pixley Seme said in 1925 of the line of descent of the House of Senzangakhona: 'It goes very far back in the history of the Zulu country, until it merges ... with the fables (*izinganekwane*) of the place.'[7] This is just as much the case with the Zulu monarchy as it with those of Benin, Buganda and every other African society relying on oral tradition to establish the ancient lineage of its kings. But even when the line of succession is relatively recent and without question – as with the eight Zulu kings from Shaka to the present – 'spin' can play its part. Charles Ballard's official history of the Zulu monarchy, published in 1988, was called *The House of Shaka*, and King Goodwill Zwelithini is regularly referred to as descending from King Shaka. Strictly speaking, that is not true. Shaka had no heir of his loins, and the present Zulu king is descended from Shaka's younger half-brother, Mpande. More correctly, therefore, the royal family should be known as the House of Senzangakhona after the father of the first three Zulu kings. But Senzangakhona sadly lacks the resonance of Shaka's name.

At the height of the battle of Isandlwana, the memorable Zulu victory

The iconic image of 'Chaka King of the Zoolus' drawn by J Saunders King, the hunter-trader who landed in the Zulu country in 1825. It was reworked for publication in 1836, eight years after King's death, and just how accurately it depicts Shaka is debatable.

(NATHANIAL ISAACS, *TRAVELS AND ADVENTURES IN EASTERN AFRICA*, 1836) over the British in the Anglo-Zulu War of 1879, Ntshingwayo kaMahole, the senior Zulu commander, declaimed the praises of Senzangakhona and Shaka. He then held his great war-shield aloft and shook it, shouting out to the *amabutho*: 'This is the *intando* of our people ... You are always asking why this person [Shaka] is loved so much. It is caused by the *intando* of our people.'[8]

Ntshingwayo's meaning would have been clear enough to the *amabutho*, but we need to know that *intando* means 'the will', 'the power of choice', and that its secondary meaning is 'love-charm'. Both meanings in their different ways apply to the war-shield (*isihlangu*), which to this day remains the great cultural icon of the Zulu people. It was held to belong to the king, and not to the bearer. *Amabutho* would 'beg' shields from the king and they were not taken home but kept stored at the *amakhanda*, to be distributed only when the *amabutho* mustered to serve there or go to war. In other words, his war-shield proclaimed that a man belonged to the king and served his will. And since an *isihlangu* was cut from the hide of one of the kingdom's wealth in cattle that were so dear to the shades of the royal ancestors, it compelled the protection in battle of the *amadlozi*, none more illustrious than that of Shaka, the great warrior and founder of the kingdom.

Indeed, the Zulu people to this day declare that their warrior nation was 'born out of Shaka's spear',[9] and his praises, or *izibongo*, celebrate him as a great conqueror:

> The nations he hath all destroyed
> Whither shall he now attack?
> He! Whither shall he now attack?
> He defeats kings
> Whither shall he now attack?
> The nations he hath all destroyed
> Whither shall he now attack?
> He! He! He! Whither shall he now attack?[10]

Yet, for all his undying fame, the reality (as Dan Wylie has deflatingly pointed out) is that 'we know almost nothing for certain about Shaka'.[11] The problem is that we have to rely on the highly embroidered and self-serving accounts of white trader-hunters who actually encountered him, on the despatches of British colonial officials who only learned of him at second hand and were predisposed to swallow and pass on any tale of his savagery, and on necessarily extremely patchy archaeological evidence. We also have the recurrently embellished *izibongo* handed down over the generations that might even 'borrow' striking elements from each other for incorpo-ration, as well as popular and oft-repeated Zulu traditions. Both of these give us a sense of how Shaka has been – and is – perceived by his people. However, neither began to be written down until the later 19th century. As for the systematically recorded oral testimony of hundreds of interview-ees taken down during the very late 19th and early 20th centuries, those interviewed had at best distant childhood memories of the Shakan period, or could only relate what the previous generation had to say of Shaka. And that in itself carries the further problem that, in their hostility, some traditions run against the contemporary trend to laud Shaka, because they come from people who considered themselves the victims, rather than the beneficiaries, of his conquests and rule.

Considering the uncertainty of the evidence, it is no surprise that we cannot be sure of the date of Shaka's birth. It is most often said to have been 1787, although Dan Wylie has persuasively argued for about five years earlier.[122] Shaka was the son of Senzangakhona kaJama, the *inkosi* of the unremarkable Zulu chiefdom in the valley of the White Mfolozi River. Senzangakhona was evidently a spirited and handsome man. His *izibongo* proclaim that

> When he lay down he was like rivers,
> When he got up he was like mountains …
> He whose body was beautiful …
> Whose face had no blemish,
> Whose eyes had no blemish,
> Whose mouth had no blemish …[13]

He was also virile, and tradition tells us that 18 sons were born of Senzangakhona's 15 wives. But here a damaging question hangs over Shaka: was the founder of the Zulu kingdom illegitimate?

This is a crucial question, central to a king's right to rule. It is true that there are societies in Africa without a chief where authority is collective and where it is exercised by a council of elders. All its members are of the same senior age-grade regiment, that is, men of roughly the same age who have gone together through the rituals of initiation into adulthood. However, for probably about the last 1 500 years most of the Bantu-speaking peoples is southern Africa have been living under some form of chieftainship whereby a chief or king imposes his authority over the whole community and takes decisions on its behalf. There are many ways in which such a ruler induces society to accept his authority, but the fundamental requirement is being legitimately descended of the royal lineage. Being of the 'blood royal' proclaims a division between the ruling house, whose members alone are eligible to vie for the chieftainship or kingship, and the great mass of commoners, who have no such claim. The line of royal descent can be matriarchal (as with the Rain Queen of the Balobedu in South Africa), but this is rare in Africa and the Zulu royal line is firmly patriarchal.

The tradition current in the 19th-century royal house, as told by King Cetshwayo, Shaka's nephew, was that when Senzangakhona began his reign, 'he was unmarried; but had a natural son, only a year or two old, by [Nandi], daughter of [Mbhengi kaMhlongo], chief of the [Langeni] tribe, named Chaka, or the "bastard."'[14] Oral testimony had it that Nandi's mother was Mfunda, sister of Phakathwayo, the *inkosi* of the Qwabe and later Shaka's formidable foe. It seems Nandi gave birth to Shaka at her father's Ngugeni *umuzi* on the north bank of the Mhlathuze River near kwaNtoza hill.[15]

The very meaning of Shaka's name gives credence to this account. The Zulu believed that a beetle called an *itshaka* caused intestinal disorders and made the stomach swell out. But this does not mean that Shaka was named after it. The expression '*itshaka*' was used to describe a girl who became pregnant before marriage, and the illegitimate child she bore was also spoken of as *itshaka*.[16] The strong belief persisted in some Zulu and colonial circles that Shaka remained illegitimate. What gave credence to this position was the tradition that Nandi, whose name means 'sweet' in Zulu, and who was described as 'dark-skinned, big, and strongly built' with small breasts,[17] could not abide seeing Shaka grow up at Senzangakhona's *umuzi* while she shamefully remained with her father as an unmarried woman. Perhaps it was then that she earned her evil reputation as a sexually frigid, bad-tempered shrew:

> She whose thighs do not meet,
> They only meet on seeing her husband.
> Loud-voiced one …[18]

So, the story goes, she eventually left to marry Ngendeyana, a man of substance among the Qwabe people – or perhaps just to enter his *isigodlo* as a concubine until Senzangakhona claimed her. What does seem well accredited is that she had a son, Ngwadi, by Ngendeyana, although the paternity of her good-tempered, light-skinned and very fat daughter, Noncoba, is disputed,[19] even if her short, wide nose was said to have been very like Shaka's.[20] To complicate matters, a tradition did persist that Ngwadi was really Senzangakhona's son and so Shaka's only full brother.

Meanwhile, as the illegitimate Shaka grew up in Senzangakhona's household, his father, according to Cetshwayo, believed he showed every sign of becoming troublesome and a possible threat. So, in about 1802, when Shaka reached his late teens, Senzangakhona decided to kill him. However, Shaka received warning and fled to Jobe kaKayi, the powerful *inkosi* of the Mthethwa people in southeastern Zululand between the White Mfolozi and Mhlathuze rivers, where the ambitious exile began to prosper as a war leader. With warfare so undeniably imbedded in African culture, military valour and expertise were the hallmarks of a man's personal honour, sexual allure and standing in society, and were the accepted avenue to power and riches.

When Jobe died in around 1807, his son Dingiswayo killed his brother Mawawe, who was his father's designated *inkosana*, or heir by his chief wife, and seized the throne. Shaka threw in his lot with Dingiswayo and remained high in his favour on account of his exceptional military prowess. According to tradition, Dingiswayo bestowed on him the praise name of *uSitshaka ka sitshayeki*, meaning 'he who beats but is not beaten'[21] – surely preferable to 'bastard' as the source of his name and well suited to his aggressive character.

At Dingiswayo's side, Shaka had ample opportunity to hone his exceptional military talents. Hunting and small-scale raiding had long been the honourable occupations of men such as Shaka in a society that espoused a warrior culture (one must put firmly aside the legend of a peace-loving, harmonious pre-Shakan Eden). Indeed, whatever else about Shaka is uncertainly known, the inborn bellicosity that never deserted him is very well attested. The hunter-trader Nathaniel Isaacs, who had many dealings with him, emphatically declared: 'War and dominion were the ruling passions of Chaka',[22] while nearly 90 years after Shaka's death Mayinga, a Zulu of illustrious lineage whose father had been one of Shaka's military commanders, stated categorically: 'He was always talking of war.'[23] Yet, it must be remembered that for Shaka, as with every other African king, being a powerful war leader was always a prerequisite for effective political leadership. The corollary was that military failure severely damaged a king's reputation and brought his right to rule into question, spawning plots to assassinate him and encouraging would-be usurpers to rebel.

It was Shaka's good fortune that as a young man he could build a military career in a period of intensifying warfare in southeastern Africa. Increasingly complex, hierarchical, centralised and very militarised states were emerging and vying with each other for regional dominance. In such states, people gave their allegiance – the Zulu word is *ukukhonza* – to a political superior in return for land to pasture their livestock and grow their crops, and for the protection to do so safely. We must be wary, however, of thinking of even the most powerful of these states as possessing the administrative means of governing all its territory in a uniform way, or of having the firm territorial boundaries customary today. The typical pattern for a kingdom, even the Zulu one at the height of its power, was a geographical nucleus firmly controlled by a central government whose authority and power faded away towards the periphery, where vague boundaries often overlapped with those of other states.

These kingdoms waxed and waned in power and extent in a manner that seems strange today. If a ruler could not provide his subjects with the security and prosperity they required, disaffected groups might hive off and *ukukhonza* to one of the neighbouring rival rulers better able to do so. Their exodus might be even more extreme. Because political power was based on a ruler's control over essentially mobile resources such as cattle and the people's agricultural labour, no chiefdom was bound inexorably to a particular territory. Thus a disgruntled unit or even an entire chiefdom might migrate elsewhere in search of improved security or better lands, accumulating or shedding adherents as it moved on.

Such mass movements were possible because Africa in this period was significantly under-populated and still offered ample territorial scope for settlement. With an environment as geographically and climatically harsh and unforgiving as Africa's, and with otherwise habitable regions rendered lethal by endemic disease, only restricted areas were suitable for the pursuit of agriculture and pastoralism, and thus for human settlement too. Southeastern Africa was one of these favoured regions, but because the population was dependent upon a vulnerable subsistence economy, it struggled to multiply appreciably. These circumstances have since changed beyond all recognition, and the population of the region is now about 25 times more numerous than it was in the early 19th century. But even though populations were then thinly scattered, all of them were naturally concentrated in the most favourable areas. This meant that when groups or whole chiefdoms migrated, they inevitably clashed with existing settlements, destroying them, incorporating them or causing them to ricochet off on their own disruptive path.

So, for a chiefdom or kingdom to protect itself from enemies, to deter defections and (it must be added) to be in a position to expand its own domain, it was absolutely essential to maintain some form of military organisation.

In 'stateless societies' where, as we have seen, political authority was exercised by a council of elders, age-grade regiments of both men and women were expected to give their labour to the community and to marry each other when the word was given. Male age-grade regiments were also mobilised to defend the community when the need arose, thus constituting part-time militias rather than standing armies. By contrast, in many centralising, hierarchical kingdoms across Africa, the king called on his subordinate nobility to provide military levies in time of war, rather as feudal lords would have done in mediaeval Europe. The king would usually also maintain a small standing army, often partially made up of slave

Migrations during the consolidation of the Zulu kingdom

soldiers, who were a common African institution except in the southern parts of the continent.

Southeastern Africa presented a unique fusion of the two types of society, which had consequences for military organisation. From the late 18th century the paramountcies and kingdoms of the region, although hierarchical and centralising, were nevertheless constructed on the institution of age-grade regiments. Youths, instead of going through the stressful experience of a circumcision school as the portal to adulthood, were banded together every few years by their ruler as cadets when enough of them of approximately the same age were available, and spent their days herding his cattle, working the fields and practising military skills. After a few years of such service, and on reaching young adulthood, their ruler formed them into a fully-fledged *ibutho*, or age-grade regiment, and bestowed on it its distinctive name. In what seems to have been a substitution for the defunct circumcision ceremony, on marriage members of an *ibutho* assumed the headring, or *isicoco*. This indicator of full adulthood was a circlet of tendons or fibres sewn into the hair with cattle sinews. It was coated with beeswax or gum and then greased and polished.

These *amabutho* were their ruler's main instrument of power and coercion. But just how they were deployed requires an understanding of the prevailing nature of pre-colonial warfare in southeastern Africa. The prevalence of horse sickness caused by tsetse flies in Africa's forested central tropical zone meant that horses, common in North Africa, did not penetrate to regions to its south until Dutch settlers imported horses to the Cape in the 17th century. Consequently, when Shaka was growing into manhood horses were all but unknown in his part of Africa, and warfare was waged exclusively by foot soldiers. Mthethwa and Zulu warriors, and those of the other African societies they fought against in the first decades of the 19th century, were all armed with various forms of spear, which was their principal weapon. Lighter javelins were cast from a distance, and heavier spears were used for stabbing at close quarters. Warriors might also wield a heavy-headed, skull-crushing club, or sometimes a battle-axe. Bows and arrows were not part of their arsenal, and throwing spears were the only projectiles employed. Combatants carried an oxhide shield that came in many designs specific to each society: small or large, winged, hourglass-shaped, apron-shaped or – most familiarly – oval, as was the body-covering Zulu shield.

Warfare in sub-Saharan Africa was all about securing territory that would provide sufficient winter and summer grazing for livestock and that would be capable of supporting agriculture. It also had as its objective the control of people necessary to serve as herders and work the land and – crucially in an underpopulated continent – to reproduce themselves. For African rulers, therefore, warfare was a zero-sum game in which your gains were precisely your enemy's loss, and fighting primarily took the form of endemic, localised raiding to impoverish and weaken rivals. Major campaigns were much rarer and short-lived on account of insurmountable logistical difficulties in supplying armies at a distance over long periods, especially if they became bogged down in besieging strongholds. Among southern African indigenous societies that lacked the wheel there were no animal-drawn wagons, and supplies had to be carried by each warrior (and sometimes by non-combatant porters) or foraged for on the march.

Still, by the later 18th century warfare in southern Africa was becoming more sophisticated, and campaigns were being mounted to control resources such as ivory, gold, cattle, animal pelts and feathers and – mainly in the region of Delagoa Bay – slaves. These goods were bartered with seaborne outsiders for foreign goods desired by the elite, such as cloth, beads, agricultural tools and alcohol. For the Zulu at the beginning of Shaka's reign, the trade route best worth controlling was northeast to Delagoa Bay, where from 1787 the Portuguese had maintained a tenuous presence in their fort and trading post called Lourenço Marques.

By the early 19th century the consolidating chiefdoms in the lands between Delagoa Bay to the north and the Thukela River to the south, bounded to the west by the Drakensberg Mountains and to the east by the Indian Ocean, were increasingly at each other's throats. In the 16th century the largest chiefdom in the region had probably been that of the Mbo. For reasons unknown, this chiefdom fragmented in the early 18th century. Several of its splinters, notably the Ndwandwe living just south of the Phongolo River, tried to rebuild their lost power. They were confronted by expanding rival paramountcies, of which the Mthethwa to their south, between the White Mfolozi and Mhlathuze rivers, was the most formidable.

By the time Shaka was serving Jobe, the Ndwandwe and Mthethwa – along with other of the more aggressive polities between the Black Mfolozi River in the north and the Mzinyathi and Thukela rivers in the south, such as the Hlubi and Qwabe paramountcies and the Chube chiefdom – were fiercely raiding each other's cattle, struggling to control the winter and summer grazing pastures, and vying to attract new adherents at the expense of their rivals.

In their endemic wars these chiefdoms all deployed *amabutho*, and Shaka served in the ranks of the Mthethwa ones. He has often been credited with inventing these 'regiments' and with devising their fighting style. In fact, although he would be instrumental in tightening the organisation of the Zulu *amabutho* under his sole command and in refining their tactics, the inception of *amabutho* (as we have seen) pre-dated him. Even their hallmark tactic of first casting long throwing-spears and then finishing off their foes with short stabbing-spears, a battle-winning 'innovation' long ascribed to Shaka, would seem to have gone back to well before his time.

What does appear certain is that the exiled Shaka earned a great military reputation among the Mthethwa. He wore the *isicoco* of a married man while serving Dingiswayo, and there is a strong tradition that he took several wives, and had even fathered a son, Zibizendlela.[24] Crucially for advancement in a hierarchical chiefly society, he enjoyed Dingiswayo's wholehearted patronage. As a mark of his favour, the Mthethwa paramount placed Shaka under the special care of his commander-in-chief, Ngomane kaMqomboli, who became the young warrior's father figure and mentor.

Shaka's rise to prominence in Dingiswayo's service coincided with the increasingly deadly struggle for regional supremacy the Mthethwa were waging against the Ndwandwe, who were pushing south across the Mkhuze River under their violent and cunning paramount, Zwide kaLanga. Weaker neighbouring chiefdoms began to take flight west over the Drakensberg and south over the Thukela River to avoid the escalating warfare. They in turn dislodged communities in their path so that the ripples of violence spread out further and further outwards.

In resisting the menacing Ndwandwe, Dingiswayo relied on the smaller, tributary chiefdoms within his orbit to give him military assistance. One of these was the Zulu chiefdom under Senzangakhona, which was strategically placed to secure Dingiswayo's northwesterly borders up the valley of the White Mfolozi. It consequently made good sense for Dingiswayo to tighten his hold on the client Zulu chiefdom. There is a robust tradition that he – himself a usurper – believed this could best be achieved if Shaka, his trusted and able protégé, were to supplant his father as the Zulu *inkosi*.

But how was this to be effected? It was first necessary to do away with Senzangakhona. It seems Shaka had no qualms about falling in with Dingiswayo's plan and playing his full and willing part in bewitching his father when he paid his overlord a visit in search of a new wife. Whatever the actual means employed (and there are differing versions), Shaka apparently gained occult ascendancy over his father. Senzangakhona began to feel mortally ill, and returned home to his *umuzi*, kwaNobamba, where he fell into a rapid decline and died, probably in 1816.

The second stage of the plot now had to be implemented because Shaka was not Senzangakhona's designated successor, or *inkosana*, and would not normally have succeeded him as *inkosi*. Indeed, the question of royal succession was a deeply vexing issue since it was not clear-cut. A king or chief shared the same problem with every man of high status in Zulu society: a large number of wives and multiple children thoroughly muddied the waters when it came to deciding who should be his heir. So the Zulu had put complex procedures into place to promote a smooth succession. However, in the royal house the customary succession of the eldest son of a man's designated great wife (who had not necessarily been his first-married wife, but was deemed of suitably distinguished lineage to carry on the line, or was excessively favoured) was not automatically adopted. It was considered too dangerous for an ageing king to have an acknowledged heir hovering impatiently outside the royal hut, so the naming of the *inkosana* was delayed until the last moment to reduce the possibility of usurpation. Yet this was no complete solution either, because the technical qualification of any male of the royal lineage to mount the throne was likely to spark a succession dispute.

Knowing this, and well before the king died, those with a possible claim would be gathering support for the looming contest. Consequently – as in many another African kingdoms – regicide and bloody civil war long characterised the royal succession in the Zulu kingdom. Tellingly, King

Cetshwayo reputedly had a dream in which he was visited by the *amadlozi* of two of his royal predecessors, Ndaba and Dingane. They said to him, '[W]e shall give you only one son, for you of the Zulu are always killing one another in disputing the kingship if there are many of you.'[25]

The reason why Shaka was not Senzangakhona's designated successor was not because he was a bastard. The recorded oral traditions are very much in agreement that some time before his death Senzangakhona had married Nandi, and that the handing over of *ilobolo* to her father had legitimised Shaka.[26] Rather, it was because even though Shaka was Senzangakhona's eldest son, he was not the son of his 'great wife'. And that person was not Nandi, but Bhibhi, Senzangakhona's eighth wife and undisputed favourite. Her son by Senzangakhona was Sigujana (otherwise known as Nomkwayimba or Mfokozana), who was of much the same age as Shaka, and there seems general agreement that Senzangakhona had recognised him as his *inkosana*.[27] However, because Shaka was now of Senzangakhona's legitimate line he was eligible to succeed his father. And that meant getting Sigujana out of the way.

The sanitised version of what happened next was recounted by King Cetshwayo, who declared that on Senzangakhona's death 'the Zulu tribe sent to him [Shaka] and begged him to be their king: he consented … and he was made king with great rejoicing. His brothers acquiesced.'[28] However, all other surviving accounts are unanimous that, with Dingiswayo's active support, Shaka first did away with Sigujana and then usurped the Zulu throne.[29]

To eliminate Sigujana, it seems Shaka turned to his half-brother Ngwadi, with whom he had developed a close rapport. Ngwadi was in Sigujana's fatally misplaced confidence, and went bathing with him in the river. Ngwadi's accomplices were stationed in the long grass along the river-bank, and when the unsuspecting Zulu *inkosi* stooped to wash they ran him through from behind with two spears. Ngwadi sent immediate word to Shaka that he had done away with Sigujana. In commemoration of his treacherous deed he would be come to be known appropriately as 'the stick of one who cuts down trees'.[30]

With Sigujana dead, it remained to implement the third stage of the plot. This is where Mnkabayi kaJama, Senzangakhona's older, unmarried sister and Shaka's aunt, showed her hand and (in King Cetshwayo's words) 'carried on all the negotiations' for her nephew's return.[31] Zulu society may have been overtly patriarchal, but subtle power was exercised from the *isigodlo* by the king's or chief's female relations, his wives and the widows of his predecessor. Royal women thus had it in their power to manipulate the outcome of succession, and of Mnkabayi it was said that the Zulu kings were 'placed' by her.[32]

Mnkabayi was taller and lighter in colour than her unmarried twin, Mmama (who was dark brown), and was described as a person whose prime-conditioned body was sleek and softly fat.[33] In her *izibongo* she was celebrated for her honest, incorruptible ability to resolve her adherents' problems and for her success in confronting any evil forces that might threaten Zulu power:

> She who allays for people their anxiety,
> They catch it and she looks at it with her eyes.
> The opener of all the main gates so that people may enter ...[34]

She had first come to prominence on the death of her father, Jama, when she ruled as co-regent with Mudli kaNkwelo kaNdaba of the Zulu royal house until Senzangakhona came of age. One tradition holds that Mnkabayi, while she was regent, saved the infant Shaka's life. The story goes that when Senzangakhona learned that he had an illegitimate child by Nandi he was enraged and ordered the infant's death, but Mnkabayi spirited Nandi and her baby away to the safety of her father's *umuzi*, where Shaka grew up.[35] True or not, this tale connects Mnkabayi to Shaka, and it suggests she and Mmama encouraged Shaka's ambitions while in exile. The two women were reputed to have been deeply instrumental in contriving Sigujana's assassination by Ngwadi and in persuading other members of the royal house to go along with them.[36] With Sigujana done to death, Mnkabayi assumed temporary power as regent (as she had once before after her father Jama's demise) until Shaka arrived from the Mthethwa country to seize the empty throne.

When Shaka arrived to take up his inheritance, it was with the daunt-ing military escort Dingiswayo had despatched under the command of

Ngomane, the Mthethwa commander-in-chief and Shaka's old mentor. Shaka at once established his rule with exemplary ruthlessness. He executed the prominent men associated with Senzangakhona's regime – including a number of uncles – as well as others whom he suspected of opposing his claim to be king. All of Shaka's remaining brothers, thoroughly cowed, gave up any immediate ambitions they might have harboured to succeed Sigujana, and tendered him their allegiance.

To consolidate his power, Shaka placed those he was beholden to in high positions. Ngomane would become his chief councillor. Ngwadi, Sigujana's assassin, would remain a close favourite of Shaka, who 'gave him authority over a large number of people' over whom he was allowed to rule in a semi-independent manner, amassing great herds of cattle and even maintaining his own little army.[37] Shaka, along with the next three kings of the independent Zulu kingdom, believed that royal women from the *isigodlo* made for dependable representatives to govern their most important *amakhanda* as extensions of the royal household. Those he appointed included two of Senzangakhona's widows, Bhibhi and Langazana, his half-sister Noncoba, and his aunt Mmama.

For Mnkabayi, the domineering woman who had assured Shaka's succession, and who he intended should be a mainstay of his rule, he reserved the most significant *amakhanda* of all. He placed her over the sacred kwaNobamba where Senzangakhona was buried, and in due course over the strategic ebaQulusini, which dominated northwestern Zululand and guarded that vulnerable frontier. She also presided over esiKlebheni, where she was entrusted with the sacred *inkatha* kept there, the ritual powers of which will be discussed in due course. Besides these *amakhanda*, eMahlabeni was also Mnkabayi's. This prestigious *ikhanda* was known as the seat of war. It was where the army used to *ukuthetha*, or go through the ceremonies of giving praise to the ancestors under her command, and where, from the reign of Shaka to that of Cetshwayo, the marching orders for a major campaign were issued. When she died during King Mpande's reign, Mnkabayi's grave near the kwaGqikazi *ikhanda* in the Mahlabathini plain became a place of secure refuge for fugitives, and her name long continued to be invoked when people took a sacred oath.

CHAPTER TWO

A GREAT WARRIOR IN THE ZULU COUNTRY

No sooner had Shaka seized the Zulu chiefdom as Dingiswayo's tributary than, in 1817, his overlord was taken captive by his great rival, Zwide of the Ndwandwe, through (it was said) occult means and put to death.[1] With the Mthethwa leaderless and Zwide ascendant, all that now stood between Ndwandwe domination was Shaka's determined defiance, which brought increasing violence down on all the peoples of the region. Angered by Shaka's refusal to acknowledge him as his new overlord, Zwide invaded Zulu territory in 1818 and laid waste to the valley of the White Mfolozi. Shaka was only just able to beat the Ndwandwe off. Badly savaged, Shaka fell back for a time on the coastal country. Yet he refused to give in. He began to regroup, carefully harboured his resources and concentrated on building up the military capabilities of his *amabutho* against future Ndwandwe attacks. Shaka celebrated his growing military and political heft by singing of himself that

> I am a great warrior there in the Zulu country,
> I am foremost in the place of headrings [in the *isibaya* where affairs are discussed].[2]

And indeed, it is as the invincible warrior that Shaka is remembered, and this image remains a great source of pride for the Zulu people.

Yet this image is double-edged, and contemporary white commentators were quick to associate Shaka and the rise of the Zulu kingdom with appalling devastation and bloodshed, which, they claimed, decimated the local population and turned many thousands into terrified refugees or desperate cannibals. Historians subsequently built on this vision to come up in the 1970s with the concept of the *mfecane* (crushing). According to this model, the explosive expansion of Shaka's militaristic Zulu kingdom was at the root of the unprecedented dislocation that spread across southern Africa in the early 19th century. However, as with all historical models, that of the *mfecane* has since been modified, and the growing consensus is that while the Zulu kingdom was a prominent player during the *mfecane*, it was neither its sole instigator nor its only motor. Furthermore, it is accepted that the scale of dislocation, suffering and death during the *mfecane*, while certainly not negligible, must be kept in perspective. Quite simply, the technological and physical capacity to massacre untold numbers simply did not exist, certainly not on the scale of millions that historians once blithely wrote about.[3]

Nevertheless, it does seem that Zulu society under Shaka was increasingly militarised, and 'only war was talked about'.[4] As we have seen, when Shaka entered Dingiswayo's service the *amabutho* were already the basis of every chief's power in the region. Once he became the Zulu ruler, however, Shaka modified and regulated the institution so that it became the central pillar of royal authority and remained so until the fall of the Zulu kingdom in Cetshwayo's time. But to make it so, Shaka had to overcome a crucial obstacle that was nothing less than the basic social and economic unit of the kingdom: the homestead, or *umuzi*.

Tens of thousands of scattered *imizi*, looking like so many tiny circular villages, dotted the rolling countryside. A married man (*umnumzane*) lived in each *umuzi* with his two or three wives and children (a man of wealth and status might have as many as a dozen wives, however). The domed, thatched huts, or *izindlu*, that made up an *umuzi* should be regarded as separate rooms in a single home. The huts were on average three metres in diameter, although that of a man of status could be double the size and with several supporting poles rather than one. The *izindlu* were erected in a crescent surrounding the central, fenced *isibaya*, where deep pits in which grain and seed were stored were carefully disguised. The arrangement of the *izindlu* was hierarchical, with that of the chief wife at the top and dropping progressively in status to those of retainers or dependants nearest the entrance. The storage huts for beer, vegetables and grain were usually built between the dwelling huts and the outer protective palisade.

Because the summer rainfall in Zulu country provided sufficient pasturage and agricultural land, each *umuzi* was a self-sufficient home where it was mainly – but not exclusively – women who tilled the small scattered fields and raised the staple crops of Indian maize, sorghum, millet, pumpkins and various other vegetables. On occasion, men also went out to hunt wild animals to supplement their diet and to garner animal pelts, and they were responsible for building and repairing the *umuzi*. But the main occupation of men and boys was herding the prestigious and valuable cattle that provided milk and meat on special occasions, as well as hides for basic items of clothing. Technically, the cattle of the kingdom, along with the land itself, belonged to the nation and therefore through the chiefs to the king himself, but for practical purposes they were in the ownership of each *umuzi*. Even the king's own cattle, which were too numerous to be pastured in one place, were entrusted through the custom of *ukusisa* to individual *imizi* as well as *amakhanda* where the herdsmen had the right to make use of them for milk or dung and to retain their calves.

Shaka proceeded to gain control of these self-sufficient *imizi* by regulating marriage. In Zulu society an adult man could not break loose from his father's *umuzi* and establish his own household without marriage, and that traditionally could not take place until the woman's father had received *ilobolo* from the prospective husband. So Shaka stepped in to regulate the lives of women more fully in the service of the state by forming girls into female *amabutho* for the purpose of marriage. At the same time, he took away the right of subordinate chiefs to form young men of the same age-group into *amabutho* of their own. Henceforth, each *ibutho* was recruited from across the entire kingdom, and not regionally. Only Shaka and his royal successors possessed the authority to bring cadets before them every few years when enough of the same age-grade had been collected, to form them into a new *ibutho* with its own distinctive name, and to command them to build themselves a new *ikhanda* as their headquarters.

At intervals the king gave the members of a female *ibutho* permission to marry, but only to suitors from those male *amabutho* he had ordered to put on the *isicoco*. As we have seen, the *isicoco* had long been the indication of a married man, but Shaka gave it a new significance. From his reign until the fall of the kingdom the *isicoco* remained the quasi-sacred symbol of the monarch's absolute prerogative over every male married subject's life, for it was regarded as belonging not to the man who wore it, but to the king. Nor was it up to an individual to assume it, as it seems to have been in the past. The king alone could grant the privilege – not to individuals, but to an entire *ibutho* when he decided it had proved itself by long service. By withholding the *isicoco* until men of an *ibutho* were between about 35 and 40 years old and approaching middle age, the king was denying them the status of an *umnumzane* and prolonging the period in which they continued to be regarded in Zulu society as *izinsizwa*, or unmarried youths. This meant that they remained conveniently under the authority of their married elders and, through them, the king.

Under Shaka and his successors the *amabutho* were obliged to serve their king by providing labour, by repairing the *amakhanda* where they were quartered, and by herding the royal cattle. They also participated in great hunts in which they amassed the precious skins, feathers and tusks that were a vital royal resource for display and trade. They collected the tribute that politically subordinate subjects rendered in return for the king and his soldiers creating the safe conditions in which to produce the goods in the first place, and they enforced internal control against recalcitrant subjects. Less frequently, they operated as the army against external enemies. Since they served the king directly for only several months a year in their *amakhanda*, they were not a standing army as white settlers and British officials so frequently averred. Yet they were always at his service, and the king alone could mobilise them for war. He was not reliant (as in many other African kingdoms) on the goodwill of his subordinate notables to supply military levies in time of war. Nor was there any need for him to maintain an elite royal guard on a permanent footing, as was the practice particularly in North and West Africa, where rulers favoured slave soldiers to protect them.

Yet while the *amabutho* system was the Zulu king's main instrument of

control over his subjects, it only worked as it did because it was a reciprocal arrangement. Not even Zulu *amabutho* were prepared to serve without
some tangible recompense, and the Zulu kings knew that to ensure their
loyalty they must keep them well fed and rewarded. In a pre-industrial
society without money of any kind, the prime indicator of wealth and the
means of paying *ilobolo* to formalise marriage was cattle. It was therefore
necessary for the Zulu king to raid neighbouring chiefdoms regularly to
acquire booty, especially cattle. The captured cattle daily fed the *amabutho*
with meat (which they rarely ate at home) when they served in the king's
amakhanda, and were redistributed to them – most lavishly to their officers
– in token of the king's appreciation.

Two things forcefully struck white observers when, in Shaka's reign,
they first clapped eyes on the *amabutho* in their magnificently lavish festival
attire, which in its myriad details differentiated one *ibutho* from another,
as did the distinctive colours and patterns of their war-shields. The first
was that the costume was made entirely of a prodigious variety of animal
skins, furs, feathers and horns that spoke to the kingdom's greater ability
to dominate and exploit both the domestic and wild animal resources of
the region than could any of its less lavishly costumed neighbours. The
second was that its purpose was to terrify, to confirm the dread reputation of the *amabutho* as eaters of men, as ravening wild beasts. As Shaka's
izibongo vaunted:

> You are a wild animal! A leopard! A lion!
> A horned viper! An elephant![5]

Indeed, certain items allowed the wearer to take on the attributes of the
animal in question. Thus a plaited head ornament of buffalo hide imbued
the warrior with that dangerous beast's fighting cunning, while the vulture
feathers worn by army commanders made them battle to the death like
that indomitable bird of prey.

Every warrior wore the basic kilt of tails. White ox and cow tails were
fastened around the neck like a cape to hang down the back as far as the
knees, and down to the waist in front. The king bestowed this cape on the
men of each new *ibutho* along with their shield, so warriors looked after it

34

with special care and wore it only at the great festivals. More cattle tails were tied above the elbows and below the knees to cover the shins. No footwear was worn. Bracelets of beads and bangles ornamented the arms. The headdress, individual to each *ibutho*, was held together by a thick, padded hide and fur headband. More skins hung from this headband as flaps or tassels on either side of the face or down the back of the neck. Combinations of feathers arranged in bunches or in single plumes, worn upright or slanting backward, completed the headgear. The king and the great men of the kingdom wore the same style of ceremonial dress as the warriors, but their higher status was indicated by the costliness and rarity of their furs and feathers and by a greater display of beads and ornaments. On campaign, much of this finery was inevitably set aside, although in Shaka's era more seems to have been retained than in later times. Always, though, officers persisted in a finer display than their men in order to be distinguishable from the rank and file.

When the king mustered them for war, the assembled *amabutho* were ritually 'strengthened' for the impending campaign. Behind the rituals was a distinctive belief system. The Zulu believed in three shadowy, distant divinities of creation and generation that could only be approached through the shades of the ancestors, or *amadlozi*. So it was to the *amadlozi* that the Zulu turned. They dwelt underground and watched over the living, who in turn consulted them in everything they did, propitiating them with offerings when they sensed their disfavour, and making contact with them through blood sacrifice in the *isibaya*. Since, in Zulu belief, an overlap existed between this world and the world of the *amadlozi*, there was dangerous scope for a mystical and contagious force, *umnyama* – darkness, evil influence and misfortune – to seep out among the living. The act of homicide and the blood of the slain formed a potent occult bridge for *umnyama* to take hold, so warriors had to be protected against its effects through occult medicines, or *imithi*. These magic potions could be either benevolent or – in the wicked hands of witches, or *abathakathi* – malevolent and even fatal. Either way they were extremely potent, because they always included snippets of the human body and its waste products, such as nail clippings or urine. (Zulu were consequently always careful to prevent their *insila*, or body dirt, getting into the hands of those who wished them harm.)

In the course of the three days of ceremonies that strengthened the *ama-butho* against *umnyama*, the central ritual occurred when an unarmed *ibutho* favoured by the king caught a black bull from the royal herds upon which all the evil influences that had accumulated in the land were symbolically cast, and strangled it to death bare-handed. War-doctors then cut strips of meat from the dead bull, treated them with powerful 'black' *imithi* intended to strengthen the warriors and bind them together in loyalty to their king, and then roasted them in a great fire of green mimosa, which the *amabutho* had collected the previous day. The war-doctors then threw the strips up into the air and the *amabutho*, who were drawn up in a great circle around them, scrambled to catch and suck them.

Meanwhile, the war-doctors burned further *imithi* and had the warriors breathe in the smoke before sprinkling them with the cinders. Then, in order to finally expel all dangerous influences, each warrior drank a mouthful from a pot of further *imithi*, and a few at a time took turns to vomit the contents into a hole dug close to a running stream. This ritual vomiting took all day to complete and its purpose was to bind all the people together in loyalty to the king. On the third day the *amabutho* and the king ritually bathed in a running stream. There they were treated with 'white' *imithi* that neutralised the mystically dangerous 'black' *imithi* that had placed them in an intensified and contagious state of *umnyama*, and so rendered them fit to re-enter normal society.

The army then marched towards enemy territory. It tried to spare its own population while marching through Zulu-held country, and for a few days it depended on food carried by women and *izindibi* (baggage-carriers, boys between six and twelve years old). When these stocks were exhausted, the women and many of the boys would return home. The army then subsisted as best it could by slaughtering the cattle they drove along with them, and by bivouacking at *amakhanda* where provisions had been stocked. All the warriors carried iron rations in a skin sack, the favourite combination being a cooked cow's liver and maize grains. However, all these supplies would eventually run out, and once the army entered enemy territory it began to forage ruthlessly.

Once the enemy was located and the decision to engage was taken, the army drew up in a circle (*umkhumbi*), to be sprinkled by war-doctors with *izintelezi*, medicinal charms to counteract *umnyama* from affecting the men with its evil influence and to give them courage. With his *amabutho* now ritually assured of victory, the commander then took up position with his staff on nearby high ground. Shaka was reputed to have usually (but not always) accompanied his *amabutho* on campaign,[6] and to have directed the course of the battle holding aloft his black war-shield (*isihlangu*) with white or grey speckles only at the lower end.[7] Besides the *isihlangu*, Zulu men used a variety of different smaller shields for dancing, courting and everyday protection. In Shaka's time the *isihlangu* reached from foot to chin, but a smaller, more easily handled version, the *umbumbulozo*, came increasingly into use after the 1850s, although the *isihlangu* continued to be carried by officers and some of the older *amabutho*. During Shaka's reign, the war-shields of each *ibutho* were of identical colour and pattern to distinguish the *amabutho* from each other, but by the 1870s the kingdom would no longer have the cattle resources to maintain this practice, and the convention was adopted of married *amabutho* carrying predominantly white shields and unmarried *amabutho* black or brown ones. The Zulu kings carried their own distinctive war-shields. Shaka's *isihlangu* has already been described, although he is also remembered as carrying a pure white one with an oval black patch across the middle. Dingane's *isihlangu* was black with a semicircular patch halfway down and on the right edge. It was also recalled as being white with a central black patch just above the middle, and that one was probably adopted when he was an older man.[8] Mpande carried an identical shield.

When the order was given for the army to advance, it was with the tactical intention – developed from the hunt – of pinning the enemy down with a frontal attack by the centre, or 'chest', while the two flanking 'horns' rapidly encircled the foe. A reserve, the 'loins', was kept back for support or pursuit. The Zulu maintained this battlefield formation, known as the 'horns of the beast' and attributed in its final form to Shaka's modifications, as late as the Zulu Uprising of 1906 (Bhambatha Rebellion).

As we have seen, the Zulu and their neighbours had long employed spears as their primary weapon, so it is hard to say just how innovatory Shaka was in their use. According to tradition, Shaka permitted his *amabutho* to carry only one spear lest they rely on throwing their spears instead of rushing in at once to close quarters. Yet the Zulu seem never to have stopped using spears as projectiles. Later in the 19th century each Zulu warrior typically carried two or three throwing-spears (*izijula*), which he normally used for hunting, and hurled them at the enemy to disrupt their ranks before charging home at a stooping run shouting his battle cry in order to engage man to man. It is in this emphasis on close fighting that Shaka's 'military revolution' most probably lies. The weapons the Zulu employed for face-to-face combat were the bone-crushing wooden knobbed stick (*iwisa*) commonly carried by Shaka's *amabutho*, and the short-hafted, long-bladed stabbing-spear, or *iklwa*. The invention of the *iklwa* has been fancifully attributed to Shaka, but it is reasonable to accept that it was he who insisted on making the already existing spear central to the Zulu way of fighting. The warrior wielding the *iklwa* made an underarm stab into the enemy's abdomen, followed by a vicious rip before withdrawing the spear. This manoeuvre, which involved hooking away an enemy's shield with one's own beforehand, required considerable skill and practice, and this is where regular training in its most effective use was crucial to Shaka's military programme. The *iklwa* certainly became a battle-winning weapon, giving the Zulu a considerable psychological advantage over their African opponents. Undoubtedly, the *iklwa* evolved into the weapon of the hero, of the man who cultivated military honour, who proved his prowess in single combat, and who – as Shaka was said to have required – bore his own wounds only on his chest.[9]

In battle, once the enemy broke into demoralised flight, the triumphant Zulu 'chest' would closely pursue them. Simultaneously, the two encircling Zulu 'horns' cut off as many of the fugitives as they could. The victorious Zulu killed all those they could lay their hands upon. They seldom gave quarter to the defeated, although it is reported that Shaka often extended amnesty to those brave survivors who would accept his rule and drafted them into his army.[10] Having disposed of the enemy warriors (and their attendant kin), the triumphant Zulu rounded up all the captured enemy cattle to present to the king. Cattle were the chief prize of combat and essential (as we have seen) for the king to redistribute as rewards to his victorious *amabutho*, as gifts to secure the loyalty of his great chiefs, and to attract new followers to his rule through largesse.

Killing a foe in battle severely contaminated the warrior with *umnyama*, and it was necessary to undertake various actions to achieve ritual purification. One was to slit open the belly of the slain foe so that *umnyama* did not affect the killer and make him swell up like the dead. Another was to put on items of the dead man's apparel instead of one's own, which would have been ritually contaminated by the victim's blood, and to wear these until ritually cleansed. On returning from war the *amabutho* could not immediately report to the king or resume domestic life until they had undergone four days of ceremonies to gain occult ascendancy over the vengeful spirits of their war victims. Only then could they present themselves before the king when they exchanged accounts of the fighting.

Every man's valour and daring in the deadly hand-to-hand fighting had been under constant scrutiny by his peers and officers. After due consideration, the king would decide to which *ibutho* went the distinction of being the first to engage the enemy at close quarters. He would also designate as heroes those of its members who had made a kill. These men the king ordered to wear a distinctive necklace made from small interlocking blocks of willow wood (*iziqu*), which was occultly associated with the *amadlozi*. The *iziqu* were looped around the neck, or slung across the body like a bandolier, and marked out the warrior hero ever after. By wretched contrast, those who failed to live up to the high ideals of masculinity, and whose courage failed them in combat, were degraded and punished. Under Shaka's successors, cowards were given the opportunity to redeem their honour, but under his stern rule they were put ignominiously to death.

Sometimes, non-combatants suffered directly in the fighting. This usually happened when a ruler and his adherents came under attack while they were attempting to migrate en masse to another region out of harm's way. Then women, children and the aged had to stand by and watch the course of the battle in a fever of apprehension, hoping fervently that their menfolk would defend them successfully. When they lost, they faced massacre alongside them in the heat of battle. 'Let no one remain alive', Shaka would order his *amabutho* before a battle, 'not even a dog or a child carried on its mother's back.'[11] It was believed that this exterminatory style of fighting began with Shaka and was known as *umbadu*, or 'people coming to a place with violence'.[12]

There is little doubt that people in general faced privation and death from starvation in the theatres where the Zulu and other armies were operating. When the Zulu attacked a community, or simply pillaged it as they marched by, many inhabitants might take temporary refuge in the surrounding bush, in caves, or on mountain tops. Once the warriors had moved on, they would re-emerge, but their situation was then dire. Their means of survival would have been destroyed or carried off: their grain-pits dug in the *isibaya* of each *umuzi* emptied (including the essential seed for the next season's planting), their vegetable gardens stripped, their live-stock rustled, and their *imizi* demolished for firewood. People would have to move off elsewhere to find food and shelter, and there is no doubt that during the course of Shaka's wars some regions became temporarily depop-ulated. As Shaka's *izibongo* graphically expressed it:

> The newly planted crops they left still short,
> The seed left among the maize-stalks,
> The old women were left in the abandoned sites.
> The old men were left among the tracks,
> The roots of the trees looked up at the sky.[13]

Ordinarily, though, there was no point in the Zulu annihilating the mem-bers of a defeated chiefdom since a functioning community could be usefully absorbed into the growing Zulu kingdom. The lot of those individuals cap-tured in raids and battles could be hard, however. There was no slavery as such, but captives would be carried off to the heartland of the kingdom where they would be incorporated into Zulu households in various menial capacities such as cattle herders or labourers if adult men, and as domes-tic servants or concubines if women or girls. Warriors were permitted to marry the young women they captured, and this had the advantage that no *ilobolo* had to be paid. Boys served their captors as *izindibi* while on cam-paign. On reaching adulthood they were permitted to become members of an *ibutho* themselves, and later to marry and set up their own *umuzi*.

Shaka's unrelenting efforts to prepare his domain for intensive fighting were absolutely necessary since the Ndwandwe were not done with him after their first campaign of 1818. The Zulu narrowly beat off a second Ndwandwe offensive and the enemy withdrew in good order, devastat-ing Zulu territory as they went. In 1819 Zwide attacked for a third time and Shaka retired before the Ndwandwe forces to the wooded and broken countryside of the Nkandla mountain range south of the Mhlathuze River. There the difficult terrain negated the numerical superiority of the Ndwandwe, and Shaka routed and scattered them in a pitched battle.

Shaka followed up this critical victory with a rapid advance across the Black Mfolozi River into Ndwandwe territory, taking Zwide completely by surprise. Thoroughly bested, Zwide and his following withdrew northwest across the Phongolo River. Shaka's *izibongo* exalted:

> I like him when he pursued Zwide son of Langa,
> Taking him from where the sun rises
> And sending him to where it set.[14]

As we have seen, it was very difficult for any African paramount such as Zwide to hold his sprawling domain together after such an overwhelming military defeat. Simmering tensions within the Ndwandwe ruling house came to the surface. Some sections of the Ndwandwe, such as the Gaza, under Soshangane kaZikode, and the Jele, under Zwangendaba kaZiguda, broke away altogether and migrated north to the environs of Delagoa Bay. The senior section of the Ndwandwe remained with Zwide on the north bank of the Phongolo, a region he had controlled for some time. He now set about considerably extending his sway further to the northwest at the expense of existing states such as the Pedi Maroteng paramountcy, which he shattered in about 1822.

Shaka would have been very aware that Zwide's fortunes were spectacularly reviving, and that the intimidating Ndwandwe presence just over the Phongolo menaced the territory the Zulu had so recently wrested from them. What made the situation even more fraught for Shaka was that he simply did not have the resources to bring Zwide's former tributary chiefdoms between the Black Mfolozi and Phongolo rivers effectively under his direct control. A section of the Khumalo, under Mzilikazi kaMashobana, rejected his rule altogether and broke away, settling in the highveld to the west of Zwide's relocated kingdom. Soon known to local Sotho-speakers as the 'Matabele', or Marauders, the Ndebele (as they proudly called themselves in their adaptation of this sobriquet) now lurked on the northwestern flanks of the Zulu kingdom, another latent threat. Other chiefdoms in the former Ndwandwe territory remained potentially rebellious. For the time being Shaka had to concede them a considerable degree of autonomy, ruling through a shrewd and ruthless viceroy, Maphitha kaSojiyisa, who was closely related to the Zulu royal house.

While watching the impatiently prowling Ndwandwe over his shoulder, Shaka was simultaneously consolidating his kingdom south of the Black Mfolozi by deploying diplomatic skill or brute force to overcome his weaker neighbours and bring them into his growing kingdom. The first of Shaka's major conquests was the Qwabe chiefdom, which, during the late 18th century, had been the most powerful polity in the coastal lands between the Thukela River and the Mhlathuze to the north. An expansionist state, it had clashed with the Mthethwa to the north and forced the neighbouring Thuli and Cele paramountcies into flight south over the Thukela. The Qwabe and the Zulu had a history of antagonism fuelled by Zulu envy of their rival's growing power and arrogance. Distinctive differences in dialect helped accentuate their differences, and the Qwabe used characteristically to *ukuthefula*, or to substitute a 'y' for the Zulu 'l' when speaking.

Tradition holds that, during his wandering youth as a despised exile, Shaka had been permitted for a while to live among the Qwabe because Mfunda, his grandmother on his mother Nandi's side, had been one of them.[15] It was said that Shaka and Phakathwayo, who later succeeded his father, Khondlo kaMncinci, as the *inkosi* of the Qwabe, had quarrelled as boys. Shaka neither forgot nor forgave an affront, and Phakathwayo woundingly insulted both his status and masculinity by calling him 'a little nothing in hiding, with a little penis that points upwards'.[16] Indeed the hurtful slur about his 'stumpy little stick'[17] of a penis would long outlive Shaka to intrigue a modern age raised on popular but facile psychological theories about his sexuality.

Accounts predictably differ as to how Shaka overcame the Qwabe. The more conventional version has Shaka attacking and defeating the Qwabe at the Hlokohloko Ridge near modern-day Eshowe.[18] Other accounts have Shaka characteristically employing treachery and magic to overcome the Qwabe.[19] Either way, Shaka took his old rival Phakathwayo captive, indulged himself by publicly humiliating him for his boyhood slights of long ago, and put him to death. With the execution of their *inkosi* the Qwabe swiftly decided to submit to Shaka and tender their allegiance. Shaka's unexpected victory over the great Qwabe chiefdom had immediate repercussions. The two largest independent chiefdoms of west-central Zululand, the Chunu and Thembu, took fright, and to escape Shaka's growing power fled south across the Thukela. Other smaller chiefdoms of the region scrambled to *ukukhonza* to Shaka to avoid being attacked.

Yet, for all this, Shaka remained insecure. Could he count on these recently subjugated chiefdoms' continuing loyal? The question always remained how best the newly subdued chiefdoms should be incorporated – chiefdoms, as John Wright reminds us, 'each with its own established ruling house, its own identity, its own body of memories and traditions'.[20]

Chiefdoms closest to the kingdom's core were most likely to be administered through royal officials (*izinduna*) ruling in the king's name like an *inkosi* over a district where the hereditary ruler had been eliminated. These *izinduna* whom Shaka appointed with the approval of his advisers were vital in carrying out his orders and performing various administrative functions. Besides that of governing an incorporated chiefdom, these could include holding important posts such as commanding an *ibutho* or presiding over an *ikhanda*. Nevertheless, whatever their power and however great the wealth they accumulated through royal rewards, *izinduna* understood that they owed their elevation entirely to royal favour rather than to right of birth, and knew that the king could just as easily disgrace them should they forfeit his favour.

For this reason, kings preferred to rely much more upon the support of their *izinduna* than upon hereditary *amakhosi*, with their long-established, hereditary power bases. Yet that was not always feasible, so the Zulu kings had to find a way of working with the subordinated *amakhosi*. In that case, the best solution for the king was to manipulate the lineage of a chiefdom. Thus, after executing the ruling *inkosi* along with the males of his direct line, Shaka might bestow the chieftainship on a junior member of the ruling house who understood he owed his elevation entirely to Shaka's favour and remained thereafter his grateful and dutiful client. A case in point was Nqetho, Phakathwayo's exiled half-brother, whom Shaka set over the Qwabe. But what to do with the *inkosi* of a defeated chiefdom situated further away from the kingdom's core? The insurmountable hindrances of distance and communication over the far-flung kingdom, with its broken terrain and many rivers, rendered tight central control difficult – and nigh unattainable along the furthermost peripheries of the kingdom. In any case, as with other southern African kingdoms, it was impossible with the prevailing social order for the Zulu monarchy to develop anything approaching a professional bureaucracy, not least because Zulu society was without writing and records were kept only in the memories of officials. The most realistic solution was to accept the formal submission of the more distant *amakhosi* and to govern indirectly through them.

Nevertheless, as a political resolution this had its flaws. The danger was that it was precisely these partially subdued hereditary chiefs on the periphery who were most likely to rebel. Essentially, there were two ways of dealing with this perennial challenge to the king's authority. One was to take violent military action against dissident chiefdoms accompanied by mass executions, the solution generally favoured by Shaka and Dingane. The alternative approach, one usually preferred by Mpande and Cetshwayo, was to accept decentralisation and confirm powerful regional notables of illustrious lineage and hereditary authority as district chiefs. The unresolved difficulty with this tactic was that patronage was power in every African kingdom. District chiefs left unsupervised in their hereditary domains were in a position to amass wealth through tribute and fines from their adherents, as well as from frequent gifts of cattle and luxuries from a king anxious to retain their loyalty. This enabled them to distribute handsome rewards to their own clients and so secure the prime loyalty of their adherents at the expense of the fealty they owed to the distant king. With monarchs weaker and less ruthless than Shaka, these great territorial magnates were tempted to exercise their old chiefly prerogatives without reference to the king, and even to maintain small armed forces of their own outside the *amabutho* system.

Nor was the influence of surviving hereditary territorial chiefs in the Zulu kingdom confined to their own domains. A select few who were distinguished by their natural competence and by the special trust the king placed in them became known as the 'great ones', or *izikhulu*. These were the men who were dominant in directing the affairs of the kingdom while simultaneously exploiting their privileged position to consolidate their personal followings in their own chiefdoms. Just how fatal this could be for the integrity of the kingdom was harshly revealed during the Anglo-Zulu War and in its sorry aftermath of civil war in the 1880s.

Indeed, despite later traditions of Shaka's well-knit, harmonious kingdom, we should never lose sight of the brutal fact that his rapidly expanding domain was in many aspects a ruthless conquest state, and that in his *izibongo* Shaka was likened to

> The threatening storm, take the children to shelter ...
> Beware, the wild beast is in the kraals.[21]

Consequently, many people in the freshly subjugated chiefdoms could never bring themselves truly to acknowledge Shaka's rule, let alone allow themselves to be more closely assimilated and take on Zulu identity. For their part, the conquering Zulu did not necessarily desire the full assimilation of all of their new subjects, and declined to consider some their true equals. Indeed, the Zulu ruling house – to whose members alone the term 'Zulu' properly applied – deliberately applied ethnic distinctions in their kingdom. On one side of the divide were the favoured 'insider' chiefdoms of the Zulu heartland, centred on the White Mfolozi. They had come under Shaka's rule early on, and their chiefly houses were absorbed into the ruling Zulu aristocracy. On the other side were the 'outsider' subject chiefdoms north of the Mkhuze and south of the Thukela. They were further away and had been subordinated later, and their chiefly houses were kept at arm's length from the centre of power.

Members of the 'insider' chiefdom came to be known as the *amantungwa*, after the *intungwa* grass that was used for thatching huts and weaving grain baskets.[22] The *amantungwa* increasingly regarded themselves as being of common Zulu descent and ethnicity. In their estimation, they were the true members of the kingdom, and it was their menfolk who primarily filled the ranks of the *amabutho*. They looked down on the 'outsiders' whose young men Shaka did not recruit into his *amabutho*, but instead deployed as lowly cattle herders and guards at outlying cattle posts. The *amantungwa* knew these 'outsiders' by a set of derogatory names such as *iziyendane* ('those with a strange hairstyle') and *amalala*. Originally meaning 'menials', in Shaka's time *amalala* became an ethnic slur, meaning inferior people with a dialect different from that of their rulers. Quite simply, they were not regarded as 'real Zulu' since they had not been 'born in the Zulu country'.[23] The reluctance of Shaka and his closely associated conquering elite to regard all their new subjects as their equals set up long-surviving differences in the kingdom that took generations to be smoothed over, if never entirely erased.

CHAPTER THREE

THE BIRDS OF
THE KING ARE HUNGRY

Shaka did not rule over the burgeoning Zulu kingdom only through the prestige of his royal descent, his firm control over the military capability of the *amabutho*, and the compliance of the new elite who formed part of the power structure of the state. His ritual powers were of equal, if not greater, importance in shoring up his right to rule.

In much of Africa it was (and sometime still is) the common belief that ritual powers – especially those of rain-making – are hereditary, and are the monopoly of the royal lineage in the person of the ruler who (as we have seen) is most often, but not always, a male. Upon his accession, and in order for him to perform his royal role, a king is endowed with the unique sacred qualities (but not the actual divinity of a living god) that set him apart from all his subjects.

Today, more people than not regard such ritual powers as merely symbolic. But in the pre-colonial period they were taken most seriously. To challenge a ruler's secular power was to run the risk of inciting retribution by the mystical forces at his command, such as preventing the rain from falling. Indeed, there was a perceived link between the health and wellbeing of the ruler and that of his kingdom as a whole, a sense that the life of a people was embodied in its king. It was therefore essential in the non-Muslim kingdoms of sub-Saharan Africa to 'strengthen' a king (and by association his people and warriors too) through regular refresher rituals and occult medicines. These renewed his potency as rainmaker to ensure the fertility of the land and the success of the harvest, protected him against evil witchcraft and assassination, and confounded his enemies.

Among all the peoples of southern Africa, the most significant of such rituals was the *umkhosi*, or first-fruits festival, which placed control of the vital harvest securely in the hands of the ruler and thereby confirmed his power over all his subjects. In the Zulu kingdom, at several crucial moments in the agricultural cycle the king was strengthened with benevolent *imithi* to ensure a good harvest, but the *umkhosi* capped all others.

In its grandeur, it was the most awe-inspiring ceremony every devised in pre-colonial southern Africa. What marked it out from similar ceremonies elsewhere was its integration with the ritual 'doctoring' of the army – an innovation traditionally ascribed to King Shaka – which turned it into a fearsome war feast. The ceremony was divided into two stages, the little and great *umkhosi*, always held when the full moon was about to wane. The little *umkhosi* took place about a month before the great one, in late November or early December when the green maize was ready to eat, and marked the beginning of the new year. It was on a relatively small, private scale. The king was ritually strengthened by 'black' *imithi* so powerful that they would (it was believed) have killed a commoner instantly. He sucked them from his fingers and squirted them out of his mouth at the rising sun to drive out evil influences from his people and to send confusion among his enemies. Especially handsome royal cattle that had been set aside in their own sacred enclosure for just such a purpose were then sacrificed to honour the shades of the royal *amadlozi*. The royal herd was then driven to the graves of the king's ancestors in the emaKhosini valley, where the king praised their shades and the people chanted *amahubo*, the great national anthems.

Here something more must be said of the royal *amadlozi*. In the Zulu spiritual universe, the living and the shades were bound together in a single community in which the *amadlozi* were the senior members. And because the shades retained the status they had possessed when alive, this meant that the *amadlozi* of the king, whom only he could invoke, were more influential than any others in the spirit world and were regarded as looking after the interests of the entire kingdom.

With the rituals of the little *umkhosi* completed, the people could now eat their crops and, full of rejoicing, begin to prepare for the great *umkhosi*. Across the kingdom the *amabutho* began to mobilise and concentrated in the vicinity of the king's chief *ikhanda*. This was the moment for the king's annual ritual hunt, when the *amabutho* sought out the fierce, powerful and venomous animals required for the *imithi* that would strengthen them during the coming ceremonies. On his return from the hunt, the king was kept in seclusion while he was ritually purified and fortified against evil influences with formidable 'black' *imithi*.

Early on the morning of the first day of the great *umkhosi* the king emerged from the great audience hut in the *isigodlo* to stand before the assembled *amabutho* and women. To his subjects, he was at his most terrible. He was dressed in the skins of eerie animals such as baboons, and his mystical association with the powers of fruitful nature was emphasised by greenish, fibrous coverings that made him resemble a tree. His face was painted in the symbolic colours of Zulu ritual medicine, with his right cheek white and his left black, while his forehead was red. To protect him from adverse occult forces he was smeared in powerful 'black' *imithi*. In his hand he carried the sacred royal spear that he wielded in blood sacrifices to his ancestors. It was an ancient throwing-spear, its shaft black with smoke and age, and its blade covered in rust.[1]

On his appearance before his people, the king was greeted by the swelling, awe-inspiring sound of the national song-dance peculiar to the *umkhosi*. As he had at the little *umkhosi*, the king spurted *imithi* at the rising sun to confound his enemies, and dashed a special bitter-tasting *uselwa*, or gourd, to the ground to exorcise all evil influences, pestilences and diseases from the nation.

The assembled *amabutho* were then purified of *umnyama* and ritually strengthened in three days of ceremonies that followed the same pattern as those they underwent when being prepared for war. On the day following the completion of these rituals, which had once more bound the warriors in loyalty to their king, there was jubilant feasting on royal cattle sacrificed to the *amadlozi*. Then followed a grand review of the *amabutho* in their full regalia with competitive military manoeuvres and dancing contests to honour the king and wish him well in governing the kingdom. If the mood took him, the king might join in the dancing and singing. Then, to conclude the *umkhosi*, the warriors formed a great crescent around the king while the monarch's chief councillor proclaimed the royal laws in his name. In response, the people would sing the praises of the king and his ancestors, and would finally disperse.

When the *amabutho* ritually vomited *imithi* into a hole during the *umkhosi*, a small amount of what they voided was added to the *inkatha yezwe yakwa-Zulu*, the only ritual object the Zulu specifically fashioned. Its possession was the ultimate legitimation of the king's authority because it was believed to possess the enormous mystical powers of rejuvenating and protecting the king and the nation, and of gathering the people together in loyalty to the king.

This *inkatha* was a circular grass coil about a metre in diameter and the thickness of a man's calf. It was wrapped in a python skin, which embodied the reptile's enormous strength and its supernatural coolness that brought the rain and the successful harvest, and was securely bound with grass rope by the leading men of the kingdom. The components from which it was made contained the supernatural essence of the living nation. The grass came from alongside the paths that had been brushed by the people and cattle as they passed, and from the doorways of huts which people rubbed when they stooped to enter. Into it went the *izinsila* of the king, his predecessors and relations. Shaka incorporated fragments of the *izinkatha* of chiefs he had conquered when consolidating his kingdom, and small pieces of the bodies of enemy leaders he had killed. The warriors' vomit has already been mentioned, but also added was litter from the ground where the king's councillors sat and discussed affairs of state, along with the hair and teeth of powerful wild animals such as lion and buffalo. And if that were not enough, potent *imithi* were inserted into the coil. It was believed that the king and his royal ancestors could transfer the occult powers of the *inkatha* to the people. So, when the king squatted upon the *inkatha*, a mystical force rayed out from it to inspire his army in battle and to prevent the malevolent shades of dead enemies from aiding the foe.

The *inkatha* was reverently handed down from king to king, swelling in size as it was continually added to. It was always kept out of sight and under guard in the great hut of an *ikhanda*, where it was entrusted to the keeping of one of the prominent widows of former kings. During King Dingane's reign it was deposited at the esiKlebheni *ikhanda* in the emaKhosini valley. This was the sacred site of Shaka's father Senzangakhona's original *umuzi*, and where he was buried. Langazana, one of Senzangakhona's surviving widows, was still presiding over esiKlebheni on 26 June 1879 when, in the final, cataclysmic days of the Anglo-Zulu War, the British burned the *ikhanda* along with the *inkatha* itself. The *inkatha*'s destruction was indubitably the symbolic end of the Zulu kingdom as founded by King Shaka, and severed the mystical link between the first four Zulu kings and those monarchs who came after them.

There was something else too besides lineage, raw power and ritual consecration that made an African king a king. This was the deeply and widely held understanding that there was (and is) an informal contract between a king and his subjects. The latter possess a clear perception of what constitutes fairness and justice, and they have an expectation of how a reasonable ruler should behave. In practice, this meant that a king's subjects required him to be constrained by the traditional laws and customs of his realm. Should a king flout these bounds, he could expect resistance, rebellion, the breaking-away of disaffected subjects, or even assassination and usurpation. To ensure that things never reached this desperate pass, and to contain the potentially destructive vagaries of royal individuals, in most African kingdoms monarchs were expected to consult their councillors when making state decisions, and to hearken to their advice.

Accordingly, the pre-colonial Zulu kings had an inner core of half a dozen or so leading advisers, a 'cabinet' or *umkhandlu*. From among their number the king selected his chief councillor and commander-in-chief whose task was to guide him and share the weight of decision. The *umkhandlu* conducted affairs by first holding a confidential conclave in the royal *isibaya* in front of the *isigodlo*. Upon reaching agreement, it then went to consult the king. Once the king had pondered its advice and come to a decision, he would summon the great council, or *ibandla*, which consisted of the leading notables of the kingdom. Its members sat in a semicircle before the king to hear what he had decided and to discuss the matter with him. If it were a truly vital decision, such as that of going to war, an even broader meeting of married men and *amabutho* might be called so that the issue could be widely aired and a popular consensus reached. Finally, after consultation had run its course, the chief councillor announced the agreed-upon decision of state to the people at large in a general assembly at one of the great national festivals such as the *umkhosi*. In times of national emergency, however, the announcement was made when necessary.

Such at least was the theory of consultative royal rule, and it was often the practice too. Nevertheless, although a king was not expected to make great state decisions without proper consultation, when rulers possessed an overwhelming and ruthless personality, their councillors were highly unlikely to question the king's wishes. Maclean described the members of a large assembly, ranged before Shaka in a semicircle, who 'squatted on the ground in a very humble posture, their elbows resting on their knees', who, at every pause in Shaka's conversation, humbly responded, '*Yebo baba, yebo baba*' (yes father, yes father).[2]

None were likely to forget that in the Zulu kingdom the ultimate decisions over life and death lay with the king alone. This was a crucial prerogative Shaka had removed from the hands of subordinate chiefs. Indeed, when it came to the administration of justice, the king was the final court of appeal and he could – and often did – overrule his advisers and act arbitrarily. If he found a person guilty, he could fine him cattle, send him 'into the wilderness to disappear'[3] or have him executed.

The execution of those the king sentenced to death was carried out at a designated place just outside the main entrance to the king's royal homestead, such as the notorious kwaNkatha at Dingane's uMgungundlovu *ikhanda*. In Shaka's time, when the king suddenly pointed his staff at an individual, the victim was instantly hauled off and usually first stunned by a blow to the head before being impaled and then thrown into the nearby bush, there to die still transfixed and in prolonged agony. During the reigns of the succeeding three kings a condemned man would normally be brained with a heavy knobbed stick, or his neck would be broken. Women were not executed in the same way; a rope was tied around the neck with a slip-knot, and it was then struck sharply with a stick until the noose tightened sufficiently to throttle the woman.

The execution of those found guilty of breaking the law was one thing, but the first Zulu kings regularly used their powers over life and death to order the apparently arbitrary killing of their subjects. Certainly, the kings may sometimes have had good reason to suspect a plot was brewing and to have moved to pre-empt it. And here we must not forget the other male members of the royal lineage, the *abantwana*, or princes of the blood, who inevitably stood high in the hierarchy of power. Some were content to live private lives, away from court, but others were ambitious, if not necessarily particularly able, and the king could not avoid sharing some degree of his power with them, inviting them onto his council, and so on. But every *umntwana*, whatever his talents, was a standing danger to any king since, on account of his lineage, he could potentially replace him. And inevitably there were a few in the ranks of the princes consumed by boundless ambition or corroding envy who coveted the throne and were willing to resort to violence if the king should be seen to falter. By the same token, in an environment where the king was capable of suddenly executing anyone he considered a danger, no matter how high his rank, *abantwana* sometimes felt compelled to strike first to save their lives.

In practice, though, kings were usually in a better position to strike first, and when they ordered apparently capricious and indiscriminate executions it was for political reasons – to strike terror and compliance into the hearts of those they spared but suspected of disaffection. In ordering the death of important individuals, the kings' command over the loyalty of their *amabutho* was of paramount importance, for it was they who carried out the killings. Sometimes (especially during Shaka's reign, as we shall see) these took the form of the mass killings of whole groups of people, but usually it was individual notables who were targeted. In that case, it was the practice to eliminate the great man's whole family along with him so that there would be none left to avenge him.

As we have seen, Zulu kings, if they were sufficiently determined, could ignore the counsel of their advisers and the traditional constraints of contractual rule and conduct themselves as despots. In this regard, Shaka's *izibongo* stated bluntly that the king was

He who refuses to be told,
He who refuses to be advised.[4]

The nature of a reign very much depended, therefore, on the character of the ruler himself, since it was he who decided in what manner he would wield his enormous power. Yet when we turn to examine Shaka's personality as a possible key to understanding the nature of his rule, we find ourselves hobbled from the start. Much of what we think we know about him personally is derived from Zulu oral traditions. Many are deeply critical of him as a bloodthirsty tyrant because they emanate from people who considered themselves his victims. By contrast, those traditions preserved among people who benefited from his sway laud him uncritically as a hero and founder of the kingdom. The observations of the white hunter-traders who were acquainted with him were deeply coloured by prejudice and self-interest. Shaka, despite his fame, must therefore remain an enigmatic and elusive figure. We don't even know how to pronounce his name. *Amalala*-speakers said 'Tshaka', and not 'Shaka',[5] as the *amantungwa* would have. This explains why the early Port Natal settlers, living as they did in *amalala* country, always wrote 'Chaka' since that spelling indicated the 'Tsh' sound.

One thing, though, we can say of Shaka without the slightest hesitation: he was incorrigibly, formidably warlike. His *izibongo* jubilantly extol him as:

> The voracious one of Senzangakhona,
> Spear that is red even on the handle …
> The young viper grows as it sits,
> Always in a great rage,
> It eats with its shield on its knees.
> The forceful one,
> The lunatic is in the eyes of men;
> He who while devouring some devoured others …[6]

Otherwise, what else can we know of Shaka's character? Charles Maclean, who spent nearly three years at Shaka's court and, as a child, was permitted a degree of intimacy with Shaka that would have been denied an adult, later wrote that 'Shaka was a man of great natural ability, but he was cruel and capricious'.[7] Zulu at the beginning of the 20th century believed that the king's character was made up of the contradictory impulses of generosity to those who had earned his favour and wanton cruelty against those who had not. And, certainly, we have seen how apparently arbitrary executions were a standard instrument of royal policy. There were Zulu who, while admitting that Shaka 'killed off frequently', shrugged it off as the king merely indulging in 'sport' as was his due.[8] Or was he in fact deriving a perverse kind of amusement from seeing people killed, as other testimony had it?[9] Certainly, indignant traditions of Shaka's callous bloodthirstiness were passed on: 'Seeing vultures flying above, he [Shaka] cried, "Wo! The birds of the king are hungry!' People were then killed and put out on a hill to be eaten by the vultures. And wu! The vultures were all out on the hill!'[10]

Disturbingly, besides remembering Shaka's insouciant pleasure in executions, people also preserved tales of various atrocities Shaka perpetrated. Of course, many of these should be disregarded as nothing more than adverse propaganda. Some Zulu wisely reflected that people relished concocting horror stories about Shaka, such as his nasty habit of impaling children on stakes.[11] So when an informant was recorded as saying that 'Tshaka did many evil things to people, like cutting open a pregnant woman to see how her child lay',[12] we are tempted to discount the tale. Except that, in this case, it was repeated by several other informants, suggesting that we should possibly give it credence.[13] It is perhaps enough, though, to take these stories of Shaka's arbitrary cruelty as indicators of popular fear and dislike among certain of his subjects, and as a subsequent justification for his assassination promoted by his killers.

Shaka the wicked despot was only part of the picture, and like any human being he had other, more vulnerable sides to his character. From talking to Zulu people when he visited King Dingane on a diplomatic mission from the Cape in 1832, Dr Andrew Smith gained the impression that 'Chaka was a man of great feeling and used frequently from grief or excessive joy to burst into a crying fit'.[14] We also learn that Shaka was 'very fond of going about visiting places. He sat very little indoors.' Late in his reign, once he had settled at kwaDukuza, about ten kilometres from the seashore, he is said to have enjoyed sitting for hours watching the waves of the Indian Ocean. At sunset he would energetically start off home 'at a run' with his courtiers – many of them plump and stately like most Zulu men of high status – scurrying and panting to keep up with him.[15] Such physical activity was not surprising, though, in a man the hunter-trader Nathaniel Isaacs noted was considered 'the best pedestrian in the country', and who in the dance 'exhibited the most astonishing activity'.[16]

The Zulu remembered that when Shaka 'got older he used to have the white hairs pulled out of his head. He always wanted to be regarded as quite young,'[17] doubtless fearing that if he were seen to be ageing his enemies would be tempted to take advantage. Indeed, his grey hairs, recalled Maclean, 'caused him great uneasiness' and, letting down his guard in private, he anxiously enquired if the white men possessed any remedy. He was thrilled when he learned they possessed the 'valuable preparation' – Macassar oil, a fashionable hair conditioner – necessary to restore his hair and beard to its full blackness.[18]

And what of Shaka's sexuality? Despite his having an *isigodlo* of hundreds of young women at his disposal, some Zulu were later prepared to declare categorically: 'Tshaka had absolutely no issue – male or female.'[19] A prurient modern age has latched onto this lack of progeny to speculate that he was sterile, impotent or homosexual. Yet there is in fact no mystery here. The Zulu agreed that their kings were simply following the practice among leopards and lions for the mother to hide a male cub for fear the father would kill it.[20] As one informant confirmed to Stuart: 'A person like Tshaka is like a wild beast, a creature that does not live with its own young, its male offspring.'[21] Cetshwayo stated bluntly that Shaka simply did not wish to have progeny.[22] Dingane, Shaka's successor, had no child either. That was because both feared the consequences of raising an heir to become a competitor and possible usurper – as Mpande, the third Zulu king, would discover when forced to share power with Cetshwayo, his overmighty son and *inkosana*.

In other words, just because Shaka had no heir did not mean he avoided sexual relations with women. It was said that 'Chaka used to sleep in company with four of his wives, one on each side and one across the feet and one at the head'.[23] To enjoy them he did not necessarily have to impregnate them. Like other Zulu men he doubtless practised *ukuhlobonga*, or external sexual intercourse, when he did not wish his partner to conceive, although it was said that in fact he always penetrated the women he slept with.[24] Besides, is it true that he fathered absolutely no children? Tradition held that he had many *izixebe*, or paramours,[25] and that whenever Shaka, while living under Dingiswayo, 'met a girl in the path he would catch her and make her pregnant', and that his indulgent patron would not punish him for the rape.[26] We have already seen that he married while serving Dingiswayo, and is reputed to have had a son, Zibizendlela, who may have survived in exile.

Once Shaka was the Zulu king, however, what did he do with a woman he had made pregnant, and with her unwanted baby? Andrew Smith asserted that if any of Shaka's women fell pregnant, they were ordered to abort the fetus. If that did not work, they were put to death.[27] Socwatsha, whose father, Papu, was a contemporary of Shaka's, had been told precisely the same thing.[28] However, as Maclean noted, white settlers relished the notion that the savage king killed any concubine he made with child. From his observation while living at Shaka's court, any *umndlunkulu* or *isigqila* the king made pregnant was sent away to live 'in great retirement and obscurity'. These banished women kept their children but 'never hinted they were of royal blood'.[29]

All we can truly say in the end of Shaka the man is that in many ways he will remain unknowable, the projection of conflicting adulatory and condemnatory traditions. Nevertheless, what does emerge about this person of such contradictory characteristics – at once vain and emotional, cruel and generous, bellicose and suspiciously fearful – was that he possessed extraordinary abilities, especially military ones. Had he not been skilful and aggressive, decisive and ruthless beyond ordinary measure, he would never have overcome his many rivals and bitter enemies to build the kingdom that was his monument.

Shaka's physical appearance remains as much a conundrum as his character. One thing we can be certain of is that he did not possess the film-star good looks of Henry Cele, who played him in the popular television series, *Shaka Zulu*. Nor do the various modern statues and numerous visual portrayals of him represent anything other than an idealised figure imagined by the sculptor or artist.

Fuze, writing his history a century after Shaka's death and drawing on tradition, described him thus:

Shaka as a grown man had a good, strong, well-built body; he had good buttocks, well-shaped but not large, unlike Mpande who had very large buttocks. He had a large body, but … he was a man of war and not sedentary. He was brown in colour, unlike Mpande who was black, and as a king, glossy with good food. He did not get stout like Mpande, but remained muscular and powerful.[30]

Possibly Shaka did indeed look like that. The problem is that no first-hand artist's image of him survives, as it has for Dingane and Mpande, and of course he was never photographed, as were the Zulu kings from Cetshwayo onwards. White hunter-traders saw Shaka close up, but left only impressionistic descriptions. Isaacs, for example, described him as 'upwards of six feet in height, and well proportioned',[31] But is that how the Zulu saw him? Once again we have to weigh up positive and hostile traditions, the problem being that the only Zulu with first-hand recorded memories of him were children at the time who had only seen him from afar,[32] while others who spoke of Shaka's physical characteristics were repeating the tales of their fathers or grandfathers second-hand.[33] In the main, Fuze's description of Shaka accords with their recorded oral testimony, although they disagree as to whether he was of only medium height or taller.[34] A few dissenting voices described him as 'slight', rather than well-built and light-brown (like a lizard in colour), rather than dark brown.[35] It seems certain that Shaka had not been circumcised as the practice had already ceased in the region where he was born.

It appears, then, that Shaka was physically well set up, strong and athletic. But how handsome was he? There is no doubt that he was unusually hirsute for a Zulu. Many of the family of Senzangakhona had patches of hair on their bodies, like spotted butterflies. Accordingly, in his *izibongo* Shaka is described as

The butterfly of Phunga
With round spots as though deliberately placed.[36]

Other descriptions of his looks are not complimentary. Shaka, declared Mayinga in his recorded testimony, 'had eyes always red, and a protruding forehead. He had a badly shaped head. His head came forward and then went back. He was not really ugly but his head was peculiar.'[37] Baleka of the hostile Qwabe was less equivocal. She told Stuart that her father said that Shaka had 'a large nose, and was ugly.'[38] Indeed, Shaka's nose was clearly not his best feature. Senzangakhona's children were known for their prominent noses, and Shaka's was clearly large and wide.[39] Unattractively, 'Tshaka's nose used to perspire', said Mayinga. 'He used to take hold of his nose from above and give it a twist as if to blow it and get sweat off at the same time.' Even more attention was drawn to Shaka's nose, added Mayinga, because 'he snuffed a good deal.'[40] Shaka was said to have had two prominent front teeth, and these may have contributed to his widely reported speech defect of mouthing his words as if his tongue were too big for his mouth, or of stuttering or lisping.[41] On the other hand, this 'defect' may simply have been a snobbish Zulu insider's take on Shaka's widely reported Mthethwa *ukuthefula* dialect, which resembled that of the Qwabe, which both substitute a 'y' for the Zulu 'l'. Very unattractively, Shaka is remembered to have laughed 'outside his mouth', which meant he had a hollow, ominously artificial laugh that struck fear into those who heard it.[42]

To his credit, Shaka does seem to have acknowledged that he was not a handsome man and to have been able to joke mordantly about it. Mtshebwe, a son of Magaye kaDibandlela, the Cele *inkosi* and a great favourite of Shaka's, recalled that the king said to his father, who was a good deal younger than him:[43]

Even though it is said I am in the habit of killing people, never will I kill you. Were I to do so ... the Zulus would laugh at me. They would say I had killed you simply for being handsome, and because I am *isinkontshela*, i.e. with a prominent, protruding forehead, and ugly.[44]

CHAPTER FOUR

❈

DO YOU HEAR THE KING?

The year 1824 was a climactic one in Shaka's fortunes, and several unconnected developments combined to shake his confidence and change the nature of his regime.

Used to an unbroken string of victories as he built his conquest state, Shaka admitted no bounds to his sway. But the disastrous Mpondo campaign of the autumn of 1824 graphically signalled the limits of his military reach.

Despite their many conquests, Shaka's *amabutho* were not invariably invincible. The further they operated away from their bases, the more their defective logistical arrangements diminished their ability to stay in the field and secure a meaningful victory. If the objective of a campaign was the actual conquest of a territory, then the strategic intention was to bring the foe to a decisive battle as rapidly as possible. On the other hand, when the more limited goal was to raid for cattle and captives, or when the enemy avoided facing battle, then the strategy was to force the enemy to evacuate their territory or take refuge in their mountain or forest fastnesses. Once that was achieved, the *amabutho* were free to scoop up the booty their foes had left behind. However, the raiders could easily become the victims of their own strategy. When unable to come to grips with the enemy warriors – or if defeated – the *amabutho* were left with no option but

60

to retire. But they had stripped the countryside of supplies and burned all forms of shelter when they advanced. Now, hungry and suffering from exposure, encumbered by their captured cattle and other loot, demoralised and eager to get home, that is when the raiders were at their most vulnerable to counterattack.

In April 1824 Mdlaka kaNcidi, Shaka's foremost commander, led an army south along the foothills of the Drakensberg and then eastwards down the valley of the Mzimvubu River into the heart of the Mpondo paramountcy ruled by the wily and experienced Faku kaNgqungqushe. This army should not be imagined as being very large, certainly nothing like the horde of Zulu warriors conjured up by the fevered settler imagination and perpetuated in the modern-day imagination. We have seen how, in the early 19th century, Africa was still underpopulated, and the total population of Shaka's kingdom would have been somewhere in the region of only a quarter of a million people. The hunter-trader Francis Farewell reported in September 1824 that he found the 'large territory he [Shaka] was possessed of ... very thinly peopled' and that 14 000 males 'might be fighting men on a push'.[1] So we must think of only several thousand warriors under Mdlaka entering Mpondoland and then busily rounding up Faku's cattle in a major raid rather than a campaign of conquest. Faku's forces retaliated, bested Mdlaka's in scattered fighting, and then harried them as they retreated northwards along the coast. Abandoning their captured cattle and completely out of supplies, the *amabutho* were obliged to subsist on wild plants and melons (*amabece*). Ever afterwards this disastrous foray was known as the *amabece impi*, or melon campaign.

As with any ruler whose reputation is built on exceptional success in war, Shaka knew perfectly well that a military reverse, even a fairly minor one, would damage his prestige and authority. Smarting at his humiliation, he immediately despatched spies into the Mpondo territory so that his forces would have better intelligence when they attacked again, as they must.

At the very moment that the *amabece impi* was disastrously playing out, quite unexpected actors entered the scene who would have a momentous and abiding impact on Shaka and his kingdom. Shaka was already familiar with the lucrative trade with the Portuguese conducted through Lourenço Marques. To secure it, he had by mid-1824 made tributaries of the chiefdoms living in the coastal plain as far north as the further side of Delagoa Bay. But Lourenço Marques was far from the Zulu heartland and Shaka cast about for an alternative trading partner. The Cape Colony, which had been affirmed a British possession on 13 August 1814 by the Convention of London, and of which Shaka was dimly aware, seemed a possibility. But it was not easy to make trading contact with it. Westwards over the Drakensberg, which marked his kingdom's western limits, the highveld of the interior was dominated by the emerging Sotho mountain kingdom and by Mzilikazi's roaming and belligerent Ndebele state, Shaka's inveterate foe. The Cape was in closer and easier reach overland southwards along the coast from Zululand than over the mountains. But the way was barred by the powerful Mpondo paramountcy that had successfully repulsed the Zulu army under Mdlaka. The only other viable trade route to the Cape was by sea, but the Zulu possessed no seagoing vessels, not even the canoes with which other African peoples further to the north plied their lakes, rivers and lagoons.

Yet, as it turned out, the Zulu did not have to take the initiative. Adventurous traders and hunters from the Cape opened up the economic possibilities of the Zulu kingdom. Fortuitously, the only viable natural harbour between Algoa Bay in the Cape Colony and Portuguese-controlled Delagoa Bay lay in Shaka's domain about halfway between the Thukela and Mzimkhulu rivers. There a great, bush-covered bluff thrust into the sea on the southern side of an extensive bay that enclosed several small wooded islands. The place's one drawback as a harbour – and it was not an inconsiderable one – was a sandbar that impeded entrance to the bay to all but small vessels.

On 10 May 1824 the 21-year-old Henry Francis Fynn and five companions made land in the bay from the tiny sloop *Julia*. Several weeks later, on about 20 June 1824, a larger group of 26 prospective settlers arrived in the brig *Antelope* under Lieutenant Francis George Farewell, RN, a naval veteran of the Napoleonic Wars. Farewell had secured the support of JR Thompson & Co of Cape Town for a permanent trading post. He and Fynn were to act as their agents in obtaining ivory, hides and maize from the Zulu, and in extending operations northward to capture some of the flourishing trade flowing through Delagoa Bay.

Fynn and Farewell both hoped that their little settlement, which they dubbed Port Natal, would be brought under the protection of the British Crown. To that end they immediately went through the motions of raising the Union Flag and firing salutes, and petitioned the Governor of the Cape Colony to annex Port Natal. They were turned down flat and the hunter-traders were on their own. This rejection left them with no option but to seek Shaka's patronage. In August 1824 Shaka summoned Fynn and Farewell to kwaBulawayo in the Mahlabathini plain, his principal *ikhanda* at the time, to make their case in person. Their outlandish garb, incomprehensible speech, light skin colour, extraordinary hair – likened to maize tassels or cattle tails – unfamiliar horses and terrifying firearms threw ordinary people and even the *amabutho* into complete consternation and astonished Shaka himself.

From the first, Shaka was able to communicate with the hunter-traders through their black interpreter from the eastern Cape, known as Jacob or Jakot Msimbithi. And as outlandish as they appeared, it is to Shaka's credit that he decided to make use of them instead of rejecting them, as he might well have done. He grasped that he could control these men trading from within his kingdom far more effectively than he could the distant Portuguese. He also saw how they might well be the conduit through which he could foster relations with the British authorities at the Cape, whose power he was beginning to appreciate. Furthermore, he foresaw that with their muskets they could make useful allies against his enemies. So he genially welcomed them to his court and conferred on them the privilege of being considered *abakwethu*, or 'people of our house', kinsmen. Next, on 8 August 1824 Shaka put his mark with due ceremony to a significant document by which he granted 'Farewell & Co' permission to occupy the land surrounding Port Natal and extending 50 miles inland and 25 miles along the coast. He also gave the settlers the right to exercise authority over this territory, as well as permission to trade.[2]

From his perspective, Shaka had neither ceded Port Natal to the settlers, nor surrendered his ultimate authority over it. He regarded the settlers as typical client chiefs, and expected them to render service to him as would other tributaries, and that included military assistance. And without any overt support from the British authorities, the traders had no choice but to abide by Shaka's terms and go along with his demands, no matter how irksome they might prove.

Daunted by the many hardships they encountered, most of the settlers at Port Natal lost heart and returned to Cape Town. By December 1824 the settlement had been reduced to only six men. A small party of reinforcements arrived when their brig, *Mary*, was driven onto the sandbar by a gale on 1 October 1825 and foundered on the beach. Their leader was James Saunders King, who liked to pose as an ex-naval lieutenant and who had failed to drum up support in England for the Port Natal project. He brought with him his 17-year-old assistant, Nathaniel Isaacs, and the nine-year-old Charles Maclean. Life in the rudimentary settlement remained basic in the extreme, and the traders were soon adapting to local dress and customs, taking concubines and multiple wives and, with Shaka's encouragement, setting up as subordinate *amakhosi* over the people in the vicinity of the port. Consequently, as was typical in Zulu political life, the power and fortunes of the various settler chiefs waxed and waned with the number of adherents they could attract to their banner.

Shortly after the arrival of the Port Natal settlers, a sensational event at esiKlebheni, the *ikhanda* Shaka's father, Senzangakhona, had established in the emaKhosini valley, deeply unsettled Shaka and threw his kingdom into turmoil.

Dancing had been going all day at esiKlebheni, and when dusk fell Shaka ordered lighted bundles of dried reeds to be lit and held up to illuminate the pulsating scene. Suddenly there was a great shriek, the lights were extinguished and the people began a great uproar, yelling and screaming that Shaka had been attacked while joining in the dancing. Zulu testimony agrees that an assassin's spear blade stabbed Shaka through the left upper arm but barely penetrated his chest beneath. Shaka himself pulled out the spear and his attendants hustled him away to the security of a small *umuzi* some distance from esiKlebheni.

Fynn was present and assisted Shaka's own *izinyanga*, or traditional healers, in treating his wounds.[3] He was witness to scenes of hysteria, particularly in the *isigodlo*, where the *umndlunkulu* dared not eat while their lord hovered between life and death. The whole great, exhausted assemblage at esiKlebheni went through the incessant motions of intense mourning, since not to weep – or to be caught feigning to do so – or to sit down, or to wear ornaments, or even to wash meant (Fynn dramatically assures us) being put to death.

The assassins escaped in the frantic turmoil, wounding several others as they fled, and it was left to Shaka to decide who the culprits were likely to have been. His suspicion fell upon two of his half-brothers, Dingane and Mhlangana, who lived at the isiPhezi *ikhanda* on the banks of the Mphembeni River a few kilometres to the west of the emaKhosini valley. These two ambitious *abantwana* might well have been plotting against him, but Shaka evidently decided it would be impolitic to take action at that moment, and so held his hand.

The hysterical throng at esiKlebheni were in no doubt regarding who was to blame for the deed, and the clamour went up that the assassins must have been sent by Shaka's inveterate foe Zwide kaLanga, the *inkosi* of the Ndwandwe. Shaka indulged the crowd by sending two *amabutho* in pursuit of the supposed culprits. On the fifth day after the assassination attempt they returned with several bodies that they claimed were those of the would-be assassins. The mob, still in its mourning frenzy, hysterically pulverised the corpses into the ground.

Meanwhile, Shaka had decided on whom it would best serve his political interests to fix the blame, and declared that the would-be killers were members of the Qwabe people, whose proud, powerful chiefdom had been his first major conquest. It is evident Shaka doubted the sincerity of their submission, and resolved to exploit the opportunity to crush them decisively. He despatched several *amabutho* to fan out across the countryside and kill Qwabe wherever they could find them. So great was the ensuing massacre that even Nandi, Shaka's tough mother, was appalled.

Shaka's ferocious breaking-up of the Qwabe doubtless gave his many internal and external enemies pause, as he intended it should, but it did not do away with them. So Shaka's response following the assassination attempt was to shift his capital away from the valley of the White Mfolozi to within Qwabe territory. By relocating the centre of the kingdom's gravity there, Shaka was better situated to keep a close and wary eye on the surviving Qwabe and the neighbouring Mthethwa, just north across the Mhlathuze River, who did not find it easy to forget their former greatness. He also put a safe distance between himself and the Ndwandwe, who were recovering their strength and were beginning to probe Zulu defences in the north and to raid their former territory south of the Phongolo. Furthermore, by moving much closer to the Thukela, Shaka was better able to consolidate his hold over the rich coastlands south of the river by quartering *amabutho* there and by establishing a string of outlying royal cattle posts.

Shaka's new capital in the Qwabe country was called kwaBulawayo. *Amakhanda* were frequently re-founded in new locations, so it is often necessary to distinguish them one from another as the first, second and even third of that name. The first kwaBulawyo was just north of the White Mfolozi. Shaka built the new, second kwaBulawayo just south of the Mhlathuze River, at the source of the Bele stream, on a ridge of hills about 27 kilometres north of the present-day town of Eshowe. Symbolically, its site was close to eMtandeni, the capital of Phakathwayo, the defeated Qwabe *inkosi*, which it was clearly intended to overshadow. According to a strand of oral testimony, kwaBulawayo means 'the "place of death", where people are killed, from the precipices near there over which people were thrown'.[4] Though, as with many other *amakhanda*, it had alternative names, and kwaBulawayo was originally known as Gibixhegu, meaning 'Defeat the Old Man'. It gained that name when Shaka defeated Zwide, because he is supposed to have said, 'I won't think of fighting with an old man (*ixegu*) who used to fight with my father.'[5]

From contemporary descriptions we can conjure up something of the spectacle and atmosphere of everyday life at Shaka's court at kwaBulawayo. It continued in much the same fashion under succeeding kings until it was finally extinguished at the end of Cetshwayo's reign.

Each pre-colonial Zulu king was like every other sub-Saharan African monarch in that the *ikhanda* in which he held court encompassed a greater complex of buildings and a larger concentration of population than elsewhere in the kingdom. As at other royal palaces, the *isigodlo* formed the heavily guarded private quarters of the king and his women. He was the only man – on pain of death – who could enter the *isigodlo* without a royal summons or spend the night there. It was typical too that of the hundreds of *umndlunkulu* kept in the *isigodlo* only a select few became his concubines. Some of the others would be given to favoured notables to cement political alliances, while the balance acted as servants, or *izigqila*, to the royal women. It was normal too that the king's chief councillors and *abantwana*, along with the king's confidential male attendants, should have their own special huts in two enclosures on either side of the *isigodlo* at the top of the two *izinhlangothi* wings surrounding the parade ground. These enclosures were known as the *izigqiki* after the carved wooden headrests that supported the neck of a sleeping Zulu, where the 'head' was the *isigodlo* and the 'body' the *inhlangothi*. All African palaces had their audience area too, accessible to councillors, deputations and select guests. In the Zulu king's *ikhanda* this was the *isibaya* in front of the *isigodlo*. He also held meetings in an especially large hut within the *isigodlo*, and he might arrange private audiences within his own sleeping hut in the *isigodlo*.

An African king was barely ever alone. In his *isigodlo*, the Zulu monarch was surrounded by hundreds of women. In the central, 'black' section of the *isigodlo* dwelt the female members of the royal house, or *amakhosikazi*. As married or senior women, they were crowned with complexly worked topknots of hair, and wore pleated leather skirts. These were shorter than those of commoners and did not reach to the knees, and were worn low down so that about five centimetres of the cleft between the buttocks could be seen. The women of the royal house decorated themselves with beads around the forehead, ankles and arms. Like all post-pubescent Zulu people of both sexes, they wore ear plugs of carved, polished wood, about two to five millimetres in diameter. These might be replaced by cylindrical earlobe snuff cases, and it was a status symbol among the *amakhosikazi* to have ones made of rhino horn. (Ivory was reserved for the elite, and commoners made do with bone and the horns of lesser beasts.) Alongside the *amakhosikazi* lived the king's favoured *umndlunkulu*. All unmarried girls across the kingdom had a front covering of beadwork or leaves to shield their nakedness, or perhaps a fringed waistband of skins, but these *umndlunkulu* were reputed to wear nothing other than strings of beads. If the king particularly favoured them, they sported brass coils around their arms, as well as four brass collars so tight that it was almost impossible to turn the head.

Unlike those unfortunate *umndlunkulu* who had failed to draw the king's fancy and who, with the widows and the *izigqila*, performed all the menial chores around the *isigodlo*, the unoccupied and unexercised favoured ones grew fat and petulant in their boring seclusion. They spent their days sitting on their mats anointing themselves with the fat from the heavy tails of sheep until their flesh glistened for the king's delectation. Of an evening they would sing and dance for him, and the most favoured would later lie with him that night.

At court, there were a number of male personal attendants, the *izinceku*, who looked after the king and who had been carefully selected for this confidential role. The king employed them as private advisers or as diplomatic agents, deployed them to report back on the activities of key subjects, and often used them as conduits through which he made his wishes known. Outside the *isigodlo* the king was forever interacting with *amakhosi* and *izinduna*, who were constantly coming and going to pay their respects, to report back, to petition or to attend the national festivals, and who always approached him in awful solemnity, in a humble, half-bent posture.

As at all royal courts worldwide and not just in Africa, esoteric protocol surrounded the Zulu king and considerable ceremony attended his public appearances. At daybreak the gatekeeper roused the sleeping *isigodlo* by loudly calling out the king's praises. The king did not emerge from his sleeping hut until the sun rose, by which time the *izigqila* had tidied and swept the entire *isigodlo*. In the company of favoured councillors and courtiers the king was washed and rubbed down either in the *isigodlo* or in the *isibaya*, where a section, called the *inhlambelo*, was divided off for his ablutions. A barber would shave him and dress his hair while he sat in the place of assembly chatting to his great nobles, all the while going through an extravagant pantomime of fear at daring to touch the royal person.

All the king's hair and stubble would be caught in a little basket and then burned, with the ashes scattered into a running stream so that his *izinsila* did not fall into the wicked hands of an *umthakathi* and be used as in ingredient in *imithi* to gain malevolent power over him and call down disease or death. For the same reason, if the king squirted saliva or coughed up phlegm, an attendant would rub it into the ground so that it could no longer be found. To thwart the machinations of *abathakathi*, kings would keep *izangoma*, or diviners, in close attendance. Their occult powers were the gift of the *amadlozi*, and they were inspired to 'smell out' prowling *abathakathi* for execution. These ominous *izangoma* consequently wielded

terrifying power over even the greatest in the land whom they could identify as *abathakathi*. They could thus subvert even the king's authority by
'smelling out' his favourites. A strong king such as Shaka would have none
of this. He put his *izangoma* to the test by laying traps for them, and
executing them if they pointed out the wrong culprit. In that way he
controlled them and ensured that they 'smelled out' only those victims he
himself wished to execute.

The king ate well of his kingdom's produce, but he touched neither the
milk nor meat from any cow that had been captured in foreign parts. At
mealtimes, *umndlunkulu* sliding on their knees presented the king with an
intricately carved wooden spoon, a fly-whisk and the finely woven grass
mat on which they deposited the large, carefully worked wooden tray for
his meat, along with the pots and baskets of his other food and drink. Like
every other Zulu, the king first drank *amasi*, sour clotted milk, served by
a manservant. It was followed by large gobbets of meat that male attendants had roasted or stewed in great black, earthenware pots in the *isibaya*
out of sight of ordinary people. Complex rules governed the status of the
individual parts of the beast to be consumed, and the king would have
received the sirloin. It was probably 'high' since they preferred it that way
in the *isigodlo* for the enhanced flavour. There were also prepared dishes in
which fat, blood clots, minced meat and grains were turned into various
forms of sausage or a rich broth that constituted the staple diet of the
isigodlo. To accompany the meat and broth, *umndlunkulu* prepared a por-
ridge of roasted or boiled ground maize, which might be of either a dry
or runny consistency. Boiled vegetables, such as pumpkin, sweet potato,
beans, ground-nuts and *indumbe* tubers (*Colocasia*), spiced with the leaves of
pumpkins and other plants, added savour. The king might drink whey or
water throughout the meal.

Water was fetched every day by women of the *isigodlo* from a pure spring
beyond the *ikhanda*. (Water from any stream nearby would have been pol-
luted by urine and excrement from the *ikhanda*. Everyone, including the
king, defecated just beyond the outer palisade, and when the king or
members of the *isigodlo* urinated into earthenware pots, the contents were
thrown out close by.) It was death to look upon these *umndlunkulu* when
they left the *isigodlo* under armed escort to bathe or to relieve themselves

at a distance, and those who accidently encountered them instantly threw themselves face down in the grass.

The king would complete his meal with *utshwala*, the tasty and nutritious beer his women brewed from water, ground sorghum and millet or maize and stored in clay pots. Pinkish in colour and with a low alcohol content of about two per cent, it was essential on all social and ceremonial occasions. The monarch would continue drinking it through the evening while his *umndlunkulu* and boon companions entertained him with songs, dancing, riddles and games.

While the king was at dinner, alone except for his attendants serving the meal, a couple of *izinceku* would walk around the *ikhanda* shouting out that the king was not to be disturbed, and an *umndlunkulu* would rapidly and continuously knock two iron hoe-heads together. The ringing hoes and the calls of the *izinceku* warned everybody not to pollute their monarch by coughing, sneezing or spitting until the sounds ceased, signifying that the king had finished eating and rinsed his mouth.

When the king wished to speak to an individual, his *izinceku* would shout out the name around the *ikhanda* until the individual heard and ran as fast as he could go to the *isigodlo*. Once the guards let him pass, he entered the royal enclosure and approached the king's great audience hut singing his praises as loudly as possible and carefully averting his eyes from the king's women. He only entered the audience hut if specifically ordered to do so, and would find the king reclining on a mat on the left side of the door. Or he might be seated on a rolled-up sleeping mat (or *umqulu*), which in Shaka's day served as a throne, or, as in the time of the later kings, on a ceremonial chair intricately carved out of a solid block of wood, which, like Dingane's throne, might be decorated with burned-in spots (*imbala*).[6] The king would be chatting and laughing with his intimates and advisers while dozens of *umndlunkulu* shuffled about on their knees attending them.

The king and his male companions would all be dressed in very similar fashion. The king (as we have seen) would wear a bizarre and unique costume during rituals such as the *umkhosi*, and when attired for war he would assume the panoply of precious furs and feathers that made up every warrior's superb and intricate ceremonial garb. But everyday dress was much simpler. In a society where there was no shame in nakedness, and where the king dried himself after washing by sitting totally nude in the sun before all his courtiers, for modesty men wore no more than a penis sheath of cowhide (after Dingane's time it was made of the woven stalks of the wild banana). Their habitual garment was a thick bunch of animal skins (such as those of monkeys and wild cats) twisted in a variety of styles to resemble tails (the elite would have afforded the more decorative spotted and banded skins of genets). Several hundred of these 'tails' might be continued all around the waist like a kilt, or be replaced over the buttocks by an oblong apron of cattle hide or by a more expensive pelt, often supplemented by further tails. On cold days Zulu men had originally thrown a cloak of skins over their shoulders. But woven woollen blankets, introduced in the early 19th century with the arrival of the first white traders, rapidly gained increasing favour, although initially they were luxury garments confined to the king and the Zulu elite. Blue cotton and calico salempore cloth from India came in from the Portuguese at Delagoa Bay, and the king and his notables delighted in draping it around themselves for show.

All men wore ornaments, as did women. Most prized were expensive, imported coloured beads woven into necklaces, armbands, waistbands and anklets. Inevitably, the elite and members of the *isigodlo* wore them in greatest profusion, and the king would have been dripping in them when he assumed his dancing costume. Besides a profusion of beads, there were other visible indicators of rank. Men of status (but never women) grew their nails long to advertise their exclusion from manual labour. The king and other leading men of the kingdom would carry a tall, ceremonial wooden staff, beautifully carved, as an indicator of rank.[7] None but Shaka, *abantwana* and a few favoured *izikhulu* were permitted to sport a bunch of red lourie (*gwalagwala*) feathers. The wearing of leopard skin was the preserve of royalty, as was a necklace of leopard or lion claws. A particularly prestigious ornament was the brass armband, or *ingxotha*, which the king alone could confer on his favourites, men and women alike. It reached from wrist to elbow and was decorated with raised concentric patterns of repoussé work. To allow it to be put on and taken off it was split along its length, but it was still a painful process to prise it loose. On a hot day, wearing *ingxotha* in the sun of the *isibaya* or parade ground could become unbearable, and water was kept handy to pour over it to cool it down.

An individual the king had summoned to his hut would be welcomed with an invitation to eat and drink. But he did not consume the food sitting down. It was placed on a wooden tray on the ground before him, and he ate it on his belly like a dog, nibbling and chewing but never touching it with his hands. A servant held out a tightly woven basket of *utshwala* for him to drink. This apparently degrading performance was part of the convention of showing respect (*ukuhlonipha*) for an authority figure, none greater than the king. A superior was supposed to be always positioned higher than his inferior, who would take care to crouch, sit or lie before him, and never show disrespect by looking him in the eye or talking loudly. When conversing, an inferior was expected to use *isihlonipho*, or avoidance speech. Thus, he never directly uttered the king's name or that of his ancestors, or even used a word that contained a syllable of the name or that phonetically resembled it. Instead, he would employ a synonym or a loanword from another language.[8]

While he was the king's guest in the *isigodlo* the visitor dared not laugh in case his mirth be misconstrued with fatal consequences. When he (or anyone) finally left the king's presence, he did so backwards – as in European courts – so that he did not turn his back on his ruler. His ordeal over and back among his comrades, the king's visitor was a figure of awe because he had been in the king's terrible presence, and survived.

When the king left the *isigodlo* for the *isibaya* to administer justice or to hold a general assembly, or *umphakathi* (as opposed to a private conclave with his councillors), a great cry of summons, led by an *inceku*, went up. The people – except for menials, who did not attend – hurried out of their huts singing his praises as they assembled in a semicircle on the parade ground facing their monarch. He was seated on a mound in the *isibaya* so all could see him, with the members of the *ibandla* sitting in front of him. The most important councillors sat a little apart and closer to him. The king was flanked by his *izinceku* and by a bevy of prominent figures at court, or *izilomo*. These *izilomo* as yet held no official administrative positions, although some may have been of high lineage. What these courtiers had in common was their personal friendship with the king and their ability to keep him entertained. An *inceku* held up a shield attached to a long pole to shield him from the sun, and another carried his snuffbox in a basket.

72

Taking snuff was surrounded by considerable ceremony, for it was associated with the *amadlozi*, virility and fecundity, and involved a display of wealth, power and generosity. Thus, if the king took a pinch of the snuff poured out for him into his ivory snuff spoon but then spoke before he had sniffed it up, he threw it away and the whole procedure began again.

Before they seated themselves, the people gathering on the parade ground saluted and acclaimed the king. The men did not squat, as they would normally have done when in the presence of the king, but sat like girls, their bottoms 'right on the ground' to acknowledge their inferiority.[9] During the assembly only the king and those of his court and council who were *izikhulu* could speak. Whenever the king said anything, the *izikhulu* would ask the assembly: 'Do you hear the King?' Whereupon the whole multitude would cry out in vehement agreement: 'Yes Father (*Yebo baba*)!'[10] The minor *izinceku* sitting in front of the semicircle of commoners facing the king then repeated to the men in the rear what he had said. When the king laughed, all laughed.

When matters of war were discussed and deeds of valour remembered and praised, men who were renowned for their courage would dance before the king. Indeed, joyous dancing and praise-singing were daily occurrences at court. The *izikhulu* danced to encourage the cows when they were brought back to be milked. Their herdsmen were armed with spears and shields, and were members of the youngest *amabutho*, whose huts were in the place of least honour near the entrance to the *ikhanda* at the bottom end of the parade ground. These young *amabutho* would join the *izikhulu* in the dance and, attracted by the bellowing of cattle and the rhythmic stamp of feet, other young *amabutho* would pour onto the parade ground, singing and capering. This was the signal for the king to take up position on a convenient anthill or rock that allowed him to peer over the fence of the *isigodlo* and appreciate the highly disciplined and intricate dexterities of the dance. Dozens of lowly servants would now appear to do the milking of the many hundreds of cows, all standing in their allotted places. With arms outstretched and held high, these menials carried off the milking vessels of carved wood, all covered with attractive basketwork.

Once the milking had begun, the *izikhulu* and *amabutho* went back to their huts to eat, loudly chanting the king's praises and shaking their hands with fingers extended in token of gratitude for the generous piles of stewed meat the king had provided. Beasts were slaughtered and skinned every day for their consumption, with the herdsmen and gatekeepers receiving the luscious kidneys as their special perk. When they ate, the *amabutho* thronged in dense circles several men deep around each carver, who apportioned a chunk of meat to every second or third man. First taking a bite, the recipient passed it on to his neighbour.

Yet for all the pageantry that attended ceremonial life at the *ikhanda* where the king was in residence, and for all its glamour as the seat of power and royal munificence, it was also a place to dread. Not only were living conditions distinctly uncomfortable and crowded, except for the denizens of the *isigodlo* and the great men of the court, but it was also the place where the king meted out justice and where those dragged out to execution were at the mercy of his whims.

※

CHAPTER FIVE

ALAS FOR MY MOTHER!

Menaced by the resurgent Ndwandwe hoping to regain their old lands south of the Phongolo, and still smarting from the failure of the *amabece impi*, Shaka began to contemplate the military potential of the Port Natal settlers. It did not escape him that, with their muskets, they were indefatigably hunting down elephant and hippopotamus for ivory, and buffalo for their hides. They had brought numbers of Khoekhoe retainers with them from the Cape who were already familiar with firearms, and the settlers were training their local African retainers in their use. A muzzle-loading flintlock musket was a feeble firearm by later standards, with an effective range of no more than a hundred metres and a rate of fire of about three rounds a minute. Moreover, without sights and with a smooth-bore barrel, its accuracy was low. But Shaka was quick to appreciate that if he harnessed the shock effect of the settlers' firearms he would be able, in future campaigns, to tip the military balance back in his favour.

In his appreciation of firearms he was well ahead of most of his *amabutho*. The Zulu, with their deeply ingrained belief that only hand-to-hand combat was honourable conduct for a warrior, proved resistant to embracing a gun culture. In comparison, the Xhosa, for example, who between 1779 and 1878 fought nine Cape Frontier Wars against colonisers bearing firearms, increasingly adopted firearms themselves and modified their tactics to make the best use of them. The Zulu, on the other hand, never went beyond regarding them as mere ancillary weapons, a form of throwing-spear. They were generally far quicker to see the potential of firearms for hunting, especially elephants for their ivory. Yet, even if Shaka's *amabutho* could have been persuaded to take up firearms, they were as yet all but unobtainable. So if he wanted muskets in his arsenal, they had to be carried by the Port Natal settlers and their trained black hunters.

Shaka first employed his white tributary chiefs and their retainers against the Ndwandwe. Zwide, his old adversary, had died in early 1825, and by 1826 his son, Sikhunyana, had won the inevitable succession struggle. Shaka seized the opportunity presented by the debilitating rivalry within the Ndwandwe ruling house to make a pre-emptive strike. A combination of pressure and the promise of booty induced Fynn and several of the traders, along with their African retainers, to join the *amabutho* Shaka was concentrating at kwaBulawayo in September or October 1826 for the coming campaign. Led by Shaka himself, the Zulu army came upon the Ndwandwe host positioned on the slopes of the izinDolowane hills overlooking the Phongolo River from the north. The battle was an overwhelming Zulu victory. There was pande-monium as the desperately shrieking Ndwandwe women and children, who were gathered to the rear of their army, were butchered along with their menfolk. Zulu *amabutho* roamed the countryside, killing the enemy wounded and rounding up their great herds of cattle as the spoils of conquest. It is not clear if the musketeers made much difference to the outcome of the battle, but their mere presence was fraught with huge significance for the military history of the region.

With his victory at the izinDolowane hills, Shaka had at last removed the most powerful and persistent threat to his kingdom. For the Ndwandwe, this time their defeat was irreversible. Their kingdom collapsed into abso-lute ruin and the survivors scattered far and wide. Some transferred their allegiance to Shaka, some to Mzilikazi of the Ndebele or to other chiefs of the region. No wonder Shaka's *izimbongi* gloated:

> As for Zwide, you have made him a homeless criminal.
> And now today you have done the same to the son,
> The people of Zwide, Shaka, you have jumped over them.[1]

With the defeat of the Ndwandwe, Shaka began the construction of a magnificent new *ikhanda* near the mouth of the Mvoti River, less than 80 kilometres north of Port Natal, or a day and a half's journey away. The colonial town of Stanger was later built over its site, and the magistracy erected on the very spot where the *isigodlo* had been. Called kwaDukuza, the *ikhanda* was known playfully to the Zulu as the place where one loses one's way on account of its great size.[2] Maclean, who inspected it closely, has left a detailed description. Its layout closely followed that of any other *amakhanda*, but it was a particularly large one, containing some 1 500 huts to accommodate about 3 000 *amabutho*. The *isigodlo* impressed Maclean especially. Built on elevated ground overlooking the whole *ikhanda*, it was about 366 metres in length and 55 metres wide and housed between 150 and 200 women in about 50 huts. These huts, Maclean enthused, were of 'unusual size and neatness in their construction', and were tidily arranged around a series of oblong, semicircular and triangular enclosures. The 'exceedingly' smooth and even floors of the enclosures were made of the same material as that of hut floors – a blackish, dark-green mixture of earth from anthills compressed with cow dung – and were polished to 'a glassy smoothness … that reflects the image like a mirror'. 'Everything', Maclean exclaimed, 'wears an air of neatness that elsewhere we had not witnessed.'[3]

For a while yet, kwaBulawayo remained Shaka's administrative centre and he only visited kwaDukuza periodically, as he did his other *amakhanda*. Yet the construction of kwaDukuza heralded a decided shift in Shaka's focus. With the final elimination of the Ndwandwe threat it was no longer necessary for Shaka to be within striking distance of the northern borders of the kingdom. Now was the moment to tighten his control over the client and tributary chiefdoms of the coastlands south of the Thukela, managed for him by his great favourite, Magaye kaDibandlela, the Cele *inkosi*. Yet it seems Shaka's greatest motivation in building kwaDukuza was to be closer to Port Natal, and by the end of 1827 there were three other new *amakhanda* in its vicinity. Still disturbed by the threat of possible plots against him, and by simmering discontent, Shaka looked to the traders' firepower to protect him, and to Port Natal as a final bastion if a revolt should break out.

Yet, in relying increasingly on the Port Natal hunter-traders, Shaka was brought up against the problem of their growing factionalism, which 'tended much to perplex' him.[4] Those who had taken part in the Ndwandwe campaign were of Farewell's party, while those he subsequently deployed in February 1827 against Bheje kaMagawuzi of the Khumalo (who had been holding out for years in his stronghold in the rugged Ngome region of the northern borderlands), belonged to James King's settlement. King and Farewell had fallen out over bad debts and commercial competition, and the settlers and their adherents divided behind one or the other, each of whom tried to build up his own little private army and gain Shaka's ear. Early in 1827 Fynn, who was of King's faction, established a station far to the south near the Mzimkhulu River with a party of his African hunters. His intention seems to have been to develop an overland route through the Mpondo country by which he could export his ivory to the eastern Cape and thus be free of the Port, which Farewell continued to dominate.

During 1827 Shaka reached a point where he had to decide which of the two factions could better help him make diplomatic contact with the British authorities at the Cape. This project that had been on his mind ever since the settlers' first arrival on his shores. Besides wishing to foster trade, he would have been aware that in the recent Fifth Cape Frontier War of 1818–1819 the British had defeated Hintsa, the Xhosa paramount whom he acknowledged as being a powerful ruler in his own league. The Cape was thus a military power to reckon with, and Shaka would appear to have calculated that if he could make allies of the British he could use their support as a counterweight against continuing opposition to his rule at home.

In the end, Shaka dropped Farewell, his initial protégé, in favour of King, who had slowly been building a 30-ton, two-masted schooner at the Port. It was still unfinished when, on 24 July 1827, Shaka summoned King, Isaacs and Fynn into his presence and informed them confidentially that once the schooner was ready he wished to send a chief with King to open negotiations with King George IV of Great Britain, know to the Zulu as 'Mjojo'. Then, according to Isaacs, 'in the most entreating manner' he charged King to obtain 'some stuff for turning white hairs black', begging him to keep his request a 'profound secret'.[5] But before the elated King could launch his schooner, an extraordinary upheaval convulsed the Zulu kingdom that in retrospect must be regarded as the great rupture in Shaka's reign.

Nandi, Shaka's mother, was held in enormous respect in the kingdom as the *iNdlovukazi*, the Great She-Elephant or Queen Mother. She presided over his *isigodlo* and, with no royal wives to dispute her sway, was omnipotent in managing Shaka's domestic arrangements. We simply do not know the true nature of his emotional relationship with her, whether he revered or resented her, or was uncomfortably ambivalent in his feelings. There is no doubting, though, that she was a central figure in Shaka's life.

On 10 August 1827 she died at the eMkhindini *umuzi* presided over by her unmarried daughter, Noncoba, which was situated on a ridge about five kilometres west of kwaBulawayo. 'No sooner did Nandi die', recounted Ngidi, who, like Nandi, was of the Langeni people, 'than Tshaka was overcome with grief and said, "alas for my mother, alas for my mother! What has killed my mother?"'[6] This is a question that has continued to perplex. Was it dysentery? Or (as so many oral traditions attest) was Shaka enraged when he learned that, against his strict orders, his mother was harbouring a male baby born of one of his *umndlunkulu* instead of immediately banishing mother and child, and that in his blind fury he stabbed her to death? Or did he order his *inceku* to kill her, either by stabbing or poisoning her?

Of course, in the final resort, it is not possible to be sure whether Nandi died of natural causes or whether Shaka was responsible for her death. Nevertheless, what the persistent and widespread rumours of matricide disclose – tales accompanied by telling and convincing circumstantial detail – is that by 1827 there was a deep swell of opposition to Shaka's rule and a readiness on the part of many of his subjects to believe the very worst of him. Moreover, Shaka's well-attested and grossly exaggerated reaction to Nandi's death, which sent out devastating seismic waves of hysteria and violence across the Zulu kingdom, smacked suspiciously of pathological remorse and guilt rather than simple grief at the death of a parent, and certainly would have fed public belief in his complicity, rather than allaying it.

Even so, the people flocked to join Shaka in his mourning, stripping off their beads and other ornaments. Their wails and lamentation were not normal even on the death of a king, and Nandi was the only royal personage remembered to be mourned in such an excessive way.[7] But everyone who gave way to excessive demonstrations of grief was doing so to establish their innocence of this terrible offence against the king and his mother, and turned violently on those who did not appear sufficiently sorrowful. To demonstrate their devotion and to express their overwhelming sorrow, Shaka's *amakhosi* sent out war parties across the land to kill people who had not proved their innocence by instantly presenting themselves at kwa-Bulawayo to join in the mourning. Desperate to prove the intensity of their grief, people from all over the kingdom drove herds of cattle to kwaBula-wayo to condole with Shaka by their lowing.

Once he had brought the first intense spasm of public mourning to an end, Shaka set about burying his mother. A boot-shaped grave was dug in the hut where she had died, and on the second day after her death Nandi was placed in it, propped up on a mat and covered with another mat. Personal articles she had last used, such as clothing, jewellery, blankets and eating utensils, would have been placed beside her. As a person of exalted rank she was accompanied in death by an *umgando*, or group of victims killed to keep her company 'down below' and to attend and cook for her there, as well as the black oxen sacrificed at the funeral. The *umgando* consisted of some ten women, girls and *izinceku*. Whether they were buried alive or killed beforehand was a matter of debate for the Zulu of a later generation, but Socwatsha, who was a youth at the time, was insistent that 'a man is never buried alive with a corpse, but killed by having his neck twisted' and was 'not stabbed'.[8] It is also likely that the dead bodies of the *izinceku* were used instead of rocks to prop up Nandi's corpse. The grave was filled in and cov-ered with stones and a wooden fence erected around it. For three months Nandi's grave was watched over by members of her Langeni people and others selected by Shaka, including a large contingent of warriors. Every year, men made sure that the thicket of trees that sprang up naturally on the grave and the thick mat of grass growing there were not burned since that would have been tantamount to burning the Queen Mother herself.[9]

While Nandi's obsequies were taking place, Ngomane kaMqomboli, Shaka's trusted Mthethwa mentor whom he had appointed his chief *ind-una*, announced a year-long programme of excessive mourning abstinence for Shaka's beleaguered people that went to the extent of forbidding the harvesting of crops and the milking of cattle. Those caught ignoring the stipulations faced execution but, in desperation, people got around them by subterfuge. Tununu, a child at the time, remembered that they buried the gourds they had harvested in the manure of the cattle enclosure and that they milked the cattle by stealth late at night.[10] There was more to this than meets the eye. Clearly, a powerful political element was involved, and it seems Shaka exploited the mass hysteria he had whipped up over Nandi's death to rouse popular animosity against his old enemies to justify purging them. Once again, the deeply mistrusted Qwabe people fell victim, suffering mass killings and loss of cattle.

Yet Shaka himself developed misgivings about the mourning purge, fearing that all he had achieved was to make new foes and conjure up fresh conspiracies. On 8 September 1827 Shaka rather desperately confided to Isaacs: 'I am like a wolf on a flat, that is at a loss for a place to hide his head in.'[11] And certainly, there are indications that, spurred on by Shaka's violent intemperance, a conspiracy was beginning to coalesce in the royal house. Shaka was able to scotch it by encouraging his *izangoma* to 'smell out', in order of seniority, his half-brothers Dingane, Mhlangana, Ngqojana, Sophane and Mfihlo. That alone was enough. Facing the threat of execution and with the knowledge that Shaka's baleful eye was trained on them, the *abantwana* scrambled to reaffirm their loyalty. Shaka was doubtless unconvinced, but for the moment he took no further action against his half-brothers.

Thanks to all these upheavals, Shaka became increasingly uncomfortable at retaining kwaBulawayo as his capital, not least because of its position in the heart of the inimical Qwabe country. So, during the last months of 1827 he quitted it in great state for kwaDukuza. As soon as the period of official mourning for his mother came to an end in September 1827, Shaka vigorously took up the stalled issue of sending a diplomatic mission to the Cape. Urged on by Shaka, King's workmen rushed to complete the schooner that was to carry the envoys there. Satisfied with their progress, in February 1828 Shaka recognised King as paramount among the Port Natal traders (thus superseding the grant he had made the now crestfallen Farewell in 1824). Shaka then put King in command of the embassy to the Cape and commissioned him to 'negotiate a treaty of friendly alliance' with King George.[12] But King had his own game to play. His intention, as his manoeuvrings once he reached the Cape would reveal, was to present

Shaka's grant of February 1828 to the colonial authorities and to lay claim to the territories it specified. However, he realised that for the claim to be effective and for him to exploit his exclusive trading rights in Zululand to the full, he needed some measure of British protection. And that in turn meant he must persuade the Cape authorities to establish some sort of authority over Port Natal.

Launched on 10 March 1828, the schooner *Elizabeth and Susan* sailed on 30 April 1828 for the nascent settlement of Port Elizabeth in Algoa Bay. On board were King and Jacob the interpreter, along with Shaka's chief emissary, Sothobe kaMpangalala, an extremely arrogant, deep-chested giant of a man who was a senior *induna* of the Sibiya people and an acknowledged royal favourite, and his aide, Mbozamboza, an *inceku* who held a confidential post as one of Shaka's official intelligence-gatherers. The mission came to nothing. In fairness to the Cape authorities, how were they to view this unexpected and undeniably odd embassy? They were understandably suspicious of the bumptious and shady pseudo-lieutenant King, who made no bones about pursuing his own, self-aggrandising agenda. And while the Zulu emissaries seemed genuinely to desire a friendly alliance with the British and good trading relations, should they, rather than King, be regarded as truly representing Shaka? And then, in May 1828, just as talks were tentatively getting under way, Shaka threw the bona fides of the mission to the winds by launching a major raid against the Mpondo.

Why Shaka mounted this inopportune campaign at such a delicate diplomatic moment remains something of a conundrum. We can certainly discern the self-interested and devious hand of King and his associates who, in order to draw Britain into the affairs of the Zulu kingdom, evidently persuaded Shaka that he would win the favour of the British by attacking their apparent enemies on the Cape frontier. Nevertheless, even if the activities and schemes of the traders complicated Shaka's management of affairs of state, he always pursued his own very definite objectives, and the Mpondo raid made good sense in very Zulu terms.

With Shaka settled in kwaDukuza, the official mourning for Nandi came to an end. It was now time to bring her spirit home, or *ukubuyisa*. The final act in the *ihlambo* (washing or cleansing) ceremonies that marked the end of a period of mourning for a royal personage was to make war against neighbouring peoples. 'As tears could not be forced from these distant nations,' declared Ngomane, Shaka's chief *induna*, 'war should be made against them, and the cattle taken should be the tears shed upon her grave.'[13] In this way, the *umnyama* associated with Nandi's death would be cast into the enemy's country. The Mpondo were selected as the target of the great raid because it was considered particularly appropriate to secure the delayed revenge for the humiliation of the *amabece impi* of 1824, in honour of Nandi's shade.

Yet, other factors would have weighed with Shaka. After the unprecedented excesses of the mourning for Nandi, the *ihlambo impi* (or cleansing army) would refocus the attention of his alarmed and fearful subjects on fresh military glories. And if great herds of cattle were captured, he could reward his *amabutho* and *amakhosi* – insatiably eager as ever for plunder – and so damp down simmering discontent and mounting internal opposition to his rule. Quite possibly, he might also have reflected that a show of military strength in the region of Port Natal and the lands to the south would remind the presumptuous traders that he, and not they, held the whip hand.

In May 1828 the *ihlambo impi* began its march southwards under Mdlaka kaNcidi, Shaka's most senior and seasoned commander. Cape border officials estimated its strength at between 2 000 and 3 000 men.[14] Shaka required the traders' supporting firepower, and on its march south the *ihlambo impi* was joined by contingents of Farewell's retainers from Port Natal and musketeers from Fynn's post on the Mzimkhulu. Having crossed the Mzimkhulu, the *ihlambo impi* advanced southwestwards through the Mpondo country. By mid-June it was raiding as far as the Bomvana country, south of the Mthatha River, seizing about 10 000 cattle as it went. It then turned back and by mid-July had retired across the Mzimkhulu. There Shaka was waiting for the *ihlambo impi*'s return. He had accompanied it only as far south as Fynn's post, where he remained guarded by an *ibutho* and in the company of a number of his *umndlunkulu* girls under the supervision of Mnkabi, one of Senzangakhona's more influential widows.[15] He would not have known it, but this was the last of the many campaigns in which he took an active part.

The Cape authorities remained extremely nervous of a Zulu incursion.

In the coming months Cape forces made their presence actively felt for the first time in the buffer zone north of the frontier as a warning to Shaka to stay north of the Mzimkhulu. Yet, from Shaka's perspective the *ihlambo impi* had been a successful operation despite its potentially adverse impact on relations with the Cape. It had reasserted Zulu predominance over his southern African neighbours, and he had the captured Mpondo herds to redistribute as necessary largesse.

Unfortunately for Shaka, the successful *ihlambo impi* was not enough for him to recapture his equilibrium and prestige. The failed embassy to the Cape returned to Port Natal on 17 August 1828. King was a broken and dying man, and when Sothobe successfully laid the blame for the fiasco on King, he and his trader associates barely escaped execution at the hands of an utterly enraged and humiliated Shaka. Dismayed as he was, though, the politically savvy Shaka tried his best to ensure that the adverse results of the mission were not widely known, and he put as positive a spin as he could on the diplomatic debacle. It is also characteristic of him that he acted immediately to retrieve the situation. King's faction had failed him, but Shaka acknowledged that he remained as dependent as ever on the traders to facilitate relations with the Cape authorities. So he turned to Farewell's recently discredited faction and chose John Cane, Farewell's principal agent, to reopen talks with the British. Cane's embassy left overland on about 6 or 7 September 1828 for the Cape. Meanwhile, Shaka decided to mend his fences with King's faction and on 17 September 1828 endowed Isaacs with the lands he had previously granted King, who had died only a few days earlier.

Cane arrived in Grahamstown on 7 October, and the British officials took Shaka's pacific overtures seriously. On 26 November 1828 Cane was informed that he was to return to Shaka with Captain RS Aitchison and an armed escort to discuss a treaty. But on 26 December 1828 the mission was countermanded because startling word finally reached the Cape: Shaka had been assassinated three months before.

CHAPTER SIX

❀

UGLY YEAR

Even before John Cane left kwaDukuza on Shaka's second embassy to the Cape, the king had despatched his army north against Soshangane kaZikode of the migratory Gaza kingdom, one of the Ndwandwe fragments making their way north after Shaka's victory over Zwide in 1819. In 1828 it was situated in the hill country 130 kilometres to the northwest of Delagoa Bay, somewhat elevated above the humid and malaria-infested bushveld south of the Olifants or Lepelle River – known to the Zulu as the Bhalule. Zulu tradition holds that Shaka was over-fond of sending out his army, 'so that that people did not sit still and did not rest'.[1] Nevertheless, launching a fresh campaign straight on the heels of the *ihlambo impi* dismayed not only the jaded veterans of that campaign who had been hoping to recuperate at home. It would appear that Shaka ordered an unprecedented general mobilisation to significantly reinforce the army operating against Soshangane, so that its strength probably came close to 15 000 men. Fifty years later, in the reign of King Cetshwayo, the war song composed for this general mobilisation was still remembered:

Go every one to war
Old birds and young!
He says this –

Who is as big as the whole country.
You who stayed at home yesterday
Won't stay at home today.[2]

Shaka was later widely said 'to have *bunguleka'd* i.e. gone mad' when he launched what came to be known as the *Bhalule impi*.[3] Nevertheless, if we dig down, several rational objectives are brought to light. Shaka knew that to keep his tributaries on the far margins of his kingdom obedient he needed periodically to reassert his power. Several tributaries situated to the west of the Swazi kingdom had been lax in following the extreme mourning he had required for Nandi, and needed to be brought sharply to order. On top of that, Soshangane had been abetting some of these disobedient tributaries and was attempting to attract them into his orbit. By sending the *Bhalule impi* along the western flank of the Swazi kingdom before it swung east towards the Gaza kingdom, Shaka was ensuring that it punished the disloyal tributaries along its line of march before vigorously reminding Soshangane to stay out of the Zulu zone of influence.

Yet even if the *Bhalule impi* made apparent political sense, surely as experienced a general as Shaka must have seen that it was militarily extremely ill-conceived. The Gaza kingdom was nearly 700 kilometres away and the Zulu army would be operating well beyond the limits of its logistical support and in totally unfamiliar, hostile and disease-ridden territory. Inevitably, the *Bhalule impi* under Mdlaka's command met with disaster. The men were laid low with malaria fever and dysentery, they were reduced to the verge of starvation, and the Gaza cannily withdrew to their strongholds and repelled the desperate Zulu assaults. Mdlaka was left with no option but to withdraw as best he could and without any booty at all for his pains, even though he knew he would have to face Shaka's furious retribution for his failure.

So why did Shaka so determinedly push forward with this risky and unnecessary campaign? It seems that what was driving him was fear that the *abantwana* were once again conspiring to do him to death. At the time of the assassination attempt in 1824 at esiKlebheni, and again at kwaBulawayo in 1827, Shaka had suspected a royal conspiracy. Most recently (if we are to accept the detailed oral testimony), it seems that at the conclusion of the *ihlambo impi* Dingane and Mhlangana, abetted by Shaka's own trusted *inceku* Mbopha kaSitayi, had resolved to kill Shaka while he was seated on a rock on the banks of the Mkhomazi River. At the very last moment they were unexpectedly disturbed, lost their nerve, and failed to strike.[4] But, clearly, they were only awaiting an opportunity to try again.

For his part, Shaka did what so many other rulers have done when confronted by treacherous but high-born conspirators. He sent them away on a dangerous military campaign to give himself a breathing space, and with the hope that they would perish. So, unlike the *ihlambo impi*, during which Shaka had accompanied his army as far south as the Mzimkhulu River, he did not leave kwaDukuza for the *Bhalule impi*. However, he made sure that all his senior brothers marched with the army. They in turn would have understood his motives and must have feared that he would execute them if they survived the campaign.

Yet, sending his enemies away on the *Bhalule impi* was not a permanent solution, and we must presume that Shaka was banking on some other development to strengthen his hand. Most likely, he calculated that his first embassy to the Cape would lead to a powerful British alliance that would strengthen his hand against his enemies. The failure of the mission dashed these hopes and left Shaka feeling ever more vulnerable. But, despite his efforts to 'spin' the outcome, word of this humiliation would have reached the *abantwana* serving with the *Bhalule impi* and encouraged them to strike while Shaka did not have his army about him. It seems, too, that they were induced to act by the incendiary tales spreading around the army that Shaka was committing intemperate and irrational atrocities against the womenfolk left at home.[5]

When the *Bhalule impi* reached Ceza, a great, looming, flat-topped mountain that dominated the Sikhwebezi River basin in northwestern Zululand, Dingane and several of his brothers secretly conferred on how they should go about killing Shaka. But that brought to the fore another crucial question: who would succeed him as king? It seems that when Shaka moved his capital south of the Thukela to kwaDukuza he entrusted the country to the north of the river to Dingane as his effective viceroy, and that by doing so he was effectively establishing Dingane as his successor. However, Dingane had a serious rival in his half-brother, Mhlangana. Genealogically,

Mhlangana was probably the rightful *inkosana* because he was born of Mzondwase, Senzangakhona's fifth wife, whereas Dingane was the son of Mphikase, Senzangakhona's sixth wife.

Dingane and Mhlangana were known to be fond of each other and to work well together as a team. At Ceza they decided to put the matter of the succession aside until after they had dealt with Shaka. However, they did not trust all of the *abantwana* serving with the *Bhalule impi* to play their part in the conspiracy. They left Mpande, the son of Songiya, Senzangakhona's ninth wife, who was born between 1795 and 1798, and whom it seems they considered too weak-spirited to be an effective assassin, to continue north with the army, along with his full brother Nzibe, who was still a stripling.

Their plans made, the royal conspirators abandoned the army and made their way back towards kwaDukuza. Once in the vicinity of the *ikhanda*, they made secret contact with Mbopha kaSitayi, Shaka's *inceku* who had been party to the aborted plot to kill Shaka at the end of the *ihlambo impi*. Mbopha was about 1.8 metres tall, dark and stout, and had an evil reputation for abusing his confidential position with Shaka, and for urging the execution of many innocent victims. Despite being high in Shaka's favour, it seems he harboured a secret desire for revenge against the king for being responsible for his mother's death. And as unsavoury as he was, the conspirators needed him again since, as Shaka's confidential body servant, he was in a privileged position to give them easy access to the king and – crucially for the planned assassination – was the only person in the kingdom allowed to carry a spear in his close proximity.

Crucially for the success of the plot, Mnkabayi, Shaka's redoubtable aunt who had twice previously acted as Zulu regent and who had secured the throne for him, gave the conspirators her active blessing. With Nandi's death, she had replaced Shaka's mother as the highly influential matriarch of the Zulu royal house, the Great She-Elephant, or *Indlovukazi*. She and her twin sister, Mmama, had been Nandi's friends and (an echo of Mbopha's grievance against the king) were convinced that Shaka was responsible for her death. Moreover, they believed that his incessant campaigns and repeated acts of violence were destroying the kingdom. Having once been Shaka's most ardent supporters, it seems that they had now become his covert and malevolent enemies. For some time, Mnkabayi had been a manipulative voice in Dingane's ear, whispering rebellion, working on his and Mhlangana's well-founded fears that they would be Shaka's next victims. She had also woven Mbopha into her plot with the promise of a large chiefdom of his own.

Once Dingane and Mhlangana had confirmed their pact with Mbopha and were assured of Mnkabayi's support, they reported back to Shaka at kwaDukuza. Unsurprisingly, Shaka was angered by their unwelcome return and deeply suspicious of the princes' motives for leaving the army. The conspirators knew they must strike immediately or suffer their own deaths.

Predictably, the circumstances surrounding Shaka's assassination are difficult to reconstruct with any precision. Not even the date of the assassination is certain. Shaka Day, which was subsumed into Heritage Day in South Africa in 1995, is celebrated annually on 24 September, but contemporary evidence makes it most likely that Shaka was killed on Tuesday, 23 September 1828. There is much more certainty where the assassination took place. As was usually the case with an *ikhanda* where the king resided, a small, separate *umuzi* was built on a slight rise about 50 metres from the *isigodlo* where he could relax in privacy with his intimates and women, or hold more exclusive meetings with councillors or petitioners. At kwaDukuza it was known as kwaNyakamubi (or Ugly Year).

Towards sundown (or so the preponderant body of evidence would suggest), Shaka was seated on rolled mats in the open space outside his hut in kwaNyakamubi complacently watching his immense herds of cattle being driven homewards, wrapped snugly against the evening chill in one of his woven blankets obtained from the Port Natal traders. Serving women from the *isigodlo* were in attendance, and numbers of courtiers, relatives and officials were keeping him company. They included Nxazonke kaMbengi, an elderly uncle of Nandi's, along with several of his Langeni kinsmen, as well as Mxamana kaNtandeka of the Sibisi people. Like Mbopha, Mxamana was one of Shaka's *izinceku* and was also his principal *imbongi*, or praise-singer.

As was ever the case, Shaka was not entirely free to take his ease and was occupied in receiving a delegation of about ten men – the sources differ as to whether they were Mpondo paying tribute, Tswana hunters or iziYendane (tributaries from south of the Thukela). Quite unexpectedly,

Dingane and Mhlangana approached the king and greeted him, pretending they had just returned from the hunt. Four or more of their brothers were with them. Finding Shaka surrounded by so many people, they dared not strike as they had intended and withdrew to consult with Mbopha. The *inceku* coolly directed Dingane and Mhlangana to take up their positions behind the fence of the calf byre in the *umuzi*, their spears held at the ready under their karosses (blankets of animal skins sewn together), while he set about creating a diversion.

Mbopha burst in unexpectedly upon the assembly and began to belabour the members of the delegation with the shaft of his spear while stridently reproving Shaka's courtiers for pestering their master. Fearing this was the signal for their deaths, the whole crowd began to scatter in panic into the surrounding bush. Shaka, who by now was standing leaning against the calf byre, was sardonically amused by all the commotion.

There are divergent versions as to what happened next, all strongly coloured by the subsequent apportionment of blame based on clashing political agendas. Who actually killed Shaka: Mbopha, Mhlangana, Dingane or all three? And were they joined by two more of the princes, Ngqojana and Sophane? Many accounts single out Mbopha, suggesting he threw his spear when Shaka had his back turned to him. Others believed it was Mhlangana who stabbed first, aiming at the armpit, which would cause instant death. But, on account of the blanket Shaka was wearing, Mbopha succeeded only in piercing him through the arm or, alternatively, the back of his left shoulder. Some accounts maintain that Dingane stabbed Shaka as he cast off his blanket and tried to break free of his assassins, but there is a strong tradition that Dingane did not actually shed his brother's blood and only laid hold of him to hinder his flight. The mortally wounded Shaka managed to escape from kwaNyakamubi and make for the sanctuary of the *isigodlo* at kwaDukuza, but collapsed and died just outside the *umuzi*.

Are we to believe (as it was said) that he begged his assassins for mercy, whimpering 'Leave me alone, sons of my father, and I shall be your menial'? Was that in his character as a great warrior? But, if it were so, it certainly would have done him no good because it was the firm Zulu belief that if you happened to be fighting your brother and he called out for mercy, you would be overcome by misfortune and would not live long should you spare him. So the assassins were remorseless with 'the evil-doer who kills the wives of men who are away' (with the *Bhalule impi*).[6]

Once Shaka fell to the ground, we can be fairly certain that the assassins did not keep on stabbing his corpse, as was done ritually (*ukuhlomula*) with an enemy who had died courageously, or with a ferocious wild beast such as a lion. Nor would they have observed the ritual of slitting open his belly so that the evil influence of *umnyama* would not make him swell up like the dead. For, in the case of killing a near relation, these rituals were not observed. Instead, their spears were not withdrawn and were left sticking into the body where it lay.

The accounts closest to the moment of his death are in agreement that Shaka only had time to gasp out incredulously, 'What is the matter my father's children?'[7] before he collapsed. However, the temptation to ascribe significant last words to celebrities is universal, especially if they can be interpreted retrospectively as prophetic. And that in turn means they must be formulated long enough afterwards to ring true. This was certainly so in Shaka's case. The most succinct, and those which most immediately came to pass, were the ones purportedly addressed to Dingane and Mhlangana, and repeated by King Mpande's grandson, Mkebeni kaDabulamanzi (born in the 1860s): 'Are you stabbing me, the king of the earth? You will come to an end through killing one another.'[8] Otherwise, Shaka's prophetic last words all refer to the impending rule of the white men, frequently referred to as 'swallows' because they 'come up from the sea' like those migratory birds,[9] and because swallows also build their houses of mud. In 1902 Mkando, who was born in about 1827, gave voice to the fulfilment of Shaka's dying prophecy in the bitterest of terms: 'When Tshaka died he said the white men would overrun the land; the whole land would be white with the light of the stars; it would be overrun by "swallows". We are your dogs.'[10]

With Shaka dead, the assassins rounded up a few men to raise the *ihubo*, a sacred ballad honouring the mighty deeds of the ancestors and, as part of the *umgando* purification ceremonies practised on the death of a king, sacrificed a black ox from the kwaNyakamubi herd in thanksgiving to Senzangakhona's mighty shade and to those of the other royal ancestors. All the *umndlunkulu* sallied out of the *isigodlo* and joined in the ceremony, some happily enough, others crying in fright, if not grief.

After the sacrifice, the suppressed rivalry between Dingane and Mhlangana came into the open. The gall of the sacrificed beast, mixed with the contents of its paunch, was drunk by those who had killed it and the remainder was sprinkled over the bodies of those present to ward off the evil taint of *umnyama*. The depleted bladder was then worn on the arm of the foremost man who had performed the sacrifice. Each of the two brothers angrily insisted on their superior right to do so. Mbopha quickly intervened and pacified the pair by suggesting that until the *Bhalule impi* returned and made known which of the princes it favoured as Shaka's successor, he, Mbopha, would act as an interim regent.

Shaka's body was left all night where it had fallen. Scavenging hyenas did not trouble it because, the Zulu believed, they never touched the corpse of a king. Next morning, Mhlangana is said to have proposed that it be dragged to a pool in the nearby river and fed to the crocodiles. However, those of Shaka's attendants who had not yet fled insisted it must be buried properly with all the ceremony that normally attended a royal funeral, and Dingane concurred.[11]

The assassins' spears were removed from Shaka's corpse and it was wrapped up in the skin of the black ox the brothers had sacrificed the previous evening. The body was then removed to a hut in kwaNyakamubi. Following the ancient custom, it was placed in a sitting position tied to the central pole of the hut. Relatives kept the body company at night, and the inhabitants of kwaNyakamubi performed the funeral rites. The corpse remained putrefying in the funeral hut and was not finally buried until all his personal belongings and private things that had ever touched him – his loin-covers, dancing dress, bead and brass ornaments, food dishes and utensils – had been collected up from across the kingdom to join him in the grave. Most were probably burned beforehand, and others (in accordance with custom) placed up against both sides of the body, but not in front or behind it.

However, Shaka's spears were not laid in the grave with him. No Zulu would ever put a spear 'in the hands of a dead man' lest his *idlozi* be angry – and Shaka's had every reason to be so – and mystically stab living people, causing them to bleed from the mouth and die. Certainly, Shaka's killers were in fear of his malevolent spirit, and ordered that all the surrounding empty grain-pits be thoroughly closed up lest his *idlozi* find a channel of escape and wreak his vengeance on them. Fynn recorded that, as an extra precaution, a piece of his buttock covering was placed in Shaka's mouth to repress his *idlozi*'s anger. The assassins issued orders that, on pain of death, there should be no mourning for Shaka for 'the evil-doer (*itshinga*) was dead, the madman from the country of the Mtetwa who had destroyed the Zulu country and caused it trouble'.[12]

When Shaka came to be buried in the ground, certainly in the customary sitting position, he was accompanied – as his royal status demanded – by a number of victims of elite status to follow him into the spirit world to wait upon him there and keep him company. This *umgando* of ten men included Nandi's elderly uncle, Nxazonke, and the king's *imbongi*, Mxamana, both of whom the assassins had killed immediately after Shaka, as well as Ntendeka, the *induna* of the kwaDlangezwa *ikhanda*. A heap of stones was raised atop Shaka's grave and a hut built over it. Those men who had had an actual hand in the burial were either put to death or banished to a far-off region on the grounds that 'they would give food to the heir with bad hands … for they had handled his father when dead'.[13] As was customary, the inmates of the *umuzi* where he had perished and the people employed at his burial were posted there as guards. They were supplied with cattle and grain for their subsistence since they were forbidden to abandon their watch on pain of death. Their isolation did not last for too long. The Zulu believed that after a few months the spirit of the dead ruler should be brought back (*ukubuyisa*) at a great feast, propitiated with copious sacrifices, and then be requested to permit itself to be conveyed to a new spirit home, or *umuzi wedlozi*.

Dingane, who was extremely anxious to evade the ravening fury of his brother's *idlozi*, performed this ceremony as soon as was appropriate. When in 1829 he established his new chief *ikhanda*, uMgungundlovu, in the emaKhosini valley, he rebuilt kwaDukuza close by as Shaka's *umuzi wedlozi*. In 1843, when King Mpande subsequently built his principal *ikhanda*, kwaNodwengu, in the Mahlabathini plain across the White Mfolozi from the emaKhosini valley, he made sure to rebuild kwaDukuza nearby as the new abode for Shaka's spirit. The British burned this third kwaDukuza on 26 June 1879 during the final stages of the Anglo-Zulu War. It was never rebuilt and Shaka's *idlozi* no longer had an *umuzi wedlozi*.

As for the grave where Shaka's body lay buried at the abandoned kwa-Nyakamubi, a small *umuzi* was built close by so that its inhabitants would be on hand to care for the site. They tended it until 1844 when the British, who (as we shall see) had annexed the territory where it lay, allocated the land to a white farmer, T Potgieter. In 1873 the Surveyor-General of Natal, William Stanger, laid out a village (named Stanger after him) on the site of the first kwaDukuza. (In 2006 the name of Stanger was officially changed to KwaDukuza.) As for the grave itself, it lay half-forgotten for decades alongside the house that WD Wheelwright, who had been the resident magistrate of the Lower Tugela division from 1887 to 1889, had built close to the magistracy erected on the site of the *isigodlo* at kwaDukuza.

KING DINGANE
kaSENZANGAKHONA

❀ ❀ ❀

CHAPTER SEVEN

꙳

OX THAT ENCIRCLES THE HOMESTEADS WITH TEARS

The Port Natal traders fell into a panic when word reached them on
24 September 1828 that Shaka had been assassinated by his brothers.
Anticipating that his violent death would unleash a civil war and that they
would be caught up in the ensuing mayhem, they scurried in from their
scattered settlements and prepared to escape on the schooner *Elizabeth and
Susan*. Four days later, messengers arrived from Dingane and Mhlangana
to assure them of their friendship and protection, and entreated them not
to leave. But, with the succession undecided, the traders decided that a
temporary withdrawal was prudent, and on 1 December 1828 most sailed
on the *Elizabeth and Susan* for Port Elizabeth. Before they left, Dingane and
Mhlangana entrusted Farewell with a verbal message for the Cape officials that assured them that 'now Chaka was dead, they wished to live on
friendly terms with every nation and by no means would do anything to
displease them'.[1]

And certainly, with the *Bhalule impi* still away on campaign and their
available military resources very limited, the *abantwana* were anxious to
avoid any external conflicts. They also feared that the Mpondo, Bhaca and
other neighbours would exploit the situation to raid Zulu territory, and
set about building up what military forces were at their disposal to protect
the kingdom. Just before his death, Shaka had raised an *ibutho* of untried

youths, the iziNyosi, or Bees. To augment the iziNyosi, the *abantwana* immediately formed a new *ibutho*, the uHlomendlini, or Home Guard, under the
command of Nongalaza kaNondela, the Nyandwini *inkosi* who would later
rise to become one of Dingane's leading generals. The uHlomendlini was a
scratch force made up of men who had evaded joining the *Bhalule impi*, and
of several hundred iziYendane, the 'mop-headed' menials and cattle guards
serving in the *amakhanda* and cattle posts south of the Thukela.

Meanwhile, Dingane and Mhlangana continued to abide by the agreement that Mbopha would function as an interim regent until the *izikhulu*,
the people and the returned army formally recognised one or the other
of them as king. While they waited, though, the two *abantwana* eyed each
other with increasing mistrust and growing antagonism. They acted as
one, though, in dealing with Ngwadi kaNgendeyana, Shaka's half-brother
by Nandi, who seemed disposed to challenge the two princes for the
throne. In late October they despatched a joint force of the uHlomendlini
and iziNyosi under the command of Mbopha to Ngwadi's kwaWambaza
umuzi, which he had turned into a veritable fortress with a thick, high
fence of tree trunks and thorns. The defenders, including Ngwadi, fought
stoutly to the death, and their womenfolk died with them. But Mbopha's
forces suffered crippling casualties, leaving the princes in a weaker military
position than ever. Everything would depend on how the *Bhalule impi*, still
making its way home and deliberately loitering for fear of reporting back
to Shaka, would take the news of Shaka's assassination.

Dingane was confident that the army would favour him, but Mhlangana
insisted he had a better claim than Dingane because he had taken the most
active part in killing Shaka, and had jumped over his corpse, thus proclaiming that he was the murdered king's conqueror and successor. Ironically, it
was this very assertion that undid him when, in late November, the senior
members of the royal house and the great nobles of the realm were summoned to meet and discuss the succession.

The consultation took place before one of the premier men of the country, Ngqengelele kaMvulana. He had been a confidant of Shaka's, and the
king had raised his protégé to great heights by appointing him *inkosi* of the
Buthelezi people. Also present were Noncoba, Shaka's half-sister by Nandi,
and his formidable aunt Mnkabayi, who dominated the meeting. The latter

came to the assembly dressed as a man, wearing an *umqubula* of blue monkey and genet tails (this was a dress formed of three girdles or kilts of tails, one of which was worn low over the buttocks, another above the hips and a third over the shoulders like a cape, thus covering the body entirely from neck to knee), and a feathered headdress with a long crane feather. She carried a white war-shield with a black spot and a bundle of spears, and used a barbed spear as her staff.

Dingane was her preferred candidate and she roundly declared: 'Yebo, Zulu people, what are you saying now that the madman from the Mtetwa country [Shaka] is dead? He was not a chief; he became chief through his madman's strength. He killed Sigujwana [sic], the real heir of Senzangakhona. As Sigujwana is no longer living, there is the son of Miyeya [the mother of Mpikase, Dingane's mother].'[2] She then went on to convince the meeting that a man who had killed his king was not fit to rule. Ngqengelele weightily agreed, and it was decreed 'The one with the red assegai shall not rule.' As for Dingane's undeniable part in the assassination, that was brushed aside on the grounds that he had only caught hold of his brother while the other two stabbed him, and was therefore not guilty of shedding Shaka's blood.

The way was now clear for Dingane to be declared king, but what was to be done with Mhlangana? He had his many supporters, and to stave off a likely civil war Mnkabayi and Ngqengelele resolved that Mhlangana must be put to death. But to act openly against Mhlangana carried its own dangers, so Mnkabayi devised a cunning stratagem. Mbopha was employed to whip up the discord between the brothers, convincing each that the other was plotting his death. Egged on and assisted by Mnkabayi, Dingane resolved to strike first. In a treacherous show of reconciliation, Dingane invited Mhlangana to go bathing with him in the Mavivane, a small stream close by kwaDukuza. Mhlangana would have done well to recall that this was precisely the ploy Ngwadi had adopted when he murdered Sigujana to clear the way for Shaka. As on that previous occasion, Dingane and Mhlangana agreed not to bring their armed followers with them. But Mnkabayi's men were concealed at the spot, and sprang out to drown Mhlangana. Magema Fuze, the first Zulu historian, who believed that 'a name reflects its owner like a person's shadow', wrote (with fine retrospect) that the name Mhlangana meant that his 'grave would be in a reed swamp [*umhlanga*], in an open place and not at home'.[3] It is said that the *umntwana*, realising too late that he had been betrayed to his death, cried out, 'Nhi! Son of Sitayi [Mbopha], have you done this to me?'[4] Dingane's *izibongo* recalled the deed in these chilling words:

> Deep river pool at Mavivane, Dingana,
> The Pool is silent, and overpowering,
> It drowned someone intending to wash
> And he vanished, headring and all.[5]

A week or so after Mhlangana's death and some two months after Shaka's assassination, the *Bhalule impi* began at last drifting home through the coastal lands in small, exhausted groups, ill and on the verge of starvation, its numbers catastrophically reduced by about two-thirds. It was, as Isaacs reflected, 'the most signal defeat the Zoolas had ever sustained'.[6]

The returning army found that Dingane, with the support of the *izikhulu*, had already stepped into Shaka's place. He was calling himself '*uMalamulela*' (Intervener) because he had intervened between the people and the madness of Shaka,[7] and his *izibongo* celebrated him as 'The one who acted on behalf of the people! Mediator!'[8] Indeed, he had moved very cannily and swiftly to win popular approval by decreeing that he would allow unmarried *amabutho* freely to enjoy premarital sex, and that he would immediately permit several of the older *amabutho* to assume the headring, take wives and set up as *abanumzane*. He also relaxed military discipline and ensured that warriors serving at the *amakhanda* were well supplied with meat. Consequently, Dingane did not find it difficult to win over the dispirited remnants of the *Bhalule impi* and persuade them to accept – or, at least, not to oppose – his succession.

With that assurance, the day of *ukubuzana* could be held. This, King Cetshwayo later explained, was the day of ceremonial questioning when 'all the great men of the country assemble and talk to one another about the heir, whom they look upon as king already'. They say to each other, continued Cetshwayo, 'You must take care of this king and not act out of an evil heart against him.' Having agreed among themselves, they would then send

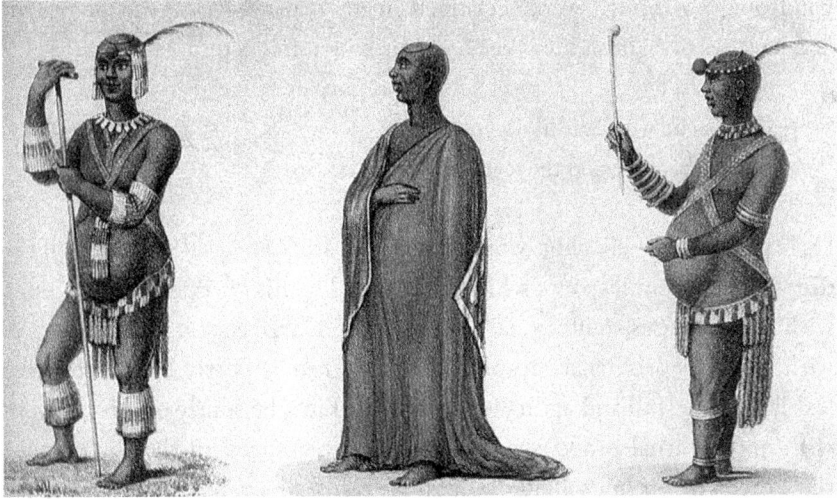

King Dingane, drawn in 1835, attired in both ordinary and dancing dress. In the central image, he is wearing a cloak of the blue salempore cotton cloth imported from India and favoured by the Zulu elite.

(CAPTAIN ALLEN F GARDINER, *NARRATIVE OF A JOURNEY TO THE ZOOLOO COUNTRY IN SOUTH AFRICA, UNDERTAKEN IN 1835, 1836*)

a deputation to the *inkosana*, inviting him to leave the *ikhanda* where he had been living as prince and to transfer to the former king's chief *ikhanda* 'as king'.[9] And so it was with Dingane, at about forty years of age the undisputed *inkosana* selected (it must be said) by Mnkabayi and acclaimed as king by the nation. As soon as Dingane heard he had been chosen, he burst out alone from the assembly and performed an energetic dance (*ukugiya*) and then entered the *inhlambelo* (enclosure where the king washes). When he emerged, 'he was covered in coloured patches … of different medicines used on him by the doctors, who were strengthening him'.[10]

What was he like, Dingane, the second Zulu king, who was known as *uMgabadeli*, the Usurper? His *inceku*, Tununu, considered him 'good-looking' and described him as 'light brown (*mpofu*) in colour' and about 1.7 metres tall.[11] Lunguza, who as a child had often seen him, remembered that he had 'the slightest show of whiskers, and a small beard' and wore the *isicoco*. Like many of Senzangakhona's descendants, Dingane had what Lunguza described as 'very large fat thighs and a large neck' but was not flabby, being 'solidly built … firm and tough'.[12] His '[p]rominent buttocks, handsome posterior!' were acclaimed in his *izibongo*.[13] As with Shaka, he had patches of hair on his body, and was hailed in his praises as

Hairy-One with hair like a lion's,
Having hair even on the legs.[14]

He had a large, fleshy chin, which always sweated. He used to scrape off the drops with his snuff spoon, which was carried by his *inceku* in a basket along with his capacious snuffbox, fashioned out of a large gourd. Isaacs observed with some surprise that, despite Dingane's heavy, portly frame, the king 'exhibited his skill and agility' at dancing, which, he sourly observed, went with his 'habitual propensity for corporeal pleasures' in the company of the women of his household.[15] For all that, like Shaka before him, Dingane did not marry or have any children who might grow up to threaten him. Whenever one of his *umndlunkulu* became pregnant, Dingane made sure that she drank a potion prepared by one of his *izinyanga* to make her abort.

Dingane has a well-earned reputation for self-indulgence. He kept court with more splendour and pageantry than any other Zulu monarch. Sivivi remembered that, even if the king was out of sight, one always knew from an *imbongi* ceaselessly shouting his praises when he was travelling on foot between his *amakhanda*, accompanied by a great concourse of all his *amabutho*, *izikhulu* and *izinduna*. As he made his stately progress the king 'would walk along with the *izinceku* on either side of him but at a distance of 50 or more yards from him. Others would be in the front, flattening grass, sweeping, cutting part, removing small pebbles. They thoroughly cleared the way. The *izinduna* would keep with the regiments, keeping the men back so as not to come too close on the king and *fudumaza* him (cause to be warm or heated).' Indeed, Dingane used to get tired when on the march: 'He would then sit down, and a large white shield would be held out over him to make a shade.'[16]

In keeping with his sense of majesty, Dingane maintained some 500 women in the *isigodlo* at uMgungundlovu, meaning 'the place that encloses the elephant', namely, the king. Situated in the cool, lowveld country of the emaKhosini valley, with its excellent grazing interspersed by acacia bush, aloes and euphorbias, the *ikhanda* was constructed in 1829 on the slopes of the stony Singonyama (or Lion Hill) in the fork between the

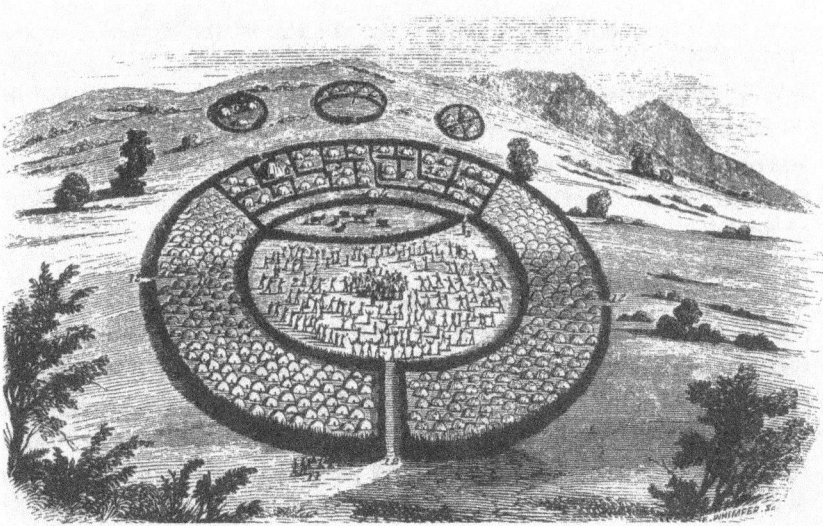

A representation of the layout of uMgungundlovu, King Dingane's principal *ikhanda*,
published 17 years after its destruction.

(REV WILLIAM C HOLDEN, *HISTORY OF THE COLONY OF NATAL, SOUTH AFRICA*, 1855)

Mkhumbane stream to the east, and the Nzolo stream to the west. The
oval-shaped *ikhanda*, with its great parade ground 600 by 500 metres, was
probably the largest and most magnificent ever constructed. It consisted
of between 1 400 and 1 700 huts (those in the *izinhlangothi* in rows six to
eight deep) that, when packed for one of the great festivals, could have held
between 5 000 and 7 000 people. The *isigodlo* at the foot of the Singonyama
hill was divided, as was customary, into two sections, the black *isigodlo*
under the charge of Mjanisi, one of Senzangakhona's redoubtable widows,
and the less prestigious white *isigodlo* under Bhibhi, once Senzangakhona's
favourite wife.

The huts of the *isigodlo* were divided into numerous triangular compart-
ments of about three huts each, separated by two-metre-high fences of
interwoven flexible branches. Dingane's exceptionally large audience hut
was in the extreme northwestern corner of the black *isigodlo*. The supreme
example of the hut-builder's art, it was supported by ten wooden poles and
could accommodate as many as 50 people. Dingane's private hut, where he
usually ate and slept, was on the eastern side of the black *isigodlo*. It had one

central pole which the *umndlunkulu* had entwined from top to bottom with patterns of red and white beads, a practice forbidden outside the *isigodlo*.

Dingane's *umndlunkulu* wore nothing except strings of large beads with an opaque white core covered with a layer of transparent red or amber (known as Cornaline d'Aleppo) imported from Cape Town through Port Natal and restricted to the king and his household.[17] He is said to have particularly favoured fat young women with pretty faces. His favourite evening's entertainment was to have about a hundred of them sing loudly and interminably to him until they were quite exhausted. Women normally stood or danced when they sang, but Dingane's *umndlunkulu* were so fat with good food and lack of exercise that they sat on the ground and moved only their arms in time to their songs.

Dingane's eyes were most expressive, revealing both his quick apprehension and volatile temperament. Isaacs noted on 1 May 1829 that Dingane's fierce glance was 'keen, quick, and always engaged, nothing escaping him, but every movement and gesture of his people was readily caught, and immediately noticed'. At the same time, he admitted to being quelled by Dingane's exceedingly 'piercing and penetrating eye', which he rolled 'in moments of anger with surprising rapidity'.[18] When he spoke it was in the *amalala* style because as a young man he had given his allegiance to the Qwabe (as Shaka had to the Mthethwa) and had lived many years among them. Thus he himself would have pronounced his name as 'Dingane', rather than as 'Dingana', as the *amantungwa* would have done.

More than any other Zulu monarch, Dingane has gained an evil reputation in the written record. John Cane lost no time in describing him to the Cape authorities as 'weak, cruel, indolent, capricious and even more prone to shed human blood than the monster [Shaka] that has been put to death'.[19] The vehement denunciations of white settlers who feared and fought him, and the horrified disapproval of the missionaries he spurned, relentlessly reinforced the negative representation of Dingane as a treacherous and bloodthirsty tyrant. Thus the mission-trained Magema Fuze characterised him as 'a greater torment than Shaka', who 'although a person in form, had the heart of a dog' and was 'truly like a poisonous snake'.[20] This hostile tradition culminated in Peter Becker's sensationalist 1964 biography, *Rule of Fear*.

King Dingane reclining in the fresh air from the doorway in his many-pillared hut in the *isigodlo* at uMgungundlovu, attended by his *umndlunkulu*. Note the scalloped hearth and eating utensils next to it.

(CAPTAIN ALLEN F GARDINER, *NARRATIVE OF A JOURNEY TO THE ZOOLOO COUNTRY IN SOUTH AFRICA, UNDERTAKEN IN 1835, 1836*)

By way of contrast, in his *izibongo* Dingane is approvingly hailed as 'Giver-of-cows-with-full-udders' and is remembered as having 'a good heart among men'.[21] And within a year of Dingane's coming to the throne, Isaacs noted with relief: 'Chaka was born and nurtured in war, which was his darling aim, but Dingane cultivates the repose of peace, and only wields his spear when necessity compels him: he is no warrior – he is a man whose soul seems devoted to ease and pleasure.'[22] Isaacs also perceived with less enthusiasm that Dingane was 'deliberative and calculating', indeed, 'reserved, even to the extreme, and in speaking seems to weigh every word before he utters it'.[23] Certainly, the Zulu recognised his deep, unfathomable nature, calling him in his *izibongo* 'Deep one, like pools of the sea!'[24] and

The reserved one he doesn't speak, he has no mouth
He is not like Shaka
Who used to finish a kraal speaking.[25]

That Dingane never laughed out loud, but merely gave an amused grunt and nodded his head to and fro, reinforced this impression, although it could be that he merely did not wish to show his ugly teeth, which were unusually small.

More positively, the Zulu read Dingane's reserve as sensible prudence and caution, and hailed him as

He who peeps over dry ravines before crossing,
Who washed his hands and they dried while he was in council.[26]

In his daily life, Tununu, his *inceku*, found him friendly and cheerful, although he could easily be provoked into terrible displays of temper. Tununu ruefully remembered the king viciously beating him all over the body with a stick and breaking several of his fingers because he suspected him of sleeping in the long grass with one of the women of his *isigodlo*.[27] Indeed, the Zulu understood only too well that underneath Dingane's reticent exterior he was cunning and brutally dangerous:

Ox that encircles the homesteads with tears;
Mamba who when he was down he was up.[28]

In Isaacs's estimation, Dingane was never cruel for cruelty's sake, as Shaka seems to have been, 'though at times he was implacable, and perhaps unrelenting'.[29] But, as we have seen, killing for a Zulu king was a necessary act of state, to be ruthlessly undertaken. Nzobo kaSobadli (also known as Dambuza), the portly and notoriously ill-tempered personage always clad in his familiar 'whiteish blanket' whom Dingane raised to be one of the two principal men in the kingdom,[30] and who seemed adept at strengthening Dingane's resolve whenever he was inclined to mercy or compromise, stated the case uncompromisingly: 'The killing of people is a proper practice, for if no killing is done there will be no fear.'[31] Nzobo was firmly supported in this position by Ndlela kaSompisi, of the Ntuli people. He was the brother of Bhibhi, Senzangakhona's favourite wife, and had risen to prominence under Shaka as a much-acclaimed warrior, successful general and fine orator. Dingane promoted him to become his chief councillor and commander-in-chief, superior to Nzobo. Older than the king and dark-complexioned like Nzobo, he was tall, with thin legs, and portentously stout. He wore a slight beard. Although reputably a kindly and temperate man who was inclined to mercy, he too saw the necessity for arbitrary executions, not least as a means of eliminating rivals and entrenching his own power. So it was widely believed that it was his two senior advisers, rather than Dingane himself, who ensured that the vultures were regularly fed with the flesh of those who attended the king's assembly. In a telling metaphor in Dingane's *izibongo*, they are seen controlling the king, likened to a goat with its proverbially skittish and unpredictable disposition:

> Goat of Dambuza and Ndlela,
> Which they held by the ear and it was patient ...[32]

Consequently, as King Cetshwayo bleakly put it, his uncle 'Dingaan commenced his career as king by killing all his brothers, except Panda [Mpande, Cetshwayo's father], also his brothers' principal chiefs and friends, with all their women and children ... At least eighty people thus perished.'[33] Unabashed, Dingane's praises crowed:

> Hornless calf of the daughter of Donda, [ancestor of Mphikase,
>   Dingane's mother]
> That went and kicked the other calves,
> And blood flowed from their nostrils.[34]

In some Zulu eyes, extensive fratricide certainly made Dingane 'a bad king',[35] and Mpande publicly declared that while Dingane 'used to say he had killed Tshaka for troubling the people; in fact it was he who finished off the Zulu house'.[36] Nevertheless, most Zulu subsequently understood that Dingane, having already had a hand in killing both Shaka and Mhlangana, naturally feared his surviving brothers would in turn conspire to assassinate him. In his *izibongo* Dingane is called 'Wizard whose liver is black, even among his father's children'. An actual *umthakathi*, or wizard, was loathed and feared, but in metaphorical terms a 'wizard' denoted a person with amazing powers, while a 'black liver' meant profound courage. Dingane was therefore being lauded for his resolve in purging his brothers whom his praises go on to list in order of seniority: Mhlangana, Ngqojana, Mdungazwe, Somajuba, Sophane and Mfihlo.[37] Of these, Ngqojana, an engaging and intelligent man with unassuming manners, evaded execution until 1835. His crime, Dingane being childless, was that he stood next in line after the drowned Mhlangana to the succession.[38]

Of his remaining brothers, Dingane spared Gqugqu, Senzangakhona's youngest, who was still a small boy and no threat as yet. Mpande also escaped execution, and for his survival was subsequently hailed in his praises as 'The brass rod which remained from the other sticks'.[39] Mpande, it will be remembered, had not been brought into the conspiracy to kill Shaka, and had instead continued to serve with the *Bhalule impi* throughout the disastrous campaign. Yet why Dingane did not now kill the 30-year-old prince along with his brothers is not entirely clear. One likely reason is that he was not considered eligible to succeed Shaka because he was 'of the *umsizi* hut'.[40] During the annual *umkhosi* festival the king was daubed with *umsizi* (powdered ritual medicines) and had sex with one of the women of his *isigodlo* in a specially prepared hut. Any child born of this intercourse was accepted as a member of the royal house, but of inferior rank. Otherwise, it seems that there was consensus that Mpande was a simpleton (*isitutana*), and Dingane's councillors, notably Ndlela, persuaded him that there was little point in killing him since he could never be a danger. So Dingane gave him a hundred cattle and ordered him to build his own *ikhanda* in the country between the Mhlathuze and Thukela rivers.

Having disposed of his brothers, Dingane next rid himself of Shaka's close associates and a number of over-powerful *izikhulu* who might resist his authority. As it was said, 'a king rarely retained the preceding king's *induna* because he was afraid lest he should … overshadow him'.[41] He permitted Mdlaka, Shaka's seasoned military commander, and Ngomane, his chief councillor, to live out their days in obscure retirement. Others fared less well.[42] Nqetho kaKhondlo, the younger brother of Phakathwayo, the Qwabe *inkosi* whom Shaka had killed, was (as we have seen) a great favourite of the dead king's. In early 1829 he and a large section of the Qwabe revolted against Dingane and migrated southward out of the Zulu kingdom to Bhaca and Mpondo territory.[43] Dingane was enraged by the loss of so many subjects and their wealth in cattle, and feared that others might be encouraged to break free of Zulu rule. He blamed Magaye, the Cele *inkosi* and Shaka's powerful viceroy south of the Thukela, for not doing enough to prevent the defection of the Qwabe through his domain, and executed him. He then entrusted the region south of the Thukela to Sothobe, who had led Shaka's first embassy to the Cape. Sothobe had astutely thrown his hand in with the conspirators before their assassination of Shaka, and was the most eminent survivor of his reign, being honoured when visiting uMgungundlovu by being quartered in the same prestigious enclosure next to the *isigodlo* (the *isigqiki*) as Ndlela and by being addressed as 'father' of Dingane because of his age and status.[44] As his viceroy of the trans-Thukela region, Dingane entrusted Sothobe in 1831 with the execution of Mkhonto, Magaye's heir, and the final elimination of the Cele.

Others whom Dingane liquidated because he feared they were too powerful and independent-minded, or who (like Magaye) had stood high in Shaka's favour, were Zihlandlo kaGcwabe of the Mkhize, whose people lived between the middle Thukela and upper Mvoti, and Dube kaSilwane of the Qadi, who also dwelt along the banks of the middle Thukela. Dingane also purged the Hlubi along the Mzinyathi River and the Khumalo on the upper reaches of the Mkhuze.

As had been promised him when Mnkabayi first drew him into the plot against Shaka, Mbopha was raised to be an *inkosi* south of the Mhlathuze. But, as a regicide who had betrayed his position of trust as Shaka's *inceku*, he could not be allowed to live and prosper. Dingane had additional cause to distrust him. He remembered just how effectively Mbopha had manipulated him and Mhlangana during the few months he had held the balance between them, and that he had contrived Mhlangana's death. Conveniently, Mbopha also made the perfect scapegoat for Shaka's death, and his eventual execution satisfied the returning *Bhalule impi*.

If Dingane's reign seemed at first to have held out the promise to be far more relaxed and pacific than Shaka's had been, it became rapidly apparent that nothing had fundamentally changed in Zululand under his rule. This was not on account of some dreadful character flaw in the new king. It was because the social structure and geopolitical circumstances of the Zulu kingdom had not altered with Shaka's death, and it was not feasible for Dingane to do other than maintain the character of the monarchy Shaka had established. For example, at the very beginning of his reign Dingane had expressed his intention to abolish his *isigodlo*, explaining that it was 'a bad institution' because it 'was the cause of people being put to death'. But his powerful *induna*, Nzobo, quickly poured water on that unroyal foible, briskly enquiring, 'How, without one, can you be a king?'[45]

Yet, even if the political and socio-economic structures of Shaka's kingdom continued unchanged under Dingane, he was still free to adopt several new policy directions without appreciably undermining them. For one thing, he was concerned about Shaka's military overreach to the south and decreed that the Mzimkhulu must be regarded as the southern boundary of the Zulu kingdom because 'the land south of the river belonged to Faku, the Pondo king'.[46] For another, he was uneasy with Shaka's centring of the kingdom in such close proximity to Port Natal because that gave the traders an inordinate degree of influence over Zulu policy. Consequently, on becoming king he immediately moved the hub of the kingdom away from kwaDukuza and back north across the Thukela to its traditional core in the emaKhosini valley. There, as we have seen, in 1829 he built his new 'great place', uMgungundlovu.

However, that did not mean he was done with the Port Natal traders. Dingane understood that they were not faithful subjects and had probably been involved in the conspiracy against Shaka. Moreover, he was correct in believing that their objective was to establish Port Natal and the surrounding region as an autonomous base for their commercial activities – although he probably did not know that Cape merchants, eager to open up his kingdom for commercial enterprise, were lobbying the British government to annex the Port. Nevertheless, he valued their trade goods and connections with the Cape too much to try and evict them from his domain. As a consequence, the traders remained ensconced at Port Natal. The settlement continued to grow, a new township was laid out on the north side of the bay, and in 1835 Port Natal was officially renamed Durban, after the Governor of the Cape, Sir Benjamin D'Urban (although it continued to be known as Port Natal for years afterwards). By 1838 there were about 40 white traders at the Port, along with numbers of Khoekhoe retainers they had brought with them as hunters and transport-riders. But, except for John Cane, who stayed on through thick and thin, most of these were new people, and almost all the original hunter-traders who had been there at the time of Shaka's assassination had died, been killed or had left the scene.

Dingane had originally intended to relax his hold on the more peripheral southern marches of his kingdom. But then he became aware that the traders at Port Natal were eagerly attracting refugees from his realm to build up their following. Not only was the Port fast becoming a troublesome nest of several thousand Zulu malcontents and refugees from his rule but, even more alarmingly, the traders were training many of them in musketry, and by the mid-1830s could field an army of nearly 300 men carrying firearms. More than Shaka, Dingane respected the military value of firearms (even if most of his *amabutho* required considerable convincing), and in his *izibongo* he was celebrated as 'Jonono who is like a fighting-stick of thunder [a musket]!'[47] Nevertheless, he was unable to obtain firearms in significant numbers. As late as 1837, near the end of his reign, the missionary Captain Allen Gardiner (who was much disheartened that the Zulu elite evinced more interest in the use of the onomatopoeic 'issibum' than in the word of God) reported that while 'muskets have been introduced as an article of barter with the Zulu by some of the European settlers at or near the port … at present this traffic is in an incipient state'.[48] The traders, knowing that Dingane equated firearms with power, retained a near monopoly of the new weapons and rationed their sale as a means of maintaining some control over the king. Like Shaka, he could call on his nominal tributaries at the Port to provide military support during his campaigns but – and this was the caveat – they might equally well turn their muskets on him.

So, to put a stop to the haemorrhaging away of his subjects to the Port, and to contain the traders and their firearms, Dingane had to reverse his initial policy regarding his kingdom south of the Thukela. He instructed the redoubtable Sothobe to bring the people of the southern reaches of the middle Thukela under his close supervision, and ordered the inhabitants of the coastal lands to withdraw north of the Thukela. The uHlomendlini were stationed in southern Zululand to guard the heartland from Port Natal and to prevent the seeping away of any more refugees to the traders. When the traders periodically became too contumacious, he imposed trade restrictions to keep them in line. On occasion, the traders' relations with the Zulu monarch were strained to breaking point. Twice, in 1831 and 1833, the traders evacuated the Port and took to the bush in fear for their lives when Dingane sent an *impi* to punish them, only for him to lure them back with soft words and assurances.

Dingane dealt in the same way with Lourenço Marques, Port Natal's great commercial rival, when he considered the Portuguese not sufficiently compliant. In 1833 he sent an army to attack Lourenço Marques, kill the uncooperative governor and ensure that his replacement toed the line. This successful foray incidentally consolidated Dingane's sway over the tributary Tsonga chiefdoms in southern Mozambique and secured the trade routes to Delagoa Bay.

Another reason for maintaining his difficult relationship with the Port was that Dingane, like Shaka before him, wished to open diplomatic relations with the British officials at the Cape to reassure them of his pacific intentions and to facilitate trade. He chose John Cane to convey this message, and his embassy reached Grahamstown overland on 21 November 1830, but got no further. This time, the officials refused to treat with Cane in any way whatsoever or to accept the 'four elephant's teeth' Dingane had sent as a present.[49] The humiliating failure of this mission infuriated Dingane, who did not attempt to negotiate with the Cape again.

In his spurned message to the Cape authorities, Dingane had expressed his intention of living 'in peace and harmony' with his neighbours, but he was no more able to do that than could Shaka. In 1830 he despatched a military expedition south against the Bhaca to recover the cattle (including royal herds) they had captured from Nqetho's fugitive Qwabe. The raid was unsuccessful, and a second attempt in 1833 fared no better. But Dingane required – no less than Shaka – to keep his *amabutho* employed and well rewarded and his *izikhulu* contented with the redistribution of booty. So attacks on other neighbours continued. To the west, in 1830 and 1832 he campaigned against Mzilikazi and the Ndebele on the highveld, and again in 1837 when his *amabutho* captured much livestock. To the north, in 1836 he mounted a major campaign against the Swazi kingdom, and when his *amabutho* stalled before the Swazi mountain fastnesses he called in 30 mercenaries from Port Natal, supported by a small unit of 40 retainers trained in the use of muskets. They defeated the Swazi in 1837 and forced them to surrender some 15 000 head of cattle.

Despite such military assistance, Port Natal continued to be a nagging thorn in Dingane's flesh. He valued the traders for their goods, but was alarmed that, despite all Sothobe's efforts, they continued to give sanctuary to refugees from his rule. In seeking a solution he turned for assistance to a new presence in the region. Christian missionaries were becoming interested in the conversion of the Zulu, and in 1835 the first evangelical to undertake the challenge was Allen Gardiner of the Church Missionary Society, a retired captain in the Royal Navy. Gardiner arrived at Port Natal in late 1835 and went straight to uMgungundlovu, where he impressed the king with his knowledge and demeanour and rapidly gained his confidence. Dingane decided he was just the man to broker a deal with the unruly Port Natal traders. At Gardiner's urging they duly agreed to repatriate any future refugees from Dingane's rule in return for his promise to respect their lives and property. In addition, Dingane gave permission for the admittance of missionaries into his kingdom. His prime interest was in the firearms and practical skills the missionaries would bring, rather than in the Gospels as such – indeed, his permission was required for those few wishing to take Christian instruction. But, in return for this concession, Gardiner agreed to take charge of Port Natal and bring order to the settlement. On 13 July 1835 Dingane proclaimed him chief over all the country between the Thukela and Mzimkhulu rivers: the very territory that would later comprise the British colony of Natal.

This attempted solution did not work. Most traders did not recognise Gardiner's new authority and continued to encourage Zulu refugees to join them in Port Natal, particularly if they were young women. Dingane once again tried trade embargoes to bring them into line, but was reluctant to go too far because (as we have seen) he needed their military support against the Swazi. Nor did the traders dare risk a complete break with Dingane because the British government still would not take them officially under its wing, and they could not count on British redcoats for protection.

Relations between Dingane and Port Natal were still at this unresolved and unsatisfactory pass when a daunting flood of organised and heavily armed migrants, determined to settle in the Zulu kingdom whether they were welcome or not, appeared at the passes over the Drakensberg. Shaka had never had to face a threat of this nature. Dingane's standing as ruler would depend on how effectively he was able to contain this dire threat to his realm, a fledgling kingdom that was only just 20 years old.

⚛

CHAPTER EIGHT

KILL THE WIZARDS!

When, in 1814, Britain formally annexed the Cape of Good Hope from the Dutch, some 27 000 white colonists were living in the colony. They stemmed from Dutch, Flemish, German and French Huguenot settlers and were beginning to develop a sense of their own 'Afrikaner' identity. Many did not take well to British rule, especially when the relatively liberal new administration interfered with their well-established and racially based conception of mastery over the African and slave majority, a belief reinforced by a Calvinistic and literal belief in the Bible. Some resolved to move away from the Cape into the interior so that they could live their lives as they had before the arrival of the alien, interfering British. Others combined this desire with a positive perception of the economic possibilities of the expanding frontier. They calculated that once they had moved far enough away into the interior, they could make contact with the various traders of the east coast and, free of the commercial network controlled by the British, set up their own sovereign republics. The great paradox is that in seeking independence from what they regarded as colonial oppression, they were themselves embarking on an act of colonisation that would have an impact on all the African societies of the interior.

By 1836 a migration of farmers (or Boers), known as the Great Trek, was proceeding northward across the Orange River in covered, ox-drawn wagons. By 1845 some 14 000 Emigrant Farmers, as they called themselves, or Voortrekkers (meaning the first ones to trek) as they are now commonly known, had left the eastern districts of the Cape. Taking with them all their livestock, goods and chattels, they set off in a series of separate household parties, each free to move on whenever and wherever they wished. Every party was organised by a locally prominent individual and was composed of that person's extended family, clients, and black servants and dependants. The Slavery Abolition Act had come into effect in the British Empire on 1 August 1834, and slaves over the age of six were redesignated 'apprentices', their servitude scheduled to come to an end on 1 August 1840. But thousands of these 'apprentices', to a number as great as that of the Voortrekkers themselves, went on the Great Trek with their masters. The males served as *agterryers*, black retainers who since the earliest days of Dutch rule in the Cape had accompanied their masters on horseback on hunting expeditions or military campaigns. So, when the Voortrekker parties collided with the African societies already living in the interior, and either violently displaced them or reduced them to labourers on the immense farms they staked out for themselves, their *agterryers* fought alongside them. But, because of the long-standing racialised narrative of the Great Trek initiated by the Voortrekkers themselves, *agterryers* have all too often remained invisible (if crucial) comrades-in-arms.

We must not allow ourselves to accept that the Great Trek was the unique, game-changing event it has been cried up to be. As Norman Etherington has so persuasively pointed out, the Voortrekker exodus was but one of the many early 19th-century 'treks' by other indigenous peoples in southern Africa that historians have seen as being pivotal to the so-called *mfecane*, and sometimes a by-product of Shaka's conquests.[1] Even before the Voortrekkers crossed the Orange River, which was the northern boundary of the Cape Colony, people of mixed-race origins – speaking a simplified form of Dutch that would become the Afrikaans language, and wearing European-style clothing – had migrated onto the highveld, where they lived in semi-nomadic hunting communities. They were sometimes called *drosters* (or runaways) on account of their ruthless cattle-raiding and slave-taking, and by the early 19th century the main bands were the Oorlams, Bergenaars, Hartenaars and Basters (or Griquas). They were already the most mobile and feared fighters on the highveld, effectively challenging even the warlike Ndebele, and in 1826 mauling a Zulu *impi* that collided with them near the Lepelle River on its return from a raiding expedition against the Pedi. The *drosters* were such effective fighters because they were mounted on horses and armed with muskets. Their military style was based on that of the formidable Boer commandos (or militia of farmers), first formalised in the Cape in 1715 when the Dutch East India Company developed a mobile mode of border defence under the command of local notables against African raiders. The Voortrekkers fought in exactly the same way, and many were seasoned veterans of the wars on the Cape eastern frontier against the Xhosa.

Because their numbers were so small, the Voortrekkers were unwilling to take unnecessary military risks. They avoided the sharp losses involved in hand-to-hand fighting by keeping the enemy at a distance with their musketry. A mounted Boer commando, when out raiding or striking at an enemy force, rode with minimum equipment and supplies to maximise the advantages of mobility and surprise. However, if the encounter went against them, the Boers used their horses to withdraw to a more favourable position, or made a swift tactical withdrawal to the convoy of ox-wagons that usually accompanied them with supplies and served as their base. The wagons, when drawn up in a tight, all-round defensive formation (or laager) lashed together end to end, formed an improvised fortification from which the Boers could keep up a devastating all-round fire and avoid being outflanked, always the greatest risk when fighting in open country.[2] As we shall see, the defensive laager would prove invulnerable against traditionally armed Africans who persisted in massed, frontal attacks. Aware of this advantage, the preferred Boer tactic was to ride to within range of the advancing African army in two ranks. The first would dismount, fire, remount and retire behind the next line of men, the two ranks repeating the procedure until the enemy was drawn into musket range of the laager. Once the enemy's assault had stalled under concentrated Boer firepower and they were thoroughly demoralised, mounted Boers sallied out again to transform their disordered foes' withdrawal into a desperate rout.

The commando system had always been under the command of locally prominent persons, and during the Great Trek the various household parties of Voortrekkers naturally consolidated around individuals who showed the greatest military leadership. This in turn was the key to successful and charismatic commanders consolidating what was never more than superficial political authority over the groups that decided to follow them – or that might hive off if dissatisfied. Because each of these personally ambitious leaders had his own preference regarding where he wished to settle his following, the Great Trek had no single political authority directing its objectives, but was a fractured movement of shifting alliances. Such lack of cohesion was potentially fatal for the Voortrekkers who, after all, were intending to settle in the territories of existing African societies, who could be expected to resist them.

Dingane had his first inkling of what was afoot when, in 1834, a party of Boers from the eastern Cape under Petrus Lafras Uys, Snr, a prosperous farmer with considerable military experience, visited Port Natal to ascertain whether the region was suitable for farming. The Zulu would call these Boers 'amaBunu', and on account of their deeply tanned, yellowish complexions would differentiate them from the more white-complexioned English.[3] Uys's Kommissietrek, or scouting mission, bore no immediate consequences that Dingane could see, but within a few months his favourable report would encourage many to join his particular party of Voortrekkers. Henceforth, the Zulu kingdom would feature as a highly desirable place of settlement for the Emigrant Farmers.

Precisely what the emerging Great Trek might mean for him became apparent to Dingane when he learned what had befallen his old foe Mzilikazi, the Ndebele ruler, whose kingdom the Zulu *amabutho* had raided successfully in 1830 and again in 1832 (although less effectively). Andries Potgieter, a powerful personality and natural leader, had provocatively led his party right into Mzilikazi's territory on the highveld, and on 16 October 1836 about 6 000 Ndebele under Mkhaliphi had duly attacked Potgieter's laager of 50 wagons at Vegkop, just south of the Vaal River. The Ndebele were roundly repulsed, and their defeat caused Dingane considerable disquiet because he knew that, to all intents and purposes, their way of war was exactly the same as that of the Zulu from whom they had sprung. Then, hard on the news of Vegkop came word that, on 17 January 1837, a swiftly moving commando led by Potgieter, and reinforced by Gerrit

Maritz's following, had surprised Mzilikazi at Mosega, his great place on the Marico River, and comprehensively routed his forces, their firepower breaking up every Ndebele attempt to rally.

Here was proof positive of the deadly superiority that the mobile, mounted Boers armed with muskets possessed over traditionally armed warriors, Ndebele and Zulu alike. But did Dingane contemplate coming to Mzilikazi's aid against what was surely a common threat? He did not, and instead, in June 1837, he sent an *impi* under the command of Ndlela to exploit his old enemy's misfortune. Such fatal political short-sightedness was not unique to Dingane, and it was to prove a common failing among the rulers of independent Africa when faced with colonial aggression. Instead of combining against the common foe, the tendency was to seize the short-term advantage against existing rivals, and even to make expedient alliances with the colonisers against other African adversaries.

As Ngidi (who took part in the successful campaign of 1837) expressed it, 'this was the army which seized everything and overcame everything. We ate up many cattle. We were "heavy" with them'; so many, in fact, 'that we lacked men to drive them'.[4] Ndlela finally brought his footsore army home in September, leaving the Ndebele weaker than ever. The Korana and Griqua of the highveld, without considering what threat the Voortrekkers would ultimately pose to them, also used the opportunity to raid the Ndebele in June and August. Next, Potgieter, now supported by Uys's party – along with *droster* allies who, short-sightedly, could not resist looting what they could from the weakened Ndebele – struck once more against Mzilikazi in the nine-day running battle of eGabeni north of Marico on 4–12 November 1837. By then, Mzilikazi's only thought was to escape north across the Limpopo River out of range of his enemies, and to do so with as many of his precious cattle as he could.[5]

Following their comprehensive defeat of the Ndebele, the Voortrekker parties had to decide on their next move. Potgieter's plan was to settle north of the Vaal and open trade with Delagoa Bay. But he soon found himself at odds with Pieter Retief (known to the Zulu as 'Piti'), who had led his party onto the highveld in February 1837. Retief was a farmer from the Grahamstown district in the eastern Cape where, despite constant financial troubles brought on through gambling and land speculation, he had gained a considerable reputation as a commando commandant in the recent Sixth Cape Frontier War of 1834–1835. For his part, Uys was also jealous of the charismatic Retief, with his frank, open demeanour. Consequently, along with Potgieter, he remained on the highveld when Retief decided in October 1837 to lead all those who would follow him over the Drakensberg passes into the Zulu kingdom.

Retief understood that if his party was to settle in the Zulu kingdom it was essential to come to accords with both Dingane and the Port Natal traders who controlled his outlet to the sea. Leaving his main party in laager on the western side of the Drakensberg, Retief first visited Port Natal, where the traders enthusiastically welcomed him as an ally and as a means of breaking free from Dingane's unpredictable control. Retief next opened communications with Dingane through the Revd Francis Owen of the Church Missionary Society, who, along with his wife and children, had in October 1837 set up his mission on the ridge overlooking uMgungu-ndlovu from the east. In his letter of 19 October 1837 to Dingane, Retief stated that he and his party desired 'to establish themselves in the country which is uninhabited and adjacent to the territory of the Zulus' – by which, it would later become clear, he meant the territory south of the Thukela that Dingane had, in 1835, already settled on Gardiner as chief. Retief emphasised in his letter that his 'anxious wish' was that he would always live 'on terms of peace and amity with the Zulu nation'. Yet his conciliatory words were ominously overlaid by the concluding reference in his missive to it having become 'absolutely necessary' for the Voortrekkers to declare war on Mzilikazi for having 'failed in every attempt to arrange our differences'.[6] The warning to Dingane was abundantly clear: negotiate and make the demanded concessions, or be attacked.

On Dingane's invitation to treat, Retief and a small party of Boers and Port Natal traders arrived at uMgungundlovu on 5 November 1837. Dingane set about attempting to overawe the strangers with days of mag-nificent displays of dancing and military exercise and with a parade of his stupendous wealth in cattle. The two parties finally got down to negotia-tions on 8 November. Owen put their terms into writing.[7]

Dingane stated that he was 'almost inclined' to cede Retief the ter-ritory he requested. However, it is clear that what he had in mind was definitely not the country south of the Thukela, which he regarded as part of his kingdom, but the territory lately abandoned to the Voortrekkers by Mzilikazi. One should understand that African societies were accommodating to foreigners and strangers seeking land. In the case of the Zulu kingdom, the land (as we have seen) belonged to the king and, through him, to the Zulu nation. Nevertheless, the king could grant the right for newcomers to live on the land and make use of it – but only provided they accepted the obligation to *ukukhonza*, or to offer loyalty and tribute for the privilege. The Port Natal settlers had complied (if erratically) with this stipulation, but would Retief? Dingane therefore put Retief to the test by stipulating that, before he would consent to further negotiations over land, Retief must first recover Zulu cattle rustled by the Mokotleng Tlokwa under Sekonyela, a people who dominated the Caledon River valley and who dressed and fought like the *drosters*. Retief agreed to undertake the task, but could not refrain from adding that he hoped he was 'dealing with a king who keeps his word'. For, as he portentously warned Dingane, the Bible taught that kings who conducted themselves like Mzilikazi 'are severely punished, and that it is not granted to them to live or reign long'.[8]

Retief's reiterated threatening allusions to Mzilikazi's fate would have left Dingane in little doubt that the Voortrekkers would have no qualms in seizing whatever territory they required. Retief reinforced this impression when, even before he had fulfilled his bargain to retrieve the Zulu cattle from Sekonyela, he sent word to his party to bring their wagons over the mountain passes into the well-watered countryside south of the headwaters of the Thukela and its tributaries – territory that Dingane had not yet ceded to them. There they were joined by Maritz's party and some of Potgieter's people too. Not only was the unauthorised presence on Dingane's soil of several thousand interlopers a deliberate violation of his sovereignty, but also they were encamped in their highly defensible laagers. No wonder that, in Zulu memory, the local inhabitants of the region became convinced that the Voortrekkers 'intended hostilities'.[9]

The pioneering Zulu scholar and member of the African National Congress (ANC) Sibusiso Nyembezi (born in 1919) believed that Dingane's touchy dread of being insulted and of having his power usurped was triggered when he grasped the Voortrekkers' real intentions. He understood all too well that to ensure his people's respect and loyalty he must be seen to defend their land against the invaders. As Dingane later put it to Owen, 'he would not allow white people to build houses in his country'.[10] In Nyembezi's view (and we must understand the apartheid context in which he wrote), Dingane's decisive response was an indication that blacks were quite capable of defending themselves from white supremacy, and that his resistance to the Voortrekkers was a significant signpost on the road to liberation.[11]

Even before Retief finally led a commando back over the Drakensberg in late December 1837 to recover the stolen Zulu cattle from Sekonyela, it seems that Dingane and his advisers had decided that accommodation with the bellicose Voortrekkers was impracticable, and that they must destroy the invaders. Perhaps at this time Dingane – as only kings were permitted to do – secretly stirred water with *imithi* in the cattle enclosure where he washed, and looking into its depths saw 'war in the water'.[12] A plot in mid-November to kill Retief and his party on their way back to Port Natal from uMgungundlovu miscarried when the agent, Chief Silwebana, failed to act and was then 'eaten up' by Dingane for his dereliction. Then, at the *umkhosi* on 22 December 1837, the *amabutho* made explicit their intention to fight the Boers, repeatedly and vehemently shouting out: 'Who can fight with thee; no king can fight with thee. They that *carry fire* cannot fight with thee.'[13]

Even the means Retief used to coerce the stolen cattle out of the Tlokwa confirmed in what scant regard he held African rulers and cautioned Dingane how he might be treated in turn. Employing a ruse at an arranged meeting, Retief clamped handcuffs onto the surprised Sekonyela and refused to release him until he surrendered the goods. To make matters worse, Retief did not hand Sekonyela over to Dingane for punishment as he had required. Nor did he send him the horses and muskets he had seized besides cattle, and this particularly affronted Dingane, who had in mind the formation of a small force mounted and armed like the Boers. And, to top it all, Retief's cavalier disregard of the terms of his agreement with Dingane over Sekonyela's cattle became known precisely when, on 2 January 1838, the king and his councillors learned of the Voortrekkers' final defeat of Mzilikazi at eGabeni the previous November. Their debate now turned on how Dingane could ward off the fate that had befallen Sekonyela and

Mzilikazi. Ndlela, who entirely distrusted the Boers' intentions, began urging Dingane to kill them while he could. Mnkabayi, the Zulu matriarch and kingmaker, was of the same opinion.

Retief, meanwhile, who on 11 January 1838 had returned to his laager in the foothills of the Drakensberg, was running into opposition from the other Voortrekker leaders. He wished to return to uMgungundlovu with a large well-armed commando to intimidate Dingane into honouring his agreement of the previous November to cede territory to the Voortrekkers. But there were many misgivings and objections that it was foolhardy to risk such a large force when Dingane's intentions were unfathomable and quite likely hostile. Retief therefore called for volunteers, and at length set out for uMgungundlovu with 69 Boers, 30 *agterryers* and 300 Zulu cattle recovered from Sekonyela.

Dingane and his councillors knew Retief was on his way. The option still lay before them of continuing to negotiate. Dingane had called on Gardiner and the Port Natal trader John Cane to be on hand to advise him when Retief rode in, but, fearful for their own safety, they declined to come to uMgungundlovu to mediate. Whether their presence would have made any difference is impossible to tell, but they might have persuaded Retief to moderate his aggressive deportment, which played a decisive part in persuading the Zulu leadership that only force would answer.

On 2 February 1838 large numbers of *amabutho* in their war-dress began cramming into uMgungundlovu in anticipation of Retief's arrival. The next morning the Boers rode right into the parade ground of the *ikhanda*, shooting off an unnerving salvo of musketry in greeting and putting on a display of mock combat, charging each other and firing away. Doubtless, the Zulu were suitably daunted, but Dingane's option of making a first strike before it was too late was surely reinforced. The Zulu responded over the next two days with their own military displays, and all seemed superficially amicable when on Sunday, 4 February 1838, Dingane put his mark to a document written in English. Only a dubious copy survives, but it spells out

> That whereas Pieter Retief, Gouvenour of the Dutch emigrant South
> Afrikans, has retaken my Cattle, which Sinkonyella had stolen; which

cattle he, the said Retief, now deliver unto me: I, DINGAAN, King of the Zoolas, do hereby certify and declare that I thought fit to resign unto him, Retief, and his countrymen (on reward of the case here-above mentiond) the Place called 'Port Natal', together with all the land annexed, that is to say, from Dogela [Thukela] to the Omsoboebo [Mzimvubu] River westwards; and from the sea to the north, as far as the land may be useful and in my possession. Which I did by this, and give unto them for their everlasting property.[14]

Apparently, the Boers did not consider it suspicious that Dingane was willing so meekly to cede such an enormous swathe of Zulu territory. Rejoicing at their God-given success, they accepted lavish Zulu hospitality on the following day and prepared to depart on 6 February. But Dingane had other plans for them. Persuasive intelligence had reached him that the Boers were intending to kill him while he slept. His night guards, the *ogqayinyanga*,[15] who were stationed near the *isigodlo*, reported that on successive nights they had spotted the Boers suspiciously moving around the *ikhanda*, particular in the vicinity of the *isigodlo*, suggesting that they had their lascivious eyes on Dingane's royal women. When confronted, the Boers protested that they had merely been going after their strayed horses. But the Zulu persisted in believing that they were attempting to surround uMgungundlovu under cover of darkness, exactly as *abathakathi*, or wizards, would have done when making evil magic against the king, and this has traditionally been accepted among the Zulu as sufficient justification for their subsequent execution.[16]

Consequently, with his worst suspicions confirmed, for Dingane the business of the treaty was nothing more than a ploy to lull any misgivings the Boers might entertain concerning his intentions, and certainly not a contract he ever intended to honour. (Incidentally, we might question whether Retief would have abandoned his plans to settle in Dingane's territory if he had failed to secure what he regarded as a legal right to it through the treaty. It is most unlikely.)

For his part, it is more than unlikely that Retief ever had in mind something so foolhardy as killing Dingane, and by the same token could not conceive that the Zulu believed that to be his intention. The now buoyant and overconfident Boers accordingly did nothing to allay Dingane's deep distrust and mounting antagonism towards them. On the contrary, on the day of their planned departure they imperiously demanded that Dingane hand over livestock that the Zulu had brought back from their last campaign against Mzilikazi, and which they now claimed the Ndebele had seized from the Voortrekkers. Dingane was deeply insulted by their gall, and was further provoked when the Boers declared they intended to fire a parting salute. He saw this as a plot to shoot him down, and this was subsequently proved to his satisfaction when the Boer muskets were found to have been loaded with shot.

Enough was clearly enough. Dingane called an emergency conclave with his inner council, his *umkhandlu*, to decide what was to be done, and it was resolved to make a pre-emptive strike against the overweening Boers. The two *izinduna* who visited Owen at his mission station the following day to articulate Dingane's reasons for taking such drastic action stated:

> All George's people, meaning the British were his, i.e., he liked them, but the Amaboro were not his people: nor were they George's. He said that all the armies that came into his country should be killed, that the Amaboro (Boers) were going to kill the king: that they had come like an army and were going to kill the king.[17]

Once they had decided to do away with the Boers, Dingane and his *umkhandlu* had to work out how precisely to go about it. Nzobo suggested that the Boers should be invited to a display of dancing, and then killed while unsuspecting and unarmed. Otherwise, he warned, they would resist and heavy Zulu casualties would ensue. Nzobo's plan was adopted, and Dingane invited the departing Boers and their servants, whose horses were already saddled up, to enter uMgungundlovu to take leave of him. Despite receiving warnings that a transparently uneasy and glowering Dingane was planning treachery, Retief's party piled their muskets as requested outside the main gate to the *ikhanda* where two euphorbias marked the burial place of Nkosinkhulu, one of Dingane's distant ancestors. This in itself was incidentally another mortal, if unintended insult: kwaNkosinkhulu was sacred and one could not even walk there touching the ground with a stick since this would be said to be 'stabbing the king'.[18]

Retief, along with his Boer comrades and *agterryers*, sat down to drink *utshwala* with the apparently friendly king, who was seated on his chair of state at the top end of the great cattle enclosure with an *ibutho* drawn up either side of him. These two *amabutho* moved out with dancing shields to perform an *inkondlo*, a lively dance with a gradual forward and backward movement. While a great crowd of other *amabutho* looked on, the dancers came closer and closer to the unwary Boers. Dingane had instructed Ndlela to inform the *amabutho* that once they had sung two songs he would give the prearranged signal for them to close in by waving his left hand over his left shoulder and giving a piercing whistle such as the Zulu did when they attacked. It fell out as Dingane had planned, and the *amabutho* rushed upon Retief's party before they could rise, while the king began repeatedly shouting out: '*Bulalani abathakathi*' (kill the wizards).[19]

The *amabutho*, who were not armed with stabbing-spears lest they alert the Boers to the danger they were in, were carrying only *izikwili*, very stout cudgels – not knobkerries – about 80 centimetres long. With these they belaboured the Boers and their *agterryers*, who slashed back at their assailants with their *herneutermesse* – vicious sheath knives with blades between 18 and 45 centimetres long[20] – and desperately tried to break free. But the *amabutho* swiftly clubbed them to death or broke their necks, and dragged them off with their feet trailing to kwaMatiwane, the stony hill of execution across the Mkhumbane stream from uMgungundlovu. There they threw down their broken bodies and left them as food for the vultures. There could be no going back now, no forgiveness by the Boers until they had wiped out the deed with Zulu blood. As Ngidi (who traced the line of his descent to Nandi's father) would later lament: 'Piti ... was killed, and the land was destroyed.'[21]

The violent operation Dingane had initiated did not end with the execution of Retief and his party. Zulu rulers always made sure to 'eat up' the whole following of people they had executed lest they seek revenge. Accordingly, Dingane took the steps required against the Voortrekkers in their encampments who, he well knew, would now be his inveterate foes. So he first ordered Retief's heart and liver to be placed as strong defensive magic in the path the surviving Voortrekkers must take to uMgungundlovu should they dare to attack him there. Next, Dingane ceremonially reviewed several *amabutho*, amounting to about half his available army, and gave them their orders. They were to surprise the scattered Boer encampments in the foothills of the Drakensberg, obliterate everyone in them, white or black, man, woman or child, and then bring back the captured livestock and other booty to the king. At about noon the *amabutho* set off at a determined trot for their objective, chanting Dingane's *izibongo* and lustily proclaiming: 'We will go and kill the white dogs!'[22] Thus began the Voortrekker-Zulu War, which Dingane intended should wipe his kingdom clean of the alarming Boer interlopers, but which ended disastrously in his overthrow and death.

While it is hardly remarkable that in Afrikaner tradition Dingane has been remorselessly excoriated for his unspeakable 'treachery' in luring Retief and his party to their deaths and then attacking the Boer encampments without warning, the ambivalence shown by many Zulu to these events is less expected. Yet Dingane's contemporaries were only too conscious of the ruin the disastrous Voortrekker-Zulu War brought upon the kingdom so recently forged by Shaka, of the humiliation and loss of territory. In King Mpande's time the royal *imbongi* used to declaim:

> Alas, O Hairy one of Mgungundlovu!
> You killed the Boers!
> You thrust an evil spear into Zululand!
> You thrust in an evil spear!
> You thrust it into your own stomach, did you not?
> What measure or courage is this?[23]

This perception was given fresh, written voice in the 1920 and 1930s by mission-educated Zulu intellectuals such as Dr John Dube and Rolfes Dhlomo, who blamed the treacherous Dingane (already denigrated as Shaka's wicked assassin) for bringing Boer vengeance down on the Zulu people and unleashing racial animosity in South Africa.

Yet, what alternatives to the menacing Boer demands had there been for Dingane other than abject capitulation or armed resistance? To adopt the first was to forfeit the loyalty of his subjects and undoubtedly to lose his throne. Only resistance would answer. This dilemma and the choice Dingane made have been well understood by later Zulu generations engaged in liberation politics. When Umkhonto we Sizwe – the armed wing of the ANC – was launched in 1961 on 16 December (now the Day of Reconciliation), its soldiers were consciously linked with Dingane's *amabutho* in a 'just war' against apartheid. By the 1980s the ANC-in-exile and its internal allies were hailing Dingane as a freedom fighter, an unheralded hero and patriot who had valiantly confronted the white invaders. This is still the position held today, and for his struggle against colonialism Dingane is now viewed as one of the heroic nation-builders of post-apartheid South Africa.[24]

※

CHAPTER NINE

THERE WAS GREAT SLAUGHTER

On 16 February 1838 Dingane's *amabutho* fell upon the scattered, unsuspecting Boer encampments along the Bloukrans and Bushmans rivers. Many they overran, but others had sufficient warning to organise their defences, and where proper wagon laagers were hastily formed, the Zulu were beaten off. The following day, the Voortrekkers under the command of Gert Maritz launched a mounted counter-offensive from four laagers and inflicted heavy casualties on the exhausted Zulu who were retiring with their booty of 25 000 head of cattle. In the scattered, desperate fighting over the two days the Boers lost 40 men, along with 56 women and a pathetic tally of 185 children. Their coloured servants and *agterryers* suffered heavily too, some 250 dying alongside their masters. For their part, the Zulu took some 500 casualties, far too many for a punitive raid against an unprepared foe. Even worse, heavy as the Boer casualties were, the Zulu had left them still intact in their laagers, but now burning savagely to avenge their slaughtered women and children. In Afrikaner historiography the event is known as the Bloukrans Massacre, and at the time the Boers bitterly dubbed the region where it had taken place Weenen, or Weeping. What Dingane and his advisers had intended as a bold stroke to eliminate the Voortrekker menace had turned out to be nothing other than the opening and only partially successful gambit in the long and bloody Voortrekker-Zulu War.

The surviving Voortrekkers, who numbered about 640 men, 3 200 women and children and 1 260 coloured retainers, did not fall back over the Drakensberg. They stayed where they were to fight on, not only because they were determined to avenge their losses, but also because the Zulu had driven off close to 40 per cent of their cattle. Not only were these beasts the Boers' main means of subsistence; they were also their draught animals, and with so few left it was difficult to move all their wagons. Reinforcements were essential, though, if they were to beat off another Zulu attack, and the survivors appealed successfully to both Andries Potgieter and Petrus Uys on the highveld. Both came nobly to their aid. Encouraged by these reinforcements, in early March the Voortrekkers opened negotiations with the opportunistic Port Natal settlers for joint retaliatory action against Dingane. The traders made the first move, and on 13 March 1838 John Cane and a force of about 2 000 African retainers and adherents raided across the middle Thukela River at Ntunjambili, the region where Sothobe, Dingane's trusted regent over the southern parts of his kingdom, was the dominant figure. Meeting little opposition because Dingane had summoned the local forces away to face an anticipated Voortrekker offensive, they destroyed several large *imizi* belonging to Sothobe, and returned to Port Natal on 2 April with 6 000 cattle and several hundred captured Zulu women and children.

Buoyed up by this easy victory, the traders rashly agreed that they would advance from Port Natal on uMgungundlovu with an even larger force while a Boer commando would attack from the southwest. On 6 April Andries Potgieter and Piet Uys led out a commando of 347 men without any wagons so as to move rapidly and surprise the Zulu, as they had the Ndebele in 1837. Their objectives were to recapture the Boer cattle and to compel Dingane to reconsider his policy towards the Voortrekkers by delivering a sharp blow against his army. But this time the Zulu, with their excellent intelligence-gathering network, were more than ready for them. On 10 April a Zulu army of around 6 000 men under the command of Nzobo himself ambushed the commando in broken country at eThaleni. Thoroughly bested and fighting without effective coordination, the Boers were eventually able to extricate themselves in a long fighting retreat, losing 10 dead, including Uys himself and his teenaged son. There was no disguising that the Vlugkommando, or 'Flight Commando' (as it was insultingly dubbed) had suffered a humiliating reverse in the open field, and that the Zulu forces had manoeuvred with skill considerably superior to that of the Boers. In an attempt to explain away their defeat, many members of the Vlugkommando unfairly accused Potgieter of cowardice in the face of the enemy, and he indignantly withdrew with his followers to the highveld. The remaining Boers absorbed the humiliating lesson that it was too dangerous to take on the Zulu in the open without the protection of a wagon laager to fall back upon.

The 'Grand Army of Natal' under Robert Biggar, a former British officer who had moved to Port Natal in 1836, suffered an even worse fate than the Vlugkommando. Apart from the 16 traders and 430 black retainers who had firearms, the rest of the army was made up of several thousand African auxiliaries carrying spears and shields. On 17 April 1837 a Zulu army under the nominal command of Mpande, Dingane's half-brother, but actually led by Nongalaza kaNdlela and Madlebe kaMgedeza, cut Biggar's men off at Ndondakusuka, on the north bank of the Thukela, and annihilated them. Clearly, the Zulu were capable of nullifying the advantage of firearms if, as at Ndondakusuka, they were able to wrong-foot their poorly disciplined enemies in the open and force them into the close hand-to-hand fighting at which they excelled. Having destroyed the traders' army, the victorious Zulu marched on Port Natal itself. The settlers hastily evacuated the Port and watched despairingly from the brig *Comet* (which was fortuitously anchored in the bay) as the Zulu swept down on the settlement on 24 April and gleefully put it comprehensively to the sack for nine days.

Greatly encouraged by his armies' victories against both the Boers and Port Natalians in their joint advance on uMgungundlovu, Dingane resolved that his *amabutho* must embark on a fresh offensive of their own to carry out his original objective of eliminating the Boer invaders. This time, in mid-August, Ndlela led out an *impi* of about 10 000 of the more experienced *amabutho* against the Boers in their great, triangular laager of 290 wagons along the ridge at Gatsrand, protected on one side by the Bushmans River. Several parties of Boers had come together there under Johan Hendrik de Lange, who had been a member of the Kommissietrek, and whose laager had survived the Bloukrans Massacre.[1] He had also been a member of the unfortunate Vlugkommando, but was nevertheless a seasoned veteran of the Cape Frontier Wars and proved an effective commander. Only about 75 fighting men were available to defend the Gatsrand laager – with some women dealing out powder and bullets – and they had to rush from one sector to another when it came under Zulu attack. Ndlela's army encircled the laager on 13 August and attempted repeatedly over that and the next day to storm it in great waves, but could find no weak point in the defences.[2] Because the Boers had dug pits to entrap the enemy crossing the river, the Zulu would call the battle emaGebeni, or 'Place of the Pits'. Baffled, Ndlela finally withdrew on 15 August, unhindered by the Boers, whose under-nourished horses were in too poor a condition for a pursuit. The battle of Veglaer, as the Boers came to call it, offered them the vital lesson that a properly formed laager was the sovereign defence against any Zulu attack, no matter how out-numbered the defenders.

Veglaer was a repulse rather than a full-scale defeat, but Dingane and his advisers were at a loss as how best to respond. Perplexed, they did not renew the offensive but waited for the Voortrekkers to make the next move. For their part, despite their victory the Voortrekkers were afflicted by disease and hunger and felt their fortunes still to be at a low ebb. So they sent a deputation to seek aid from Andries Pretorius, a gifted organiser and experienced commando leader who had taken part in the fighting against the Ndebele, and who was planning to lead a new party over the Drakensberg. On 26 November 1838 at the Sooilaer on the Little Thukela River the Voortrekkers elected Pretorius their Chief Commandant.

Pretorius decided to advance east from Sooilaer towards uMgungundlovu in order to force a decisive battle on the Zulu. He planned his offensive with great thoroughness, taking into account all that was to be learned from previous encounters with the enemy. Since eThaleni showed it was too dangerous to search out the Zulu on their own ground with a mounted commando, he decided to march with 64 wagons, carrying only supplies and ammunition. The wagons would laager every evening when the commando halted, and the horsemen would undertake thorough scouting for the enemy ahead.

The Wenkommando (Victory Commando, as it came to be known) halted on the western bank of the Ncome (Blood) River on 15 December and formed its wagons into a laager on a spit of land between the river and a donga (dry watercourse). Dingane had received early warning of Pretorius's advance. He fully grasped the grave threat it posed him and prepared to make a supreme military effort for what he foresaw would be the decisive clash of the war. With that objective, he raised the largest army the Zulu were capable of fielding, an *impi* of between 12 000 and 16 000 *amabutho* – the 'flower of the nation', as Tununu, Dingane's *inceku*, called it. A large number of persons of rank joined it – 'the fellows with big bellies' in Tununu's unflattering phrase.[3] In earnest of the significance of its mission, Dingane placed the great *impi* under the joint command of Ndlela and Nzobo.

Efficient Boer scouting warned Pretorius that the Zulu host was closing in on him, so he had sufficient time to prepare properly for the coming onslaught. Defending the perimeter of the laager were 472 Voortrekkers, three Port Natal settlers and about 120 Port Natal African levies under Alexander Biggar, who was aching to revenge the death of his two sons at the battle of the Thukela. Crammed inside the laager were 700 restive oxen and 750 horses controlled by some 130 black wagon-drivers and 200 *agterryers*. The battle opened at dawn on 16 December with a series of poorly coordinated assaults by different elements of the Zulu army that unsuccessfully attempted to envelop the laager. As at Veglaer, the Zulu could find no weak spot in the laager's defences and the defenders' uninterrupted fire from muskets and several small cannon prevented them ever getting close enough to employ their spears and knobbed sticks. What was different from Veglaer was that this time the Boer horses were fresh and fed. So, when the Zulu attack finally faltered, about 160 mounted men sallied out and turned the Zulu retirement into a total, disastrous rout. The Boers admitted to three wounded in the battle, including Pretorius himself. Probably well over 1 000 Zulu were killed, and the Boer tally of 3 000 Zulu dead was likely exaggerated. The Zulu corpses bloodied the waters of the Ncome River, which the Boers grimly renamed Bloedrivier, or Blood River. Tununu, who was present at the battle, lamented that 'there was great slaughter, especially in the dongas there … The *izikhulu* of the Zulu died at Ncome … So great was the slaughter that there was no mourning in Zululand. No one went to mourn with others.'[4] Indeed, the Zulu were stunned by the military catastrophe and awaited the consequences with trepidation.

For the Boers, their great, God-given victory affirmed their right to rule over the heathen Zulu, just as God had delivered the Canaanites into the hands of the Children of Israel. Moreover, revenge had been exacted for the 'murder' of Retief and his men, and for the Bloukrans Massacre. During their advance, on 9 December 1838 Pretorius's commando had made a covenant with God – which they repeated every evening until the battle was won – that their descendants would keep the anniversary of their victory as a day of thanksgiving to God. Indeed, the Covenant and Blood River duly became cornerstones of Afrikaner nationalism. With the Union of South Africa in 1910, 16 December was proclaimed a public holiday. It was called Dingaan's Day, not to celebrate the Zulu king, but rather to serve as a reminder of his supposed perfidy.[5] For the Zulu people, on the other hand, the battle became a symbol of Afrikaner domination and the racial ideology of apartheid. In 1995 the new democratic government of South Africa renamed the holiday the Day of Reconciliation, and acted to make the contentious battle site more acceptable. An impressive laager of bronze-plated, life-sized wagons had been erected in 1971 to commemorate the Boer victory; to redress the balance, a new monument, shaped like the horns of a Zulu battle formation, was opened on 16 December 1998 by King Goodwill Zwelithini just across the Ncome River from the bronze laager. It is dedicated to the brave Zulu who fell in the battle defending their independence.[6]

Despite the triumphalism of the Boer monuments at Blood River and the annual celebration of their victory, the truth is that the battle was not nearly as decisive as the Boers made it out to be, and did not end the Voortrekker-Zulu War. Certainly, it was a crushing defeat for the Zulu army, and the subsequent dispersal of his dispirited *amabutho* momentarily crippled Dingane's ability to carry on the war. He himself, once frantic messengers informed him of the Boers' victory, abandoned uMgungundlovu and the emaKhosini valley the very same night. With his reserve *amabutho* and the *izikhulu* who had remained with him, he retired northward out of reach of the Boers. He was consequently unable to resist the forced march of the Wenkommando that reached uMgungundlovu on 20 December. But Dingane denied them the satisfaction of capturing his capital intact. Before withdrawing across the White Mfolozi, the king ordered his men to consign uMgungundlovu and two neighbouring *amakhanda* to the flames, leaving the Boers to sift through their charred remains for loot.

Dingane's *izinduna* and *amabutho* were reportedly 'tired' and demoralised by their terrible setback, and many voices were counselling Dingane to make peace with the Boers and to pay them tribute.[7] Dingane, however, was not yet ready to treat and still planned to draw the Boers into an ambush and so destroy them. He could not have known that Pretorius was intending to call a halt. The Boer commander had envisaged the campaign as a punitive expedition to punish Dingane and force him to honour the territorial concessions he had agreed to with Retief. The objectives of the Wenkommando were therefore not to conquer the Zulu kingdom but to crush Zulu military capability in battle so that Dingane had no option but to treat, to destroy uMgungundlovu, Dingane's capital and the site of his treachery, and to give the 'martyred' Retief and his party proper burial. Once all of these objectives were met, one more remained. The Voortrekkers' pastoralist economy depended on livestock, and they felt it essential to recover the herds the Zulu had captured in the earlier battles of the war. It proved a step too far and nearly brought the Wenkommando to destruction.

On Christmas Day 1838, near their laager at uMgungundlovu, the Boers seized an apparent Zulu spy, Bhongoza kaMefu. He was in fact a decoy, and persuaded the Boers that all of Dingane's cattle were in the valley of the White Mfolozi to the north. The Wenkommando quickly moved camp on 26 December to the Mthonjaneni heights overlooking the Mahlabathini plain. The next day, Bhongoza guided about 300 mounted Boers under Karel Pieter Landman, the second-in-command of the Wenkommando, who had fought in all the battles of the war, as well as about 70 Port Natal African levies on foot under Alexander Biggar, down into the valley of the White Mfolozi. The Boers mistook Zulu creeping among the rocks and bushes with shields on their backs for cattle, and were completely taken by surprise when the Zulu attacked them from all sides. The mounted men broke out of the ambush and fell back westwards across the open plain, alternately firing and retiring. When they tried to cross the river they were ambushed again by an *ibutho* lying in wait for them, and four Boers were killed. Nevertheless, they broke through, and, although closely pursued, regained their camp 23 kilometres away. Being on foot, the Port Natal contingent was not so fortunate. Almost all were killed, including Biggar.

This severe setback notwithstanding, on 28 December the commando raided the emaKhosini valley and dramatically burned three *amakhanda*. On 1 January 1839 they captured 5 000 Zulu cattle and 1 500 sheep. These were not nearly as many as they had hoped for, but were enough to persuade Pretorius that the exhausted Wenkommando had achieved all its objectives. On 2 January it withdrew towards the Sooilaer, which it reached on 8 January. With that, the active campaign ended, the Boers confident that they had done enough to pressure Dingane into concluding a peace favourable to them.

Indeed, the Boers were already determinedly spreading out into the territory they insisted Retief's treaty with Dingane had ceded them on 4 February 1838, carving out enormous farms for themselves. They began to set up a rudimentary administration with an elected – and inevitably fractious – Volksraad to govern their fledgling state (the very first of the Voortrekker republics), which they named the Republiek Natalia, with a diagonal red, white and blue flag. The Republiek required a seat of government, and Retief had already identified a suitable site in January 1838 on the banks of the Msunduze River. By October 1838 a rudimentary township was beginning to arise there. It was named Pietermaritzburg in honour of Piet Retief and Gert Maritz. Earlier, in terms of Retief's treaty with Dingane, on 16 May 1838 the Boers had annexed Port Natal to the Republiek. There they started laying out their own settlement of Congella a kilometre to the west of the bay to rival the devastated Port, which the chastened traders were beginning to rebuild.

The British, who had in the past resolutely refused to take the Port Natal traders under their wing, now intervened. The Boers were still technically British subjects, and authorities at the Cape were concerned that their aggressive policies towards the Africans of the interior would destabilise their eastern frontier.[8] Accordingly, on 4 December 1838 a detachment of the 72nd Highlanders under Major Samuel Charters occupied Port Natal and built Fort Victoria on the Point. The extraordinarily tactful Captain Henry Jervis succeeded to the command on 7 February 1839 and maintained amicable relations with the Boers, even if they would not accept his

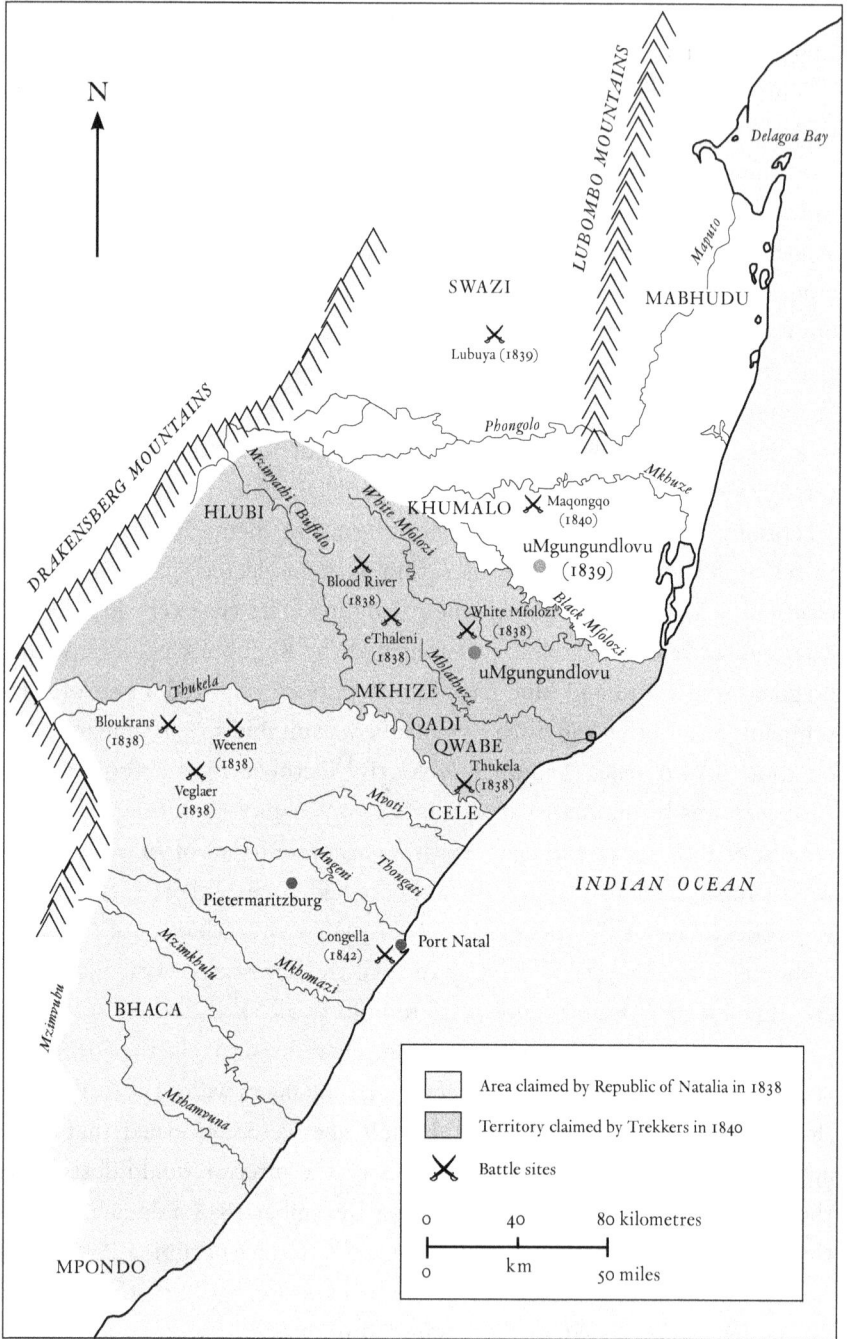

The Zulu kingdom and the Republiek Natalia, 1838–1840

authority, and did his level best to mediate a lasting treaty between the Boers and Dingane.

From the Zulu perspective, the battle of the White Mfolozi had given Dingane some consolation and proven that his military might was not irreparably broken, while the subsequent Boer withdrawal south of the Thukela had made it obvious that the invaders did not believe they possessed the military capability to conquer more of the Zulu kingdom. As a result, Dingane could proclaim to his subjects that he had in fact successfully repelled. Yet the dismal truth was that, by the same token, Dingane was in no position to retake those parts of his kingdom that now formed the Republiek Natalia. How he could reassert his shaken prestige and authority consequently remained problematic.

Dingane's first instinct was to widen the geographical distance between him and the Boers so as to allow him scope to regroup without fear of attack. After the Wenkommando retired he did not return to the emaKhosini and rebuild uMgungundlovu there. Instead, he pulled back northeast to the valley of the Hluhluwe River where he began the construction of a smaller uMgungundlovu in the territory of the Mdletshe chiefdom. But malaria was endemic in the dense valley bushveld, and Dingane moved the site of the new *ikhanda* northwest to a higher, healthier locale, just south of where the Vuna stream flows into the Black Mfolozi, a region that had once been the Ndwandwe heartland.

Once re-established at his new uMgungundlovu, Dingane decided that, until other options presented themselves, his best course would be to reach some accommodation with the Boers. Theophilus Shepstone, the son of a Wesleyan missionary from the eastern Cape who had accompanied Major Charters to Port Natal, and an accomplished linguist, was despatched to begin informally sounding out whether Dingane was amenable to negotiations. He reported in February 1839 that Dingane was willing to treat, although his execution of African peace messengers sent by the Boers was at the same time provoking them into contemplating a fresh campaign. To stave off this eventuality, Captain Jervis despatched Henry Ogle, a leading Port Natal trader well known to Dingane, to open negotiations. In response, Dingane sent Gambusha, a trusted *inceku*, to Port Natal. Gambusha made clear that Dingane hoped the British would help him expel the Boers.

Jervis refused to do so, but assured Gambusha that Britain would permit no further Boer aggression against the Zulu. With that the *inceku* had to be content.

A month after he had returned to Dingane with the British assurance, Gambusha arrived back at Port Natal with two chiefs, Gikwana and Gunwanga, who had Dingane's full authority to negotiate on his behalf. Jervis brokered a meeting between the envoys and Andries Pretorius, the Chief Commandant of Republiek Natalia, and peace was concluded on 25 March 1839. By its terms Dingane would restore all the firearms, cattle, sheep and horses captured from the Boers and would permit them to live unmolested south of the Thukela.[9] The British government, satisfied that the mission of the British force at Port Natal had been accomplished, contemplated withdrawing it once it was certain the peace would hold.

And hold it did, despite doubts it would not, with Dingane doing all he could to avoid a breach with the Boers. The reason is that he wanted no trouble along his Thukela frontier while he seriously pursued the option of expanding northward across the Phongolo River into the Swazi kingdom. He calculated that even if the land-hungry and rapacious Boers succeeded in conquering the rest of Zululand, he would thereby (like Zwide of the Ndwandwe before him) have another kingdom to sustain him. Ndukwana believed he must also have had in mind the new kingdom Mzilikazi had carved out for himself across the Limpopo after his shattering defeat by the Boers.[10]

To execute this plan, during the winter of 1839 Dingane mobilised his entire remaining military resources under Klwana kaNgqengelele – the powerful Buthelezi *inkosi* in north-central Zululand and a former favourite of Shaka's – for a determined attempt to conquer and occupy southern Swaziland. As Ngidi (who was about 22 years old at the time) put it, 'We went to open the way, to kill the Swazi along the way, so that the king could go by safely.'[11] Realising that Dingane had in mind far more than a raid and was 'removing', the Swazi did not resort to their usual strategy of taking to their mountain fastnesses until the danger was past. This time, their army under Mngayi Fakudze met the Zulu in the open field in the valley of the Lubuye stream. The hard-fought battle was a famous Swazi victory, and even though Dingane rushed reinforcements north, the campaign foundered and had to be abandoned.

This new defeat, coming so soon after the disastrous Voortrekker-Zulu War and the cession of so much territory to the Boers, drastically damaged Dingane's remaining prestige as king, besides destroying his hopes of creating a safe haven north of the Phongolo. However, it was neither the Boers nor the Swazi who finally brought him down, but his brother, Mpande, whom Dingane had so unwisely spared when he eliminated his other rivals in the royal house following his assassination of Shaka.

CHAPTER TEN

THE BRASS ROD WHICH REMAINED FROM THE OTHER STICKS

Mpande has often been written off as an unworthy successor to Shaka, obese and indolent. Yet these external attributes disguised a shrewd and determined survivor. As a boy, his father, Senzangakhona, sent him to be reared by the Cele chief Dibandlela, an ally of his overlord, Dingiswayo. In 1819 Mpande was enrolled in the umGumanqa *ibutho* in his half-brother Shaka's emerging kingdom, stationed at the kwaKhangela *ikhanda* presided over by Nandi and situated in Nqetho's Qwabe chiefdom. Belying his later reputation for being no soldier, Mpande took part in a number of campaigns, and Shaka rewarded him with several wives. As we have seen, Mpande was in the gravest danger following Shaka's assassination. His continued survival seems to have been principally at the urging of Ndlela, who persuaded Dingane that for lack of heirs by him or Shaka, only Mpande's legitimate offspring could ensure the continuity of the royal line.[1]

Although permitting Mpande to live, Dingane still saw him as a potential threat, and Mpande cannily deflected Dingane's distrust by broadcasting that he had no aspirations to be king, and by adopting a humble demeanour in his presence. For example, when he visited uMgungundlovu to pay his respects to Dingane, Mpande occupied a hut in an inferior position down by the gate instead of one close to the *isigodlo* as appropriate to one of his rank. Even so, there was no disguising that Mpande was an *umntwana* and

A distant view, drawn in 1835, of the kwaKhangela *ikhanda* in the emaKhosini valley.
(CAPTAIN ALLEN F GARDINER, *NARRATIVE OF A JOURNEY TO THE ZOOLOO COUNTRY IN SOUTH AFRICA, UNDERTAKEN IN 1835*, 1836)

– deny it as he might – quite possibly Dingane's *inkosana*, or heir. At his own great emLambongwenya *ikhanda*, between the Mlalazi and Thukela rivers in southeastern Zululand, Mpande maintained an *isigodlo* and lived in unashamedly regal style. This was the country where he had grown up, and he sedulously built up his adherents, especially from the survivors of the Cele and Qwabe chiefdoms scattered by Shaka and Dingane.

Chillingly aware of his vulnerability, Mpande also set about forging further alliances. One such was with Ndlela, Dingane's chief councillor and commander-in-chief, whose chiefdom had been carved out of territory abandoned by the Qwabe when they fled from Dingane. Ndlela's reason for taking Mpande's part so actively was at least partially due to their regional affiliations. And just as Mpande had himself been sent as a child to live among the Cele to create political bonds, so he despatched Cetshwayo, his son by Ngqumbazi, to dwell with Sithobe, the Sibiya *inkosi* and determined survivor who dominated the middle reaches of the Thukela. He also paid diligent court to Senzangakhona's widows, those formidable power brokers and kingmakers. Significantly, he also fashioned links with the *isikhulu* Maphitha kaSojiyisa of the Mandlakazi branch of the royal house, whom Shaka had appointed his viceroy over the former Ndwandwe territory in northeastern Zululand. Under Dingane, Maphitha continued to rule his

territory as an almost independent potentate, impatient of any royal control and, as Socwatsha recounted, 'was of such high rank that he used to
address the ancestors with cattle in the same way that the king did.'[2] As
Mpande would discover, Maphitha made for a very difficult ally, though a
crucial one.

Despite ever-present tensions between the brothers, with each convinced (not without reason) that the other was working secretly against
him, relations did not break down until the collapse of the Swazi campaign
in mid-1839. When Dingane demanded reinforcements from Mpande and
ordered him to prepare to move north with all his people to help colonise
the lands across the Phongolo he still hoped to conquer, Mpande jibbed.
Angered by Mpande's temporising excuses, and made increasingly suspicious when he suspended his customary visits to pay his respects, Dingane
decided that Mpande must be planning to usurp the throne. Once again,
Dingane resorted to one of his favourite pre-emptive strikes. He sent
Mpande a gift of a hundred heifers, knowing that Mpande was bound by the
rules of etiquette to come to the new uMgungundlovu to express his gratitude. Once he was there and in Dingane's hands, it would be an easy matter
for Dingane to put him to death. Unfortunately for Dingane, the *izinduna*
who drove the cattle to Mpande were in the service of Ndlela, the *umntwana*'s
protector, and one of them, Mathunjana kaSibhaca, took the considerable
risk of secretly tipping him off to beware of the king's intentions.[3]

With imminent execution hanging over him, Mpande consulted with his
izinduna and his mother, Songiya. All advised him to flee and seek sanctuary
among the Boers. Taking heed, Mpande sent out word to all his adherents between the Mhlathuze and Thukela rivers to accompany him in his
flight with all their livestock. Disillusioned with Dingane's discredited and
increasingly onerous rule, and fearful of his retribution if they stayed once
their *inkosi* had fled, in September 1839 some 17 000 joined the *umntwana* in
streaming into the Republiek Natal with 25 000 cattle. Dingane urgently
summoned his forces from the borders of Swaziland, where they were
deployed to turn back as many of the refugees as they were able. But they
arrived too late, singing 'We know of the Zulu who departed in our absence',[4]
and pulled back for fear of an armed confrontation with the Boers. The Zulu
called the great rupture of Mpande's defection 'the breaking of the rope of

government (*umbuso*) in the Zulu country.'⁵ His adherents praised him as

> He who crossed afterwards
> Of the house of Shaka;
> The swallow that gets lost in the sky,
> He who appears in his feather head-dress
> Between the English and the Boers.⁶

Certainly, it was with good reason that his adherents hailed him as 'You who crossed all the rivers on the way to restoring yourself'.⁷ For if Mpande was initially concerned only with saving himself and his adherents from Dingane's vengeance, he very quickly grasped how he might benefit from an alliance with the Boers and turn the tables on his vindictive half-brother.

Mpande's host and its great herds of cattle encamped near the Thongati River, not far up the coast from Port Natal. Mpande immediately opened preliminary negotiations with the Boers and then proceeded to Pietermaritzburg – still only a stockaded camp of wattle and daub shanties – to put his case to the Volksraad on 15 October 1839. With him were his young son, Cetshwayo, and other prominent men including Sothobe, Dingane's former viceroy in the south, who had thrown over his old master. Mpande requested of the Boers only that he be allowed to settle between the Mvoti and Mhlali rivers (a region that had been the southern part of the original Cele chiefdom and his childhood home), and undertook to abide there as a loyal Boer subject. As a sop to Boer religious sensibilities he also promised to allow Cetshwayo, whom he declared to be his chief son, to be educated by Christian missionaries.⁸ So they would recognise his young heir in future should Mpande be killed by Dingane, the Boers cut an identifying 'snip' out of the top of Cetshwayo's left ear, with little more ceremony than if he had been a calf.⁹

Mpande then returned to his encampment, leaving the Boers perplexed and highly suspicious. They knew next to nothing of this obscure Zulu prince except that, by crossing the Thukela in force, he had broken the terms of their March treaty with Dingane and might well be playing out a ruse by the treacherous Zulu king to regain his former territory. Some wished to attack the 'refugees' and drive them back across the Thukela, but, being covetous Boers, advocated retaining their precious cattle. Moderate counsel prevailed, and the Volksraad resolved to send a 28-man deputation under the hard-bitten F Roos to Mpande to negotiate further, even though they were only too conscious of the dire fate that had befallen Retief in similar circumstances.

Mpande used the days before the deputation's arrival hastily to erect an *ikhanda* built to the usual pattern, and received it in impressive royal style with displays of dancing by his warriors and much feasting. The Boers struck an alliance with Mpande on 27 October 1839 in a long tent they erected for the ceremony, and recognised him as the 'Reigning Prince of the Emigrant Zulus'. The two parties then agreed to combine in attacking and overthrowing Dingane. Once that had been effected, Mpande was to be established as the Zulu king, and in return he was to pay the Boers the cattle they believed Dingane still owed them and to cede them St Lucia Bay, a potential harbour further up the coast.[10]

Tununu was surely right when he reflected that 'had Mpande not crossed over, D. would have ruled' for he would have continued to seek accommodation with the Boers.[11] Predictably, Dingane was enraged and alarmed in equal measure when he learned of Mpande's defection and pact with the Boers, and bitterly taxed Ndlela for 'harbouring a snake' and for ever advising him to spare such 'a swollen, scrofulous thing'.[12] Otherwise, there was nothing Dingane could do about the situation except to send to the Volksraad advising it not to put its trust in such an obvious and unreliable turncoat. In fact, while British troops were still stationed at Port Natal with instructions to prevent further conflict between the Boers and Dingane, the Boers could do nothing to implement their treaty with Mpande. However, the British authorities soon came to the conclusion that the garrison's task was done (quite wrongly, as events would prove), and on Christmas Eve of 1839 Captain Jervis and his men sailed away to a mocking Boer salute of musketry.

The way was now open to launch the delayed joint attack on Dingane, but not before the Boers (who paid scrupulous attention to the legal niceties of contracts and treaties they entered into) had on 4 January 1840 formally repudiated their treaty of 25 March 1839 with Dingane.[13] Thus began the first of the three great civil wars that ravaged Zululand

between 1840 and 1884. The strategy the allies adopted for their campaign was for Mpande's army of about 5 000 men under the command
of Nongalaza kaNondela – the same general of Mpande's army that had
utterly defeated the Port Natal forces at the battle of the Thukela in April
1838 – to advance by the coastal route on the new uMgungundlovu at the
Vuna River. Simultaneously, a Boer commando of 308 Boers and some 500
agterryers under Commandant-General Andries Pretorius (who had grown
inexpressibly self-important) would follow the route north taken by the
Wenkommando in December 1838. Shamefully, this commando would earn
the name of the Beeskommando ('Cattle Commando') for treating the campaign primarily as a hunting expedition and for putting the rounding-up of
cattle ahead of fighting. Mpande, instead of marching with his own army,
remained effectively a hostage with the Beeskommando so that Pretorius
could be sure he would not betray his new-found allies.

The mutually mistrustful allies opened their campaign on 14 January
1840, even though it was the height of the rainy season and the going was
consequently difficult. Dingane recognised he was in an impossible fix.
Flight to the north was barred since the failure of the Swazi campaign, and
he knew he was not strong enough to fight both the armies closing in on
him. Calculating that the Beeskommando presented the greater threat, he
attempted to assuage the Boers, sending no less a personage than Nzobo
with a gift of 200 cattle to negotiate. Here Dingane gravely miscalculated.
Instead of respecting Nzobo's inviolability as an ambassador and according
him the courtesies he anticipated as a man of such high rank, the Boers,
who loathed him for being one of the main instigators of Retief's execution,
put him in chains. Mpande hated him as vehemently for repeatedly advising
Dingane to have him killed, and reportedly said to him, with lethal courtesy:
'Give me some snuff from your snuffbox, the snuff you used to take when
you sat at the gate of Mgungundlovu remarking as you did so that the king
had no younger brothers left.'[14] At Nzobo's rigged court martial, which the
Boers convened on 31 January 1840, the hostile witnesses included Mpande
and some of his *izinduna*. Nzobo was sentenced to death by firing squad and
died bravely, affirming his loyalty to Dingane to the end.[15]

That evening, while the Boer commando was still halted just south
of the White Mfolozi River, messengers from Nongalaza's army arrived

THE EIGHT ZULU KINGS — DINGANE

to report that the previous day, 30 January 1840, a great battle had been
fought at the Maqongqo hills a hundred kilometres away, and that Dingane
had been defeated. It was doubtless rash of Nongalaza to have engaged
before Pretorius could bring up the Beeskommando, and so to have forgone
the overwhelming tactical advantage of Boer firepower. His reasons for
taking such a risk were undoubtedly political, and must surely have been
decided upon in consultation with Mpande. To defeat Dingane without
Boer military assistance was to diminish their hold over Mpande as their
client. It was also to signal to the Zulu people that Mpande laid claim to
the throne through his royal lineage and by unaided force of arms, and that
to recognise him as king was not to submit to the Boers.

Dingane had few options left him in the final stages of the First Zulu
Civil War. Believing that his latest uMgungundlovu *ikhanda* at the confluence of the Vuna and Black Mfolozi rivers was not well situated for a
defensive battle, he had it put to the torch, like the first *ikhanda* of that
name, and retired 50 kilometres to the north, to Magudu Mountain, some
dozen kilometres south of the Phongolo River. Ndlela, his close adviser
and his veteran general of so many campaigns, took up a defensive position
with about 5 000 men a few kilometres southwest of Magudu Mountain at
Maqongqo, a group of rounded knolls in the open plain. The two sides in
the battle that decided the future of the Zulu kingdom were about equal
in number and engaged each other in the old way, without the white man's
muskets, going shield to shield and with the stabbing-spear. Because both
armies were identically accoutred, as a distinguishing mark Mpande's followers wore two thongs of white cowhide suspended from the neck and
hanging over the back and chest. Morale in his army was high, far better than that in Dingane's, and was bolstered by Mahlungwana kaTshoba,
the leading *isangoma* of the Zulu kings, who had abandoned Dingane's
cause and, before the battle, made powerful magic to ensure the defeat of
Ndlela's army. Even so, Tununu, who was with Mpande's forces, later drew
an unusually candid picture of the pre-battle nerves that seized even men
of high rank: 'The *izinduna* themselves were agitated and they defecated
and urinated, for an assegai would not be forgiving ... even though they
were *izinduna* they would not escape.'[16]

The battle, which began in the early afternoon and continued until darkness fell, was extremely tough and closely fought. It seems Dingane and Ndlela were at odds over what strategy to adopt. The king wanted to mount an all-out attack with his entire army, but his general went his own way and opted for a cautious, piecemeal approach, keeping back a large division in reserve. In the end, defections from Ndlela's forces finally turned the tide. Both sides suffered considerable casualties so that when Dingane's army eventually retired, not entirely defeated, Nongalaza's men were too mauled to conduct much of a pursuit. Nevertheless, they still finished off the wounded in the vicinity of the battle and mercilessly flushed out and killed members of Dingane's household who had not managed to get away with the retreating *amabutho*. One of these unfortunates was no less a personage than Bhibhi, Senzangakhona's widow and Ndlela's sister, who only a short while before had been one of the leading women of the kingdom.

As for her brother Ndlela, he was wounded in the thigh during the retreat but still made it back to where Dingane was sheltering with the survivors of his household and the remnants of his army. Dingane was fuming because he 'entertained utter contempt' for Mpande and had been sure that his brother would be 'no match whatever for him'.[17] So he put his unanticipated defeat down to Ndlela's partiality for Mpande and his treachery in deliberately not following the battle strategy the king had laid down. And, certainly, it is not inconceivable that Ndlela was playing a double game, and that he was not the only grandee in this time of civil war to be hedging his bets. Be that as it may, when he crawled humbly before Dingane, the king was furiously shouting out: 'Woh! Where is Ndhlela? He too must die. It was he who used to say that Mpande was less than nothing. I see it is he who has ruined my army as well.'[18] On Dingane's command, Ndlela was cruelly executed for 'spoiling' his *impi*. A contingent of warriors first cast a volley of spears at Ndlela while the already wounded man sat on the ground, and he was then strangled to death with an oxhide noose. The body of the man who had been second only to Dingane in the Zulu kingdom was finally thrown aside as unworthy of burial.[19]

It would seem that Dingane only finally decided to retire north across the Phongolo River with the remaining intact units of his army, the surviving women of his household and all his cattle when he was informed that, on 3 February 1840, 201 men of the Beeskommando had set out in pursuit of him. He is reported to have said, 'Never again will I face up to guns.'[20] Nor did he have to. Once the Boers, who were contending with horse sickness and heavy rains, learned that Dingane was across the Phongolo, they decided to turn back on 8 February and to leave it up to Nongalaza to keep up the pressure on the fugitive king. His forces pursued Dingane for about 50 kilometres and captured his mother, Mphikase. She was too old and exhausted to keep up any longer with the women of the *isigodlo*, and her son, determined to break free from his pursuers, pitilessly abandoned her to her fate. Dingane led his people northeast into the dense, malaria-ridden bushveld, making for the western slopes of the Lubombo Mountains. Confident that Dingane had been forced sufficiently far away from the Zulu kingdom to pose no future threat to Mpande, Nongalaza called a halt to the gruelling chase through the inhospitable terrain.

The Zulu used to say that 'a king who left his home and went to the mountains was finished'.[21] That certainly held true for Dingane. Significantly, after the battle of Maqongqo the greatest *izikhulu* of the north, Klwana of the Buthelezi and Maphitha of the Mandlakazi, rapidly indicated that they wished to make their peace with Mpande and, despite Dingane's efforts to retain their loyalty, abandoned his cause. Those of his defeated *amabutho* who had not accompanied him across the Phongolo began to disperse and straggle home, disgusted that their king had fled. These defections within the Zulu kingdom told Dingane that his authority there had all but dissipated. Nevertheless, all was not entirely lost while he still had a following about him, for he might still emulate Zwide, Soshangane or Mzilikazi and carve out a new kingdom elsewhere.

On the rugged slopes of the Hlathikhulu hill below the Lubombo Mountains Dingane ordered the erection of a makeshift but classic royal residence with an *isigodlo* section where he was determined to maintain as much royal state as he was able. He called it eSankoleni, or 'The Secluded Spot'. It was in the territory of Silevana, the regent for Sambane kaNhlolaluvalo, the heir to the Nyawo chiefdom. Silevana was a tributary of Dingane's inveterate foe, King Mswati II of the Swazi. At first, Silevana had no choice but to welcome Dingane to his domain because of the number of armed men still with him. Soon enough, though, the Nyawo became eager to be rid of Dingane because his presence brought with it the danger of a Zulu attack, and because his followers were eating up their supplies at the point of the spear.

For their part, the Zulu notables still with Dingane were becoming increasingly disaffected with their lot. In Socwatsha's words:

> The great men when alone said to each other: 'Where are we going? We are being killed by fever ... We are leaving the country of our people, the country of the Zulu.' They said, 'Let us kill him [Dingane], and go back to our own country.' But some asked, 'which people ... will kill him?' They said, 'Let the *amankengane* [an *inkengane* is a poor, destitute common fellow, a term contemptuously applied to any member of a foreign tribe] be decoyed into doing it. Let them kill him for us, while we go back. For Mpande is a son of Senzangakhona; he will rule us.' They said, 'Wo! Let amaSwazi be fetched.'[22]

The plotters' opportunity arose when Dingane dispersed the bulk of his remaining *amabutho* to forage, and even despatched some to retrieve as many as possible of the valuable baubles of royalty he had abandoned during his rapid withdrawal after the battle. Dingane retained only the iziToyatoyi at eSankoleni, an *ibutho* of young lads—not unlike the iziNyosi whom Shaka had kept by him at the last – to act as his guards. The disloyal *izinduna* let on to Silevana that Dingane was almost defenceless. Silevana in turn alerted a roaming Swazi patrol under Sonyezane Dlamini of the situation, and they agreed to work together to liquidate Dingane.

A picked force of Swazi and Nyawo surrounded eSankoleni in the early hours of the morning, and it was said that some of the inhabitants had a sudden, strong whiff of birds, not realising they were smelling the feathered headdresses of a war party. Some of the *impi* crept into the *isigodlo* section where Dingane slept. He had always kept a number of large dun, red or black dogs by him, acquired during Shaka's campaigns in the Mpondo country, and the fat and notoriously sluggish Magilwana (or Makwedlana), much favoured by the king and fed on only beef and milk, gave the alarm before being run through. Dingane strode resolutely out of his hut, spear in hand. A cast spear struck him, and he is said to have snarled, 'Fellow (*umfokazana*, a term of contempt meaning common person, menial), are you stabbing me with an assegai?'[23] Wounded as he was, Dingane managed to escape into the bush, valiantly protected by a few attendants, including Makhanda, whose job it was to sew on his *isicoco*. His assailants caught and killed a number of the women of Dingane's *isigodlo*, including his sister, Nozilwane. According to Socwatsha, the redoubtable Mnkabayi, who had stuck resolutely by the prince she had raised to be king, rallied the surviving women and led them and a great number of cattle back across the Phongolo to find sanctuary with Maphitha.[24]

The Nyawo and Swazi war party melted away before the surprised iziToyatoyi could rally to their king's defence, shouting as they retired: 'Your people called us to come and kill him because he has tired you out.'[25] The iziToyatoyi finally found Dingane as dawn was breaking. And here accounts begin seriously to diverge.[26] Ngidi attributed Dingane's death to his humiliation and remorse at having to wander the hills a fugitive, and to being stabbed by common people.[27] Others held that Silevana himself, and no commoner, had cast the spear that passed through Dingane's thigh and pierced his lower intestines. The iziToyatoyi were said to have carried Dingane back to eSankoleni where they inspected his deep wound and saw it was fatal. Rather than prolong his agony, they enlarged the wound with a spear so that he quickly died. The Zulu historian Magema Fuze reflected that they 'did well' to do so, 'so that he too should feel the spear as he made his great brother Shaka feel it'.[28] Socwatsha held that Dingane suffered only from a single wound in the upper arm. On being brought back to eSankoleni he sent an *induna* to fetch a narcotic potion to allay his pain. Dingane always carried an assortment of antidotes and poisons with him, and whether by design or by mistake (who can tell?) he was administered a deadly draught. The moment he drank it, insisted Socwatsha, 'his colour changed to a darker hue, a perspiration came over him and in a short time he expired'.[29] What final thoughts passed through Dingane's mind as he suffered his painful and ignominious death are known to none, but he must surely have reflected that Shaka's *idlozi* was finally exacting its revenge. Truly, as Dingane's *izibongo* lamented of the three half-brothers, 'The wild beasts of Jama have killed one another.'[30]

Dingane's faithful attendants buried their king at eSankoleni. Perhaps he was laid alone in his grave like a commoner, but some maintained that the royal funeral customs were adhered to, and that an *umgando* of killed attendants accompanied him into the next life and black cattle were sacrificed at the funeral.[31] The site of the grave was known to the members of the Nyawo ruling house, who courteously placed ritual stones on top of it. But, fearful that the Zulu royal house might exact revenge for their part in killing Dingane, for more than a century they kept it a closely guarded secret, known only to a few.[32] On 18 June 1983 King Goodwill Zwelithini unveiled a monument erected by the KwaZulu Monuments Council at the supposed location of Dingane's grave. The site is remote and difficult to reach and, like so many other out-of-the-way monuments in Zululand, King Dingane's has been vandalised.

Magema Fuze wrote somewhat fancifully that 'the name Dingane meant he would suffer from want [*dinga*] and that he would ... in the end come to a country which was not his own, where his bones would be buried'.[33] So it was, but it was hardly Dingane's inevitable fate. It was the Boer invasion that set Dingane upon the disastrous path that led to the loss of his kingdom and his hard death as a fugitive. Yet one must question whether Shaka would have been any more successful in staving off the battle-hardened Boers, with their firearms, horses and wagons. After all, the interlopers presented an entirely unprecedented military challenge, while the structure of the Zulu kingdom and the Zulu way of war continued unchanged from Shaka's reign to Dingane's. Nor is it impossible that Dingane and the Republiek Natalia might have managed to coexist relatively peaceably. In the end, it was dynastic conflict within the Zulu royal house that gave the Boers the opening to intervene to their advantage in the First Zulu Civil War and bring down final ruin on Dingane.

KING MPANDE
kaSENZANGAKHONA

❀ ❀ ❀

⁂

CHAPTER ELEVEN

THE ROOT OF THE ZULU NATION

With Dingane's flight and death, Mpande was left with several daunt-
ing goals. One was that of imposing his authority over the rump
of the Zulu kingdom. Just how difficult this was going to prove was indicated by the high-handed and provocative behaviour of Maphitha, the
great *isikhulu* in northern Zululand. When Mnkabayi led the remnants of
Dingane's household of women through his territory on their way to join
Mpande, Maphitha insolently detained half the women for his own *isigodlo*
and seized all the cattle they had with them. For the moment Mpande
allowed this insubordination to slide, because the most immediate problem was what to do with Dingane's erstwhile followers who had stuck by
him to the end, and who were now disconsolately drifting back to offer
their submission. Many of Mpande's councillors believed that such people
should be summarily 'cleared out of Zululand'. They were reflecting the
popular sentiment among those on the winning side of the civil war who
were derisively referring to the losers as '*umdidi ka Ndhlela*', or 'Ndlela's
arsehole', and were patting themselves on the back as the '*geja* of Mpande',
the reversible plough of the Europeans that had ploughed them under.[1]
Mpande ordered such talk to cease, for he was determined to heal the bitter
rifts of civil war and to live up to his name that meant (so Fuze believed)
'that he was the root [*impande*] of the Zulu nation'.[2]

Mpande's greatest challenge, however, was how to accommodate his rapacious allies, the Boers. On the morning of 10 February 1840 he and his chief councillors apprehensively obeyed the summons to appear before Chief Commandant Pretorius in the intimidating encampment of the Beeskommando on the southern bank of the Black Mfolozi. They would have feared that the Boers were not intending to honour the terms of the treaty they had struck with Mpande on 27 October 1839 whereby they undertook to recognise him as king once Dingane had been overthrown. Initially, they must have been relieved when Pretorius, speaking in the name of the Volksraad of the Republiek Natalia, did indeed proclaim Mpande 'king or chief of the Zulus'. But it would quickly have dawned on them that the way in which the proclamation was couched constituted an unexpected affront. Rather than hailing Mpande as king by right of his royal lineage, it instead indicated that he was the new Zulu monarch thanks entirely to the favour of the Boers who 'were instruments in the hands of God' in putting 'an end to the indescribable cruelties and murders committed by Dingaan'. Mpande diplomatically indicated he was overjoyed to be so honoured by the Boers. But he must have been inwardly seething, not merely because his unaided victory over Dingane at the Maqongqo hills had been conveniently ignored, but also because the Boer proclamation effectively reduced him to the status of the vassal of his 'great ally', the Republiek Natalia.

Nor was Pretorius yet done. On the morning of 14 February he raised the flag of the Republiek Natalia and caused a proclamation to be read informing the dumbfounded Mpande that the Boers were now going to annex all the Zulu territory between the Thukela River to the south and the Black Mfolozi River to the north, including St Lucia Bay, a vast territory that encompassed about two-fifths of the kingdom Mpande had thought was his. This time, Mpande could not manage to disguise his chagrin and disconsolately made off from the Boers' camp while they cheered in self-congratulation and fired victorious salutes. As for the Boers, their business done, the Beeskommando withdrew south of the Thukela with an enormous booty of 31 000 head of cattle, leaving Mpande another 15 000 to distribute among those *amakhosi* who had supported him in the civil war.[3]

Yet, despite appearances to the contrary, the Boers did not leave Mpande – king as they supposed by their favour and under their sufferance – as undermined as might be supposed. Nor did they prove to be the great obstacle to the secure establishment of his rule they initially promised to be. For one thing, the Boers simply did not have the manpower or capacity to make good their annexation of the territory between the Thukela and Black Mfolozi. So Mpande found he could continue to govern the region as if were still his, and not the Boers', and continued to reside in the heart of the Zulu kingdom, in the valley of the White Mfolozi.

For his part, Mpande had many attributes and circumstances much in his favour. Contrary to the abiding myth that he was weak and foolish, this was by no means the case at this stage in his reign (although, as we shall see, he went into eclipse in his old age). He was remembered by later generations as being naturally good and kind, not possessing the 'wicked heart' of either Shaka or Dingane, whom Fuze described as 'wild beasts' by comparison.[4] We have seen how he had the acumen and decisiveness to survive Dingane's suspicion and enmity, and the diplomatic dexterity to work with the Boers and not to break with them despite their arrant breach of faith in depriving him of so much of his kingdom's territory. Above all, the Zulu still steadfastly accepted the institution of the Zulu monarchy established by Shaka and recognised Mpande's right to the throne through his indubitable royal lineage, according him all the respect and deference due to the monarch. As king, therefore, Mpande continued to perform all the royal functions exercised by Shaka and Dingane. He enrolled the *amabutho* and gave them permission to marry, maintained the *amakhanda* (still often under the command of women of the royal house), as well as the royal *isigodlo*, and was regularly confirmed in his ritual powers at the national ceremonies. He presided over his royal council, administered justice, and sent out his *amabutho* to levy fines, punish wrongdoers, collect tribute and raid his neighbours.

Not least in assuring his acceptance as king by the Zulu was that, at the time of his accession, Mpande looked the part and comported himself accordingly. The acute and sharp-eyed French naturalist Adulphe Delegorgue, who closely observed Mpande in October 1839, was struck by his royal bearing and patent intelligence, and approvingly noted his shining, stout body, jutting brows, high square forehead, generous mouth and firm square chin. What most caught his attention were his large and well-shaped brilliant eyes, which, he declared, 'shone like black diamonds'.[5] Mpande is often remembered nowadays as being so fat that he could barely walk and having to be dragged to the assembly 'in a little wagon'.[6] But that was only in his old age, and in 1839 he was sufficiently active to lead his host on foot into the Republiek Natalia when he 'broke the rope', and then to walk the whole way to Pietermaritzburg and back from his encampment at the Thongati River. There is no denying, though, that he had the typically heavy thighs of Senzangakhona's sons and that in 1840 he was already running to fat, with pendulous breasts. He had no peculiar vocal quirks and spoke fluently, maintaining a measured and controlled royal delivery even when angered or excited. His most obvious foible was his extreme fondness for ostentatious and expensive dress with a profusion of ornaments — but that was seen as an essentially royal whim, as was his love of dancing and interest in breeding cattle.[7]

Despite all the points in his favour, Mpande must nevertheless be considered fortunate that, thanks to no initiative on his part, his rapacious and unreliable neighbours, the Boers of the Republiek Natalia, were very soon replaced by a colonial power with which he could establish stable relations.

It had not been long before the British authorities became genuinely concerned about the expansionist activities of the Republiek Natalia, which menaced neighbouring black societies to their south and so threatened the stability of the Cape's eastern frontier. Humanitarian dismay with the Boers' racial policies combined with these strategic interests and with economic aspirations to persuade Sir George Napier, the Governor of the Cape Colony, to intervene once more in Natal's affairs. British troops raised the Union Flag over Durban on 4 May 1842. The Boers resisted and defeated the British in a skirmish at Congella on 23 May, forcing them to take refuge in their fort. But reinforcements under Colonel Josias Cloete were shipped in and relieved the fort on 25 June. The Boers fell back on Pietermaritzburg and on 5 July 1842 the Volksraad submitted to the Queen. Then followed a curious period of shared rule between the British and Boer authorities while the British government pondered what to do with the territory it seemed to have acquired. On 12 May 1843 it was reluctantly annexed to the Crown as the District of Port Natal, but it was not until 31 May 1844 that the Republiek Natalia was finally extinguished and Natal annexed as

King Mpande, as depicted in 1847 by George French Angus,
seated on his chair of state in the *isigodlo* at kwaNodwengu,
his principal *ikhanda*.

(GEORGE FRENCH ANGUS, *THE KAFFIRS ILLUSTRATED IN A SERIES OF DRAWINGS*, 1849)

a separate District of the Cape Colony. (Only on 15 July 1856 would Natal
finally be created a separate British colony.)

Most of the Boers of the former Republiek Natalia could not accept living
under British rule (after all, they had trekked away in the first place to escape
it) and by 1848 had trekked back over the Drakensberg to the highveld. There,
by the Sand River Convention of 17 January 1852, the British recognised the
full independence of the Boers living north of the Vaal River, and by September
1853 they had established the Zuid-Afrikaansche Republiek (ZAR).[8]

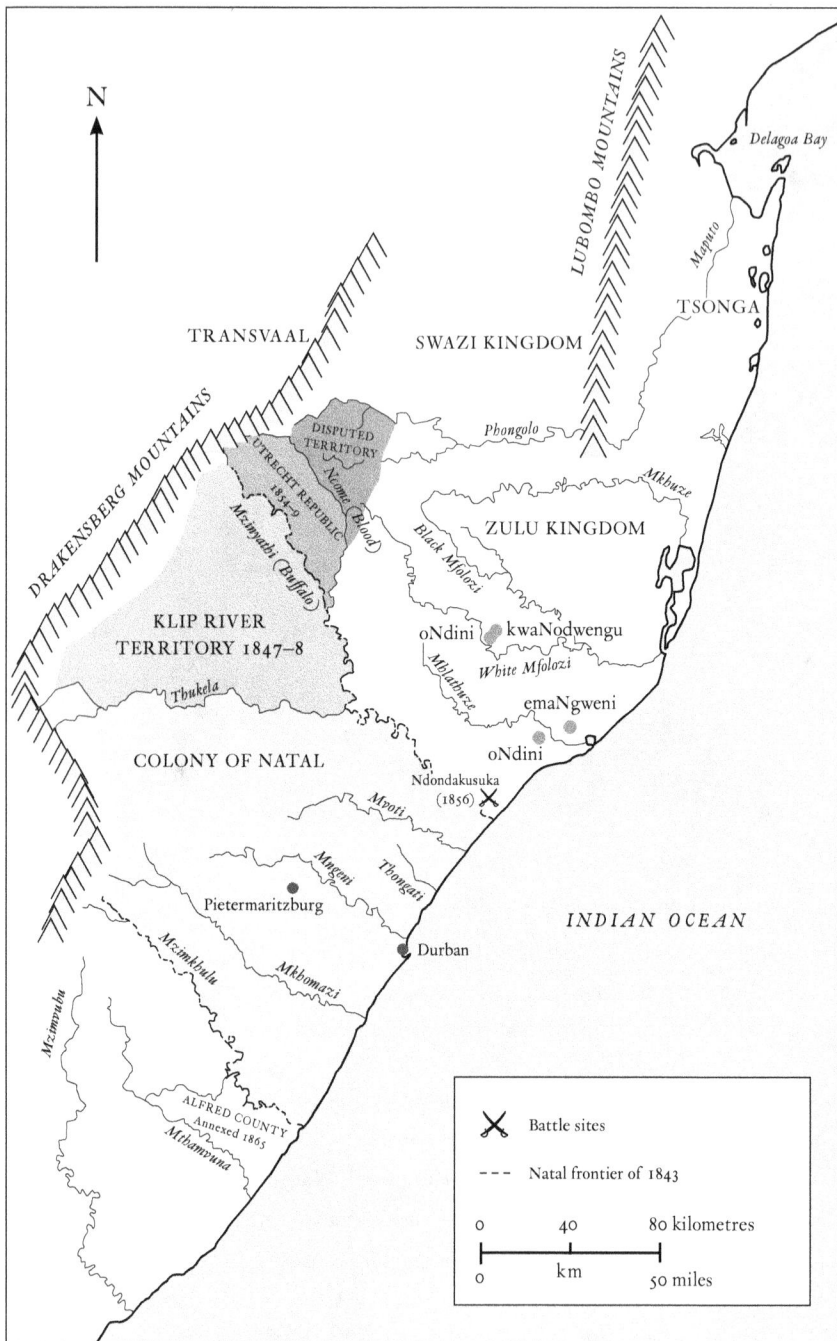

The Zulu kingdom and the Colony of Natal, 1840–1879

Mpande trod cautiously and with great skill during the nebulous period of the British takeover of Natal. He quickly divined that by cultivating the British he could undo the Boers' titular control over the southern part of his kingdom. His efforts bore fruit when, on 5 October 1843, in his esiKlebheni *ikhanda* in the emaKhosini valley (technically right in the middle of the territory annexed by the Boers), Mpande assented to a document written in English that Henry Cloete, Her Majesty's Commissioner in Natal, had translated for him word for word. By its terms Mpande recognised British sovereignty in Natal, and the British in turn recognised him as 'King of the Zulu Nation'. This was vital, for unlike the Boers, who had 'proclaimed' him king at their discretion, the British 'recognised' him as the monarch of a sovereign kingdom. The Boer annexation of southern Zululand was annulled, and a new boundary line between the Zulu kingdom and Natal drawn northwest from the sea along the Thukela and Mzinyathi rivers to the Drakensberg. With dire implications for the future, however, the treaty did not specify Zululand's northwestern and northern boundaries since this region was not yet of concern to the British.[9] It was destined to become so with the establishment of the ZAR a decade later, and the undefined boundary between the Zulu kingdom and the Boer republic would (as we shall see) assume explosive qualities.

Meanwhile, Mpande saw that close, cordial relations with the British must be the cornerstone of his foreign policy, not least because they would serve to frustrate future ZAR territorial ambitions at the expense of the Zulu kingdom. So, after a few hiccoughs that taught him that the boundaries set by the British were meant to be observed,[10] he embarked on a consistent line of approach in his dealings with the British in Natal to ensure that they looked favourably on him. Thus, while he was careful never to acknowledge that the British held any authority over him, he nevertheless (as his son, Cetshwayo, would later put it) treated them 'like relations', keeping them as frankly informed as he would members of the royal house and his *izikhulu* of everything that went on in his kingdom.[11] At the same time, he won British favour by permitting ever greater numbers of white traders and hunters to operate in his kingdom so long as they paid him for the privilege in firearms, kept to his rules, and did not contest his tight control of the external trade in ivory and other valuable animal commodities.

What Mpande did soon discover, though, was that while the British were prepared to give him a free hand in Zululand itself, they did concern themselves whenever his foreign policy or military adventures threatened to destabilise the region. Yet the problem for Mpande was that, as with both Shaka and Dingane, he needed to send his *amabutho* out on regular forays. These not only gave them necessary combat experience and helped to keep them occupied, but also allowed them to seize the booty essential for redistribution to ensure the loyalty of the *amabutho* themselves and of the great men in the kingdom. Mpande was not therefore the peaceful ruler of legend, averse to war. He was still a Zulu warrior-king – even if he no longer went on campaign himself – but he no longer enjoyed his predecessors' freedom to launch military operations at will. The established presence of the British in Natal and the Boers in the ZAR meant that he could no longer wage war against other African states to his south or on the highveld to his west without clashing with them too – which he was determined to avoid. This meant that the only field of operations left open to his armies was to the north. Yet, even then, he was reluctant to launch a campaign in that region without first overcoming British objections (which weighed far more heavily with him than Boer disapproval) through concerted diplomatic activity.

The British official with whom Mpande primarily negotiated was Theophilus Shepstone, known by Africans as *Somtsewu* or *Somtseu*, 'father of the white man'.[12] Of 1820 Settler and missionary stock, in 1845 he was appointed Diplomatic Agent to the Native Tribes in Natal. In 1853 his post was upgraded to Secretary for Native Affairs, and he held it until 1875. For thirty years, from his understaffed and dingy office in Pietermaritzburg, he almost single-handedly administered the lives of Africans living in Natal with energy and assurance, maintained a network of diplomatic relations with neighbouring African states and trained up a school of colonial administrators in his own image. His was a system of indirect rule designed to cushion the shock of a sudden transition from African rule to colonial administration. Hereditary African chiefs were therefore retained in the 'native locations' that he created, but were permitted to exercise only a modicum of their former powers under the supervision of colonial officials. Courageous, secretive and reticent, Shepstone understood the power of silence and an inscrutable gaze, and cut an unfailingly commanding and imperturbable figure. It did not take him long to establish himself as a sort of father-figure in African eyes, and his praises declaimed:

> Pure of heart is he whose ears glow with the rays of the sun.
> The young and hornless bull that has repeatedly silenced other young
> bulls.
> The bird that devoured other birds, some in one way and some in
> another.[13]

Indeed, to Africans on both sides of the Thukela he was the one true ruler of Natal, not the distant and fabled monarch in England. As Xaba explained, Natal and Zululand 'knew only Somtseu; they did not know the Queen ... As for the Queen, those of Zululand used to look on her as someone in a story ... simply an image (*isitombe*).'[14]

Consequently, when Mpande contemplated going to war, he consulted Shepstone first. When Shepstone withheld his permission, Mpande and his councillors obeyed, for, as Socwatsha expressed it, 'the great bird – bigger than them – had spoken; were they to disobey they would be killed'.[15] Yet, despite Shepstone's disquiet and regular orders to desist, in the early years of his reign Mpande's armies went out frequently on campaign. As it had been for Dingane, the Swazi kingdom was Mpande's most promising source of booty and remained a potential region of refuge should he ever be driven out of Zululand. A Swazi dynastic dispute and civil war that spilled into Zulu territory gave Mpande his opportunity, and when he invaded in early 1847 he was able to persuade Shepstone that he was acting in self-defence. His armies swept across much of Swaziland, but withdrew in July, baffled by the usual Swazi tactic of taking to their fastnesses and resorting to irregular warfare. Mpande invaded Swaziland again in 1848 with far more success than had Dingane in 1839, this time forcing King Mswati II to submit and even become his tributary. Only British alarm prevented Mpande from consummating an out-and-out conquest. When in 1852 Mswati attempted to break free from Zulu overlordship, Mpande responded with a full-scale invasion, sweeping Swaziland from end to end and driving off great herds of cattle. Under British pressure, Mpande withdrew once more, giving the hard-pressed Swazi time to regroup. In 1858, and again in 1860, Mpande planned a fresh Swazi campaign, but drew back when he met strong British disapproval. Mpande was also militarily aggressive along his northeastern border, raiding the Mabhudu chiefdom in 1851 and forcing its ruler to become his tributary and ally. The most distant of Mpande's campaigns was the raid of 1851 against the Pedi Maroteng paramountcy to the northwest of Swaziland, which resulted in the capture of a considerable number of cattle.

Inevitably, much of Mpande's attention as a ruler was focused on consolidating his position in Zululand itself, where the recent shattering experiences of Boer invasion, civil war and usurpation had deeply unsettled the existing political structure and created opportunities that fuelled ambitions among many of his over-mighty subjects. Consequently, he was only too aware that he must be prepared to curb those *izikhulu* who might rebel or attempt to break away from his rule, and that he must be on his guard against potential rivals and usurpers in the royal house.

So Mpande, for all his reputation for benevolence, could not afford to be any different in this regard from his ruthless two half-brothers and predecessors, Shaka and Dingane. As he ruefully admitted towards the end of his life to the Natal colonial official John Shepstone, 'The Zulu people are ruled through killing'.[16]

To ensure that he could make his will felt, Mpande surrounded himself with a coterie of loyal advisers and favourites. One such was Nongalaza, the victor of the Maqongqo hills and now rich in years and cattle, whom he confirmed as his commander-in-chief. Another was Mnyamana kaNgqengelele, the brother of Klwana, the renowned warrior and Buthelezi chief who had been one of the great *izikhulu* of the north. Early in his reign Mpande had Klwana killed, certainly at the instigation of his ambitious sibling, Mnyamana, on whom Mpande conferred the Buthelezi chieftainship. In Mnyamana Mpande consequently gained a significant ally in the north as well as an extremely shrewd councillor who was destined to play a significant role in the unfolding history of the kingdom. Yet nothing speaks better to Mpande's astuteness than his choice of Masiphula kaMamba as his chief *induna*. It did not matter that Masiphula had been a Dingane loyalist whom that king had raised to the chieftainship of the emGazini over the rightful heir, and that he had been one of Dingane's *izinceku* at uMgungundlovu. What Mpande saw in him was that he was excessively, even unnaturally, cruel, and was possessed of such a ferocious, unforgiving temperament that he was likened in his frequent rages to 'a wild animal'.[17] Yet for a king who deliberately fostered his own reputation for mercifulness and magnanimity in order to help heal the scars of civil war, it was extremely useful to have a much-feared, even loathed, chief *induna* who willingly took responsibility for implementing Mpande's less popular policies, and apparently relished shouldering the odium of ordering executions.

Nevertheless, executions – although sometimes unavoidable – were not Mpande's first choice. In bringing his great nobles to heel he preferred the carrot over the stick. For example, he wooed influential dependants by freely loaning out royal cattle (*ukusisa*), and exploited the institution of the royal *isigodlo* to bind them to him through marriage. This requires some explanation. In 1843 Mpande built kwaNodwengu as his principal *ikhanda* in the midst of the Mahlabathini plain. The *isigodlo* section there was very large, but not large enough to accommodate the 500 or more women in the royal establishment, some of whom were dispersed across various other *amakhanda* in the close vicinity. Their number was unprecedentedly large because it had been swollen when Mpande combined his existing *isigodlo* with the remnants of Dingane's that made their way back to him from the Lubombo Mountains. The young *umndlunkulu* of the *isigodlo* were undoubtedly highly decorative, and were described by one admiring African visitor as being 'very fat and pretty' and to be wearing 'very slight loin covers ... say 2 inches square'.[18] Of more significance than their beauty, however, was their significance as political pawns. The *umndlunkulu* were the daughters of men of power and influence who had presented them to the king, and he in turn gave some of them in marriage to other men of importance. That tied the husband to Mpande through the marriage alliance, and had the additional benefit of augmenting Mpande's wealth because the *ilobolo* was paid to him rather than to the father.

And if such amiable methods did not work, Mpande could always impose heavy cattle fines on those men of status who challenged his authority, send his *amabutho* to 'eat them up' along with all their dependants, or execute them when they ventured to kwaNodwengu to pay their respects. In

King Mpande reviewing his *amabutho* in 1847 in the great parade ground at kwaNodwengu. Note the large huts of the *isigodlo* at the top end of the *ikhanda*.
(GEORGE FRENCH ANGUS, *THE KAFFIRS ILLUSTRATED IN A SERIES OF DRAWINGS*, 1849)

1848 (to cite a notable example of punitive action of this kind) he sent his *amabutho* to attack Langalibalele kaMthimkhulu, the tributary *inkosi* of the Hlubi in southwestern Zululand, who was presumptuously usurping the royal powers of rain-making. They drove him and his ally, Phutini of the Ngwe, into Natal where the British settled them in the foothills of the Drakensberg.

While powerful, independent-minded *izikhulu* undoubtedly posed a threat to Mpande's authority, it was rivals within the royal house itself that he most feared. After all, Shaka's brothers had killed him, and he himself had overthrown Dingane. When Mpande mounted the throne, only one other of Senzangakhona's sons was still alive, his half-brother Gqugqu. He had been only a child at the time of Shaka's death, so the assassins had spared him. They had shown misguided pity, for Gqugqu had grown up to be an *umntwana* of considerable power and popularity. He kept his own *isigodlo* in royal style at his homestead among the Sigubuthu hills across the Black Mfolozi, and raised his own *amabutho* like an independent *inkosi*. And because his power base was in the north, precisely where Mpande's grip on *izikhulu* such as Maphitha was its weakest, he inevitably became a

166

rallying point for the opposition. Among those who joined this dissident circle was Mawa, a daughter of Senzangakhona and sister of the still powerful Mnkabayi, who had her homestead at Ntonteleni in the southeast of the kingdom. It could not escape Mpande's notice that Gqugqu was assuming precisely the same subversive role he himself had adopted during the final stage of Dingane's reign.

Yet Mpande was loath to kill Senzangakhona's only surviving son besides himself. Nevertheless, events came to a head when Gqugqu was visiting Mpande to pay his respects. According to tradition, Gqugqu sneezed and his attendants exclaimed '*Thuthuka Mageba*' ('Good luck Mageba'). '*Thuthuka*' was an acclamation reserved solely for the reigning monarch, and in uttering it Gqugqu's followers were publically and provocatively acknowledging him as king.[19] Mpande could no longer ignore the challenge Gqugqu posed. Vehemently urged on by the uncompromising Masiphula, in June 1843 he ordered the death of his half-brother and his entire household, down to babies in the womb, and at the same time sent out his *amabutho* to purge all of Gqugqu's presumed co-conspirators. Mawa and others of note managed to escape across the middle Thukela with as many as 3 000 followers and as many cattle.

The Zulu long remembered the 'Crossing of Mawa' as a memorable event in their history, but it was part of a less dramatic but persistent drift of cattle and people out of the Zulu kingdom into Natal. Indeed, it seems that by the mid-1840s the British in Natal ruled over more Zulu-speakers than did Mpande in the Zulu kingdom. Driving the process was the realisation by young Zulu men that they could marry much earlier in Natal and set up their own *umuzi* there without having first to serve the Zulu king as the member of an *ibutho*; while fathers grasped that their daughters would obtain a much higher *ilobolo* in Natal than in the Zulu kingdom, where the herds of cattle were now appreciably smaller thanks to Boer depredations.

Even so, despite problems such as these, it seemed to Mpande that by the early 1850s he had achieved an effective equilibrium in his external relations while at the same time reasserting Zulu military potential in the region. Crucially, his rule no longer appeared to be challenged at home and his most obvious rivals were dead or in exile. So confident had he become that in 1850 he even permitted Christian missionaries, whom he had expelled in 1842 as a threat to his authority, to resume their evangelising in his kingdom. Could it be that Mpande had succeeded in navigating the Zulu kingdom into calm waters, and that he would at last be allowed to enjoy his reign in peace?

🌑

CHAPTER TWELVE

THIS OLD MAN
IS FULL OF TRICKS

The Zulu historian Magema Fuze enquired why, had it not been for Mpande, the Zulu royal house would have ceased to exist. The answer is because he alone of all his brothers 'produced progeny'.[1] Yet, the truth of it was that his sons ruined Mpande's longed-for peace of mind and destroyed the tranquillity of the kingdom he had attempted so diligently to ensure. The princes brought down on Zululand the horrors of the Second Zulu Civil War of 1856, which they waged to decide the royal succession. Of course, if like Shaka and Dingane (who had deliberately sired no acknowledged offspring) Mpande had had no sons, there would have been other, collateral members of the royal line to dispute the succession, and war between them would then inevitably have been the consequence. Zululand's misfortune was that, because of the lack of a truly settled line of royal succession, Mpande's having nearly 30 sons by his many wives did not prevent conflict either.[2] Rather, because his senior sons calculated they were in with a chance for the crown, the consequence was vicious civil strife. In the aftermath, once the victor was firmly established as his successor, Mpande would reflect on the nature of his own succession, and of Shaka's and Dingane's too. He ruefully acknowledged 'Our house did not gain the kingship by being appointed to sit on a mat [the *umqulu*, or rolled-up mat that originally served as the

Zulu throne] ... Our house gained the kingship by stabbing with the assegai.'[3]

Nonetheless, was it not the case that Mpande did in fact have an acknowledged heir? Did he not, on 15 October 1839, present his boy Cetshwayo to the Volksraad in Pietermaritzburg as his *inkosana*, his heir by his chief wife? At the time, it may have been politic for Mpande to make this announcement in the course of forging an alliance with the Boers, but it was against both custom and good sense. With a king, as with any man of substance, it was imprudent to name an heir too soon lest he defy or overthrow his father in his weak old age. Cetshwayo naturally grew into manhood arrogantly secure in the belief that he was Mpande's *inkosana*, and inevitably attracted a self-serving following with their eyes on the rising, rather than on the setting, sun. For his part, Mpande grew both resentful and fearful of his prematurely identified heir. So in the early 1850s he began deliberately to tangle up the apparently clear line of succession by advancing the dynastic claims of another son. If he hoped thereby to hobble Cetshwayo's aspirations – at least for a while – he was fatally misguided, for Cetshwayo no more shrank from securing the throne by force of arms than had any of his royal predecessors.

Cetshwayo was born in about 1832 at Mpande's emLambongwenya homestead in southeastern Zululand. Why he should have been given his name, which signified that he would be slandered (*cetshwa*), is unclear. His mother was Ngqumbazi of the Zungu chiefly house, and Shaka himself paid the *ilobolo* for her on Mpande's account, thus assuring her status as his great wife. As an *umntwana* and grandson of Senzangakhona, Cetshwayo's position from birth was one of both elevated status and great peril. Indeed, by Cetshwayo's own account Shaka ordered the death of his elder brother Mlanjwane,[4] and he and his father lived in fear that Dingane would destroy them. As we have seen, Mpande took Cetshwayo with him when he 'broke the rope' in 1839. Once Mpande became king in 1840, Cetshwayo could at last grow up in the security of his position as *umntwana*. Even though he was a prince, he was raised like any other Zulu boy, and in 1850 or 1851, when he was about 18 years old, he was recruited into the newly formed uThulwana *ibutho* along with seven other princes of his age-grade. Their presence in its ranks made the uThulwana the most prestigious and arrogant of the *amabutho*, notorious for its unruly behaviour. In 1852 the uThulwana fought in the Swazi campaign, and Cetshwayo was blooded in combat, an essential experience for a future Zulu king and war leader.

Crucially for the future, while serving with the uThulwana Cetshwayo developed an intimate accord with its *induna*, Mnyamana kaNgqenge-lele, the *inkosi* of the Buthelezi. An *isikhulu* and one of the great northern magnates, Mnyamana was high in Mpande's favour and rich in cattle. Apparently never photographed, he was described as being tall and of slight build, with a dark complexion, and sporting a little pointed beard. His deep, resonant voice was always attended to with great respect in the king's council, for he was an astute politician of coolly reasoned purpose. He was steadfastly hostile to white traders and missionaries because he correctly gauged the threat they posed to the established Zulu order. Nevertheless, he comprehended the power they potentially wielded, and always advised exercising caution when dealing with either the British or Boer authorities because he was sensibly opposed to risking war with them. The young Cetshwayo absorbed his political philosophy and would follow it when in due course he became king and Mnyamana his chief *induna*. More immediately, Mnyamana's friendship and material support would be vital in Cetshwayo's coming conflict in the succession dispute with his brothers.

At the time of the Swazi campaign of 1852, Cetshwayo was already growing into a handsome, heavily built man with a powerful chest. In his maturity he was the first Zulu king to be photographed, so we have a far better idea of what he looked like than is the case with either Mpande or Dingane, of whom rather rudimentary artist's impressions survive, or of Shaka, of whom no contemporary, first-hand likeness was made. Reputedly, Cetshwayo took after his mother in looks, with a broad face and large lus-trous eyes that sparkled when he was animated, and he possessed the same pleasant smile and open, good-natured expression. Unlike many other Zulu men, he wore a beard and moustache. He was darker in colour than most other Zulu, and flushed deeply when angered or distressed. In later life he would become fat, but his flesh always remained firm – never flabby – and he worked to maintain his fit, hard condition through long, daily walks even when he became king. No amount of exercise, however, could reduce the size of his immense thighs, a feature he shared with many others of the

House of Senzangakhona. Cetshwayo always held himself erect in a royally dignified manner, with his head thrown slightly back, a habit acquired from long regarding all those about him as his inferiors. Nevertheless, he unfailingly treated others with courtesy and was genial and engaging in his manners. He said what he thought and spoke in a strong, deep voice. Generally, he was convivial, relishing good cheer and witty conversation – even, some thought, being too willing to gossip for hours with his intimates – but he would sometimes lapse into an intimidating taciturnity.

As he grew into manhood, Cetshwayo began to consolidate a power base in northern Zululand. Mpande had placed Cetshwayo's mother, Ngqumbazi, as head of the kwaGqikazi *ikhanda* close to where Dingane had built his final uMgungundlovu. From there she could exert royal influence over the powerful northern *izikhulu*, some dependable like Masiphula and Mnyamana, others more refractory, such as Maphitha. Mpande fretted that Cetshwayo spent too much time at kwaGqikazi, correctly suspecting that the prince was cementing his ties with the northern *izikhulu* who were looking ahead to when he became king. Cetshwayo also fostered good relations with the northern *amabutho* serving at kwaGqikazi and the associated kwaBazeni *ikhanda* just to its south, while his sterling service and valour in the Swazi campaign of 1852 promoted his popularity in the army as a whole.

The son whom Mpande began to promote as his heir in preference to the overweening Cetshwayo (whom he was beginning to fear and positively dislike) was Mbuyazi, like his brother a member of the elite uThulwana *ibutho*. Mpande rationalised his partiality for Mbuyazi by explaining that when he had pointed out Cetshwayo to the Boers as his heir he had still been 'an ordinary person', but now that he was king, Mbuyazi was better suited to succeed him.[5] His reasoning was that Mbuyazi's mother, Monase, had been an *isixebe*, or paramour, of Shaka's, and that Shaka had taken her from his *isigodlo* and given her to Mpande in marriage along with a large number of cattle and a specially built *umuzi*. One tradition has it that Monase was already pregnant by Shaka, and that her son Mbuyazi was his, not Mpande's.[6] Another tradition insists that Shaka was deliberately invoking the custom of *ukuvuza* whereby the biological father – in this case Mpande – 'raised up seed' for Shaka, who feared any offspring of his own would be killed. Either way, that made Mpande and Monase's child Shaka's legitimate heir, 'the king of the earth' (as Mpande phrased it).[7]

There is another aspect to Mpande's increasing championing of Mbuyazi's claim to the throne: he admired and deeply loved this particular son, and in his mind it was only right that the warrior-like young man should gain the throne, 'being so like Tshaka, moreover tall, and athletic'.[8] Mbuyazi was a light-skinned young man with distinctively fleshy eyelids, a large mass of hair on his head and a tuft of hair growing low down on his back. This explained his praise-name, bestowed on him by Mpande himself: 'the elephant [denoting his royal status] with a tuft of hair'.[9] Unfortunately for his chances, Mbuyazi lacked Cetshwayo's natural tact and affability. He was foolishly arrogant towards Mpande's councillors and courtiers, and failed to disguise his aspirations to succeed to the throne. Nor did it help him when Mpande, conscious that not enough people were rallying behind Mbuyazi, deliberately slighted Cetshwayo at public ceremonies to show where his preference lay.

But it was already too late to pressure Cetshwayo into making way for Mbuyazi. The former was too popular, and the northern *izikhulu* and *amabutho* were coalescing into a powerful faction to defend his interests. Its members became known as the uSuthu – 'with the long horns' – after the large 'Sotho'-type cattle Cetshwayo's adherents in the Zulu army – particularly those associated with the ekuBazeni *ikhanda* – had captured from the Pedi in the campaign of 1851. Their battle cry was 'uSuthu!'[10] As a distinguishing mark, each member of the uSuthu sported an *umshokobezi*, an ornament made of the bush of a cow's tail and worn erect in two pieces on the crown of the head. Mbuyazi also began to mobilise his support at iNtengweni, the homestead of his mother, Monase. His faction became known as the iziGqoza from the word meaning 'to drop down like the drops of water from a roof', indicating a steady trickle to his cause.[11] Their insignia, according to Tununu, consisted of a notched flap of skin over each ear with a small oxtail standing erect at the top of each flap,[12] and their battle cry was '*Laba, laba, laba, ba yoze ba si bone!*' [Those people are really going to see who we are!]'[13]

To Mpande's disappointment, it soon became apparent that the trickle joining the iziGqoza could not match the number of uSuthu rallying around Cetshwayo, and that he must try another ploy to support Mbuyazi. So he tried geographically separating the rival princes, with himself in the Mahlabathini plain between them. He placed Mbuyazi to the north of the White Mfolozi and pried Cetshwayo loose from his power base in the north by building an *ikhanda* for him called oNdini on the southern bank of the lower Mhlathuze. The plan did not work because Masiphula strenuously supported Cetshwayo's objections to Mbuyazi being settled in the north. By this stage the whole country was becoming polarised, and it seemed to Mpande that the two princes must have the matter out before the kingdom lurched into out-and-out civil war. He accordingly approved their request to hold a joint hunt in the wild country at the confluence of the Black and White Mfolozi rivers. Everyone understood that this was a mock hunt, and that the members of the two factions, who set off carrying war-shields instead of hunting ones, were in fact intent on fighting a relatively contained duel in the dense bush of the wilderness. But the iziGqoza, finding themselves badly outnumbered, lost their nerve and retired without a blow being struck.

Following this debacle, an increasingly alarmed Mpande did what he still could to support the cause of his favourite son. He refused Cetshwayo's request to discuss the succession and his prior claim as heir before the king's full council. Instead, in November 1856 he allocated Mbuyazi and the iziGqoza a slice of territory in southeastern Zululand, south of the Mhlathuze. This was the selfsame region where he had had his power base before the 'breaking of the rope', and Mpande calculated that it was likely to be loyal to his preferred heir. The region was also close enough to Natal for Mbuyazi to flee to the British for sanctuary, just as Mpande had fled to the Boers in 1839. Mbuyazi accordingly moved south into the territory Mpande had designated, provocatively raiding Cetshwayo's adherents on the way.

Increasingly angered by Mpande's blatant preference for Mbuyazi, Cetshwayo complained bitterly that 'this old man is full of tricks'.[14] The northern *izikhulu* who supported him – Masiphula, Maphitha and Mnyamana – urged Cetshwayo to make war on Mbuyazi, with Maphitha brusquely telling him: 'You will never be king if you do not act at once.'[15] Cetshwayo heeded their advice and mobilised the uSuthu at oNdini. The majority of his brothers rallied to his cause, reckoning that since his supporters greatly outnumbered Mbuyazi's he was bound to be victorious. Mpande tried to intervene, letting it be known that he favoured Mbuyazi's cause and calling on his subjects to join his side. But Masiphula stymied him, sending out word that all should join Cetshwayo and kill Mbuyazi, and that Mpande was 'mistaken' in favouring Mbuyazi, who was an '*ixoki*', that is, a person intolerable to others on account of his quarrelsome nature and the trouble he caused.[16] To a southern chief who was considering obeying Mpande's order to fight for Mbuyazi, his advice was blunt: 'Wo! Do not go. You will die. Cetshwayo will kill you.'[17]

Saluted in his *izibongo* as 'The restless black one ... leaning on his barbed spear',[18] Cetshwayo marched south at the head of his intimidating host of between 15 000 and 20 000 fighting men. Terrified, Mbuyazi gathered up all his people and livestock and retreated southwards towards the drifts across the lower Thukela to Natal and petitioned the British authorities for military assistance. The Second Zulu Civil War was afoot, and there were many on Cetshwayo's side who knew only too well that civil conflict meant rich rewards for the victors and the acquisition of vast herds of cattle as booty.

Mbuyazi had only about 7 000 fighting men, but on 28 November he secured the aid of 35 Natal Frontier Police and about 100 African hunters and some white hunter-traders. Known as the iziNqobo, or the 'Crushers', all were armed with muskets and were under the command of John Dunn, an adventurous transfrontiersman. Even so, Mbuyazi intended to cross over to safety in Natal as his father had in 1839, but the Thukela was swollen with the summer rains and was impassable. So he had no choice but to stand and fight with his back to the river. On 30 December the uSuthu encamped about eight kilometres to the northwest of the iziGqoza. Dunn advised Mbuyazi to attack, and late on the stormy afternoon of 1 December he gingerly advanced his forces while his noncombatants and their cattle took refuge in the heavily wooded stream-beds flowing into the Thukela. Darkness fell before the two sides could fully engage, and they both withdrew to their respective camps.

The early morning of 2 December was cold and drizzly when the two sides both drew up in the traditional chest-and-horns formation. The terrible battle they were about to fight came to be known as Ndondakusuka after the highest hill in the region. In terms of the numbers engaged on either side it was most probably the greatest battle ever fought on Zulu soil, and was certainly among the most deadly in lives lost.

Cetshwayo took up position on a low rise behind his forces as was normal practice with Zulu commanders. He carried a dark-brown or black shield with a small white patch at the side, and his headdress was a band of otter skin with tassels of blue monkey skin and the tall blue crane feather of the uThulwana. As battle was joined he ritually kneeled on a shield that had belonged to Mbuyazi to achieve supernatural mastery over his rival. While the uSuthu were cheered by the sight, the already dispirited iziGqoza were dismayed when a gust of wind blew off Mbuyazi's ostrich plume – a bad omen if ever there was one.

The uSuthu battle plan was a classic 'hammer and anvil' manoeuvre. Their right (the 'anvil') would outflank and hold down the iziGqoza left, preventing any escape across the river, while the centre and left (the 'hammer') drove the rest of the iziGqoza back onto their own left. Surrounded, the iziGqoza would be destroyed. However, the iziNqobo stationed on the iziGqoza left flank foiled this manoeuvre with their firepower, and although Cetshwayo reinforced his right, it was repeatedly hurled back. (It was there that the uSuthu suffered their greatest casualties of the day.) Seeing that he was losing the battle on his right, Cetshwayo changed his strategy and moved reinforcements from the chest to the left horn with the intention of turning the iziGqoza right. The veteran Mandlakazi contingent of Maphitha's people took the lead, and it was they who were subsequently credited with the uSuthu victory – something Maphitha would not allow Cetshwayo to forget. They smashed the iziGqoza right horn and the remainder of the iziGqoza army began to fall back, fearing encirclement. But their initially orderly withdrawal turned into a rout when they became entangled with the panicking noncombatants in their rear. A general stampede towards the river began with the remnant of the iziNqobo doing their best to cover their flight with musket fire. Dunn escaped across the river, but most of his men and the bulk of the iziGqoza were cut down along the north bank of the Thukela, where for decades their white bones starkly littered the path of their flight (and are still being ploughed up to this day), or died in in the river's flooded, crocodile-infested waters. Only some 2 000 of the iziGqoza warriors escaped, along with about a quarter of the noncombatants. In his memoirs, John Dunn described the uSuthu moving through the heaving, terrified mass of fugitives and cattle 'with terrible earnestness, hard at work with the deadly assegai ... pinning babies to their mothers' quivering forms.'[19]

Cetshwayo himself took part in the pursuit to the Thukela and was praised as

He who caused people to swim against their will,
For he made men swim when they were old.[20]

Among the latter were Nongalaza, Mpande's venerable commander-in-chief, who had obeyed his king's order to stand by Mbuyazi and died for his loyalty. Mbuyazi, along with two of his full brothers and three of his half-brothers, died in the rout, including Shonkweni, whom Mpande had fathered as Dingane's heir through the *ukuvuza* custom. Mbuyazi's corpse was never identified, which gave rise to the rumour that he had escaped and would one day return to claim his own. But the Natal official John Shepstone was convinced that he had been 'pursued and run down', although the men who had killed him would not have owned up to it.[21] As Socwatsha explained, all those who participated in killing him did so with their faces hidden behind their shields in deference to Mbuyazi's royal status, and then fled the kingdom for fear of being put to death for daring to slay him, just as Mbopha was executed for stabbing Dingane.[22]

The battle of Ndondakusuka and Mbuyazi's death reaffirmed Cetshwayo's position as Mpande's *inkosana*, loath as the king was to accept the unpalatable fact. Nevertheless, in November 1857 he and Cetshwayo reached an agreement whereby the prince, who was still only in his late twenties, would be allowed to play a major part in ruling the kingdom, the only condition being that Mpande would remain the ultimate authority. In practice, though, it was Cetshwayo who increasingly took up the reins of power at the expense of his ageing and ailing father. As Socwatsha expressed it, 'Practically speaking, Mpande was killed by Cetshwayo, for he used to speak of him as the little old man (*ixegwana*), and he became thus disrespectful.'[23]

Even so, and despite appearances to the contrary, Cetshwayo's position as Mpande's heir was not entirely settled. The king could change his mind again, and there were still potential rivals among Mpande's many other sons. The most insidious and persevering among them was the self-indulgent, physically flabby Hamu kaNzibe, notorious for his violent and overbearing manners. He possessed the immense thighs of the House of Senzangakhona, and wore a hard, disdainful expression on his impassive face. He was Mpande's first-born son by Nozibhuku, the niece of Monase, Mbuyazi's mother. Despite being Mpande's eldest son, through the *ukuvuza* custom he was heir to Nzibe kaSenzangakhona, Mpande's beloved younger full brother who had died of fever in 1828 during the *Bhalule impi*. Hamu inherited Nzibe's great kwaMfemfe homestead in northwestern Zululand, strategically placed between the Swazi kingdom to the north and the ZAR to the west, and ruled as *inkosi* over the Ngenetsheni people. He too was one of the great northern *izikhulu*, and Cetshwayo was grateful for his support in the Second Zulu Civil War. But Hamu was a man of enormous, restless ambition who patently resented that, on account of his genealogical descent from Nzibe, he ranked behind the rest of Mpande's sons. Consequently, he played up his royal status, courted popularity, maintained a huge *isigodlo* of 300 women and celebrated his own *umkhosi*. As with Maphitha, the greatest of the other northern *izikhulu*, he administered his domain like a quasi-independent ruler and brooked no interference from Mpande. Cetshwayo was not prepared to put up with Hamu's pretensions, and in June 1857 his and Cetshwayo's forces actually clashed. There was no conclusive outcome, and the two princes agreed to make up their differences and keep the peace. But Hamu had put Cetshwayo on notice, and thereafter Cetshwayo (with good reason) had always to keep a wary eye out for his half-brother's disloyal machinations.

Cetshwayo faced a more immediate threat from Mbuyazi's surviving brothers than from Hamu, and acted brutally to eliminate it. Mkhungo, Mbuyazi's 13-year-old full brother, fled to the safety of Natal when he learned that Cetshwayo, intent on killing his adolescent rival, was approaching his *umuzi* with a large armed force. There he joined his mother, Monase, and Sikhotha, a half-brother, who were already in exile in Natal. The Natal authorities saw that the two *abantwana* might prove useful counters in their future dealings with the Zulu kingdom. So they were placed in the care of John William Colenso, the Anglican Bishop of Natal from 1853 until his death in 1883, who enrolled them in his school for the sons of chiefs at Bishopstowe, close to Pietermaritzburg.[24] A liberal but stubborn theologian who was an incorrigible controversialist, Colenso would be excommunicated for heresy in 1866, although retaining his bishopric (which caused a local schism in the Anglican community). He stood uncompromisingly for justice as he conceived of it, and this led him increasingly to support the rights of Africans in Natal and Zululand against the colonial authorities. The Zulu came to recognise in him a true champion, calling him *Sobantu*, or 'Father of the People'.

Cetshwayo understood that so long as Mkhungo and Sikhotha lived in Natal under government protection, Mpande could always use their status as potential heirs to the throne as leverage against him. Nor were they the only pawns in that game. The Boers of the ZAR had their covetous eyes on the rich grazing lands of northwestern Zululand and were steadily infiltrating the territory ruled by Hamu. On the one hand, they saw that if they supported Cetshwayo against rival claimants he might in return look favourably on their land claims in Zululand. Conversely, if they could lay their hands on a few exiled *abantwana* as Natal had done, then they could use them to extract concessions from a nervous Cetshwayo.

And, as it happened, Mpande found a new favourite in Mthonga (whose praise-name was 'Wave of the Sea'), born of Mpande's great favourite, or *intandokazi*, Nomantshali. She had been his *isixebe* (or lover) when she was a girl, and was now a junior wife with two more sons by the king, Mgidlana and Mpoyiyana. She was tallish, plump, light-skinned and very pretty. Her praise-name was 'Somapa, thigh that becomes the centre of attraction!'[25] Mpande, who was finding it increasingly difficult to walk and was suffering from memory loss, was utterly besotted by her allure and bestowed on her an old man's devotion, forsaking all his other wives for her. Nomantshali was consequently accused of bewitching him with love-charms and of unduly influencing his decision-making. Indeed, Nomantshali was clearly growing spoiled and wilful while she led Mpande by the nose, and it was said that 'at times she would take a stick and smash a man on the head with it'.[26] Rumours also abounded that she was bewitching Mpande's other wives, including Cetshwayo's mother. But these were the hothouse tales of the *isigodlo*. Much more dangerously for Cetshwayo, Mpande was chafing increasingly at having to share power with his overweening *inkosana*, and by 1861 was beginning to confide to his intimates that he was intending to thrust Cetshwayo aside and proclaim Mthonga his heir.

Cetshwayo reacted savagely. He despatched an armed force under his trusted *inceku*, Bhejana kaNomageje, to Nomantshali's emDumezulu *umuzi* in the Mahlabathini plain with orders to kill her and her sons. But by lucky chance she was not there, and neither were the 14-year-old Mthonga and his younger brother, Mgidlana. Unfortunately for Mpoyiyana, the youngest boy, the raiders scooped him up and dragged the terrified child with them to kwaNodwengu. There they aggressively confronted Mpande without any of the respect due to him as their king and demanded that he surrender Nomantshali and her other two sons to them. But they were not at kwaNodwengu and the stunned and appalled old king could not comply. Thwarted, Cetshwayo's men dragged the pitifully wailing Mpoyiyana out of Mpande's arms where he had crept for safety, and killed him outside the *ikhanda*. Mpande, aware that he himself had escaped assassination only by a hair's breadth, was overcome by impotent despair, and cried out to Sonkehlenkehle, his *inceku*, 'Give me an assegai that I may kill myself.'[27] As for Nomantshali, the killers soon tracked her down in a little *umuzi* close by esiKlebheni, betrayed (some said) by Senzangakhona's widow, Langazana, who was in charge of the *ikhanda* and was trying to gain Cetshwayo's favour. Nomantshali died pitifully engulfed in grief because she presumed all her sons were already dead. But Mthonga and Mgidlana had made good their escape to the ZAR, and Cetshwayo's latest rival to the throne was still at large.

This appalling – and bungled – affair did Cetshwayo no credit at all. Public opinion in the kingdom was outraged, and it was said that on the day of the abominable deed 'the earth shook and the mountains thundered'.[28] Mpande, wallowing in grief and resentment, could never bring himself to forgive Cetshwayo, and was heard to say that he could not believe that the *amadlozi* would ever allow Cetshwayo to become king after acting so monstrously.[29] They did permit it, but perhaps it could be said that the coming disasters of his reign were their punishment. People certainly believed it to be so, and glumly reminded each other that in his anguish Mpande cried out to Cetshwayo: 'We shall see when you are king Cetshwayo. The stars will be bright in the daytime. The country will be overrun by the white people.'[30]

As for the refugee *abantwana*, the Boers received them with open arms. Cetshwayo marched to the Ncome River, which marked the southeastern boundary of the ZAR,[31] with a large force to demand their extradition. By the Treaty of Waaihoek of March 1861 (to which Cetshwayo put his mark, although he later strenuously denied he had), the Boers agreed to hand over Mthonga and Mgidlana. In return, Cetshwayo promised to spare their lives and – with dire consequences for the future – to recognise indeterminate Boer land claims east of the Ncome River. In the short term, though, Cetshwayo could afford to ignore the implications of this concession because, in the course of the negotiations, the Boers publicly recognised his claim to be Mpande's *inkosana*. This not only strengthened Cetshwayo's position in the kingdom, but also compelled the Natal authorities not to be outdone by the ZAR. They feared that if Cetshwayo's rapprochement with the Boers became too close he might concede them a corridor to the sea through northern Zululand. Ever since the Great Trek the British in southern Africa had done their best to thwart Boer ambitions to gain economic independence through the acquisition of a port not in British hands. Clearly, a diplomatic initiative was required to prevent them from doing so now.

So, on 8 May 1861 Theophilus Shepstone arrived at kwaNodwengu with the intention of shoring up Mpande's authority to diminish that of Cetshwayo and his Boer allies. Things did not work out that way. Tempers ran extraordinarily high during the turbulent negotiations and Cetshwayo arrived at the meeting in full war dress at the head of the uThulwana *ibutho*. His men were in ugly mood, and when they started dancing before the dignitaries they closed in menacingly on Shepstone, just as Dingane's *amabutho* had on Retief and his party. Other *amabutho* joined the furious uproar and for some desperate moments it really did look as if Shepstone would suffer the same fate as Piet Retief. But with extraordinary resolution the indomitable Shepstone sat unflinching, earning the admiration of the spectators, who exclaimed, 'Hau! The wild beast has courage!'[32] Mpande's *izinduna* finally quietened the worked-up *amabutho* while the king berated them for their shameful behaviour. In the ensuing calm Shepstone abandoned his original aim of supporting Mpande against Cetshwayo, and instead persuaded the old king to proclaim Cetshwayo unequivocally as his heir before all the assembled notables of the kingdom. His revised plan was that, by being seen to have played a leading role in ensuring that Cetshwayo's ambitions were at last requited, he had weakened the *inkosana*'s reliance on the Boers and reaffirmed Natal as the Zulu kingdom's patron and ally.

Shepstone departed, confident that he had successfully undercut the Boers. As for the exiled princes, although the Boers returned them to Zululand, Mpande believed they were not safe and advised them to flee at once. By 1865 they were both settled in northern Natal, provocatively close to the borders of Zululand, and were joined there by three more of Mpande's sons. Mkhungo in particular continued to plot against Cetshwayo and gathered iziGqoza refugees about him. Nevertheless, the exiled princes had ceased to pose a meaningful threat to Cetshwayo, whose position as *umntwana* was at last unassailable. Yet power was not yet entirely in Cetshwayo's hands. Although Mpande was relieved to shed many of the cares of state into Cetshwayo's hands and desired to live out his days in tranquillity, he was still the king. This meant he continued to perform all the royal rituals and exercise all the royal prerogatives, so Cetshwayo still had to refer important decisions to him for approval and defer to him in public. Moreover, to keep his arrogant and cordially loathed heir in check, Mpande continued to manoeuvre behind the scenes. He permitted increased missionary activity in the kingdom to gain the approval of the colonial authorities in Natal, and employed missionaries as political advisers and diplomatic intermediaries.[33]

To counter his father's courting of the missionaries, Cetshwayo turned to the rough hunter-traders active in Zululand – precisely the class of men most disapproved of by the missionaries. Through them he obtained the battle-winning firearms that had been so lacking at Ndondakusuka, and luxuries such as sugar, salt and coffee. The most prominent among these transfrontiersman allies was John Dunn (the Zulu called him Jantoni), who had fought against Cetshwayo at Ndondakusuka but now became Cetshwayo's friend and adviser. He was the conduit through whom

Cetshwayo dealt with the Natal authorities, writing his communications and reading the replies to him. Cetshwayo settled him in a large tract of territory in southeastern Zululand where the 'white chief' accumulated wives, cattle and adherents in such numbers that he became one of the leading chiefs in the kingdom.

In the final decade of Mpande's reign, while he and Cetshwayo continued to spar with each other, the greatest threat to the integrity of the kingdom remained the Boers of the ZAR. Shepstone had barely returned to Natal in May 1861 before both Mpande and Cetshwayo repudiated the Treaty of Waaihoek and the cession of Zulu territory east of the Ncome. But Boer parties moved in anyway, provocatively forming defensive wagon laagers. When Cetshwayo mobilised his *amabutho* in response, Natal succumbed to an irrational 'invasion scare' and rushed what few troops it had to the border with Zululand. Fearing in turn that the British intended to invade the Zulu kingdom, in July Cetshwayo redeployed his *amabutho* to guard the Natal border, leaving the Boers free to consolidate their incursion onto Zulu territory. By August 1861 the 'scare' was over, since neither the British nor Zulu wished to fight each other.

During the course of the crisis Mpande came to the conclusion that if he worked with the Boers he would discredit Cetshwayo, who so strenuously opposed them, and invoked his authority as king to honour the Treaty of Waaihoek after all. Cetshwayo was outmanoeuvred, but the consequences of Mpande's short-sighted policy, which put confounding his detested heir ahead of the greater interests of his kingdom, were serious. By throwing in his lot with the Boers, Mpande had turned his back on his British patrons, while the Boers, in return for their continued support of the old king, made ever-growing demands in the coming years for land concessions in Zululand. Cetshwayo responded to Mpande's diplomatic about-face by turning to the British in Natal for diplomatic assistance in staving off Boer land claims. Nevertheless, the question of the Disputed Territory, as the region of Boer territorial infiltration became known, continued dangerously to simmer on, poisoning Zulu-Boer relations and unsettling the whole region. The issue was still unresolved when, in the spring of 1872, Mpande finally breathed his last at kwaNodwengu.

KING CETSHWAYO
kaMPANDE

❆ ❆ ❆

༈

CHAPTER THIRTEEN

WE LOOK TO ENGLAND TO SUPPORT CETSHWAYO AS KING

Mpande was the first of the Zulu kings to die a natural death. When precisely he expired is unknown since his councillors and the women of the *isigdlo* kept his death a closely guarded secret, only letting on that the frail old king was 'indisposed'.[1] The people understood by this that Mpande had died, but to ensure an undisputed succession his demise was not officially acknowledged until Cetshwayo had his hands firmly on the levers of power. At length, on 22 October 1872 he summoned all the *abantwana* and *izikhulu* to kwaNodwengu to announce his father's death.

Unlike Dingane, whose interment had been a scrambling affair, Mpande was accorded all the traditional funeral rites and honours due a king – as it turned out, the last Zulu monarch to receive them in full. In the weeks between Mpande's death and his burial, his body – except for the head, which was left uncovered – was kept wrapped up in the reddish skin of a freshly slaughtered young ox and propped up bound in a squatting position against one of the wooden poles of his hut in the *isigodlo*. A fire of aromatic wood and bones was kept blazing to mask somewhat the stench of decomposition endured by the unfortunate councillors and attendants who kept watch in the hut, as well to dry out the corpse. Once it was desiccated and odourless it was finally ready for committal. The actual moment of burial was kept a secret among the senior members of his household. Shortly after sunrise a select few placed Mpande (who was wrapped in four blankets of different colours and a kaross of jackal skins) in the toe of his deep, boot-shaped grave, dug between the top left-hand end of the cattle enclosure at kwaNodwengu and the *isigodlo*. As was customary, the body was propped up by stones, and his personal items such as loin-covers, ornaments, bead-work, sleeping mats and eating spoons were laid beside him. Mpande's four great wooden chairs were burned, and four of his spears were buried among the rocks of the Ntukwini River nearby lest the king's *idlozi* wield them to mystically injure the living.

As with Shaka and Dingane, an *umgando* accompanied Mpande into the spirit world. Cetshwayo chose two of his father's wives to be his companions, but it seems that Masiphula, uncharacteristically moved by compassion, earned Cetshwayo's deep displeasure by sparing one of them. Cetshwayo also selected Makhanda, the body servant who had sewn on the headrings of both Dingane and Mpande. But Mpande had warned Makhanda of his likely fate, and the moment the king died he made good his escape. So the unfortunate Nhlangano kaLubaca, Mpande's notably portly chief *inceku*, was seized instead and became the 'mat' on which Mpande's corpse was laid. Rumour had it that several more attendants joined their late lord's *umgando*.

By his own account, to avoid ritual pollution Cetshwayo did not attend his father's funeral.[2] Instead, Masiphula, the late king's chief *induna*, con-ducted the rites. The grave was then filled in, covered with stones and fenced off with poles. The great kwaNodwengu *ikhanda* was abandoned, and Mpande's grave was put into the care of the head of a small *umuzi* in the vicinity. An *ibutho* was detailed to burn the grass around the grave every year, leaving only a thick patch on top of it where a thicket of bush and trees soon sprang up.

It does not seem that Mpande's remains were allowed to lie undisturbed for long. There is compelling evidence that in September 1879, once the Zulu had been defeated in the Anglo-Zulu War, British soldiers opened the grave and removed some bones for 'scientific' purposes.[3] Whether they were the king's or those of a member of his *umgando* is impossible to tell. So Mpande is presumed still to lie where he was buried. His grave is marked by an austere but dignified tier of black granite slabs in the Nodwengu

Museum complex, right in the midst of the unlovely modern town of Ulundi, where it is largely unheeded in the daily bustle.

Mpande's funeral rites ended with the slaughter of a small herd of oxen as sustenance for the *amadlozi* of the king and his *umgando* in the spirit world. Cetshwayo was then free to commence the business of being king. His first act was to despatch an embassy to Pietermaritzburg on 26 February 1873. Its mission was inform the Natal government of Mpande's death and to request that Theophilus Shepstone, the Secretary for Native Affairs, visit Zululand to acknowledge Cetshwayo officially as king and to cement the existing ties between the colony and the kingdom. This initiative was not without precedent, for in 1840 his father, Mpande, had been proclaimed king by the Volksraad of the Republiek Natalia, and then recognised as such in 1843 by the British rulers of the Colony of Natal.

Cetshwayo needed Natal to support him as the legitimate Zulu king on two different fronts. Externally, he looked for diplomatic backing in the matter of the festering standoff with the ZAR over the Disputed Territory. Internally, he hoped that if he gained Natal's wholehearted support for his reign it would assist him in bringing the great *izikhulu* back into line. The problem for Cetshwayo was that he was beholden to a number of the northern *izikhulu* for their crucial support in the civil war against Mbuyazi. Besides which, they and other great regional chiefs had exploited the dysfunctional period of Mpande and Cetshwayo's joint rule to reassert many of the local powers they had surrendered under Shaka and Dingane.

If Cetshwayo hoped to manipulate Shepstone for his own purposes, that wily official perceived how he might exploit the situation to strengthen colonial control over the affairs of the kingdom. He accepted Cetshwayo's invitation with alacrity and announced that he intended to bestow Britain's sanction on Cetshwayo by crowning him king. On 8 August 1873 Shepstone entered Zululand, flamboyantly escorted by 110 mounted men of the Natal Volunteer Corps in their blue and white uniforms. But before reaching the Mahlabathini plain, where the ceremony was to take place, he was most put out to learn that Cetshwayo had already gone through a Zulu coronation.

Cetshwayo's hand had to some extent been forced. Until he declared the period of official mourning for Mpande over in July 1873, he had been living in his oNdini *ikhanda* near the Mhlathuze River in southern Zululand.

He then moved in state with all the women of his *isigodlo* and nearly half his army — the 10 000 or so *amabutho* all in festival attire — towards the Mahlabathini plain to his agreed-upon rendezvous with Shepstone. On the way, the *amabutho* undertook the ritual purification of the *ihlambo*, or Great Hunt, the final ceremony connected to Mpande's obsequies. Yet for all the majesty of his progress north, Cetshwayo became increasingly anxious that the great northern magnates might still dispute his succession or attempt to make him their instrument. When he reached the Mthonjaneni heights overlooking the emaKhosini valley and the Mahlabathini plain below, he apprehensively paused in the rain and mist to await the arrival of the northern *izikhulu*. Meanwhile, Masiphula and his other senior councillors made known to Cetshwayo that they considered his being 'crowned' by Shepstone, a foreigner, utterly demeaning, and insisted that he submit to Zulu rites to secure the blessings of the royal *amadlozi*.

Cetshwayo accepted Masiphula's vehement counsel, for he apparently did not see why one form of coronation should preclude the other. Accordingly, he led his host down into the emaKhosini valley to emaKheni, a hallowed *ikhanda* founded by Ndaba and rebuilt by Mpande. The Zulu coronation was to take place in an open place nearby, and Cetshwayo and his following drew up there, waiting for the northern chiefs and their contingents to make their appearance. The first to materialise was Zibhebhu, born in 1841, the new Mandlakazi *inkosi* who had succeeded his father, Maphitha, the most powerful of the northern barons, soon after Mpande's demise. In later years the coolly intelligent, forceful and ambitious Zibhebhu, with his signature lopsided little *isicoco*, would become the nemesis of the royal house. Now, for a heart-stopping moment at emaKheni it seemed that he intended to attack Cetshwayo when his Mandlakazi warriors menacingly formed up in battle order.

Cetshwayo would have been half-expecting Zibhebhu to attempt a coup since he knew him to be a formidable rival. Zibhebhu was of the royal Zulu lineage, descended from Jama kaNdaba, and it was known that he 'practically looked upon himself as his [Cetshwayo's] equal'.[4] He already enjoyed a high reputation as a war leader (which the coming years would amply confirm) and his Mandlakazi had a good claim to have played a crucial role in winning the battle of Ndondakusuka for Cetshwayo. Zibhebhu was also busily forging close contacts with white traders and Natal officials who admired his 'progressive' attitude to European ways and could be counted on to support him (as they actively would in the future during the Zulu civil strife of the 1880s). And even if Zibhebhu did not actually have his eye on the throne, his appearance in battle array gave Cetshwayo due warning that he intended to uphold his late father's aspirations to ensure greater independence for the Mandlakazi chiefdom from royal control. Yet, at this critical moment Cetshwayo knew that his insubordinate, over-mighty subject owed him a great favour. While he lay dying, Maphitha had suspected Zibhebhu of attempting to poison him, and, according to the testimony of Mpatshana, only Cetshwayo's intervention had dissuaded Mpande from permitting his execution.[5]

While Cetshwayo faced off uneasily with Zibhebhu, the two other great northern magnates, Hamu of the Ngenetsheni and Mnyamana of the Buthelezi, come into view and took up position with their armed followers on the opposite side of Cetshwayo's party. The king appeared to be surrounded by potential foes, and panic began to assail his followers. But Cetshwayo, who was nothing if not brave, kept his composure and sent forward reliable *izinceku* to negotiate with the Mandlakazi and calm them down. Doubtless, the presence of Cetshwayo's ally, the hunter-trader John Dunn, along with some 200 of his black hunters brandishing their firearms, also had a salutary effect. In the event, the crisis passed and all present finally formed a great circle around Cetshwayo, who sacrificed 20 cattle to the royal *amadlozi*. These were special beasts, for they had first been driven to kwaNobamba, Jama's *umuzi* where the *inkatha* was stored, and had there been imbued with the mystical spirit of the strength and unity of the birthplace of the nation. Through their sacrifice Cetshwayo bound together his throne and his people under the blessings of his royal ancestors. Following the sacrifice, the assembled people then joyously celebrated the new reign throughout the night. The next morning Masiphula formally proclaimed Cetshwayo king, and all the great men of the realm, even Zibhebhu and the chronically disaffected Hamu, publicly affirmed their loyalty and obedience.

Masiphula's proclamation of the new reign was his last public act. Cetshwayo could never forgive his father's chief councillor for his

A photograph taken of King Cetshwayo's 'coronation' on 1 September 1879. The king, wearing his 'crown', is sitting forward on his padded chair of state with Theophilus Shepstone on his left in his court uniform and cocked hat.

(KILLIE CAMPBELL AFRICANA LIBRARY, UNIVERSITY OF KWAZULU-NATAL, DURBAN)

ambivalent role during the succession crisis of 1856 and Second Zulu Civil War, while his unabated arrogance, disregard of royal commands and notorious ruthlessness made him a dangerous presence. Yet Cetshwayo shrank from publicly executing a man of such prominence. Instead he turned to three trusted women of the *isigodlo* responsible for serving Masiphula millet beer out of his personal drinking gourd. He ordered them to poison the beverage with *umuthi* he had allegedly procured from John Dunn and which he personally measured out. After drinking deeply in the king's presence one noon, Masiphula began to sweat excessively and tremble. As he staggered from the hut, the girls at the entrance called mockingly after him: 'Farewell father!'[6] Masiphula, who had appreciated that his days were most likely numbered in the new reign, was dead before midnight. Cetshwayo duly ordered four days of official mourning for him, but no one was fooled. Mnyamana, whom Cetshwayo had flagrantly been grooming to replace Masiphula,[7] immediately assumed the post of chief *induna*, and would retain it until the fall of the kingdom in 1879.

Shepstone, meanwhile, was left kicking his heels until Cetshwayo was at last prepared to receive him on 28 August. He did so at the emLambo-ngwenya *ikhanda* in the Mahlabathini plain, the home of his grandmother Songiya. The two men discussed what form the 'coronation' ceremony should take and what announcements should be made to the gathering. (They also reached agreement on economic matters, of which more below.) Duly, on 1 September the somewhat farcical 'coronation' took place at emLambongwenya, where Shepstone's men had erected a large marquee at the top of the great cattle enclosure. There Cetshwayo and his councillors – many of whom considered the ceremony an insult to the monarch's dig-nity and a threat to the independence of the kingdom – received Shepstone, who was in court uniform at the head of a procession consisting of a toot-ling military band and the mounted Natal Volunteers. Jostling *amabutho* in all their finery were ranged around the cattle enclosure. Speaking in flu-ent Zulu, Shepstone declared that he recognised Cetshwayo as king in the name of Queen Victoria. He then went on to proclaim a number of 'laws' he expected Cetshwayo and his people to abide by. These boiled down to affirming that the power over life and death in Zululand was exclusively in the king's hands. In Cetshwayo's own words, his chiefs then publicly assented to Shepstone's 'laws', declaring: 'We will so govern the country under Cetywayo, our king; and we look to England to support and recog-nise Cetywayo as the king of the Zulu nation.'[8]

Shepstone then ushered Cetshwayo into the marquee, where he invested him with a tawdry scarlet and gold mantle and a bizarre feathered diadem, presumably intended to appeal to perceived African taste. Shepstone then led Cetshwayo out of the marquee to take his seat upon a plushy uphol-stered armchair to be photographed for posterity hemmed in by a motley crowd of colonials. A 17-gun salute from the two artillery pieces Shepstone had brought with him to Zululand concluded the affair.[9] On 3 September Shepstone set off back to Natal.

What did the trumpery 'coronation' actually amount to? As the Colonial Office made clear to Shepstone, it did not commit Britain to forming a protectorate over Zululand. Nevertheless, in the long term, Shepstone's 'laws' would backfire on Cetshwayo. British officials seeking reasons to wage war on him would eventually come to assert that they limited his right to execute his own subjects, and that his failure to abide by them was a justification for deposing him. In the short term, though, Cetshwayo was the gainer because, as his great chiefs were quick to recognise, the 'coronation laws' confirmed that the new king now had Natal's backing in reasserting the royal prerogatives Mpande had allowed to slip away into their hands. Thoroughly disgruntled, and determined to do their best to thwart Cetshwayo's efforts to re-concentrate power into his own grasp, most *izikhulu* packed up immediately after the 'coronation' and set off for home as an indication of their displeasure. Even Mnyamana was heard to say of Cetshwayo as he left: 'So he is a good man, one who pisses with his legs apart; he plants one leg on the other side of the Thukela, and the other in the Zulu country!'[10]

Thereafter, Cetshwayo would attempt increasingly to rule through the loyal favourites he raised up – men such as John Dunn and the self-important Qungebe chief, Sihayo kaXongo, who was involved in trade with Natal and favoured European dress – rather than through the great regional chiefs and princes on his council, whose influence he intended to curtail, and who deeply resented the elevation of the king's creatures.

The moment Shepstone returned to Natal, Cetshwayo set about constructing his new great place, oNdini. Sited in the Mahlabathini plain between his father's kwaNodwengu *ikhanda* and emLambongwenya, it was double the size of Cetshwayo's first oNdini *ikhanda* built on the south bank of the lower Mhlathuze River when he was heir-apparent, and was intended to replicate Mpande's kwaNodwengu in every particular except one. At emaNgweni, Cetshwayo's small *ikhanda* northeast across the Mhlathuze from the first oNdini, the principal hut in the *isigodlo* had been built under missionary influence like a European three-roomed house with glazed windows, wooden doors, whitewashed walls and a thatched roof. Likewise, in the 'black' *isigodlo* at oNdini Cetshwayo employed mission-trained Zulu artisans to build him a rectangular, four-roomed, thatched house of audience out of sun-dried bricks with verandas at front and back. Its rooms were wallpapered and contained European furniture, including a large mirror and a washstand. Cetshwayo regularly spent part of the day there consulting his councillors. At night, its two exterior doors were locked and guarded by women of the *isigodlo*.

Cetshwayo possessed *umndlunkulu* in superabundance because he had

A view drawn in 1878 of King Cetshwayo's chief *ikhanda*, oNdini, looking across the great parade ground towards the *isigodlo*.

(GRAPHIC, 22 FEBRUARY 1879)

inherited his father's *isigodlo* and persons of rank regularly presented their daughters to him as a sign of their allegiance. He himself estimated that there were 400 *umndlunkulu* at oNdini alone, and that a good many more were housed at other *amakhanda* presided over by his wives or by Mpande's widows.[11] It was said that Cetshwayo preferred to sleep with his *umndlunkulu* rather than with his wives,[12] and in 1868 he had sired an heir, Dinuzulu, by such a woman. Dinuzulu's mother was Nomvimbi, the daughter of a commoner, Msweli of the Nzimela people. She had been one of Mbuyazi's *umndlunkulu* and was captured at Ndondakusuka and taken to emaNgweni where she worked in the *isigodlo* as a menial *isigqila*. There Cetshwayo forced himself upon her. She became pregnant, and Cetshwayo later made her his wife once Mpande permitted the uThulwana *ibutho* (of which Cetshwayo was a member) to marry. Hence, there were those who persisted in regarding Dinuzulu as an *umlandwana*, or illegitimate child.[13] A tradition was passed down in the royal house that, soon after Dinuzulu's birth, Cetshwayo had a dream in which Ndaba and Dingane and some other, unidentified, former Zulu king appeared to him. In it they notified him that, to put an end to members of the royal house habitually slaughtering each other to gain the throne, they would permit only Dinuzulu to survive into adulthood and reign as king.[14] In fact, Cetshwayo did have another son, the 'orphan' Manzonwandle, conceived in 1883 after his return from exile, and born posthumously in 1884. Manzonwandle always insisted that he, not Dinuzulu, was Cetshwayo's chief son and heir since his mother,

Mfumatha, was the king's '*intombi*', or sweetheart, and not a raped captive such as Nomvimbi had been.[15] Manzonwandle never abandoned his claim to be Cetshwayo's true heir, and the colonial authorities manipulatively persisted in considering him 'a good trump card' to be used against Dinuzulu.[16]

At oNdini and his other *amakhanda* Cetshwayo carefully maintained the domestic routine and daily ceremonies observed by his predecessors, even if the adoption of colonial artefacts modified some of the details. Such were his Western-style 'black house' in the *isigodlo* at oNdini and his special runabout, a small, four-wheeled horse-drawn carriage known as a spider phaeton – not to mention Shepstone's coronation regalia, which he carefully stored away. And when he went out of the *isigodlo* to defecate on a hillock nearby, Nomguqo Dlamini remembered that he put on European clothing, donning a black overcoat with red facings, a black hat and shoes.[17]

Despite these exotic trappings, and with a disdainful disregard of colonial expectations concerning how he should comport himself as king, Cetshwayo was determined to rule no differently from his ancestors. Indeed, since it was his intention to resuscitate the power of the monarchy, which he felt had been dissipated during his joint rule with Mpande, he deliberately set about sternly imposing his will on his subjects and inspiring in them a real terror of incurring his displeasure. Thus, at oNdini he dealt harshly with his attendants and members of his household, sentencing miscreants to death even for minor misdemeanours. Once he gave the word they were dragged across the White Mfolozi from oNdini to the flat, bushy place of execution known as kwaNkatha, the same name as the dread place outside Dingane's uMgungundlovu *ikhanda*.

In order to revive royal power to the same level it had been during Dingane's reign, Cetshwayo needed not only to tame the great magnates, but also to enhance his control of the main institution through which a Zulu king exerted control over his subjects: the *ibutho* system. The two objectives were connected. It is quite clear that by the early 1870s the system was beginning to fray, with many insubordinate *amabutho* increasingly reluctant to undergo all the hardships of service. Yet, more than that, it seems that some of the great *izikhulu* like Hamu and Zibhebhu were deliberately obstructing the system by keeping their young men in their own service rather than allowing them to fulfil their obligations to the king.

Cetshwayo ultimately had much success in tightening up the *ibutho* system, although not without periodic crises. A crucial element of the whole institution was the king's right to give an *ibutho* permission to assume the *isicoco* and marry young women from a designated female *ibutho*. As Cetshwayo later expressed it, if his consent was flouted, he 'would be a shadow instead of a king'.[18] He consequently acted sternly in the affair of the 'marriage of iNgcugce' in late 1875 and early 1876, when many girls of the female *ibutho* of that name – who had already given their affections to young men of their own age – jibbed at marrying the much older men of the male *ibutho* Cetshwayo had promised them to. Public opinion in Zululand rallied behind Cetshwayo in enforcing the marriages and in executing runaway couples who continued to defy his orders, although there was much settler censure in neighbouring Natal of Cetshwayo's perceived savagery.

An even more damaging crisis erupted in December 1877 and highlighted Cetshwayo's difficulties in controlling both the *amabutho* and his *izikhulu*. Cetshwayo always celebrated the annual *umkhosi* festival at the new kwaNodwengu he had built south of his father's abandoned *ikhanda*. The *amabutho* were tightly packed for the festival into the 16 *amakhanda* in the Mahlabathini plain and in the emaKhosini valley, or in temporary shelters. The married uThulwana, of which Cetshwayo was himself a member, was quartered as usual at oNdini. But Cetshwayo insisted on cramming the iNgobamakhosi – a turbulent unmarried *ibutho* he had enrolled during his reign and which was now his favourite – in alongside them. The iNgobamakhosi failed to show the respect due to their elders, and in the cramped quarters tensions ran increasingly high and insults were exchanged. Eventually, on 25 December, as the *amabutho* formed up at the gates of oNdini to proceed to kwaNodwengu for the *umkhosi*, rancour exploded into fighting. Since no *ibutho* carried spears to the *umkhosi*, the fracas began as a stick-fight and the younger men drove the uThulwana back inside oNdini. Humiliated and infuriated, the older men grabbed their spears from their huts and counterattacked in earnest. The iNgobamakhosi, who had only their sticks, were beaten back in turn, and Cetshwayo was heard to cry out in alarm, 'My boys are being finished off!'[19] Fighting continued until nightfall, by which time 60 or 70 men lay dead, twice as many iNgobamakhosi as uThulwana.

Cetshwayo was enraged by the affair. He fined the iNgobamakhosi for starting the fighting and packed them off home. But this time public opinion was thoroughly against him. He was blamed for provoking the event by quartering the two *amabutho* together in the first place. Hamu, the *induna* of the uThulwana, was especially infuriated. He had suffered the indignity of being badly beaten about the shoulders, and demanded the execution of the *induna* of the iNgobamakhosi, Sigcwelegcwele kaMhlekehleke. But Sigcwelegcwele was one of Cetshwayo's personal favourites and he let him off with a fine. Hamu was predictably affronted by the king's leniency, and was further aggrieved when Cetshwayo reproached him for encouraging the uThulwana to take up their spears to defend themselves. Indeed, the king probably subscribed to the widely held suspicion that Hamu had actually fomented the whole business as an assertion of his power, and that it was further proof of his envious half-brother's intention to usurp his throne.

Be that as it may, Hamu left oNdini in high dudgeon for kwaMfemfe, his great place in the northwest, and Cetshwayo could not induce him to return to oNdini until the crisis of the impending British invasion in late 1878. Yet Cetshwayo was not daunted by Hamu's sulks. He exploited the disgraceful affair of the *umkhosi* to tighten his control over the *amabutho* and to forcefully remind his chiefs that ultimate power in the kingdom resided in his hands, and absolutely nowhere else.

Besides intensifying his internal control over the Zulu kingdom, Cetshwayo understood how essential it also was to ensure and maintain good relations with neighbouring Natal and to embrace elements of Western technology that strengthened the monarchy. This is not to say he necessarily welcomed the intrusive and unsettling presence of traders and missionaries (indeed, he considered the latter particularly subversive to his authority), but he was sufficiently pragmatic to deal positively with the encroaching colonial world.

Shepstone's 'coronation', for all its ambiguities, was Cetshwayo's first step in this direction. On that occasion, he struck an agreement over the recruitment of migrant labour for Natal from the Tsonga chiefs to the northeast who were in a tributary relationship with the Zulu crown. Tsonga work-seekers (several thousand a year) were to be allowed unhindered passage through the kingdom in return for Cetshwayo receiving a fee for every migrant who registered for work in Natal. In addition, Cetshwayo levied a tax amounting to a third of their wages to migrants returning home. The revenue they brought in was all the more welcome since the kingdom's store of wealth in terms of its herds of cattle fell by half in the same period. The reason was an ill-fated consequence of Cetshwayo's traditional Zulu coronation. Integral to the ceremony was a demonstration of his wealth. That required rounding up 100 000 head of royal cattle from every corner of Zululand so that they could be paraded before the new king, who used the occasion to reapportion them to *amakhanda* and honoured individuals for pasturage (*ukusisa*) and to present some of them to his favourites as gifts. Unfortunately, during the week these vast herds were together the handful of beasts already suffering from deadly lung-sickness transmitted it to thousands of others, with devastating consequences.

This calamity occurred at precisely the moment when Cetshwayo believed he required all the sources of revenue he could lay his hands upon to buy firearms to preserve his throne against internal rivals and external foes. Muskets (as we have seen) first entered Zululand in 1824 with traders and hunters from the Cape Colony, yet their full potential only became apparent during the Voortrekker invasion of 1838. Nevertheless, the Zulu made scant use of them during the two civil wars of 1840 and 1856, not only because thus far they had not embarked on a concerted effort to acquire them, but also – and more significantly – because their military culture remained steadfastly traditionalist. Consequently, any warrior who sought military honour was still required to achieve it in face-to-face combat with the stabbing-spear, the weapon of heroes.

Nevertheless, Cetshwayo understood that the new weapons technology must not be ignored, because firearms served as an expression of his military muscle vis-à-vis other states. From the late 1860s firearms had begun to spread rapidly throughout southern Africa thanks in large part to the demand for African labour at the diamond fields, which allowed migrant workers such as the Pedi to buy firearms. While still co-ruler with his father, Cetshwayo had perceived that the Zulu should not fall behind in the burgeoning arms race between African societies. Yet because no Zulu man was permitted to leave the kingdom, since he had to serve the king in his *ibutho*, firearms could only be acquired through traders. The enterprising hunter-trader John Dunn, who had gained Cetshwayo's ear as his adviser, cornered the lucrative Zulu arms market early in his reign, buying from merchants in the Cape and Natal and bringing in the firearms through Portuguese Delagoa Bay to avoid Natal laws against gun trafficking.[20] The Zulu paid mostly in the depleted stocks of cattle, which Dunn then sold off in Natal.

It is not possible to gauge how many firearms entered Zululand during Cetshwayo's reign because the statistics given by different contemporary sources differ widely. Even so, the informed estimate by a colonial news-paper correspondent that by August 1878 there were 20 000 firearms in Zululand is a useful indication. Of these firearms, he reckoned that 500 were superior breech-loading rifles, 2 500 good percussion-cap rifles, another 5 000 second-hand rifles of various types and the balance anti-quated, muzzle-loading muskets.[21]

Not only was the bulk of the Zulu arsenal acquired by Cetshwayo thus obsolete, but not many of these firearms – not even the outmoded ones – found their way into the hands of the *amabutho* until the king dispensed them to his warriors on the outbreak of hostilities, along with his care-fully hoarded stores of gunpowder and ammunition. Cetshwayo's reason for restricting the distribution of firearms was because he regarded them as instruments of power and as a valuable form of largesse over which he was determined to maintain his control. He set aside the most modern fire-arms as rewards for the elite, but even then the problem was that the king and other men of status tended to value them primarily for their associ-ated mystique of power, rather than as actual weapons. Thus Cetshwayo's bodyguard of young women from his *isigodlo* at oNdini, whom he armed with 'short carbines' and who accompanied him as he moved from *ikhanda* to *ikhanda*, had an entirely ceremonial function.[22] When defeat loomed in the Anglo-Zulu War, Cetshwayo would disband his 'amazons' before they could fire a single shot.

It was the case that a handful of men of status, along with several hundred individuals recruited and trained in the use of firearms by white hunt-ers such as John Dunn, had the desire and sufficient ammunition at their disposal to practise and perfect their shooting skills. Otherwise, the bulk of the *amabutho* were largely unaccustomed to firearms and unpractised in their use. Little wonder, then, that when they went to war in 1879 most would regard their unfamiliar firearms in the same light as their throwing-spears, to be jettisoned before getting down to the real business of fighting hand-to-hand with the *iklwa*.

Acquiring firearms was a precaution and a ploy in a power play, and Cetshwayo's relations with his neighbours remained at first as they had been under Mpande. The key was maintaining British friendship and support as a counterweight to Boer expansionism and their designs on the Disputed Territory. Yet for Cetshwayo, as it had been for his royal predecessors, it was right and proper for a Zulu king to 'wash his spear' against an enemy. His *amabutho*, especially the turbulent younger ones, were eager for glory and booty, while for Cetshwayo a successful campaign was the most obvious way to replenish the depleted royal herds. But this was no longer the age of Shaka, and the British and Boers hemmed Zululand in from the south and west. That left only the Swazi kingdom north across the Phongolo, the traditional raiding ground of the Zulu kings, as a possible target. But since the 1850s, when the British had restrained Mpande from further campaigning there, the Swazi kings had exploited the respite to consolidate their kingdom and were no longer easy prey. Besides, Mnyamana and most of Cetshwayo's other principal councillors were determined to keep in step with the British, and they knew that the Natal government remained opposed to the instability a Zulu campaign in Swaziland would unleash in the region. So in 1874, 1875 and again in 1876 Cetshwayo's council dissuaded him from invading Swaziland, and the king had to be content with making small, low-key territorial gains along the northern margins of the kingdom.

Mnyamana was in any case correct in keeping on the right side of the British, because the Boers were clearly determined to expand into the Disputed Territory. In 1875 officials of the ZAR unilaterally proclaimed a new boundary line that took in a large chunk of Zulu territory south of the Phongolo, and in 1876 began attempting to levy taxes from the Zulu living there. Cetshwayo responded by sending a force of several thousand men to support his subjects, and the Boers backed off. Cetshwayo then successfully petitioned the Natal authorities to arbitrate between him and the ZAR. But before anything could come of this diplomatic initiative, the march of events in southern Africa unexpectedly and dramatically over-turned the longstanding amicable relations between the British and the Zulu and cleared the way for war.

CHAPTER FOURTEEN

THE WHITES HAVE COME
TO FIGHT WITH ME

In January 1877 Sir Theophilus Shepstone, the newly appointed British Special Commissioner in the Transvaal and previously the Secretary for Native Affairs in Natal, entered the ZAR with a small escort of 25 Natal Mounted Police. He carried in his valise secret instructions entrusted to him by the Earl of Carnarvon, the Secretary of State for Colonies, to annex the republic to the Crown.

Shepstone's *démarche* had its roots in the anxieties of Tory imperial strategists. They regarded the intensifying jostling among the rival European powers to acquire new territories abroad as a perilous moment for Britain, urgently requiring them to consolidate and defend the Empire. To their way of thinking, India, rather than Africa, was central to British commercial interests and its status as an imperial power. Nevertheless, India's security depended on the Royal Navy's control of the African sea routes through the Suez Canal and around the Cape. It was essential, therefore, to secure South Africa as a strategic link, and Carnarvon argued that this could best be achieved through knitting together a politically stable British confederation of the subcontinent's white settler states.[1] Thanks to the discovery of diamonds in 1867 in the northern Cape and the enormous wealth being generated at the Kimberley diggings, the whole region was being sufficiently transformed economically to support the edifice of the envisaged confederation.

Nevertheless, serious obstacles would have to be overcome. The Cape, Natal and Griqualand West were already British colonies,[2] but British rule would have to be extended over the Boer republics of the interior. Of the two, it would be more difficult to incorporate the isolationist ZAR than the Orange Free State, with its close social and economic ties to the Cape.[3] A further challenge was posed by the endemic wars with African neighbours along the frontiers of the Cape and the Boer republics. These conflicts threatened to destabilise the whole region and to be an ongoing drain on British and settler military resources. The Tory administration was attempting to economise on the costs of empire, and the last thing it wanted was to be compelled to maintain large garrisons of British troops in South Africa to prop up the new confederation. So it was clear to Carnarvon that it was imperative that he also break the military power of the remaining independent African kingdoms, disarm them, and impose some form of British supremacy over them to keep the peace.

The Boer-Pedi War of 1876–1877 gave Carnarvon the lever he was seeking. When he learned that the Pedi of the Maroteng paramountcy, ruled by Sekhukhune woaSekwati and bordering the eastern ZAR, had inflicted a decided reverse on the inept forces of the anarchic and bankrupt republic, he seized on the Boer military debacle as an excuse to annex the ZAR preparatory to dealing conclusively with the recalcitrant Pedi.

Shepstone, his chosen instrument to bring about this political coup, did not disappoint. The ZAR, overwhelmed by the burden of its national debt, was paralysed by divisions between political factions. So, when at 11 am on 12 April 1877 Shepstone proclaimed the ZAR the British Transvaal Territory and ran up the Union Flag in Church Square in Pretoria, Boer opposition was muted. The Volksraad did resolve to send a delegation abroad to make its objections to annexation widely known, but meanwhile appealed to citizens to refrain from violence so as not to prejudice their mission.

Shepstone immediately set about attempting to persuade Sekhukhune to accept the Queen's protection without further hostilities. While the Maroteng paramount equivocated in an attempt to maintain his independence, Shepstone prepared to perform a complete somersault in his relations with the Zulu kingdom. As we have seen, while Secretary for Native Affairs in Natal, Shepstone had always lent the Zulu crucial support against Boer claims to the Disputed Territory because he feared the ZAR's territorial ambitions were inimical to British interests. But now, as Administrator of the Transvaal, his prime concern was to placate the Boers and further the cause of confederation. So, when the issue of the Disputed Territory came to the boil again, he calculated that if he asserted the Transvaal's claims he might convince the intransigent Boers of the benefits of British rule. And there was more to it than that. Shepstone was of the erroneous but deeply held belief that Cetshwayo was supporting Sekhukhune in his obduracy, so he reasoned that if he were to assert British power over the paramount's presumed 'ringmaster', it would 'produce a good effect on him [Sekhukhune] as upon all the other native tribes'.[4]

On 18 October 1877 Shepstone and a handful of Transvaal officials, guarded by a small military escort, met a large Zulu delegation of 300 councillors, chiefs and other men of rank, accompanied by 200 attendants. The increasingly acrimonious encounter, which lasted several hours, took place on a large, flat-topped hill (subsequently called Conference Hill) in the wide plain overlooking the west bank of the Ncome River. Shepstone was taken aback by the 'haughty' bearing of the Zulu delegates, and he indignantly reported that 'they were evidently excited, and in a very self-asserting humour, and it seemed difficult for them to treat me with the respect they had usually paid me'. Mnyamana, who headed the Zulu delegation, mortally affronted Shepstone with his mulishness and 'violent and threatening manner' in refusing on behalf of the Zulu nation to abandon any Zulu land claims whatsoever.[5] Yet it must be understood that the Zulu felt themselves betrayed by Shepstone's bewildering change of stance. Sigcwelegcwele, the *induna* of the iNgobamakhosi, stood up and indignantly asked Shepstone:

Is it so then, Mr Shepstone, that after two men have been friends, and then one of them dies, and leaves his son fatherless, that the reviving [sic] man ought to be harsh with the son of the deceased? This Cetwayo [sic] whom you have come to trouble and not to help is Mpande's son, and Mpande was your friend.[6]

If the Zulu were dismayed at having lost the British support they had so long relied upon, then Shepstone rode away from Conference Hill more convinced than ever of Cetshwayo's warlike intentions and his leading role in coordinating African efforts to undo white rule in the subcontinent. Perilously for the future of Cetshwayo and his kingdom, Shepstone's viewpoint came to be shared by Sir Bartle Frere, who in March 1877 Carnarvon had appointed the High Commissioner in South Africa with instructions to consummate confederation.

Frere, who had a distinguished career as a senior administrator in India, sincerely believed that confederation was nothing less than a Christian duty and moral objective which would bring the myriad benefits of British civilisation to all the peoples of southern Africa. But (and here his thinking tracked that of Carnarvon, his superior) for so long as independent, warlike African states existed, they would stand in the way of a prosperous, modern South Africa. With this in mind, he immediately focused on closing down arenas of endemic conflict. One running sore was the eastern Cape frontier, where eight wars had already been waged against the Xhosa people. Another, more recent one was the unresolved relationship between the Transvaal and the Pedi, which Shepstone warned him was potentially all the more dangerous because Sekhukhune was acting 'as a kind of lieutenant' to the baleful Zulu king.[7]

It took nearly a year, from September 1877 to July 1878, for Frere to achieve his first objective and conclusively crush the Xhosa in the Ninth Cape Frontier War.[8] Then, after a series of minor frontier skirmishes during the course of 1878, in October 1878 a British force finally invaded Sekhukhune's territory in what came to be known as the First Anglo-Pedi War. The campaign proved an embarrassing fiasco for the British, and they quickly withdrew. Sekhukhune lived to fight another day, one that would come in November 1879 when he was defeated and captured in the Second Anglo-Pedi War. Meanwhile, only weeks before the first Pedi campaign was launched, on 9 August 1878 the British Officer Commanding in South Africa, Lieutenant General Sir Frederic Thesiger (who in October succeeded his father as second Baron Chelmsford), established his headquarters in Pietermaritzburg to begin preparing for the campaign Frere was determined to wage against the Zulu kingdom.

The British repulse in the First Anglo-Pedi War only hardened Frere's resolve to have done with the Zulu because he and Shepstone were more convinced than ever that Cetshwayo and Sekhukhune were working hand in glove. What made this apparent alliance so dangerous in the minds of British administrators and local 'experts' – an alliance that in fact never went beyond a vague common understanding, with no military commitments – was the obsessively held belief that the Zulu kingdom was the political and military lynchpin of African resistance to British rule. By the end of 1878 Frere would be melodramatically yoking all the African states of the sub-continent together in what he characterised to his superiors in London as 'a common purpose and general understanding that the time was now come for the black races to shake off the domination of the white and to expel them from the country'. Needless to say, he cast King Cetshwayo as 'the head and moving spirit' of this alarming combination.[9] As for the Zulu king himself, in increasingly luridly phrased and alarmist despatches Frere characterised him as an 'ignorant and blood-thirsty tyrant', one who had at his ruthless disposal a 'frightfully efficient manslaying war-machine' that was a standing menace to his neighbours.[10] It was only stating the obvious, therefore, for Frere to insist that the key to solving the entire South African 'native ques-tion' was to settle with Cetshwayo once and for all and destroy the infamous Zulu military system. As he wrote to Shepstone on 30 November 1878, he was determined to 'draw the Monster's teeth and claws'.[11]

Naturally, Cetshwayo and the members of his *ibandla* were increasingly aware that the British were building up menacing concentrations of troops along their Natal and Transvaal borders. Yet they were understandably at a loss to explain what they had done for the British to threaten them thus. They had been heartened when, earlier in 1878, Sir Henry Bulwer, the Lieutenant Governor of Natal, had offered to mediate in the fester-ing Zulu-Transvaal border dispute lest it get out of hand and draw Natal into undesired hostilities. A Boundary Commission duly began sitting at Rorke's Drift on 17 March 1878 and delivered its scrupulous report on 15 July 1878. To Frere's exasperation, its findings largely vindicated Zulu ter-ritorial claims. Knowing that the report would be dynamite in the volatile Transvaal, Frere decided to sit on it until he could neutralise it by drawing Zululand into the war he was already determined upon.

Unaware of Frere's devious strategy, and impatiently awaiting the suppressed boundary award, the Zulu leaders were perplexed by his intemperate reaction to a number of minor border incidents, not understanding that he was deliberately playing them up so as to present his superiors in London with a *casus belli*. One in particular engrossed Zulu attention. On 28 July 1878 Mehlokazulu, the chief son of Cetshwayo's unpopular and pushy favourite, Sihayo, crossed into Natal with two of his brothers and an armed band to seize two of his father's unfaithful wives who had fled to the colony. He apprehended the two women, dragged them back onto Zulu soil and killed them there. The British authorities insisted that Cetshwayo must surrender Mehlokazulu and his associates for trial in Natal to answer for their unlawful killings. But Cetshwayo would not even consider giving up Sihayo's sons, even though the large majority in his council were in favour of surrendering them to placate the British and were dismayed by his pig-headedness in refusing to do so. Instead, he offered to pay compensation for the offenders' misdeeds, a proposition the British summarily dismissed.

Perplexed, in September 1878 Cetshwayo sent to the Lieutenant Governor of Natal, Sir Henry Bulwer, challenging him to 'tell him plainly what wrong he has done to the English'.[12] During the ensuing November the king's pacific protestations to the authorities in Natal, in which he was earnestly encouraged by the majority of his councillors, grew in number and urgency in proportion to the pace of British military preparations. They culminated in his plaintive protestation that 'Cetywayo hereby swears in the presence ... of all his Chiefs, that he has no intention or wish to quarrel with the English'.[13]

Unfortunately for the Zulu king and his subjects, Frere was not prepared to 'decline the contest'.[14] Neither surrendering Sihayo's sons (which his councillors continued to insist he should do) nor anything else Cetshwayo could have done would have diverted Frere from his adamantine intention to destroy the dreaded Zulu military system. And to do so successfully, Frere was convinced, required brute force. In his estimation, fair words and negotiations simply would not have the desired, long-term effect.

Only the British government could have prevented Frere from taking the final steps to war, and he deployed all the bureaucratic wiles of a seasoned proconsul of empire to circumvent the wishes of his superiors and get his way. In London, the government was becoming increasingly uneasy with his bellicosity since it faced other, more pressing dangers. The Second Anglo-Afghan War broke out in late 1878, and relations with Russia were becoming dangerously strained in Central Asia and the Mediterranean. At the Colonial Office Sir Michael Hicks Beach (who had succeeded Lord Carnarvon in January 1878) made it clear he wanted no war in Zululand complicating the already alarming scenario.

But Frere pushed ahead with the military plans he knew the British cabinet would not sanction while coolly exploiting the conveniently slow communications with London to keep the ministers in the dark.[14] He knew he risked his distinguished career, but he had been assured by his military advisers, made perilously overconfident by their recent victory in the Ninth Cape Frontier War, that a Zulu campaign would be swift, cheap and decisive. Consequently, Frere calculated, any censure for diso-beying instructions would be wiped away by his triumphant clinching of confederation. By late 1878 he had also worked out how a defeated and disarmed Zululand would be slotted into the new British order in South Africa. Drawing on his extensive administrative experience in India, he did not envisage Zululand being annexed. Rather, he saw it taking its assigned place in the confederation like an Indian 'subject ally', or princely state, ruled indirectly through a compliant chief under a British resident.[16]

With growing numbers of British troops massing along the king-dom's borders and Frere winding the political crisis to breaking point, King Cetshwayo and his *ibandla* discussed the threatening situation with mounting concern. In September and again in October 1878 they par-tially mobilised the *amabutho* in response to border alarms. Cornelius Vijn, a white trader who found himself detained in Zululand during the war, noted that ordinary Zulus were increasingly directing their ire against those 'very bad people', the British. Rapidly swelling rumour insisted that the Europeans were coming 'to capture all the males, to be sent to England and there kept to work, while the girls would all be married off to (white) soldiers, and their cattle would, of course, all belong to the English gov-ernment'. Warriors responded by declaring that 'when it came to fighting, they fought not for the King only, but for themselves, since they would rather die than live under the Whites'.[17]

As 1878 drew to a close, Lord Chelmsford put the finishing touches to his plans for the invasion of the Zulu kingdom. His main striking force would be his battalions of British infantry supported by the African levies raised in Natal and the Transvaal, who made up 52 per cent of his army. Regular cavalry would not be made available until the closing stages of the campaign, so Chelmsford had to rely for reconnaissance and raiding on a motley collection of colonial mounted units. The general appreciated that when he invaded Zululand his slow-moving and vulnerable supply trains — which averaged no more than ten miles a day over the broken and rain-sodden terrain of the summer months — considerably compromised his manoeuvrability. So he decided he must send in a number of smaller columns with the strategic intention of converging on oNdini as well as protecting sectors he believed vulnerable to Zulu counterattack. The columns were organised as follows: No 1 (Right) Column of 4 750 men under Colonel CK Pearson would protect the Natal coastal plain; No 3 (Centre) Column of 4 709 men under Colonel RT Glyn — reinforced by the 3 871 African levies of No 2 Column under Brevet Colonel Durnford — central Natal; No 4 (Left) Column of 2 278 men under Brevet Colonel HE Wood the Utrecht District of the Transvaal; and No 5 Column of 1 565 men under Colonel H Rowlands the volatile eastern Transvaal, which abutted the Pedi, Swazi and Zulu kingdoms.

In devising his strategy, Chelmsford was much influenced by Shepstone, who had convinced him and Frere that under the stress of invasion existing opposition to Cetshwayo within his kingdom would grow, and that political disarray, compounded by military defeat, would bring the kingdom to its knees. Shepstone could point to Hamu, Cetshwayo's dissident and envious half-brother, who had returned to oNdini from his self-imposed absence to take part in the deliberations of the king's council, but who was already treasonously plotting to abandon the Zulu cause. In early November Hamu sent a letter penned by a compliant trader to officials in the neighbouring Transvaal Territory promising that should hostilities break out he would 'run over with all his people to the Government, if Government [would] receive and protect him'.[18]

Encouraged by Hamu's overture, Chelmsford fully intended to encourage other disaffected chiefs to defect, and instructed his commanders to accommodate surrendered Zulu notables and their followers behind their lines. Yet this political strategy would only work, and the Zulu kingdom unravel, if the British secured the military ascendancy, and Chelmsford was determined to avoid the desultory, protracted warfare he had experienced in the Ninth Cape Frontier War. Therefore, he intended to conclude the campaign expeditiously with a decisive pitched battle, and was confident that the Zulu, true to their heroic warrior traditions, would oblige him. So Chelmsford's operational gambit of dividing his army into several columns was also bait intended to entice the Zulu into attacking these small and deceptively vulnerable forces. Then, as the Xhosa had previously discovered, the Zulu warriors' mass attack would be shattered by the disciplined, superior firepower of the British soldiers.

With the advice of Shepstone, Bulwer and other colonial administrators, Frere drafted an ultimatum to the Zulu king that was coupled to the long-awaited boundary award and effectively negated it. Shepstone's younger brother John (the Acting Natal Secretary for Native Affairs) met Cetshwayo's emissaries on the Natal side of the Thukela River on 11 December 1878. The Zulu emissaries' delighted satisfaction with the boundary award turned to deep dismay on learning the terms of the ultimatum. Indeed, Frere's ultimatum was a deeply disingenuous document, not least because the British were fully aware that Cetshwayo's *ibandla* was strongly in favour of keeping negotiations open and avoiding war. However, the ultimatum was deliberately intended to elicit Cetshwayo's rejection of its terms. Among other stipulations was the demand that Cetshwayo abolish the Zulu military system and submit himself to the authority of a British resident – in other words, jettison everything that made him a Zulu king. Cetshwayo's despondent and fearful representatives had the unenviable duty of conveying these impossible conditions back to their master, as well as telling him that the ultimatum left him only until 11 January 1879 to comply fully. Otherwise, the British would invade.

In this supreme crisis, the princes and the king's inner council vented their frustrations on John Dunn and accused him of betraying Cetshwayo over his negotiations with the British. Realising that some were demanding his execution, and calculating that his survival lay in throwing his lot in with the British, on 31 December Dunn began crossing into Natal with all his followers and cattle. Dunn's significant defection stunned the king and his councillors and they were left to respond to the ultimatum quandary without his advice. All were agreed that the military system could never be abandoned and that they must fight to preserve it, but hoped the British could still be placated by other concessions. It seems many councillors continued to believe against the odds that if they surrendered Sihayo's sons somehow the British would be placated. Yet, in the end, they faced up to the inevitable conclusion that they had no choice but to go to war to preserve Zulu independence.

In early January Cetshwayo sent out orders for his *amabutho* to assemble at oNdini without their ceremonial dress and to be prepared for immediate active service. Kumbeka Gwabe recalled: 'The regiments gathered there had so many men in them that they seemed to stretch right from there to the sea. The first thing our king did was to give us cattle and beer to drink.'[19] During the days following the expiry of the British ultimatum the *amabutho* mustered in the *amakhanda* in the Mahlabathini plain were 'doctored' for war. Weapons were incorporated into the ceremonies of ritual purification and strengthening, and with firearms mystical forces were expected to compensate for lack of practical skill in hitting a target, just as they would protect a man from wounds and death. Mpatshana described in detail how before the opening campaign an *isangoma* who had obtained his *imithi* from the distant Rain Queen of the Balobedu 'made all those with guns hold their barrels downwards on to, but not actually touching, a sherd containing some smoking substance, i.e. burning drugs, fire being underneath the sherd, in order that smoke might go up the barrel. This was done so that bullets would go straight, and, on hitting any European, kill him.' The *isangoma* also 'made marks on our faces ... and declared that the Europeans' bullets would be weakened ... and not enter'. Unhappily for the *amabutho*, the *isangoma*'s charms proved entirely ineffective.[20]

We are so habituated to buying into the notion of Frere's 'man-slaying war-machine' that it is difficult to accept just how unprepared the *amabutho* were for the impending campaign. The last time they had actually fought against whites had been in the Voortrekker-Zulu War during Dingane's reign, 41 years before. It had been 27 years since Mpande's final raid in 1852 against his Swazi neighbours. Ironically, the most recent campaign in which the *amabutho* had been heavily deployed was the Second Zulu Civil War of 1856, 23 years before, in which Cetshwayo had triumphed over his rivals for the throne. Consequently, no Zulu general in 1879 had previously led an army as a senior commander, while of the 16 *amabutho* who were to fight in the Anglo-Zulu War, 12 had never previously seen the field of battle. This does not mean that the *amabutho* were not desperately eager to face the British in battle and were not confident of their ability to beat them. But that was precisely the problem. Who among them had any experience in confronting disciplined soldiers armed with modern rifles? It is true that four *amabutho* had fought at Ndondakusuka, where they had faced the fire-power of John Dunn's iziNqobo. But these hunters and policemen had been carrying flintlock or percussion-lock muzzle-loaders, not nearly as effective as the modern rifles and artillery the *amabutho* would be facing in 1879. With a gun culture failing to take deep root in their military culture, and with no experience in encountering modern weaponry, is it any wonder – in the shamed words of Ndungungunga – that in 1879 the Zulu would ulti-mately find themselves 'completely beaten off by the artillery and bullets' despite their undoubted courage and tenacity?[21]

From the spies he deployed in Natal, the Transvaal and Delagoa Bay, Cetshwayo learned the precise strength and intentions of the British col-umns poised to cross his borders.[22] Fully apprised of the threat they posed, he cast about for allies, sending out emissaries far and wide. His failure to secure a single one conclusively debunked the chimera of the 'black con-spiracy' and demonstrated that African rulers – even when faced by the forces of colonialism – continued to place sectional advantage ahead of wider, common interests.

Consequently, despite making friendly overtures in late 1878 to King Mbandzeni, there was no prospect of Swazi support. On the contrary, the Swazi looked eagerly forward to the elimination of the long-standing Zulu military threat. The Mabhudu-Tsonga, who paid tribute to the Zulu, also welcomed the prospect of the breaking of Zulu power. The distant Sotho and Pondo were not interested in becoming involved. Cetshwayo's most likely ally was Sekhukhune, but the Pedi ruler decided that it was too dangerous to allow his unresolved conflict with the Transvaal to be sucked into Cetshwayo's cataclysmic confrontation with the British.

With no African state willing to step forward as an ally, and not being confident of waging a successful aggressive campaign across the Zulu borders, in January 1879 Cetshwayo and his advisers opted for a defensive strategy. This approach made sense both militarily and politically. Cetshwayo learned from his white advisers – in particular from John Dunn – that the British had limitless resources and were capable of remaining in the field far longer than could the Zulu. This was a crucial advantage, for (as we have seen) Zulu logistics were rudimentary and a Zulu army could not long maintain itself in the field. So, in purely military terms, a Zulu campaign had to be decisive if it was to be kept short. A decisive campaign was essential too from a political perspective. Cetshwayo believed that the only chance he had of obtaining a cease-fire and making a deal that would save his kingdom from destruction was through negotiating from a position of military strength. Yet here was the catch-22 situation. The king rightly suspected that the British would never enter into any negotiations with him if his armies followed up a victory on their own soil by invading British territory. Consequently, Cetshwayo had to convince the British that he had absolutely no hostile intentions against neighbouring British colonies, and to do that it was therefore essential to fight entirely within the borders of Zululand. Only in that way could he present himself as the victim of an unwarranted attack, legitimately defending his own. As he would later declare to Cornelius Vijn: 'It is the Whites who have come to fight with me in my own country, and not I that will go to fight with them. My intention, therefore, is only to defend myself in my own country.'[23]

Having decided on this broad strategy, the next issue was how best to deploy Zulu forces for the coming war. The problem was that the kingdom faced attack from every quarter and there were not enough fighting men to go around. The numerical strength of the *amabutho* is difficult to estimate with any certainty, but in 1879 they probably had a nominal strength of about 40 000 men. However, some of the senior *amabutho* were past active service, and actual effectives – those who were in an age band between their early twenties and late forties – were unlikely to have numbered more than 29 000. In addition, Cetshwayo could count upon an approximate

5 000 irregulars from the margins of the kingdom joining the *amabutho* on campaign.

In making his dispositions, Cetshwayo correctly decided to discount the possibility of a seaborne invasion.[24] The king was far less confident in leaving his borders with the Swazi kingdom undefended. Nevertheless, he gambled rightly that Mbandzeni would not risk entering the conflict allied to the British until he was absolutely certain they would win. Consequently, Cetshwayo could safely ignore his northern border and coastline to concentrate on the British forces to the south and west. His spies correctly informed him that the British No 3 (Centre) Column operating out of Rorke's Drift was the strongest, and that Chelmsford himself was accompanying it. This intelligence persuaded Cetshwayo that the Centre Column was the main British force and that the maximum effect would be gained by defeating it. He consequently resolved to direct his main army against it, while a subsidiary army would break away to confront No 1 (Right) Column preparing to advance up the coast across the lower Thukela River. He also sent some reinforcements to support the irregulars in the northwest who were confronting both the No 4 (Left) and No 5 Columns.

Once these strategic decisions had been made, Cetshwayo issued his departing generals with precise tactical instructions.[25] He was enough of a soldier to evaluate the dangers involved in trying to storm prepared positions similar to the Boer wagon laagers in 1838. He therefore categorically forbade his commanders from attacking any form of entrenchment where they would be pitilessly exposed to concentrated firepower. Rather, according to Nzuzi of the uVe *ibutho*, he cautioned them to bypass defensive works and to threaten the British lines of supply and the territory to their rear. This would force the enemy out to protect them. Then, Cetshwayo instructed them, 'if you see him out in the open you can attack him because you will be able to eat him up'. After all, it was in a pitched battle in the open field that the heroic virtues of the *amabutho* were most likely to prevail.

Nzuzi further recalled that before the Zulu army finally marched out to war, the king addressed it as it stood around him in a great circle:

'I have not gone over the seas to look for the white men, yet they have come into my country and I would not be surprised if they took away our wives and cattle and crops and land. What shall I do?' … 'Give the matter to us,' we replied. 'We shall go and eat up the white men and finish them off. They are not going to take you while we are here. They must take us first.'[26]

꙳

CHAPTER FIFTEEN

WE ARE THE BOYS FROM ISANDLWANA!

With the expiry of the ultimatum on 11 January 1879, the British No 3 (Centre) Column, already concentrated at Rorke's Drift on the Mzinyathi River, began its laborious advance into Zululand over the rain-sodden ground. On 20 January Chelmsford halted and set up camp at the eastern base of the sphinx-shaped Isandlwana Mountain while he prepared to reconnoitre the way forward. The position of his extended camp was potentially difficult to defend because it was overlooked by a spur of the Nyoni hills to the north, but since Chelmsford considered a Zulu attack most unlikely, no attempt was made to entrench it.

The Zulu response to the British invasion was rapid. After parading past the graves of King Cetshwayo's ancestors to secure the blessings of the *amadlozi*, the whole Zulu army began its march on 17 January. In words that require glossing, when Cetshwayo addressed his warriors as they set out, he declared: 'Son of Sonzika [Sir Theophilus Shepstone], you have poured *inkovu* on your head today. Now we shall see.' The king singled out Shepstone because, as Socwatsha explained, the Zulu all thought Shepstone 'was the great king of Europeans. They knew nothing of the Queen [Victoria] at that time.'[1] *Inkovu* is the water in which vegetables have been boiled, and to have it metaphorically thrown over you means you have been abused to your face. So, in modern idiom, Cetshwayo was telling his gleefully responding *amabutho* that Shepstone had gone and stuffed himself in taking them on.

With its morale exuberantly high, on 20 January the main *impi* of 24 000 men under the joint command of Chief Ntshingwayo kaMahole and Chief Mavumengwana kaNdlela bivouacked by Siphezi Hill, only 20 kilometres east of Isandlwana. Chelmsford had no inkling of the enemy's close proximity, and on 21 January sent out a reconnaissance in force to scout the area southeast of Isandlwana. During the early hours of 21–22 January Chelmsford himself reinforced the reconnaissance force since he believed that reports of Zulu movements indicated that the main Zulu army was pushing down the Mangeni valley to the east. He left Lieutenant Colonel Henry Pulleine and about half his force (67 officers and 1 707 men, some half of whom were African levies) to hold the camp during his absence.

Meanwhile, the joint Zulu commanders, who had indeed been considering a flanking march to Chelmsford's east to cut the British column off from Natal, decided instead to take advantage of the general's division of his forces. On the evening of 21 January and during the next, in a truly masterful manoeuvre, they transferred their army undetected in small units across the British front to the deep shelter of the Ngwebeni valley northeast of Isandlwana.

Late on the dull, cloudy morning of 22 January the Zulu *impi* was still bivouacked in the valley of the Ngwebeni stream while small parties were out foraging and scouting. Its commanders were in conclave, discussing their next move. At that moment a party of mounted British scouts suddenly came over the Mabaso heights overlooking the valley. The mettlesome younger *amabutho* at once charged forward, and the Zulu commanders had difficulty in keeping back four of the more experienced *amabutho* in reserve. As it drove on towards the British camp, the *impi* deployed into its time-hallowed chest-and-horns formation with the intention of enveloping the extended British firing line in front of their camp.

When the Zulu centre spilled over the Nyoni heights, where the Zulu commanders halted to take up their stations, it was exposed to the British firing line. Even though the British troops were in open skirmishing order, the weight of their fire was quite heavy enough to stall the daunted *amabutho* who had never, ever experienced the like. The Zulu commanders

Ntombe Drift

Ntombe Caves ✕✕

Luneburg ○

Ntombe

SWAZI KINGDOM

Disputed Territory

Phongolo

Bivane

Utrecht ○

KHAMBULA ◎✕

ebaQulusini ●

Mkhuze

Hlobane ●

HLOBANE ∧∧∧✕

TRANSVAAL
TERRITORY

Ngome Forest

● kwaDwasa

∧∧
CONFERENCE
HILL

Ncome

Black Mfolozi

LANDMAN'S DRIFT ◎

○
Dundee

Prince Imperial killed ✕

NHLAZATSHE ∧∧∧

NQUTHU ∧∧∧

White Mfolozi

kwaNodwengu ●
oNdini ●

kwaSogekle ● ∧∧∧

Zungeni ✕

Ulundi ✕● ● kwaMbonambi

RORKE'S DRIFT ◎✕

Isandlwana

Mzinyathi

esiKlebheni ●

Mfolozi

HELPMEKAAR ◎

∧∧∧ BABANANGO
∧∧∧ ◎ MTHONJANENI

SIPHEZI

ZULU KINGDOM

Nkandla Forest

emaNgweni ●

Mhlathuze oNdini ●

◎ FORT ESHOWE

FORT CHERRY ◎ Middle Drift

Nyezane ●

Nyezane

◎ PORT DURNFORD

COLONY OF NATAL

✕ Gingindlovu

Matigulu

Greytown ○

Thukela

FORT PEARSON ◎

● Ikhanda

◎ Fort

0   miles   20

0   km   20

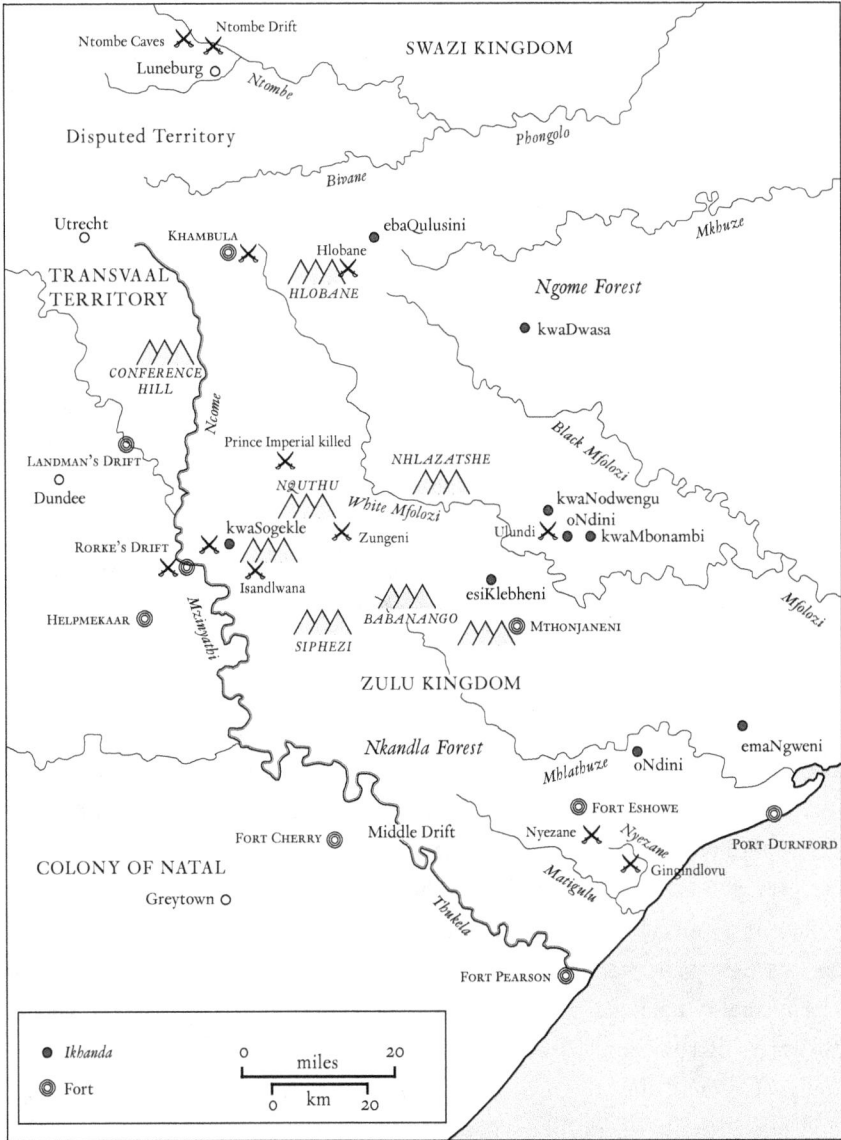

The Anglo-Zulu War, 1879

sent officers running down the hill to rally the *amabutho*. One exhorted them: 'Never did his Majesty the King give you this command, to wit, "Lie down upon the ground!" His words were: "Go! And toss them into Maritzburg!"'[2] Then, as a 'Warrior of the uMbonambi' recalled, 'they all shouted "uSuthu!" [the national battle cry during Cetshwayo's reign] and waving their shields charged upon the soldiers with great fury'.[3]

The British tried to fall back from their exposed forward positions, but the Zulu allowed them no opportunity to rally. Mehlokazulu kaSihayo remembered 'When the soldiers retired on the camp, they did so running, and the Zulus were then intermixed with them, and entered the camp at the same time … Things were then getting very mixed and confused … what with the smoke, dust, and intermingling of men.'[4] The *amabutho* finally had what they so ardently desired, a brutal hand-to-hand struggle as they drove the British through the camp. The Zulu horns almost succeeded in encircling the camp and entered it from the rear. Some of the British mounted men, pursued and harried the entire way by the Zulu, succeeded in getting away down the treacherous 'Fugitives' Path' to the Mzinyathi River, which was lethally swollen by the summer rains. Small units of British infantry attempted to rally and fight their way out, or at the very least to make a gallant last stand. Nzuzi grimly recalled that as the Zulu fell upon the white men, 'many … said to us in our own tongue: "… Spare our lives. What wrong have we done to Cetshwayo?" "How can we give you mercy," we replied, "when you have come to us and want to take our country and eat us up? … uSuthu!"' And with their eyes 'dark' in battle fury the warriors 'stabbed everything we came across'.[5] As one of the special ritual precautions necessary to gain ascendancy over the vengeful sprits of the slain, it was customary for Zulu warriors to slit open the belly of a dead foe, to *qaqa*, so that *umnyama* would not affect the killer and make him swell up like the dead. The British, when they later found the disembowelled bodies of their comrades, naturally saw their mutilation in a very different light. To them it was a horror and abomination that changed the whole nature of the war and justified merciless retaliation.

Once the fighting around Isandlwana had died down, somewhere after 2 pm, the exultant *amabutho* set about comprehensively looting the camp in the sickly light of a partial solar eclipse.[6] Firearms and ammunition were the most highly prized booty, especially the modern Martini-Henry rifles. About 800 fell into Zulu hands, and in later encounters Zulu marksmen familiar through hunting with modern firearms were able to make effective use of them. Pillaging continued until, towards evening, the *amabutho* saw that Chelmsford was at last approaching his stricken camp in battle formation with the remaining half of his force. Sated, and with no further stomach for fighting, the Zulu pulled back with their booty to their bivouac at the Ngwebeni. For the loss of about a thousand men, including many chiefs and prominent men, the Zulu had killed 52 of the British officers left to defend the camp, along with 739 white troops (almost all of those in the camp), 67 white NCOs of the Natal Native Contingent and 471 recorded black troops. This was a 75 per cent casualty rate, an utter rout – the rarest of rare occurrences in a colonial campaign, all the more shocking for that.

While their comrades were relentlessly pursuing the British fugitives or exuberantly pillaging their camp, Dabulamanzi kaMpande (Cetshwayo's mettlesome half-brother) led between 3 000 and 4 000 of the Zulu reserve who had not taken part in the battle across the Mzinyathi into Natal, precisely what Cetshwayo had instructed his commanders not to attempt. But having missed the battle at the camp, it seems their intention was to salve their honour and reputation by overrunning the small British supply depot at Rorke's Drift, formerly a mission station. However, its small garrison of eight officers and 131 men had enough advance warning to improvise rudimentary fortifications from wagons and sacks and boxes of supplies with which they linked up the scattered buildings. The Zulu commenced their attack at 4.30 pm, assailing different sectors of the perimeter in separate waves rather than in a concerted assault. After ten hours and prolonged periods of desperate hand-to-hand fighting, the Zulu disconsolately withdrew in the early hours of 23 January.

For the Zulu, Rorke's Drift was a painful reverse. Not only were 350 or more killed in the failed assault to 17 of the British, but when Chelmsford brought his surviving troops back across the Mzinyathi after spending a frightful night among the disembowelled dead, some vented their homicidal fury on the hundreds of wounded or exhausted Zulu they found in the vicinity of the post or hiding in the fields and undergrowth. Rorke's Drift was, moreover, a double defeat for the Zulu since its successful defence against overwhelming odds provided the British with a welcome propaganda coup to offset the Isandlwana disaster.

The day after the Zulu *impi* marched out on 17 January, a force of about 4 000 men detached itself from the main body and headed off southeast to confront Colonel Pearson's No 1 (Right) Column, picking up several thousand local reinforcements as it went. Its commander, Chief Godide kaNdlela, was nearly 70 years old and most likely had fought the Voortrekkers in 1838. What he had learned then was probably in his mind when he attempted to ambush the British in the hills to the north of the Nyezane stream early on the morning of 22 January – the very same day as Isandlwana – while they were strung out on the march. The Zulu called this encounter Wombane after the hill that was the key to their position, and what they attempted was certainly a sensible and appropriate military ploy. It failed largely because Godide was in command of second-rate troops, since most of the crack *amabutho* were with the army fighting at Isandlwana. Godide's forces had neither the stomach to press home the attack, nor were they sufficiently disciplined to coordinate their movements effectively.

Pearson was therefore able to close up his convoy, form a steady skirmishing line and bring superior, concentrated fire to bear. The warriors consequently never got close enough to fight hand-to-hand as their comrades would do later that day at Isandlwana. Daunted, Godide called off the Zulu attack and Pearson pushed on to the abandoned mission station at Eshowe where he halted and which he immediately began to fortify.

While the Zulu armies were engaging Chelmsford's and Pearson's columns in the south, in northwestern Zululand local forces – notably the Qulusi under Msebe kaMadaka (who formed a distinct *ibutho* drawn exclusively from the men living in the vicinity of the ebaQulusini *ikhanda*), irregulars under Mbilini waMswati (an exiled Swazi prince who had given his allegiance to Cetshwayo), and the Kubheka of Chief Manyonyoba kaMaqondo – did their best to harass Wood's No 4 (Left) Column and Rowlands' No 5 Column. However, Wood's forces had thoroughly gained the advantage over them when news of Isandlwana persuaded him it would be prudent to retire northwest to Khambula hill. He formed a strong entrenched camp there on 31 January and waited on events.

Chelmsford's appalling defeat at Isandlwana had indeed comprehensively dislocated his invasion plans. More than that, it had severely compromised British standing in South Africa, leaving Chelmsford with no option but to resume and prosecute the campaign until the Zulu were utterly defeated and British prestige and honour restored. But he could not do that until he had regrouped and reinforced his forces and assembled fresh transport. Until then, he would have to stand on the defensive and do his best to rally the defences of Natal where panicking colonists were in daily expectation of a Zulu invasion.

Paradoxically, the Zulu were the victims of their own spectacular tactical victory at Isandlwana. Firstly, it ensured the overthrow of Cetshwayo's political strategy. At first, he did not realise that it had absolutely ruled out any possibility for a compromise settlement with the British, and with Mnyamana's urging opened up negotiations again while he held the military advantage. And secondly (ironies of ironies), Isandlwana also meant that there was no longer any hope of an ultimate Zulu military triumph. The Zulu success in enveloping and breaking through the extended firing line at Isandlwana taught Chelmsford that the only way to concentrate fire effectively and stem the enemy's rush was – as at Rorke's Drift – to place troops in prepared all-round defensive positions such as fieldworks, wagon laagers or infantry squares. Henceforth, the British would do their best to entice the Zulu into destroying themselves against such fixed positions. The Zulu *amabutho*, by contrast, seemed to have remained too embedded in their established military culture and buoyed up by their victory at Isandlwana to envisage alternative tactics, and they would oblige the British by persisting in hurling themselves in mass attacks against prepared positions.

Meanwhile, the Zulu had to come to terms with the heavy cost of the first round of battles. The senior women of his *isigodlo* blamed Cetshwayo for the limited success of his armies and the dire number of casualties because he had failed to perform the required rituals unswervingly. In particular, they 'scolded' him for not punctiliously keeping his seat on the *inkatha* once he heard battle had been joined in order to radiate his supernatural influence and that of the royal *amadlozi* out to his warriors.[7] Besides the 2 000 or more who had perished on the field of battle, untold numbers of the wounded, suffering massive tissue damage and splintered bones inflicted by Martini-Henry bullets, which flattened on impact – injuries beyond Zulu medical skill to heal – died as they tried to drag themselves home. So many succumbed in this way that the Zulu understandably came to believe the British bullets were poisoned. The few survivors from gunshot wounds were left scarred and crippled for life. Cornelius Vijn described mourners who 'kept on wailing in front of the kraals, rolling themselves on the ground and never quieting down; nay, in the night they wailed so as to cut through the heart of anyone. And this wailing went on, day and night, for a fortnight.'[8] The deadliness of British firearms left Zulu warriors – even those who had been victorious – severely shaken, and most of them immediately dispersed to their homes instead of returning to oNdini to report to the king, as was expected of them.

Cetshwayo was consequently cast down by the opening round of battles, despite the Zulu success at Isandlwana. He was shocked by the casualties and particularly displeased with his commanders for not religiously obeying his instructions and provocatively invading Natal. Furthermore, he blamed them for failing to prevent the army from dispersing and carrying home the bulk of the plunder they had taken (especially the firearms) instead of bringing it to him for the customary distribution. Dispiritedly, he perceived that – his fresh diplomatic feelers notwithstanding – he would have to fight and win another round of battles to preserve the independence of his kingdom.

For the time being, though, a temporary stalemate took hold. Chelmsford, who for a while had been on the verge of a nervous breakdown, urgently requested the British government to send considerable reinforcements. While he waited for them to arrive before mounting a second invasion of Zululand, low-intensity and inconclusive fighting continued on the coast and in the northwest, where Pearson's and Wood's columns were hunkered down at Eshowe and Khambula respectively.[9]

In the second week of March, Hamu, Cetshwayo's discontented rival, decided to defect to Wood's camp with many of his Ngenetsheni adherents. This act of treason sent shock waves through the Zulu kingdom, for it was the first clear indication that some Zulu notables had decided that the game was up, and that it would be politic to come to terms with

224

the British. In the aftermath of Isandlwana Cetshwayo had (as we have seen) been adhering to his political agenda by pressing ahead with rather half-hearted and tardy peace overtures to the British, but these had all been brusquely dismissed. This failure – although the king seems to have anticipated it – coming on top of Hamu's deplorable defection, persuaded him, his councillors and all the *abantwana* and *izikhulu* whom he summoned urgently to oNdini to advise him, to seize the initiative and go over onto the offensive before the British were ready to invade again. The great assembly decided that Wood's camp at Khambula would be the objective since his energetic and destructive raiding presented a graver threat to the kingdom than Pearson's passive defence at Eshowe.

So, in the second half of March the *amabutho* began to reassemble at oNdini for the new offensive. The king and his council gravely knew that the very existence of the kingdom would hinge on its success. As Cetshwayo later admitted, he was more involved in the meticulous planning for this campaign than in any other operation during the war, and consequently never imagined that the outcome could be defeat.[10] In earnest of the seriousness of its mission, the *impi*, whose strength was on a par with the one that had fought at Isandlwana, was placed under the supreme command of Mnyamana, Cetshwayo's chief councillor and the second man in the kingdom. Ntshingwayo, the tough victor of Isandlwana, would lead it into battle.

The Zulu leadership envisaged the attack on Wood's camp as a tactical reprise of Isandlwana, thereby ignoring the effectiveness of the flexible skirmishing tactics employed by the Qulusi and irregulars in the course of the fluid war of raid and counter-raid in the northwest. (Indeed, in the long run these fighters would prove more militarily successful than the *amabutho*, for Wood would never manage to subdue them entirely and at the end of the war they would be the very last Zulu units still fighting in the field.) In March these irregulars scored two successes that came second only to Isandlwana in the number of casualties they inflicted on the British. On 12 March, Mbilini overran a convoy and its escort at the Ntombe River, killing 61 officers and men besides 18 wagon drivers. Then on 28 March the Qulusi and Mbilini's men entrapped a strong force Wood had led out of Khambula camp to raid the enormous, flat summit of Hlobane Mountain for Zulu cattle. In their ignominious rout the British lost 94 officers and men and over 100 African auxiliaries. The Zulu success was partially due to a detachment of the great Zulu army advancing towards Khambula that cut off many fugitives at the base of the mountain.

The Zulu commanders were naturally exultant at this unanticipated victory, but they had forfeited any chance of taking Wood by surprise. While the *impi* bivouacked for the night near the Black Mfolozi River, at Khambula Wood grasped the short respite to ready the 2 086 men under his command (only 132 of whom were African) in his defensive complex of fort, wagon laager and stone kraals. Cetshwayo had repeatedly warned his *amabutho* to sidestep this sort of fixed position and 'not to put their faces into the lair of the wild beasts, or else they would get clawed'.[11] Rather, with the lesson of Rorke's Drift before him, he exhorted his commanders to attempt to manoeuvre in order to draw Wood out of his fortified camp and then to fight him in the open, as at Isandlwana. But, as Mehlokazulu recounted, 'the regiments were anxious to attack, but we went there cross, our hearts were full, and we intended to do the same as at Isandwhlana [sic]'.[12]

Indeed, the *impi*, especially the pairs of fanatically competitive rival *amabutho*, was too buoyed up by victory at Hlobane to heed caution. Consequently, when on 29 March the advancing *impi* halted at midday just over six kilometres south of Khambula, the firebrands had their way. As Cetshwayo later complained, 'an insubordinate regiment – the iNgobam-akhosi – said they would attack, and actually advanced to do so, contrary to orders. Mnyamana seeing this, then decided to attack with the whole army.'[13] Deploying into a fearsome crescent extending over 16 kilome-tres, at about 1 pm some 20 000 warriors began their menacing, deliberate advance on Khambula from the southeast. Full of bravado, they began to sing out as soon as they came within earshot of the apprehensive defenders: 'We are the boys from Isandhlwana! [sic]'[14]

But this time the outcome would be very different for the *amabutho*, even though the impending battle would be by far the most prolonged and fierc-est they would ever fight. The combat began at about 1.30 pm, and for four grinding, murderous hours the *amabutho* launched a series of uncoordinated attacks from three directions, which (as had been the case at Rorke's Drift, but on a much smaller scale) allowed the British to meet each one in detail. Even so, there were moments when the Zulu scented victory and almost broke through Wood's defences. But by about 5 pm all the *amabutho* were exhausted and dispirited and the Zulu army commenced an orderly withdrawal under fire. That was the moment for Wood to launch his mounted counterattack. A Zulu *impi* had last experienced a mounted sortie at the battle of Ncome, 41 years before, and once again its commanders could not rally their demoralised *amabutho*. Retirement broke down into headlong flight. The remorseless British pursuit, in which no prisoners were taken, continued as far as Zungwini Mountain 16 kilometres away, and was only called off with the fall of darkness.

Up to 2 000 Zulu perished. The Zulu calculated that more men of high rank were killed at Khambula than in any other battle of the war. The British lost only three officers and 25 men. Mnyamana did his best to keep the shattered Zulu army together to return in some order to the king, but for the most part the men were too shocked and daunted by defeat to obey. As Sihlahla of the uMxhapho later expressed it, 'Not one in our force doubted our being beaten, and [they] openly said they had had enough and would go home.'[15] Lamentation engulfed the land, and Cetshwayo was distraught. He understood only too well that any hope of winning the war in the field had been swept away, and that any realistic hope of negotiating a settlement with the victorious British had vanished too.[16]

Then, four days after the battle of Khambula, on 2 April 1879, Chelmsford scored a victory of his own. He had resolved that, before launching his second invasion, he must first relieve and withdraw the blockaded Eshowe garrison. On the early morning of 2 April, a day's march from Eshowe, the 5 670 men of the Eshowe Relief Column routed the Zulu force of 10 000 men mustered to intercept his advance under the command of Somopho kaZikhala. Thanks to Chelmsford's painstaking precautions, the Eshowe Relief Column was securely positioned within its entrenched laager near the burned-out kwaGingindlovu *ikhanda*. The Zulu attack developed at about 6 am. The warriors came on at the double in two divisions deployed in open order and taking advantage of the coastal bush for cover. They all but surrounded the laager, but under concentrated British fire their determined assaults all broke down at about 18 metres from its perimeter. By

7 pm the Zulu attackers were pinned down everywhere, and Chelmsford ordered out his mounted men. The Zulu had suffered enough and broke, hotly pursued. The 2 000 men of the Natal Native Contingent, who had been kept in reserve during the Zulu attack, were now unleashed to mop up behind the mounted men and to kill all the Zulu wounded – a task they performed with gusto. In all, the Zulu lost somewhere close to 1 500 dead to nine British soldiers and 17 African troops. Chelmsford relieved the Eshowe garrison the day after the battle and then evacuated it to the Natal border to regroup.

If Chelmsford was now readying himself for a second major thrust into Zululand to finish the war, the situation was very different for the Zulu. Their crushing, almost simultaneous defeats at opposite ends of the king-dom exposed the inadequacy of their tactics and spelled nothing but ruin for their cause. Not without reason 'the King was very angry with us when we went back', later admitted a warrior of the uThulwana. 'He said we were born warriors, and yet allowed ourselves to be defeated in every battle.'[17]

Meanwhile, on 28 May the British cabinet, lambasted by indignant pub-lic opinion, anxious to end the war and uncertain that Chelmsford was the man to do it successfully, placed the chief civil and military authority in southeastern Africa in the hands of the incorrigibly thrusting General Sir Garnet Wolseley. He outranked and superseded Chelmsford, and as Governor of the Transvaal and High Commissioner for South East Africa he sidelined Frere (now in great disfavour for beginning the disastrous war) to the Cape Colony. When Chelmsford learned that Wolseley was on his way out to South Africa to take command, he resolved to bring the Zulu to a final, victorious battle before his rival could rob him of the credit for winning the war.

✻

CHAPTER SIXTEEN

THE ZULU HOUSE
MUST GO TO THE GROUND

In Zululand, so Sibhalo kaHibana revealed under interrogation, rapidly spreading word of the devastating defeats at Khambula and Gingindlovu, 'where so large a number was killed, shook the country'.[1] With his *amabutho* scattered in disarray to their homes and his strategy for prosecuting the war in ruins, Cetshwayo was left perplexed by what to do next. In mid-May he once again summoned the leading men of the kingdom to oNdini for their counsel. They strongly urged suing for peace, but the *amabutho* were unwilling to give up without further resistance. So Cetshwayo compromised. He undertook to enter into further negotiations with the British, but promised to fight the British once more if they came as far as the Mahlabathini plain.

Chelmsford too was in a dilemma. He knew he had entirely regained the initiative, but he was uncertain how best to employ the embarrassing number of reinforcements rushed out to him by an anxious British government. Of one thing Chelmsford was certain: this time he would exercise extreme caution in his advance to avoid a repetition of Isandlwana. Eventually, he decided to deploy two widely spaced columns to screen the Transvaal and Natal from a possible Zulu counter-blow. The 1st Division of 7 500 men under Major General Henry Crealock was to advance on oNdini up the coast. The 2nd Division of 5 000 men under

Major General Edward Newdigate (accompanied by Chelmsford) was to march on oNdini from the northwest instead of following the route of the ill-fated No 3 Column. It would take longer and the unfamiliar route required considerable reconnaissance, but for reasons of morale it was considered wise to avoid the stricken field of Isandlwana. On the way, the 2nd Division was to rendezvous with Wood's 3 000 men, now renamed the Flying Column.

Zulu resistance to the new British two-pronged advance that began to gain momentum during May was distinctly muted. The *amabutho* were still dispersed, and only small, irregular units occasionally skirmished with the invaders, sometimes exhibiting (as at eZulaneni on 5 June) good use of terrain and cover and a more effectual deployment of firearms. One small skirmish on 1 June resulted in the death of the young Prince Imperial of France, the pretender to the Bonapartist throne, who was accompanying Chelmsford's headquarters as an observer. The Prince's death occasioned as much consternation in Britain as had the battle of Isandlwana.

Embarrassing as they were, disastrous skirmishes such as these were as mere pinpricks. Chelmsford's ultimate objective was to break the neck of the Zulu power in one final, cataclysmic pitched battle from which it would never recover. At the same time, though, he set about weakening Cetshwayo's authority through continuing to encourage disaffected chiefs and their adherents to follow Hamu's example, and defect. This strategy required both a carrot and a stick. The carrot comprised the easy terms of surrender he offered to Zulu notables while insisting that Cetshwayo submit absolutely to the tough terms of the British ultimatum. The stick took the form of the harsh measures he adopted against the civilian population in the hope that their hardships would provoke Cetshwayo's desperate subjects into deposing their king and surrendering. In this he was no different from other commanders in Queen Victoria's 'small wars' who accepted civilian suffering as an unfortunate ancillary to victory. So, besides systematically destroying as many as they could of the *amakhanda* in Zululand – which, as rallying points for the *amabutho* and depots for Zulu supplies, could be considered legitimate military targets – the British also remorselessly attacked the Zulu people's basic means of survival, sending out patrols to pillage and burn far and wide. Even allowing for the fact that great stretches of Zululand were never visited by British patrols, they nevertheless destroyed many hundreds of *imizi* and captured tens of thousands of cattle and other livestock. It should be noted, though, that the British perpetrated very few recorded atrocities against Zulu civilians, and this can plausibly be attributed to the usual Zulu reluctance to wage guerrilla-style warfare. Consequently, the British were not stung (as is typical in counterinsurgency operations) into wild reprisals against civilians who might be harbouring fighters.

As the two British divisions crept over-methodically but remorselessly towards oNdini the previous trickle of Zulu defections and submissions became a flood. This was particularly the case along the coastal plain, where the wholesale surrender of the disheartened civilian population – even before the final battle of Ulundi had been fought on 4 July – was not simply a consequence of the dispiriting record of the absolute lack of Zulu military success in that theatre. Rather, the easy terms offered to chiefs increasingly willing to lay down their arms worked their effect, and leading figures such as Dabulamanzi and Mavumengwana entered into negotiations.

For weeks Cetshwayo and his advisers seemed to have been paralysed by the inexorable British advance before finally reacting. In the king's own recorded words:

> During June and July Cetshwayo had decided on no definite plan of operations. He received information that Lord Chelmsford's division and General Crealock's would meet on the Mthonjaneni [heights] and move together on oNdini. On the arrival of Lord Chelmsford's force there [29 June], he saw it was impossible for General Crealock to come up in time, so he decided to give his whole attention to Lord Chelmsford. He called up men from all the districts, leaving only a few in the coast country to protect the cattle.[2]

While waiting for the *amabutho* to muster, which they did with grim foreboding and greater reluctance than in the past, Cetshwayo made repeated and increasingly desperate efforts to negotiate with Chelmsford, asking again and again what he had done wrong and begging for peace. But Chelmsford knew that Wolseley was straining every sinew to reach the front in order to take up his command, and he was determined that Zulu resistance should continue until he achieved the crushing victory in the field he believed essential for polishing his tarnished reputation. So, while he continued to advance, Chelmsford deliberately spun out negotiations by insisting on terms he made increasingly crushing and impossible for Cetshwayo to accept. By 25 June all that Cetshwayo could say through his messengers was that there was 'nothing left but to try and push aside a tree that [was] falling upon him'.[3]

By the third week of June the bulk of the Zulu army was assembled once more at oNdini in defence of their king. He was at the *ikhanda* by 24 June, and his presence indicated he would fight if he had to. Chelmsford continued to advance, and on 26 June his mounted patrols burned the *amakhanda* in the emaKhosini valley. When esiKlebheni went up in flames, the *inkatha*, the symbol of nationhood and Zulu unity handed down from King Shaka, was also consumed. Its destruction was the unmistakable forewarning of the imminent fall of the Zulu kingdom.

On 30 June Chelmsford moved down to an entrenched camp just across the White Mfolozi from oNdini. In a last-ditch effort, Cetshwayo tried to send a herd of his prized royal white cattle to the British as a peace offering. To his frustration, as he later informed the Governor of the Cape, the uKhandempemvu *ibutho* 'drove them back and said they would fight ... I then asked [them] why they would not allow the cattle to be taken to the English. And they said, "We will all rather die."'[4] So, to the very last, the *amabutho* were determined to assert their heroic honour, no matter how terrible the likely cost. But, as Cetshwayo grimly warned them, 'If you prod the ground with your stick, the earth will be hard.'[5]

And so it proved. Chelmsford was determined not to confront the Zulu army from an entrenched position as he had at Gingindlovu, but in a great, hollow infantry square. By finally defeating the Zulu in the open field that favoured their style of warfare, he hoped to impress on them the invincibility of British arms. On 3 July he sent a large mounted patrol across the

White Mfolozi River to reconnoitre the best location in the Mahlabathini for the climactic battle he planned to fight there in the midst of the great *amakhanda*. At about 1.30 am that night the British were awakened by the *amabutho* at the kwaNodwengu *ikhanda* 'singing a war song, thousands of voices and a grand chant, it came echoing up the river magnificently ... as more and more voices swelled it'.[6] Although the awed listeners could not know it, never again would the gathered manhood of the Zulu kingdom join in raising their stirring *amahubo*, the soldierly ballads honouring the mighty deeds of the ancestors and great warriors of the past, for the coming day would see them scattered in final defeat.

At first light on 4 July, Chelmsford advanced his square to a position two and a half kilometres west of oNdini itself. His force totalled 5 170 men, a thousand of whom were African. Between 15 000 and 20 000 Zulu under the command of Prince Ziwedu kaMpande, Cetshwayo's brother, were concentrated in the plain. At about 8 am they advanced on the square in loose undulating lines with large masses in support, preceded by waves of skirmishers, and within half an hour they had completed their encirclement. Experience in previous battles had given the *amabutho* a chastened sense of the effectiveness of close-range, concentrated fire. Zulu veterans admitted that, after their recent severe defeats, 'we did not fight with the same spirit, because we were then frightened'.[7]

Increasingly daunted and disordered under withering rifle, artillery and even Gatling-gun fire, at about 9.20 am the discouraged *amabutho* began a demoralised, ragged withdrawal. That was the moment for the British cavalry and colonial mounted troops to sally out of the square in a devastating counterattack. Supported by artillery fire, they drove the Zulu from the field in complete disarray and did not rein in until they reached the hills three kilometres away. The African levies then gleefully burst out of the square to assist the irregular horse in despatching the Zulu wounded and in putting all the *amakhanda* in the plain to the torch. Thirteen men died on the British side, compared to some 1 500 Zulu.

Grimly satisfied, Chelmsford could be assured that British arms had been vindicated throughout southern Africa, and that Isandlwana had been avenged. As for the defeated Zulu, Ndungungunga kaNgengene spoke for them when he declared immediately after the battle 'We were completely beaten off by the artillery and bullets … The army is now thoroughly beaten, and as we were beaten in the open, it will not reassemble or fight again.'[8]

Nor did it. After Ulundi, the Zulu army speedily dispersed all over the country and no organised forces remained in the field. King Cetshwayo himself did not witness the battle because he had left oNdini the day before for the kwaMbonambi *ikhanda*. Once runners informed him that his army had been routed, he immediately retired northwards with the idea of making a further stand. But his *amabutho* would not respond to his order to reassemble, and Cetshwayo accepted that the game was up. So he sent further word for them to disperse for, as Magema Fuze reported, 'he did not wish his people to come to an end, for they had now fought a good deal and had suffered greatly'.[9] Travelling disconsolately north on foot, he accepted Zibhebhu's offer to give his son, Dinuzulu, the women of his household and the royal cattle accompanying them sanctuary in Mandlakazi territory in the far northeast of the kingdom and out of range of British patrols. The king did not follow them to kwa-Bangonomo, Zibhebhu's main residence, but struck northward across the Black Mfolozi to Mnyamana's ekuShumayeleni *umuzi* on the Sikhwebezi River. Cetshwayo reached ekuShumayeleni on the third day after the battle and stayed there for a month, attempting fruitlessly to come to terms with the victorious British. But with his army scattered and his authority shattered, he had no bargaining counters left. He might abjectly beg the 'English' to 'take pity on him and leave him the country of his fathers',[10] but, realistically, all he could hope to parley for was his personal safety and future liberty. Meanwhile, the great men of the kingdom, 'deadened like stones', saw that 'the Zulu house must go to the ground'[11] and made ready to treat with the conqueror.

It would not be with Chelmsford, however. Having won his great victory before Wolseley could arrive to supersede him and rob him of the credit, Chelmsford promptly resigned his command on 5 July 1879. Wolseley took dynamic charge the moment Chelmsford left Zululand and hastened the process of Zulu submission. On 19 July he accepted the formal surrender of the coastal chiefs who had already submitted to General Crealock, but further efforts were needed to persuade the other great chiefs to give in. Accordingly, on 26 July he let them know that all who surrendered with their arms and royal cattle would be permitted to retain their own herds,[12] land and chiefly status in the new Zululand, where both the monarchy and the military system were to be abolished. Wolseley thus placed the chiefs in a position where they could preserve or even augment their local positions by coming to terms with the British, while the livelihood of their adherents would not be disrupted.

With symbolic intent, on 10 August Wolseley moved his headquarters to the kwaSishwili Camp amid the burned-out *amakhanda* in the Mahlabathini Plain and hard by oNdini, where only ten huts of the thousands remained standing. There, in this landscape of carnage and devastation, between 14 and 26 August Wolseley received the submission of most of the important chiefs of central and northern Zululand, including Mnyamana, Ntshingwayo, Ziwedu (the king's favourite brother) and finally Zibhebhu too. Simultaneously the chiefs in the southwest surrendered at Rorke's Drift. Nevertheless, it remained imperative for Wolseley to kill or capture Cetshwayo to prevent him from providing a rallying point for renewed resistance. He candidly wrote to his wife that he 'should be quite happy if some kind friend should but run an Assegai through him'.[13] But, since no one would oblige, he had to track down the fugitive king who, abandoned by his chiefs, had taken fright on learning British patrols were fanning out and vying with each other to capture him, and was fleeing further north, almost unattended, to the remote, broken countryside of the Ngome forest.

Wolseley had already sent the greater part of the British forces in Zululand marching home, but he retained two reduced columns to enforce final pacification and corner Cetshwayo. He also called on Hamu's Ngenetsheni to assist in the northwest, along with Swazi warriors. At this very late stage King Mbandzeni had finally decided it was safe to come out on the British side against his people's traditional foe and – incidentally – take a share of the spoils.

The Zulu chiefs were conscious that they would not secure a final peace with the British so long as Cetshwayo remained at large, and were pragmatically looking towards their future in a British-dominated Zululand. Revealingly, on 26 August Mnyamana told the British:

> [W]e lost all regard for & interest in him [Cetshwayo] after the last fight [the battle of Ulundi]: we fought them [the British] & were beaten & we felt we had done all that could be required of us for him & that he had no further claim on us. We were not afraid to kill Chaka & Dingaan, & Panda was saved because we feared the white men who were his friends, so why should we therefore be afraid of Cetewayo?[14]

The king's former chief councillor was always the political pragmatist, so it is hardly a surprise that he then elliptically gave the information necessary for a patrol to run Cetshwayo to earth. On 28 August Major RJC Marter captured the king at the remote kwaDwasa *umuzi* belonging to Mkhosana kaSangqana, one of Mnyamana's adherents, deep in the Ngome forest. Taken by surprise with only a handful of companions and women, Cetshwayo (who was wearing his leopard-skin loin covering, beadwork and a small shawl over the shoulder) surrendered with considerable dignity. The interpreter, Martin Oftebro, remembered that when the party escorting Cetshwayo south came to the Black Mfolozi and the king entered the water to cross, a number of the Natal Native Contingent on the bank began to chant the war-song, 'The bones of the Ndwandwe'. That, declared Oftebro, 'was too much for Cetywayo. His humiliation was complete ... All the "Majesty" went out of him, leaving him extremely dejected.'[15]

On 31 August, to the sound of drums and bugles, the fallen king passed through Wolseley's camp in a cart under escort, impressing all with his imposing royal bearing despite his unbearable humiliation and physical exhaustion. Until Oftebro reassured him, he was inclined to believe the rumour that Mbuyazi, the brother he had defeated and killed in 1856, was with the British and would supplant him. Keenly conscious of 'the courtesies due to his rank', he was dismayed that he was treated as 'a fugitive from law and order' rather than as a 'defeated monarch.[16] Already insulted that no officer would shake hands with him and that Wolseley refused to see him, when John Shepstone curtly informed him that he had been deposed and that he would not be allowed to remain

King Cetshwayo (wrapped in a tablecloth) sketched on 4 September 1879 embarking on a surf-boat at Port Durnford that will take him out to HMS *Natal*. His *inceku*, Mkhosana kaSangqana, and a group of *umndlunkulu* who will share his exile, await their turn to board.

(*ILLUSTRATED LONDON NEWS*, 18 OCTOBER 1879)

in Zululand, his resolution finally slipped, and the tears ran down his cheeks. The next day Cetshwayo set off under escort in an ambulance wagon drawn by ten mules mournfully murmuring: 'I am no longer a King; let me go and live in Pietermaritzburg like any other poor Zulu,'[17] for he supposed his exile would be in Natal. But to his mounting dismay he realised he was being taken towards the coast, to exile across the sea. He had never before been on a boat of any kind, and on 4 September could not entirely disguise his nervousness when, wearing a red and green tablecloth as a shawl, he was taken off through the surf at Port Durnford and put on board the steam transport *Natal*, which was under the escort of HMS *Forester*. One of those watching him go on board was Mapelu Zungu, who later remembered 'When we saw them taking him away, dead went our hearts, saying within us that never more should we see Cetywayo.'[18]

Cetshwayo's destination was Cape Town, and while being driven on

TRANSVAAL TERRITORY

Phongolo

Bivane

MGOJANA

Mkhuze

QULUSI

NGENETSHENI

emGAZINI

NDAWANDWE

kwaBangonomo

HAMU

kwaMfemfe

Bende

MPHANGISWENI

MDLALOSE

BUTHELEZI

Mahashini

Meniya

MAJDLAKAZI

SEKETHWAYO

KHOZA

uSUTHU

KwaGqikazi

ZIBHEBHU

oSuthu

ekuVukeni

ekuShumayeleni

ekuBazeni

ekuXedini

MDLETSHE

NTSHINGWAYO

Ncome (Blood)

QUNGEBE

MBATHA

ZUNGU

HLABISA

BlackMfolozi

SEBENI

MFANAWENDLELA

SOMKHELE

Somkhele's

HLUBI

FAKU

uMzinyathi

MPHUKUNYONI

MCHUNU

NTOMBELA

WhiteMfolozi

Somopho's

Mfolozi

MGITSHWA

MTHETHWA

(Buffalo)

Sokwetshatha's

SITHOLE

GAWOZI

MPUNGOSE

THEMBU

MLANDLELA

JOHN DUNN

CUBE

emaNgweni

NTULI

BIYELA

emaNGWENI

MAGWAZA

BIYELA

Mblathuze

JOHN DUNN

Eshowe

NTULI

DUNN

NATAL

Thukela

INDIAN OCEAN

N

Boundaries of the 13 chiefdoms

GAWOZI   Appointed chiefs

NTULI   Chiefdoms

0   10   20 km

0   10   20 miles

The First Partition of Zululand, 1 September 1879

238

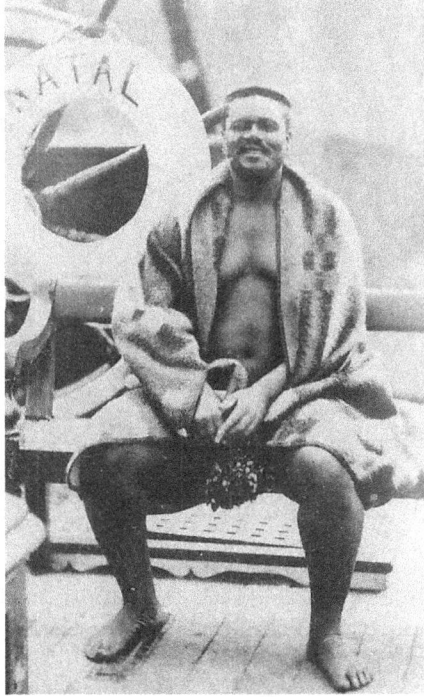

King Cetshwayo, on board HMS *Natal* in September 1879 on his way to
exile in the Cape, summons up a rueful smile for the camera.

(KILLIE CAMPBELL AFRICANA LIBRARY, UNIVERSITY OF KWAZULU-NATAL, DURBAN)

15 September to the Castle of Good Hope, where he would be incarcer-
ated, he was overwhelmed by the extent of South Africa's largest city and
all the shipping in the bay. He winced at his presumption in ever pitting
his kingdom against such evident power. 'I am now a very old man,' he was
heard to mutter to himself.[19]

With Cetshwayo bound for exile, the chiefs could with relatively clear
consciences publicly accept Wolseley's terms for a settlement, which he
imposed on them at an assembly at kwaSishili on 1 September. The Zulu
monarchy was suppressed, and its main prop, the military system, abolished. In line with Frere's preference for indirect rule in the style of that
practised in the princely states of the British Empire in India, Wolseley
did not annex Zululand, but divided it up into 13 independent territories
under the nominal supervision of a British resident. Following considerable

239

On 1 September 1879 Gawozi kaSilwana, one of the 13 chiefs appointed by General Sir Garnet Wolseley to supplant King Cetshwayo at the end of the Anglo-Zulu War, puts his cross to the treaty. Wolseley faces him across the table, left hand on hip.

(*GRAPHIC*, 25 OCTOBER 1879)

consultation with colonial advisers, Wolseley appointed a rag-bag of likely chiefs to rule over the 13 fragments of the former kingdom. He cynically calculated that, out of self-interest, most of them could be relied upon to uphold his settlement (also known to later historians as the First Partition of Zululand) and to ensure that there would be no resurgence of the centralised Zulu monarchy.

Disregarding prescient rumblings that his railroaded settlement had consigned the Zulu people to civil war and ruin, Wolseley and his staff departed Zululand for the Transvaal. The final spark of Zulu resistance fizzled on 1 September when in northwestern Zululand the Qulusi, who had remained unswervingly loyal to Cetshwayo, submitted on receiving a secret order from him to lay down their arms because he was now a prisoner. The last British troops marched out on 21 September, and the war was over.

Already, civilians were back planting in their fields for the new season and rebuilding their burned-out *imizi*. Still, even if the normal patterns of everyday life were resuming in Zululand, none could ignore the aching gap left by the men who had died in battle defending their kingdom. There were at least 6 000 of them – and quite probably thousands more who did not survive their wounds – all in the productive prime of their manhood. Yet, from another perspective, the British–Zulu ratio of casualties was 1:3, quite astonishing in a colonial 'small war' where losses in battle against 'savage' enemies were expected to be minimal. No matter how one views such figures, they testify to the relative success of the completely out-gunned Zulu war effort against colonial aggression.

Almost as telling a blow to the familiar fabric of Zulu society as the death of so many men in battle was the spectacular destruction of the *amakhanda*, those centres of royal authority and the barracks of the *amabutho* who had sustained the monarchy. Thanks to Wolseley's settlement, political power was devolved once more to the great chiefs and British appointees, and the young men of Zululand, rather than serving the king in their *amabutho* as they had since the days of King Shaka, fell once more under their chiefs' localised authority. As for the kingdom itself, forged first in war in King Shaka's day, a scant 60 years later it had been undone by war in the reign of his nephew, King Cetshwayo, and was no more.

CHAPTER SEVENTEEN

❄

MOST VILLAINOUSLY USED

When Cetshwayo stepped ashore at Cape Town, at his desire he was wearing a light suit of European clothes and a tall black hat squeezed over his *isicoco* so as not to appear before colonial onlookers as some naked savage. Nevertheless, he was not anticipating the crowd that had gathered to gawp at him despite the early hour, and certainly not the tentative cheer that went up to greet him. Cetshwayo responded to his reception with gratified humour and dignity. Indeed, ever since his capture the deposed king had been determined to keep up a front of royal serenity despite occasional black bouts of understandable depression.

It was a front not easy to maintain with the same sangfroid once the gates of the Castle of Good Hope slammed behind him and there was no ameliorating the stern fact that the British were indefinitely holding him prisoner. He was allotted quarters in the Flagstaff Bastion and a length of parapet where he could take exercise. His military custodian, Captain J Ruscombe Poole, Royal Artillery, was a sympathetic man, as was the interpreter, Henry Longcast, who had been brought up at a mission station in Zululand and had known Cetshwayo for many years. More essential for the king's wellbeing were his Zulu companions. The outspoken Mkhosana kaSanqana, who had been one of Mpande's councillors, and who had continued as Cetshwayo's friend and adviser, had elected to join the fallen monarch in exile. So too had four attractive and vivacious *umndlunkulu* from Cetshwayo's *isigodlo*, every one of them the daughter of a great chief. Three male attendants, including the royal hairdresser, looked after their personal needs.

Very conscious that he was the king of a sovereign kingdom, Cetshwayo did not find it 'fair' that he should be exiled and imprisoned in precisely the same manner as had the Hlubi chief, Langalibalele kaMthimkhulu (c 1814–1889), who (as Cetshwayo put it) had been a mere 'insurgent' in 1873 against colonial rule in Natal before being captured and banished to the Cape for life.[1] And there was indeed a difference between Langalibalele's case and Cetshwayo's. However unjustly, Langalibalele had been found guilty of treason and rebellion against colonial Natal, whereas Cetshwayo had committed no crime against the British – except to resist their invasion of his kingdom.

Yet, the hard truth was that the British of the imperial era made no hard-and-fast distinctions in their treatment of either deposed independent rulers or defeated rebels against colonial rule, especially when the distinction between the two categories was somewhat blurred. Thus (to take three substantiating African examples) when in 1896 the British invaded Asante to forestall both the French and the Germans and secured control of the kingdom, they smartly exiled the ruling Asantehene, Prempeh I (1870–1931), along with his immediate family and leading councillors, to the remote Seychelles Islands in the Indian Ocean. Yet the British meted out precisely the same fate to Mwanga II (1868–1903), the Kabaka of Buganda, who unsuccessfully rebelled in 1897 against the protectorate the British had proclaimed over Buganda in 1894.[2]

Sekhukhune, the Pedi ruler, was in a more anomalous situation than either Prempeh or Mwanga. When they annexed the Transvaal in 1877, the British asserted their sovereignty over him, a claim he strenuously rejected. Yet whatever his status actually was made no difference when Sekhukhune surrendered on 2 December 1880 at the end of the Second Anglo-Pedi War. The British promptly deposed him and held him in jail in Pretoria pending a final decision over his place of exile. For Sir Garnet Wolseley, who had captured him, there was no dilemma. He urged that

Sekhukhune must join the rebel Langalibalele and the deposed King Cetshwayo in the Cape and, like both of them, be kept far enough away from his previous domain to foment no future mischief.[3]

It was not long, however, before external events affected the circumstances of both Cetshwayo's and Sekhukhune's imprisonment. No sooner were the two deposed rulers prisoners of the British than the whole structure of South African confederation, raised at the expense of so much blood and treasure, came crashing down. In September 1880 the Sotho, who since 1871 had been administered by the Cape, broke out in a full-scale rebellion known as the Gun War. In February 1881 the Sotho and Cape forces concluded a ceasefire that marked the first step towards the dismantling of colonial rule in Basutoland.[4] The Gun War was the sole instance of a successful African revolt against colonial rule in 19th-century South Africa, and shook the basis of confederation. Yet what really demolished it was the Transvaal Rebellion (the First Anglo-Boer War) that broke out in December 1880 while British attention was focused on Basutoland. Culminating in the British humiliation at the battle of Majuba on 27 February 1881, the irreconcilably disaffected Boers bloodily repulsed several attempts by British forces to break through from Natal to relieve their besieged Transvaal garrisons. By the complex Pretoria Convention of 3 August 1881, the Liberal government (it had replaced the Tory administration in the general election of April 1880) at one stroke ceded the restored ZAR its independence and abandoned the Tory programme of South African confederation.

Article 23 of the Pretoria Convention benefited Sekhukhune, who was released from British custody and allowed to return to live in his former territory – now an integral part of the ZAR – although no longer as Pedi paramount. As for Cetshwayo, now that the Anglo-Zulu War was over, it no longer seemed proper that he should be kept a prisoner of war. Yet the British had no intention of setting him free or of allowing him to return to his former kingdom. So the Cape parliament enacted a bill in July 1880 authorising his detention, although it was not until February 1881 that he was formally transferred from military to civilian custody. The Cape government then moved Cetshwayo out of the Castle to the farm Oude Molen on the desolate Cape Flats several kilometres

east of Cape Town. It upset Cetshwayo's *amour propre* that on the adjoin-
ing farm, Uitvlugt, he had Langalibalele as his neighbour, held on much
the same terms as he, his superior and a king.[5]

At Oude Molen the conditions of Cetshwayo's captivity were ame-
liorated and he was allowed to keep cattle and hunting dogs, to course
jackals and rabbits and bring down birds with his hurled knobkerrie
(at which, to his satisfaction, he was considerably more skilled than
Langalibalele). He went for long walks with his new interpreter, RCA
Samuelson (who, like Longcast, had been brought up at a Zululand mission), went on carriage rides and railway excursions, and even attended
the theatre and society dinner parties in Cape Town. Yet he did not
allow these diversions, which helped keep his despondency at bay, to
distract him from pursuing his overriding goal, namely, his restoration
to the Zulu throne.

In captivity Cetshwayo proved remarkably adept at cultivating influential sympathisers while at the same time keeping mere snoopers at
arm's length. He quickly grasped that there were those who saw him as
the victim of an unjust war and advocated his restoration to his kingdom.
Devoted supporters like Bishop Colenso and Lady Florence Dixie (writer,
explorer, war correspondent and big-game hunter) kept his situation constantly before the public eye through their ceaseless stream of articles,
pamphlets, books and letters, and determinedly lobbied politicians, army
officers, officials and public figures, even Queen Victoria herself. The
British government was in any case increasingly embarrassed by growing
public indignation in liberal quarters over the injustice of Cetshwayo's
continued imprisonment, especially since Sekhukhune – whose circumstances were much the same as Cetshwayo's – had been released and
returned home. But like any other administration, the Liberals could
have snubbed public sentiment if it had been in their interest to do so.
However, the increasingly disastrous state of affairs in Zululand, where
Wolseley's First Partition of Zululand was rapidly unravelling, was pres-
suring them into radically reassessing their Zululand policy and the role
Cetshwayo should play in it.

At Oude Molen too, Cetshwayo's days were troubled and his nights
disturbed by progressively alarming word of the disorder and bloodshed

engulfing Zululand. As we have seen, Wolseley's prime objective in making his settlement had been to leave Zululand divided and no further threat to its colonial neighbours. He firmly stuck to the view that the 13 insecure 'kinglets' he had appointed to replace the centralising monarchy could be counted on to collaborate with the British to stifle any revival of royalist influence. Wolseley's reliance on collaborators was hardly novel, however. It was a common device among imperial administrators to depend on the cooperation of collaborators when they aimed to avoid the responsibility and expense of direct annexation of a territory while simultaneously maintaining a measure of control over it. During the coming decades in Africa, the British would increasingly adopt the political philosophy of 'indirect rule', a system by which subject kingdoms were administered through traditional authorities under the colonial overlord. The precedent was India, where indirect rule was the basis of British rule over the princely states.

Sir Frederick Lugard (1858–1945), the famous administrator of the British Nigerian protectorates and territories between 1900 and 1919, is usually credited with being the apostle of indirect rule in Africa. However, Sir Theophilus Shepstone had long anticipated him with his administration of African locations in Natal, and he had played a major hand in advising Wolseley to base his settlement of Zululand on indirect rule and the deployment of collaborators. Indeed, through a loyal school of officials who looked to him as their mentor, Shepstone ensured that indirect rule would continue to form the core of the various settlements the British were to impose on Zululand over the following decade.

The problem with this policy was that it provided for no effective means of dousing internal conflict or rebellion should a settlement fall apart, and ultimately required outside military intervention to restore order – precisely what the British government wished to avoid. And the fatal flaw in Wolseley's settlement was that, by its very nature, it made internal strife all but unavoidable. The appointed 13 'kinglets' were bound to clash with the demoted and frustrated members of the royal house. What made out-and-out conflict inevitable was Wolseley's provocative appointment of Hamu and Zibhebhu to rule over the two northern chiefdoms, where the presence of resentful royalist supporters (or uSuthu, as they were known) was particularly strong. His intent was to ensure that uSuthu aspirations there would be suppressed by the two collaborating chiefs in their own interests, but all he was doing was laying an explosive charge.

Cetshwayo's son, Dinuzulu, had (as we have seen) taken refuge with Zibhebhu after the battle of Ulundi, and Zibhebhu saw the political advantage of keeping him firmly under his control. But Dinuzulu, although only 11 years old, was proud and short-tempered and rapidly developed a deep aversion towards Zibhebhu. He resolved to escape, and Mnyamana (who had declined when offered one of Wolseley's chiefdoms) spirited him away and placed him under the guardianship of Ndabuko kaMpande, his father's full younger brother.[6] Zibhebhu was enraged and in retaliation took punitive measures against the uSuthu in his chiefdom. Ndabuko did nothing to endear himself to Zibhebhu or Hamu when in May 1880, along with his brother, Shingana kaMpande, he led a deputation of leading uSuthu on foot all the way to Pietermaritzburg to plead for Cetshwayo's restoration. He was rebuffed. By then, violence was already breaking out, although the factions still drew back from a major military clash. The future battle lines were clearly drawn at the meeting at Nhlazatshe Mountain in central Zululand on 31 August 1881. There the Acting High Commissioner for South East Africa, Major General Sir Evelyn Wood, met the representatives of the contending Zulu factions with as much military pomp as he could muster. The uSuthu leadership present, including Dinuzulu and five of his exiled father's brothers, heard Wood's uncompromising support of Wolseley's settlement with consternation while the six appointed chiefs present gloated over their discomfiture.

Nevertheless, the British government was even then preparing to make a drastic U-turn with regard to the settlement of Zululand. The Anglo-Zulu War was now widely regarded as having been ill-advised and unfortunate, Cetshwayo 'most villainously used',[7] and Wolseley's settlement fatally misconceived. On 6 September 1881 the Secretary of State for Colonies, the Earl of Kimberley, declared, 'Had we left Cetywayo on the throne, or annexed the country, we should in either case have taken up an intelligible course. As it is, we neither control the affairs of

The first uSuthu deputation that walked to Natal in May 1880 to plead for King
Cetshwayo's restoration, photographed with the king's full brother, Ndabuko kaMpande
(standing in the centre with his hands crossed over his staff). His half-brother, Shingana
kaMpande, is to his right. Ngcongcwana kaMagunde, Cetshwayo's uncle, stands to
Ndabuko's left. He would accompany Cetshwayo to London in August 1882.

(PIETERMARITZBURG ARCHIVES REPOSITORY, C. 868)

Zululand nor are we free from responsibilities for them.'[8] The upshot
was that, on 26 September 1881, Cetshwayo was informed that all the
lobbying on his behalf had borne fruit, and that he was permitted to
travel to London to plead his case in person. Obstructionist and unsym-
pathetic officialdom prevented his sailing until 12 July 1882. Meanwhile,
in April 1882 a second, large uSuthu deputation of 800 notables walked
to Pietermaritzburg to appeal once more for Cetshwayo's restoration. It
had no more success with Natal officials than had the previous effort, but
it did succeed in further alerting the Colonial Office to widespread Zulu
dissatisfaction with Wolseley's settlement.

Cetshwayo used the time awaiting his journey to England to prepare
his case, with Samuelson's assistance.[9] Since August 1880 the Governor

of the Cape had been Sir Hercules Robinson, who had replaced Sir Bartle Frere when the latter was recalled, his once illustrious career terminally blighted by the Zululand imbroglio he had initiated. In the clearest terms, Cetshwayo succinctly informed Robinson of his position:

> I was King of the Zulus, had my country invaded by the Queen's troops, tried to defend my country, but was beaten, taken captive and brought here by the Queen's orders. Here I intend to remain until the Queen restores me to Zululand.[10]

Accompanied by Mkhosana and several attendants, King Cetshwayo arrived at last in England on 5 August 1882 on board the steamer *Arab*. The Colonial Office believed it should treat even a defeated indigenous ruler with official decorum, and in London rented a pleasant house for him at 18 Melbury Road, overlooking Holland Park.[11] Instead of the savage they expected, the cheering London crowds discovered the notorious victor of Isandlwana to be a gracious, dignified monarch fashionably dressed in British style – although he retained his *isicoco*, that essential indication of his full adulthood. Indeed, Cetshwayo's exposure to British manners and customs at the Cape allowed him to mix easily in fashionable society where, crucially for his cause, he charmed many important public figures – and their wives. Among those who lionised him were Lord and Lady Edward Spencer Churchill, who presented him with an inscribed horn, silver and glass goblet and spoon.[12] The newspapers now referred to the 'unfortunate King of the Zulu nation' as a 'brave and honourable Native African Prince who was maligned and unfairly treated', one who had defended his country 'against the invading British army with admirable courage'.[13] Only once in public did Cetshwayo permit his diplomatic mask to slip when he declared 'in most emphatic tones, that there never ought to have been any war, and ascribed the fact there was war to "the little grey-headed man" [meaning Sir Bartle Frere]'.[14]

On 14 August Queen Victoria, two of whose grandsons Cetshwayo had received in Cape Town, granted him a brief, ten-minute audience at Osborne House on the Isle of Wight. Lazarus Xaba, who was present, remembered that Cetshwayo 'was trembling' when he entered the

King Cetshwayo, fashionably dressed in smart frock coat and gloves, photographed in August 1882 by Alex. Bassano of Old Bond Street, London, during his visit to England when he was lionised by smart society.

(PIETERMARITZBURG ARCHIVES REPOSITORY, C. 683)

Queen's presence, and that when she realised he was very nervous, she immediately began to make small talk to put him at his ease.[15] In her journal, the Queen wrote that through the interpreter she told the Zulu king: 'I recognized in him a great warrior, who had fought against us, but rejoiced we were now friends.'[16] The Queen presented Cetshwayo with an inscribed, magnificent three-handled loving cup, a leather-bound Bible with brass mounts and a richly engraved gold ring with a 'C' engraved on a shield-shaped plaque.[17] She also commissioned Carl Rudolph Sohn, Jnr, to paint a fine, sympathetic portrait of Cetshwayo wearing a lion-claw necklace and fur kaross.[18]

The meetings Cetshwayo held with the Queen's ministers went less successfully, and he was dashed to learn that he was not to be restored to the entire Zulu kingdom as it had existed before 1879. Still, he had no choice but to accept what was offered him, even if the boundaries of his reduced kingdom remained undefined for the moment. So it was with joyful expectations that he arrived back in Cape Town on 24 September 1882, imagining that he would immediately travel on to Zululand. It was not to be, and Cetshwayo's return was delayed for over three months while the Natal colonial administration strenuously canvassed the British government to ensure that, in the interests of Natal's safety, the conditions of Cetshwayo's restoration would be severely circumscribed. And while Cetshwayo waited to learn what these terms would be, he could not have been encouraged to learn that Sekhukhune, as he slept in a shelter outside his hut on 13 August 1881, had been stabbed to death by a band of assassins despatched by his brother and bitterly envious rival, Mampuru.[19] Would a similar fate await him when he returned to Zululand?

CHAPTER EIGHTEEN

THE KING'S DOG, NOW HIS BITTEREST ENEMY

It was with heavy foreboding and disappointment that on 11 December 1882 Cetshwayo assented to the terms of his restoration.[1] In this, the Second Partition of Zululand, his authority was confined to the central portion of the old kingdom, and he was deliberately hemmed in by two other segments of Zululand designed to frustrate any ambitions he might have to enlarge his power. Zibhebhu, the arch-collaborator and the only one of the former 13 chiefs favoured with an independent territory, was awarded an enlarged domain to the northeast that encompassed the uSuthu heartland and many of Cetshwayo's staunchest supporters.[2] To the south, as a further check to Cetshwayo's aspirations, the Reserve Territory was created out of two of the former 13 chiefdoms (one of which was John Dunn's) as a military buffer for Natal, and as a place of sanctuary for those Zulu who wished to avoid the king's reimposed rule. It was to be administered by officials recruited from Natal ruling indirectly through Zulu chiefs and paid for by a hut tax identical to that levied on Africans in Natal. Technically an independent territory, this meant that the southern third of the Zulu kingdom was actually placed under the rule of colonial Natal. To make things worse for Cetshwayo, not only was he wedged between Zibhebhu (the bane of the royal house) on the one side and antagonistic Natal officials on the other, but he had to contend with the animosity of

King Cetshwayo, shown seated at left, receives a delegation of his relatives on the Mthonjaneni heights a few days before his installation as king of central Zululand on 29 January 1883. Note the members of the British military escort looking on.

(GRAPHIC, 10 MARCH 1883)

nine of the 13 deposed 'kinglets' who found themselves in his territory, none more hostile than Hamu, his old rival and enemy.

Further, Cetshwayo was placed under the supervision of a Resident, Henry Francis Fynn, Jnr, an experienced Natal colonial administrator. The son of the hunter-trader of Shaka's day, Fynn was fluent in Zulu, and had enjoyed a close friendship with Cetshwayo since 1873. He was consequently sympathetic towards Cetshwayo's difficulties, but as the representative of the British government he was supposed to keep the peace between the restored king and his enemies, and his neutrality was not always appreciated. In any case, his ability to sway events would prove to be minimal since he had no armed forces at his disposal.

Cetshwayo agreed to rule with the advice of the British Resident, to keep the peace with Zibhebhu (no matter how reluctantly) and to respect the boundaries the British had assigned to his territory.

SOUTH AFRICAN REPUBLIC

QULUSI

NGENETSHENI

emGAZINI

kwaBangonomo

MPHANGISWENI

MDLALOSE

NDWANDWE

kwaMfemfe

ZIBHEBHU

Bende

Mahashini

Meniya

Nkunkwini

KHOZA

BUTHELEZI

oSuthu

kwaGqikazi

eku Vukeni

ekuShumayeleni

ekuBazeni

ekuXedini

uSUTHU

Ntshingwayo's

ZUNGU-MANDLAKAZI

MDLETSHE

MBATHA

HLABISA

SEBENI

QUNGEBE

CETSHWAYO

Somkhele's

MPHUKUNYONI

Ondini

MCHUNU

NTOMBELA

Somopho's

MTHETHWA

Sokwetshatha's

SITHOLE

CUBE

MPUNGOSE

THEMBU

emaNgweni

NTULI

RESERVE
TERRITORY

MAGWAZA

BIYELA

BIYELA

emaNGWENI

Mhlatbuze

Eshowe

Port Durnford

NATAL

NTULI

DUNN

INDIAN OCEAN

Thukela

N

0   10   20 km

0   10   20 miles

The Second Partition of Zululand, 11 December 1882

254

Critically, he also undertook not to revive the military system, to allow all men to marry when they chose, and to encourage them to seek work as migrant labourers in the burgeoning capitalist economy of white-ruled southern Africa. How he was to rule with the main pillar of royal authority and power in the old kingdom – the *ibutho* system – knocked away was a conundrum to be solved. Nor did it help that the royal wealth in cattle was largely dissipated and in the hands of others. As Lord Kimberley (who was highly critical of the terms of Cetshwayo's restoration insisted upon by Natal) understood well, a king with empty hands was no king at all. He foresaw that Cetshwayo would have no option but to seize back the royal herds, in itself an infallible recipe for conflict.[3]

Thus it was that Cetshwayo sailed back to Zululand, not with a soaring heart, but in deep trepidation, afflicted by all the almost insuperable challenges he would have to overcome in establishing his rule over his reduced kingdom. On 10 January 1883 he came ashore from the *Algerine* at Port Durnford in the Reserve Territory. There he was met by Sir Theophilus Shepstone, once his ally and 'father', and now a man he detested as his betrayer. Shepstone had been brought temporarily out of retirement to supervise Cetshwayo's restoration, and had with him a detachment of British cavalry to provide a guard of honour and to indicate clearly that the king was returning to Zululand under British protection and not by his own volition. On 17 January Cetshwayo reached the Mthonjaneni heights. As in 1873, at the time of his coronation, he waited there until the gathering assembly of some 5 000 prominent Zulu had agreed to an installation ceremony on 29 January in the emaKhosini valley below. His supporters were full of anxious misgivings about the terms of his restoration, and Zibhebhu deliberately snubbed him by paying his respects to Shepstone, but not to him. As Zibhebhu left, brushing rudely by the king, Cetshwayo's wives added fuel to the flames by reviling him in obscene language: 'Weu! There goes the cunt (*unhlunu*) of his mother Kundhlase. He will not die and be buried; the rocks will disappear and he will still be here.'[4]

Moreover, Zibhebhu was not content with insulting Cetshwayo. He also started a rumour that what the British had brought with them was not the

Hamu kaNzibe, a member of the Zulu royal house who ruled over the Ngenetsheni people in northwestern Zululand, coveted the Zulu throne and hoped to supplant King Cetshwayo. He defected to the British in the Anglo-Zulu War of 1879 and vigorously resisted Cetshwayo when they restored him as king of central Zululand.

(COURTESY IAN KNIGHT)

king but a waxwork doll (*isithombe*) dressed up in Cetshwayo's European clothes. It was not until the king stepped forward and addressed the assembly that his joyful followers saw it was indeed he. In his usual didactic style, Shepstone laid down the terms of Cetshwayo's restoration to the assembly, and the uSuthu leaders enraged him by complaining bitterly and at length about how unworkable they would prove. All were relieved when, the moment the unhappy ceremony was over, the British rode off, leaving Cetshwayo to manage as best he could.

Cetshwayo and his entourage moved at once to the Mahlabathini plain where in 1879 the British had burned all the *amakhanda* clustered there, including oNdini, his great place. His adherents immediately rendered him service by beginning to build a new, third oNdini a kilometre to the east of its predecessor. With about a thousand huts it was roughly half the size of its grand forerunner; nevertheless, all the traditions of the royal household were revived there. A European-style house of audience, such as had existed in the *isigodlo* at the second oNdini, was not constructed, however; instead Cetshwayo made do with a tent pitched in his new *isigodlo* from which he conducted his official business. Fynn took up station as British Resident on the hills overlooking the latest oNdini from the north. He saw from the first that his commission to keep the peace between Cetshwayo and his many enemies would prove nigh impossible since their animosities ran so deep.

Although Cetshwayo had undertaken not to revive the military system, he instantly made a half-hearted attempt to do so, reconstituting an *ibutho*. It was not a national formation such as *amabutho* had been until 1879, but only a military unit of the uSuthu faction, since its members were recruited solely from young men living in the king's truncated territory. In that sense it was no different from the regional *amabutho* that great chiefs like Zibhebhu were raising in their own territories, just as their predecessors had done before Shaka created a centralised Zulu kingdom. This fragmentation also meant that when hostilities broke out Cetshwayo was unable to muster many members of his old, pre-1879 *amabutho*, since large numbers had by then given their loyalty to other chiefs and were enrolled in their regional *amabutho*.

Cetshwayo had barely been installed when raiding and counter-raiding broke out between the king's supporters on one side and Hamu's Ngenetsheni and Zibhebhu's Mandlakazi on the other. Both sides set about utilising natural fastnesses in forests or on mountains as secure bases from which to maraud against their enemies, pillaging their goods, burning their *imizi* and fields, sweeping off their cattle and even driving them off their lands. It was Zibhebhu, though, who precipitated full-scale fighting in this, the Third Zulu Civil War of 1883–1884, by ruthlessly expelling the uSuthu from his new chiefdom. Fynn noted in his diary on 20 February 1883 that Cetshwayo, 'much excited', had declared:

> Zibebu was his Cetshwayo's dog and now land of the Zulus had been
> given to him and he was bragging over Cetshwayo, how could this
> continue, the people could not stand all this, nothing could have been

done more likely to cause bloodshed, than to deprive the Zulus and
their king of their own land and give it to the king's dog, now his bitterest enemy.[5]

The uSuthu leadership comprehended that the current skirmishing would
never force a conclusive result, and that only full-scale operations and a
pitched battle would drive out their enemies. In March, an uSuthu force
of about 5 000 men mustered on Ndabuko's orders in Mnyamana's territory in territorial units under their various chiefs, rather than in *amabutho*
as would previously have been the case. They advanced east, deep into
Mandlakazi territory, aiming at kwaBangonomo, Zibhebhu's principal
umuzi. Zibhebhu had only some 1 500 men and a handful of hardened white
mercenaries to resist them. He cannily fell back to the Msebe valley where
he prepared an ambush into which the uSuthu plunged completely unprepared on 30 March.

The battle of Msebe was characteristic of the major engagements of
the Third Zulu Civil War. The armies the two sides fielded were considerably smaller than those that had fought in the Anglo-Zulu War. At
first glance, though, tactics seem to have been remarkably little affected
by that disastrous war. Whenever they had the chance, the two sides
deployed in the traditional chest-and-horns attacking formation, and
izindibi accompanied the columns of advancing forces carrying their
baggage. What was different, though, was that ambush and surprise
were used to much better effect and that horses and guns (especially
among the Mandlakazi) played a much more prominent role alongside
spears and shields. The Mandlakazi in particular employed mounted
riflemen to take their enemy in the flank and to transform a retreat into
a stampede. At Msebe the consequence was a shattering victory for the
Mandlakazi, who lost only ten men to the thousand or more uSuthu
who died in the protracted pursuit over the open countryside, leaving
their bones to litter the plain for years to come. Most of the prominent
uSuthu managed to escape the slaughter, even though the Mandlakazi
picked off as many men of high lineage as they could with their rifles,
including Makhoba kaMasiphula, the uSuthu commander and son of
Mpande's chief councillor.

Msebe was more than a fatal setback for Cetshwayo's attempt to reassert his authority over his foes; it also doomed the Zululand settlement of 1882 to failure. Following the crushing uSuthu defeat, the Ngenetsheni and Mandlakazi ravaged the northern and central areas of Cetshwayo's territory and the uSuthu struck back inconclusively. To break the stalemate, Cetshwayo called on his allies to mount an all-out offensive against Zibhebhu from every point, and in late June began ritually preparing his main force of about 4 000 men mustering at oNdini for war. Threatened from all sides, Zibhebhu resolved to employ his fabled combination of speed, surprise and discipline to steal a march on Cetshwayo. As Herbert J Nunn, Hamu's resident white trader and adviser, put it: 'Zibebu is the Napoleon of North Zululand, and his army have named him Matshetshe or "one quick in his movements".'[6]

On 20 July Zibhebhu mustered about 3 000 Mandlakazi and Ngenetsheni at his ekuVukeni *umuzi*, supported by ten or twelve mounted white mercenaries. The uSuthu mistakenly believed this concentration was aimed at attacking Mnyamana, who was directly to its west and who was mustering his forces at his ekuShumayeleni *umuzi*. But Zibhebhu's objective was oNdini, and he brilliantly took the uSuthu completely by surprise with a night march. At sunrise on 21 July his lightning thrust caught the king's army completely unprepared and easily scattered it when it tried to form up. As two survivors of the ensuing deadly rout put it:

> Our men rushed out to meet the enemy, not as an *impi*, in fighting array, but just as working people hurrying from their work and all abroad, and there was not time even to marshal those who were there. So the enemy with their horses soon scattered them, and reached the kraal [oNdini], and burned it, killing Chiefs and old men, women and children, the Royal female attendants, and numbers of the working women, killing the King's own wives and children.[7]

Certainly, when the uSuthu fighting men fled, they left Cetshwayo's family and great chiefs who had been in attendance on the king quite defenceless. Grosvenor Darke, a hunter-trader who took part in the battle as

Zibhebhu kaMaphitha, who ruled over the Mandlakazi people in northeastern Zululand, was King Cetshwayo's greatest foe in the civil war of 1883. He is shown withdrawing in triumph after sacking oNdini on 21 July and scattering the king's army. Two of his hardened white military advisers are portrayed riding behind him.

(COURTESY IAN KNIGHT)

one of Zibhebhu's white mercenaries, later contemptuously said of the 59 or more eminent chiefs they slaughtered: 'Being all fat and big-bellied, they had no chance of escape; and one of them was actually run to earth and stabbed to death by my little mat-bearers.'[8] Among them were Ntshingwayo, the victor of Isandlwana, and Godide, who had commanded at the battle of Nyezane. Indeed, the list of distinguished men who were cut down that day reads like the roll call of the elite of the old Zulu kingdom. Jeff Guy is surely right to have concluded that this slaughter – rather than the Anglo-Zulu War – marked the true end of the old Zulu order.[9]

As for the king's family members and *umndlunkulu*, a number of them found sanctuary in Fynn's camp on the hills to the north. Cetshwayo's teenaged son, Dinuzulu, manged to make good his escape mounted on a horse, as did his uncle, Dabulamanzi, who had commanded at Rorke's Drift. Others were not so fortunate. In their despairing flight three of

Mpande's widows were cut down, as well as three of Cetshwayo's wives. His infant son, Nyoniyentaba, was stabbed to death in the arms of his mother, Majiya.

And what of the king? During the days after the battle, with the burned-out ruins of the last oNdini still smouldering, Fynn went in search of him. In a pool at the junction of the Ntukwini and Mbilane streams he found the body of a woman of Cetshwayo's household who had accompanied him in flight. Nearby, a cluster of small trees was pointed out to him as the place where Cetshwayo, whose horse had been unable to bear his considerable weight, had taken shelter alone while his companions hurried on their way to draw away the pursuers who were closing in. Nevertheless, as Fynn learned, a number of Mandlakazi soon flushed Cetshwayo out. Mkhosana (who had been with his king through all his vicissitudes) heard them call upon Cetshwayo to stand up, before throwing four spears at him. Two of them pierced the king in his right thigh. In shock and pain but deeply angered, Cetshwayo recognised one of his assailants and indignantly cried out, 'do you stab me, R[H]alijana, son of Somfula, I your king?'[10] Cetshwayo's words brought home to his attackers how terrible a thing it was to stab a king, and they lost all their bravado. They meekly approached him with all the courtesies due to a monarch and feebly tried to excuse themselves by saying that they had mistaken him for his brother, Ziwedu. After tending his two wounds as best they could, they let Cetshwayo go on his way. Cetshwayo next took shelter in a cave near the left bank of the White Mfolozi with a small number of his attendants who found him there. A pitiful fugitive once again, as he had been in the dark days after the battle of Ulundi, he lurked in his cave until 1 August when he mounted a horse sent him by his brother Shingana and made his way south into the Reserve Territory.

Deep in the Nkandla forest, between the Mhlathuze and Thukela rivers, Cetshwayo found sanctuary in the traditional stronghold of the Cube people, who were royalist supporters. Secure for the moment from Mandlakazi pursuit, Cetshwayo hunkered down in the eNhlweni *umuzi* that Luhungu of the Shezi people built for him near caves where, if necessary, he could take final refuge. Members of his household and numbers of his displaced supporters drifted south to join him there. From his hideout Cetshwayo waited on events, ineffectually attempting to rally resistance against his enemies in central Zululand, and unsuccessfully negotiating with the officials of the Reserve to act against Zibhebhu, who was now entirely in the ascendant the length and breadth of the King's former territory. In the following months Zibhebhu relentlessly raided far and wide, driving off uSuthu cattle while their owners fled before him, reduced to homeless refugees sheltering in caves and forests. The extent and degree of devastation was coming to rival, if not exceed, that suffered by the Zulu people in the Anglo-Zulu War. And, as an ominous sign of things to come, Boers from the ZAR under Cornelius van Rooyen, covetous of the rich pasturelands of northwestern Zululand, took advantage of the turmoil to declare that the land belonged to them. They began building houses and drove away the Zulu inhabitants – another wave of hapless refugees.

Melmoth Osborn, the Resident Commissioner since April 1883 of the Reserve Territory where Cetshwayo had taken refuge, was an experienced if habitually dilatory Natal official with a considerable grasp of the Zulu tongue and customs. As a confirmed disciple of his mentor, Shepstone, he was committed to limiting the aspirations of the Zulu royal house. He was consequently concerned that Cetshwayo was using his base in the Nkandla forest to regroup his followers and gather support in the Reserve. In order to deter Cetshwayo and keep the peace in the Reserve, Osborn requested military support from the British troops of the Natal garrison quartered at Fort Napier in Pietermaritzburg. The 'Etshowe Column', as it was called, duly moved forward and by the end of September was established at Fort Curtis at Eshowe. Zibhebhu, meanwhile, was keeping his eye on developments. Knowing that the British tacitly supported him, he was emboldened in late September to advance in force as far south as Babanango Mountain on the very border of the Reserve Territory. There Zibhebhu halted, uncertain whether he quite dared invade the Reserve finally to settle accounts with Cetshwayo.

Cetshwayo, meanwhile, was losing his nerve, while his demoralised supporters took refuge in their fastnesses. Believing his position to be hopeless, he sought the protection of Melmoth Osborn at Eshowe, and his messenger, Zeize, relayed his pitiable request:

> Ceywayo hears that Usibebu gives out that he is coming as far as Babanango in pursuit of his prey which escaped him with two wounds, and is now hiding in Nkahndhla ... Cetywayo says he wants to come to you, but he cannot walk all the way, he therefore, asks you to give him a horse to ride, also a pair of trousers, a shirt, and a hat.[11]

Cetshwayo's box of European clothes had been looted by the Mandlakazi at the battle of oNdini, along with all his valuables,[12] and he was determined not to appear among the British humiliatingly dressed as a 'native'. Fynn, considerate to the last, escorted the fallen king into Eshowe on 15 October. Zibhebhu, when he learned that Cetshwayo was now under British protection, withdrew north and resumed his protracted operations against the uSuthu in the territory Cetshwayo could no longer pretend was his to rule. The Second Partition of Zululand was as dead in the water as was the First, only ten months after Cetshwayo had acceded to it in London.

Osborn granted Cetshwayo and his attenuated household a small house near the site of Mpande's kwaGqikazi *ikhanda*, close by Eshowe. His royal brothers and supporters visited him there where all could deplore the ruin of his every hope and the pitiful plight of his adherents at Zibhebhu's hands. Then, at about 2 o'clock on the afternoon of 8 February 1884, suspiciously soon after he had eaten, Cetshwayo was overwhelmed by convulsions, collapsed and died. His family members would not permit a post-mortem, and the military doctor stationed at Fort Curtis could only surmise that Cetshwayo had died of a heart attack. However, the king's household were convinced that he had been killed by poison poured into his beer (as Masiphula had been poisoned on Cetshwayo's orders in 1873) or mixed in with his snuff.

Without an autopsy, the true nature of Cetshwayo's death must remain uncertain, but poison does seem to have been the likely cause, particularly since at much the same time Mnyamana only just survived a determined attempt to kill him by the same means. The question then was: in whose interest was it to eliminate the fugitive king, along with the man who had been his chief councillor and who remained the person most capable of rallying uSuthu resistance in central Zululand? Cetshwayo wives were initially in no doubt. About a dozen of them invaded Osborn's house in Eshowe while he made his undignified escape out of a side door, crying out: 'Give us our husband. He was killed by you with medicine from Misjana.'[13] 'Misjana' was John Shepstone, who had preceded Osborn as the Resident of the Reserve Territory, and the women believed that the Natal officials were all involved in a plot to do away with the inconvenient Cetshwayo after luring him to Eshowe from his refuge in Nkandla. However, the men of Cetshwayo's family (and his son Dinuzulu in particular), along with the rank and file of the uSuthu, all pointed their fingers at another, far more likely culprit: Zibhebhu. And so the deep animosity between the uSuthu and Mandlakazi took another, even more bitter twist.

The dead king's attendants followed royal custom and placed his body in a sitting position tied to the central post of closed hut, wrapped (except for the head) in a fresh bull's hide and layers of blankets. But with most courtiers and the bulk of his former household absent, it was not possible to perform all the funerary rituals that had attended his father, Mpande. Nor, despite his followers' wishes, was it possible to bury Cetshwayo in the emaKhosini valley alongside his ancestors. Osborn refused permission for fear of exciting uSuthu demonstrations, and there was the real danger that the Mandlakazi would attack the burial party. Instead, the king's by now desiccated body was placed in a huge coffin, still in its sitting position, and taken by ox-wagon deep into the Nkandla forest. On 10 April 1884 it was interred near Luhungu of the Shezi's *umuzi* in a valley below the rolling slopes of Bhobhe ridge. Cattle were slaughtered to bring the spirit of the king home, and the assembled mourners, all dressed in their ceremonial finery, chanted the great royal *ihubo* and pointed their sticks towards the emaKhosini where the royal *amadlozi* dwelt. Finally, so that it would not be profaned by further use, the wagon that had transported the king was broken into pieces and these were laid on the grave.[14]

And there, in this remote, nigh inaccessible place, surrounded by a grove of sheltering trees, and watched over to this day by Luhungu's descendants,

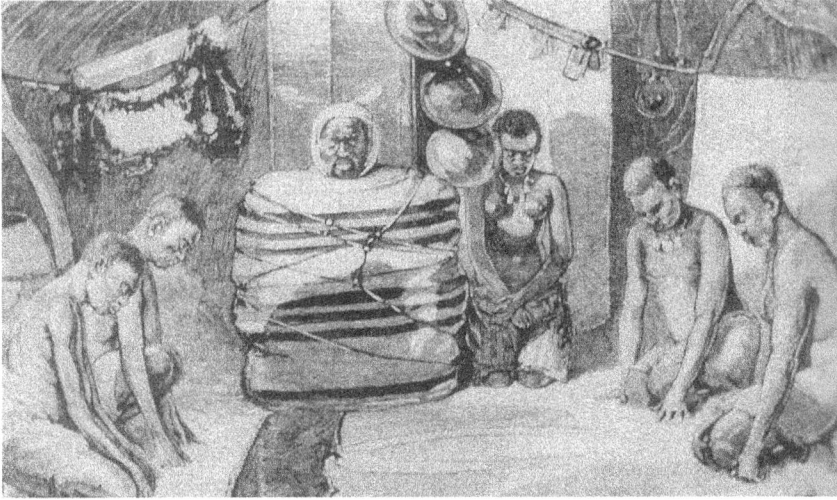

A drawing of King Cetshwayo's corpse in February 1884, wrapped and in traditional
sitting position, being watched over by his mourning attendants.

(COURTESY IAN KNIGHT)

Cetshwayo's bones still lie buried. In 1980 the KwaZulu Monuments
Council placed a low tier of three simple black granite slabs over the grave,
with an inscription. Eight diminutive obelisks stand around it, and a chain
strung between them cautions the visitor to maintain a respectful distance.

At the time of Cetshwayo's visit to England in 1882, a strange legend
began to circulate in Zululand. It was said that the white people made him
go into a pond with wild beasts in it. The beasts surrounded and licked and
licked him, but then fell back because he had overcome them. Other kings
who had been defeated were also taken there, but they were killed by the
breath of those beasts because their chiefly powers (*ubukosi*) were weak.
The point of the story was that it proved 'that Cetshwayo had the strongest powers of all the black kings of the earth'.[15] Alas for the king and for his
people, the tale was but a tale, and Cetshwayo proved no more able than
other African kings to withstand the always disruptive and all too often
destructive forces of European imperialism.

KING DINUZULU
kaCETSHWAYO

❀ ❀ ❀

❀

CHAPTER NINETEEN

THE PRICE OF BLOOD
IS ALWAYS A HARD PRICE

King Cetshwayo was the last king of a truly independent Zululand, and with him died any hope of restoring the kingdom as founded by Shaka. The divisions ran too deep and the vested interests of those opposed to the aspirations of the royal house were too strongly entrenched. In such inimical circumstances the status of Dinuzulu, Cetshwayo's son and heir, was at best perplexing. He would spend his days vainly but with great resilience endeavouring to secure his royal birthright in the teeth of his enemies, both black and white. Yet, despite the tribulations and disappointments that dogged Dinuzulu's steps, what Pixley Seme (the renowned lawyer and African political activist and the driving force behind the formation of the South African Native National Congress in 1912) best remembered of him was that

> though he was caught up in the great bloodshed of the men when he was still young, [he] did not lose his good heart, his heart which stood above all the great misfortunes which ... overtook him. He had a heart which quickly cast away and forgot unhappy things. He greatly liked to create happiness.[1]

And as Magema Fuze, the Zulu historian, put it, Dinuzulu was moreover 'clever with the qualities of the young of the Lion',[2] inclined to insist upon the respect due to his royal rank, of fiery and imperious temper, indisputably brave in battle, a competent horseman and a good shot with his rifle. In his physical appearance, he was unmistakably of the House of Senzangakhona, with large hips and heavy thighs. Plump as a young man, with a flabby upper body, in his mature years he would grow decidedly portly. Later in life he cultivated a fine beard and mustachios that added authority to his serene and determined countenance.

Dinuzulu did not stand at the graveside of his father, since he had not yet come of age, but his uncles Ndabuko, Ziwedu, Shingana and Dabulamanzi were all present, along with Mnyamana. All these uSuthu leaders had known that a disputed succession would conclusively fracture the royalist party, so it was essential to rally around Dinuzulu and proclaim him Cetshwayo's successor.[3] So only three days after the king's death the royal brothers let it be known that they had been present to hear their king's dying words, and claimed they were as follows: 'I, Cetywayo, leave the country to my son Dinuzulu for him to have when I am no longer here … The questions about my country are not ended yet. They exist still, and will remain until the Government settles them.'[4]

Ndabuko and Mnyamana, as Dinuzulu's official guardians until he came of age, took command of the uSuthu party. It was a dreadful responsibility. Fighting escalated in the Reserve Territory where the uSuthu, concentrated in the Nkandla forest under Dabulamanzi's command, resisted Osborn's efforts to collect the hut tax. Months of skirmishing and cattle raiding followed, with troops of the British garrison assisting Osborn's local levies and erecting a string of forts to contain the uSuthu. This strategy worked, and by 9 September 1884 the uSuthu in the Reserve had given up hostilities. However, it was not in the Reserve but in central Zululand where decisive events were occurring.

Despite the abject failure of the settlement of 1882 and the anarchy into which most of the former Zulu kingdom was falling, Gladstone's Liberal government in Britain brushed aside Cetshwayo's dying plea to shoulder its obligation to solve the Zulu question. Instead, it resolutely declined to take any responsibility for what was happening in the Zulu country north of the Reserve. Any possibility of extending its protection – let alone sovereignty – over this unfortunate territory was rejected out of hand.

Yet the situation in central Zululand was dire. Zibhebhu and his ally, Hamu, refused to recognise Dinuzulu as their king and militarily dominated all of the Zulu country north of the Mhlathuze. Dinuzulu's supporters there were threatened with starvation and utter ruin. A trader, Alfred Moore, reported on 9 April 1884: 'I saw [Mnyamana's followers] in the rocks and caves ... dying in dozens from deprivation and dysentery ... and if nothing is done to relieve them before the winter sets in there will be scarcely a soul alive, for all their crops were then cut and trodden by Usibepu's [sic] forces.'[5]

Brought to desperation by their plight, the uSuthu leadership came to a reluctant but fateful decision that would bring untold change and hardship to their fellow Zulu. With Mnyamana voicing the gravest misgivings, they undertook to strike a deal with the land-hungry Boers bordering northwestern Zululand. In return for Boer military assistance and their recognition of Dinuzulu as the Zulu king, they would cede them great swathes of the old Disputed Territory, and more. The pact rapidly took shape. At the beginning of April 1884 his guardians spirited Dinuzulu away from the Nkandla forest, where he had been sheltering, to a Boer farm just within the ZAR. Meanwhile, with the tacit approval of the ZAR government, leading Boer farmers along the borders of Zululand had established the Committee of Dinuzulu's Volunteers and were forming a commando of white volunteers. On 1 May this commando escorted Dinuzulu into northwestern Zululand to their laager of tented wagons at Nyathi Hill, near Hlobane Mountain.

There the Boers intended to crown Dinuzulu, just as they had his grandfather, Mpande, in 1840, and as Shepstone had crowned Cetshwayo in 1873. Yet Cetshwayo had been installed beforehand as king with traditional rituals, and again at his restoration by Shepstone in 1883. Likewise, on 20 May Ndabuko, Ziwedu and Shingana invested Dinuzulu as their king according to Zulu practice preliminary to the Boer ceremony.

The following day, 21 May, Dinuzulu, dressed in Boer-style riding clothes and wide-brimmed hat, and accompanied by four members of the Boer Committee, mounted a platform laid across two wagons on which an upended box served as a throne. The 350 men of the Boer commando were ranged in two semicircular lines behind, while facing Dinuzulu some 9 000

The leading Boers of the Committee of Dinuzulu's Volunteers are depicted proclaiming
Dinuzulu King of the Zulu on 21 May 1884 to the assembled uSuthu.
(PIETERMARITZBURG ARCHIVES REPOSITORY, C. 4758)

Zulu were massed in a great horseshoe. What followed next amounted to a
parody of a European coronation ceremony. Dinuzulu first signed the proclamation written in Dutch confirming him as 'lawful heir and successor of
the late Ketewayo ... [and] as King of the Zulu nation and of Zululand'.[6]
Then he kneeled and the four Boers placed their hands on his head and
swore to protect him from his enemies. One of them, Andreas Laas, then
anointed his head with castor oil in lieu of the consecrated oil (chrism)
applied by a bishop in one of the most sacred moments of the Christian
coronation rite. The Zulu throng – unaware that they were witnessing an
extraordinary burlesque – roared out the royal acclamations. Two days
later the king – for so he now was in the eyes of his Zulu supporters and
Boer allies, even if he was not recognised as such by his Zulu enemies and
the British – put his mark to a document by which the Boers bound themselves to give him military assistance in return for land sufficiently large to
establish 'an independent self-government'.[7]

Alarmed by the alliance being built up against him, Zibhebhu fell back
towards kwaBangonomo where he concentrated about 3 000 Mandlakazi

272

and a few white adventurers. It was his turn to feel betrayed by the British, and through John Eckersley, the mercenary who was also secretary both to him and Hamu (and whose Zulu name was Dambuza, or 'one who walks carefully'), he sent a reproachful message to Osborn in the Reserve:

> The chief begs me to say that he blames you very much for not helping him in his trouble. He has fought against his own nation for the British Government, and now that the Boers are coming you will not help him ... I do not know what I have done wrong to you or the British Government.[8]

By the beginning of June the uSuthu had gathered an army of more than 6 000 men near ekuShumayeleni and were supported by 100 or so Boers under Commandant Lukas Meyer and about 20 mounted volunteers from the German mission community at Luneburg commanded by Dinuzulu's secretary and political adviser, Adolf Schiel. Outnumbered, Zibhebhu retreated from kwaBangonomo with all his women, children and cattle to make his stand on the slopes of Tshaneni Mountain, just south of the Mkhuze River where it flows through a gorge in the Lubombo Mountains.

With their rout some 14 months before at the battle of Msebe in mind, on 5 June 1884 the uSuthu gingerly approached the redoubtable Mandlakazi in classic chest-and-horns formation. The 16-year-old Dinuzulu, in this his first battle, courageously commanded the uSuthu chest. The Mandlakazi predictably came on with great determination and the uSuthu began to waver. But Meyer's men stationed behind them threatened to shoot them if they retreated, and fired over their heads from their saddles at the Mandlakazi. Their telling volleys forced Zibhebhu's men back, and when the Mandlakazi forces attempted to break away, the mounted men outflanked them and the uSuthu succeeded in pinning them against the banks of the river. A great slaughter ensued, not only of Mandlakazi fighting men – including six of Zibhebhu's brothers – but also of hundreds of their non-combatants, who had been encamped north across the Mkhuze. Zibhebhu and a number of his men managed to escape up the Lubombo Mountains, but he left behind between 40 000 and 60 000 cattle, which the uSuthu leaders and Boers divided between them.

Buoyed up by their great victory at Tshaneni, the uSuthu and the Boers ravaged Mandlakazi territory, and Zibhebhu could do no more. On 7 September 1884 Osborn gave him sanctuary in the Reserve, along with about 5 000 to 6 000 Mandlakazi men, women and children (about a third of his adherents) and settled them far to the south, on the banks of the Thukela. For the time being, Zibhebhu had been eliminated as a player in Zululand. Hamu, his staunch ally and the bane of Cetshwayo's house, was likewise knocked out when the Boers who were blockading him in his caves forced him to surrender.

Yet victory for Dinuzulu and the uSuthu over their mortal adversaries came at an excessive cost. Following the battle of Tshaneni, hundreds of white adventurers and land-grabbers flocked in, all demanding farms, while the Boer leaders raised their sights and set them on a republic of their own stretching across Zululand to the Indian Ocean. The uSuthu tried to resist these demands, but they dared not attempt to stand up to the Boer militarily, and caved in. On 16 August 1884 at the Boer encampment at Hlobane, Dinuzulu issued a proclamation granting the Boers 1 355 000 morgen for the establishment of a Boer republic. Furthermore, Dinuzulu conceded that the remaining portion of Zululand north of the Reserve, and all the people living there, would be subject to this new Boer state.[9] As Sir Henry Bulwer, the Governor of Natal, later reflected on this, the Third Partition of Zululand: 'The price of blood is always a hard price; and to encompass the destruction of Usibebu the Usutu leaders bartered away the best part of the inheritance of the Zulu people'.[10]

As soon as Dinuzulu had made his proclamation, Lukas Meyer, who was swiftly elected the president of the fledgling New Republic, formally proclaimed its protectorate over the Zulu people north of the Reserve.[11] The Boers then immediately fanned out to claim the farms they had allocated themselves, even before the boundaries of their republic were fixed or recognised.[12] The uSuthu, suddenly finding themselves labour tenants on Boer farms, or unceremoniously driven off them, again took refuge in their strongholds and began to resist.[13] Their new masters retaliated savagely, driving off their livestock and burning their crops, so that famine once again stalked the land. This was altogether a more damaging development for the future of Zululand than Wolseley's settlement had ever been. Then

the kingdom founded by Shaka had been partitioned and centralised political power abolished, but at least the land itself had stayed with the chiefs
and their people. Now, under Dinuzulu and thanks to his fatal deal with the
Boers, even that was forfeit across great swathes of Zululand.

And what of the 'King of the Zulu nation' the Boers had crowned at
Nyathi Hill? As far as the Boers were concerned, by proclaiming a protectorate over Dinuzulu on 16 August 1884 they had revoked his status as an
independent ruler. The British government saw it the same way, deciding that he was 'no more than a nominal ruler in the hands of the Boer
invaders'.[14] Indeed, Dinuzulu was unable to prevent the Boers from occu-
pying the very graves of his ancestors in the emaKhosini valley and driving
their guardians away. He could not even stop them from burning down the
fourth oNdini, which he had ordered to be constructed near Nhlazatshe
Mountain, since its site fell within the boundaries of the New Republic.

With Zululand north of the Mhlathuze on the brink of a major disaster,
it might be supposed that the British government would have taken some
responsibility for its series of failed Zulu settlements, and intervened. But
under the Liberals this was a time of imperial retrenchment, and the abandoned chimera of confederation no longer spurred them on to take further
action in Zululand. Nevertheless, wider imperial geopolitical concerns –
not sympathy with the plight of the Zulu people – at last drove the British
to take action.

Newly unified Germany was sniffing about for African footholds to
secure its imperial 'place in the sun'. Its growing interest in the coast
of Zululand led to British fears of a German territorial link-up with
the landlocked and anti-British ZAR by way of the New Republic. So,
very reluctantly, Gladstone's administration asserted British claims to
St Lucia Bay on 21 December 1884. Next, successive proclamations by
the New Republic in October 1885 and April 1886, greedily claiming
even more of Zululand and provocatively pushing its boundaries right to
the coast, led to sharp Liberal protests. Yet it took the coming to power
in August 1886 of Lord Salisbury's Conservative administration before
Britain at last decided to take direct action over Zululand to safeguard its
imperial interests in southeast Africa. In return for British recognition
of the New Republic on 22 October 1886, the Boers agreed to limit their

The British Colony of Zululand, 1887

territorial pretensions to the northwestern third of Zululand and to drop all claims of a protectorate over Dinuzulu in what remained of the Zulu country outside its control. They also ceded control over a block of territory in central Zululand, known as Proviso B, but were allowed to retain ownership of the farms they had already laid out there, which encompassed the emaKhosini valley and the graves of the Zulu kings. A boundary commission completed the task of defining the New Republic's boundaries by 25 January 1887.

But what was to become of the rump of Zululand between the Reserve and the New Republic? As early as January 1886 Mnyamana and the other uSuthu leaders had begun to petition Osborn to request the British government to take them under its protection. Meanwhile, to his deep distress, Dinuzulu was powerless to help his people in the territory occupied by the Boers. He felt himself vulnerable not only to the prospect of future Boer expansionism but also to increasing agitation by Natal settlers that all of Zululand outside of Boer control should be thrown open to white settlement. And to add to Dinuzulu's fears, Zibhebhu, restlessly chafing in his location in the Reserve, was vociferously demanding to be allowed back to his old lands in northeastern Zululand.

Alarmed by this turbulent and deteriorating situation, Osborn took the initiative and on his own authority notified the uSuthu leadership on 5 February 1887 that British protection had been extended over what he termed Eastern Zululand. Dinuzulu and his advisers acquiesced with some relief. The British government, faced with the accomplished fact, felt it had no choice but to agree to the annexation of Eastern Zululand, Proviso B and the Reserve Territory as the Colony of Zululand, officially proclaimed on 19 May 1887. White traders and missionaries were permitted to live and operate in the new colony, but the land was reserved for sole Zulu occupation, and the Natal land-grabbers were thwarted, at least for the time being.

As an economy measure by the Colonial Office, the Governor of Natal, Sir Arthur Havelock, was made Governor of Zululand as well. He administered the new colony through Melmoth Osborn, whom he appointed Resident Commissioner, with his seat at Eshowe. White Resident Magistrates, all of them recruited from Natal and imbued with the Shepstonian orthodoxy that the Zulu royal house represented the greatest threat to the peaceful establishment of British rule, were put in charge of the six districts into which the colony was divided. These officials were expected to adhere to the Shepstonian principles of indirect rule and embodied a superior administrative layer over the traditional authorities whose powers were curtailed. To enforce their authority, they relied on a small paramilitary force recruited from among the Zulu and styled the Zululand Police (or Nongqai). This skeleton administrative machinery was not supposed to cost the British taxpayer a penny, and was to be financed by a hut tax, as was the practice in Natal. The British garrison stationed at Fort Napier in Natal was available to reinforce the Zululand Police in ensuring order, and from the outset maintained small garrisons in the new colony.

What of Dinuzulu's status under this colonial dispensation? Was he still the Zulu king? Settler opinion was in no doubt, and as the Durban newspaper the *Natal Mercury* put it: 'The Queen's Government is free to administer Zululand just as it likes. It has not to consider the shadowy but troublesome claims of kingship on the part of Dinuzulu or anybody else.'[14] From the perspective of the uSuthu leadership that had accepted British annexation for fear of worse, the new administration was alien. There was much resentment at loss of status and power under the indirect rule of the Zululand administration, summed up in the message they sent to the authorities: 'Dinuzulu says, he does not understand this placing of white Magistrates all over the country … that they have not been used to Magistrate's offices and do not know how to get on with them, and that they are afraid they will not be able to do so.'[16]

Havelock, an experienced administrator of proven humanity and sense, had anticipated such resistance by the Zulu elite, and had instructed his officials to take a conciliatory approach during the delicate transition to British rule. Their forbearance was largely rewarded, and in many parts of the colony the chiefs fell in with the new order, accepting the monetary stipends offered them as functionaries of the new order. Even Mnyamana and Dinuzulu's uncle, Ziwedu, decided that this was the best course to adopt, since the British had clearly swept the old Zulu monarchy away.

However, Dinuzulu did not see it like that at all, and was not prepared to abandon his royal status. Sympathetic handling might have placated him, but unfortunately RH (Dick) Addison, the Resident Magistrate of Ndwandwe District where Dinuzulu, Ndabuko and most of the uSuthu leadership had their *imizi*, proved himself incapable of being sufficiently conciliatory. He responded to Dinuzulu's defiance of his authority by slapping cattle fines on him and his supporters, and this only hardened the uSuthu resolve to resist the new regime. Seeing that his officials were proving unable to deal successfully with Dinuzulu's recalcitrance, Havelock summoned the uSuthu leaders to Eshowe. There, on 14 November 1887, he imposed a heavy cattle fine on them and in unequivocal and graphic terms emphatically reminded them that the Zulu monarchy was no more:

> Dinuzulu must know, and all the Zulus must know, that the rule of the House of Chaka is a thing of the past. It is dead. It is like water spilt on the ground. The Queen now rules in Zululand and no one else. The Queen who conquered Cetywayo has now taken the government of the country into her own hands.[17]

Dinuzulu was not persuaded. Armed supporters flocked to oSuthu, his *umuzi* at the upper reaches of the sluggish Vuna River, and he persisted in provocatively testing and flouting Addison's authority. In Eshowe, Osborn feared that Dinuzulu's successful defiance would encourage resistance elsewhere in Zululand. British troops were consequently brought up to the Ndwandwe District in support of the Zululand Police, but Havelock was reluctant to use them in suppressing the uSuthu since to do so would be a humiliating admission that his civil administration had failed. Instead, under the influence of his Zululand officials, all of them disciples of Shepstone, Havelock embraced a disastrous expedient. He turned to Zibhebhu, the scourge of the uSuthu and loyal ally of the British until they had abandoned him and the Mandlakazi at the time of the battle of Tshaneni. They were to be sent back from their location in southern Zululand to their old territory in northeastern Zululand, which was now situated in the Ndwandwe District. The officials reckoned that Zibhebhu's hostile presence so close to the uSuthu would bring them to their senses. Predictably (although this seems not have occurred to the Zululand officials), Zibhebhu's arrival in the Ndwandwe District in November 1887,

openly thirsting for revenge against the uSuthu, only inflamed the situation. Addison made the situation worse by blatantly taking the side of
the Mandlakazi in every dispute, and by demarcating an unjustifiably large
location for them from which (with his connivance) they forcibly expelled
all the uSuthu dwelling within its borders.

The frustrated and passionate Dinuzulu became convinced that the
uSuthu would never receive any redress from the partisan Zululand administration except through the resort to arms. On 15 February 1888 he took
the fateful step of crossing into the New Republic to seek Boer military
assistance — an action that was treasonable for a British subject such as he
now was. Dinuzulu was unsuccessful in this quest, but while in the New
Republic he did rally to his cause the ardently royalist uSuthu (particularly
the Qulusi) who had been cut off there from the rest of Zululand. These
adherents began to muster on the looming, flat-topped Ceza Mountain, a
traditional fastness that was bisected by the boundary line.

Having raised this support, Dinuzulu returned home, and during March
oSuthu became a sanctuary for those defying British authority and that
of their collaborator, Zibhebhu. Between 5 April and 13 May Dinuzulu
was once more in the New Republic, this time to rally support among
Zulu living north of the Phongolo River. While he was absent, on 26 April
Addison attempted with the backing of the Zululand Police to arrest those
uSuthu leaders sheltering at oSuthu. To his intense humiliation, Addison
was thwarted in his mission by the appearance of a thousand uSuthu in
battle order under the command of Ndabuko. With Addison's authority
openly defied, the situation in Ndwandwe lurched towards open conflict,
and at kwaBangonomo Zibhebhu began to mobilise his forces in support
of the Zululand Police and British troops. Sensing that they had crossed
the Rubicon and assessing the odds against them, in early May the uSuthu
leadership decided on a strategic withdrawal to Ceza Mountain with all the
forces they could muster.

With that, the uSuthu Rebellion (as it came to be known) had begun.
From their base on Ceza, the uSuthu proceeded to raid far and wide for
supplies and struck against those they considered guilty of collaborating
with the British. Victims of these raids included Mnyamana and Ziwedu,
and they and their people took refuge at the British military camp at

Nkonjeni in western Zululand and at Addison's magisterial post at Ivuna. Faced with open rebellion, the Zululand administration attempted to regain control of the situation. On 2 June, with a force of Zululand Police and African levies drawn from Mnyamana's Buthelezi, and supported by British troops, Addison advanced on Ceza with the objective of arresting Dinuzulu and the other uSuthu leaders. To protect his magistracy and little fort at Ivuna during his absence, he ordered up Zibhebhu and his Mandlakazi to encamp on Ndunu hill close by.

There were approximately 2 000 uSuthu bivouacked on Ceza under Dinuzulu, Ndabuko and Hemulana kaMbangezeli. When Addison and the Zululand Police moved up the mountain to execute his warrants of arrest, Dinuzulu (now an intrepid young warrior of 20) himself led the uSuthu in traditional battle formation to confront and outflank them. In the ensuing running skirmish, the uSuthu succeeded in forcing the Zululand Police down the mountain, and drove them, Mnyamana's auxiliaries who got caught up in the retreat, and the British troops who had moved up in support to cover their withdrawal, back the whole way across the Black Mfolozi River, over 15 kilometres away. Casualties were minor, but though the blow struck against the British administration was a resounding one, it should be noted that Dinuzulu's success in this encounter was the last ever achieved by the Zulu over regular British troops.

Their comprehensive victory in the Ceza skirmish undoubtedly greatly emboldened the uSuthu in their armed resistance. The jubilant uSuthu forces on Ceza swelled to about 3 000, and free-booting Boers joined them in raiding Mnyamana's and Ziwedu's cattle. Dinuzulu's uncle, Shingana, was encouraged to concentrate on Hlophekhulu Mountain in central Zululand with about another thousand uSuthu, and from this base raided 'loyal' Zulu in the vicinity. In response, more British troops were despatched to Zululand (by early June they amounted to 22 officers, 515 infantry and 455 mounted men), and Osborn busied himself raising several thousand African auxiliaries in southern Zululand.

From his camp at Ndunu Hill close by Addison's magistracy at Ivuna, Zibhebhu was occupied in plundering uSuthu *imizi* in the vicinity. But Dinuzulu was preparing to take a leaf out of the book of the 'Zulu Napoleon'. With Zibhebhu's surprise night march on oNdini in 1883 in mind, he decided to strike an identical blow against him. After dusk on 22 June, about 4 000 uSuthu under Dinuzulu's personal command set off from Ceza for Ndunu hill. Just before daybreak on 23 June, the uSuthu in traditional formation swept towards Ndunu hill, where the Mandlakazi were taken totally by surprise and scrambled to form a battle line. Dinuzulu led his crack force of about 30 or 40 horsemen (most of whom had firearms) straight at the Mandlakazi centre, where Zibhebhu had deployed his best fighters, and they threw Dinuzulu's horsemen back in confusion. But the uSuthu foot were in close support, and though they wavered for a moment, their superior numbers told. Outflanked, taken in the rear and in fear of having their retreat cut off, the Mandlakazi disintegrated in flight. The uSuthu, although fired upon by the small garrison of 50 Zululand Police in the Ivuna fort, prevented the fleeing Mandlakazi from taking shelter there, and pursued the broken foe and Zibhebhu himself beyond the Mona River over eight kilometres away. Two dozen or more uSuthu died in the battle of Ivuna, but nearly 300 Mandlakazi perished.

For the second time Dinuzulu had personally defeated the great foe of his house in battle, and could return to Ceza brimming with satisfaction. Thereafter he proudly wore the *iziqu*, or amulet necklace of willow wood, to ward off the ritually polluting effects of killing a man in battle, and to demonstrate that he had performed deeds of valour in hand-to-hand combat. His praises exalted:

> He who fought bald-headed with the assegai at Dick's,
> The wreath of smoke being the smoke of cartridges,
> Fired off by the Nongqais,
> At the fort at Nongoma …
> The Swift one like lightning,
> On the occasion he went to Ndunu.
> He who anticipated the sun before it rose
> At Nongoma.[18]

In consequence of Dinuzulu's stunning victory, the British forces in Zululand abandoned the magisterial post at Ivuna and evacuated Zibhebhu's surviving warriors to their camp at Nkonjeni. In doing so, they abandoned all the country north of the Black Mfolozi to the uSuthu. This was the high point of uSuthu success in the rebellion, and inspired uSuthu supporters in the coastal Lower Umfolosi District to emulate the battle of Ivuna. On 30 June nearly 2 000 Mphukunyoni led by their *inkosi* and Cetshwayo's first cousin, Somkhele kaMalanda, along with a few hundred men of Bhejana kaNomageje and Somopho kaZikhala, the *izinduna* of the emaNgweni, attacked Fort Andries, the magistracy of the Resident Magistrate, Andries Pretorius. As at Ivuna, the post was defended by a few Zululand Police and by the anti-uSuthu chief Sokwetshatha kaMdlandela of the Mthethwa, who was playing the same collaborating role Zibhebhu had. This time, though, the uSuthu were driven off, although they were not broken and continued to threaten the post.

With such a general collapse of British authority in much of Zululand, a thoroughgoing military solution to the uprising could no longer be avoided. Lieutenant General HA Smyth, the General Officer Commanding in South Africa, sailed from Cape Town and on 28 June took personal command of the British forces operating in Zululand. He acted with decision, and on 2 July his forces successfully stormed Hlophekhulu Mountain and drove off and scattered the thousand or so uSuthu holding it. Shingana himself fled to the sanctuary of the New Republic. This was the last engagement of any significance during the uSuthu Rebellion. Henceforth, British operations had the objective of dispersing the rebels still in the field, pacifying Zululand and re-establishing the civil administration.

Although it made political sense to strike first at Dinuzulu on Ceza Mountain, the precarious situation of Andries Pretorius in the Lower Umfolosi District made it necessary to march first to his relief. The so-called Eshowe Column successfully subdued the coastal region by 13 July, burning 180 deserted uSuthu *imizi* as it went. Havelock did not consider doing so 'a judicious means of inflicting punishment for offences committed by British subjects living within British territory',[19] but the military ignored such scruples. Smyth's next step was to initiate joint operations to regain control of Zululand north of the Black Mfolozi. The Coastal Column advanced up the coast, accepting uSuthu submissions as it went, including that of Somkhele on 30 July. On 6 August the Coastal Column reached Ivuna, where it was joined the next day by the Flying Column advancing from Nkonjeni. Under their joint pressure the uSuthu in central Zululand began to disperse home.

Dinuzulu and Ndabuko were still hunkered down on Ceza, but they decided their situation had ceased to be tenable. On 6–7 August they disbanded the remnants of the forces still on the mountain and sent them home. They themselves and 22 of their followers resolved to seek sanctuary in the ZAR. Since 20 July 1888 the unviable New Republic had been incorporated into the ZAR as the Vryheid District. Its former president, Lukas Meyer, was now the Border Commissioner committed to cooperating with the British in preventing uSuthu from crossing the frontier. However, Dinuzulu and his party succeeded in evading the border guards and making their way into the ZAR.

In Zululand, the two British columns began a joint march back to the coast on 18 August and eliminated the last pockets of uSuthu resistance on the way. By the end of the month loyalists such as Mnyamana and Ziwedu felt it sufficiently safe to return home. With the rebellion suppressed, General Smyth and his staff sailed for Cape Town on 7 September. The African levies were disbanded and the British troops no longer required in Zululand returned to Natal. By 2 November the Zululand garrison had been reduced to its normal level, and it was up to the civil authorities to reassert their authority in the colony and to resettle those uSuthu who had surrendered.

This conciliatory policy did not extend to the leaders of the late rebellion. They could not be allowed to escape punishment if British rule were to be seen to be vindicated, and their messengers were informed that they must surrender unconditionally. Ndabuko surrendered on 16 September, hoping to make terms on his nephew's behalf, but was taken summarily into custody. The British then put diplomatic pressure on President Paul Kruger of the ZAR to detain Dinuzulu and Shingana. Learning that they were to be handed over to the British, on 1 November the two escaped from their lax custody in the Utrecht District bordering western Zululand and returned to the Mahashini *umuzi* in the uSuthu heartland. But if it had been their intention to surrender there to the Zululand officials, they rapidly lost their resolve. The very next day Dinuzulu rode off for the Natal border accompanied by 20 horsemen. Shingana made for his old stronghold at Hlophekhulu, where the authorities apprehended him on 6 November.

A dejected Dinuzulu photographed in the Eshowe jail in late 1888 or early 1889
after the failed uSuthu Rebellion. He is wearing *iziqu*, the strung, interlocking
wooden beads worn by men who had killed in battle.
(KILLIE CAMPBELL AFRICANA LIBRARY, UNIVERSITY OF KWAZULU-NATAL, DURBAN)

Dinuzulu and his companions led the pursuing authorities a merry
chase through Zululand, back into the ZAR, and then into Zululand again
before crossing into Natal at Rorke's Drift. Dinuzulu and a dozen faithful
izinduna next boarded a train at Elandslaagte and journeyed on by rail to
Pietermaritzburg. They alighted there in the early hours of 15 November
and made their way across the sleeping town to Bishopstowe on its eastern outskirts. This was the home of Harriette Colenso, who had taken on
the mantle of her late father, Bishop Colenso, as the staunch defender of
Dinuzulu's cause as Cetshwayo's successor as king. Through her tireless
lobbying she had made herself the effective lash of the colonial officials
and their Zulu collaborators, whom she blamed for Zululand's descent into

bloodshed. Dinuzulu submitted to her advice to surrender to the Natal Mounted Police and to run no farther. His legal counsel wished him to stand trial in Natal, where witnesses would less likely be intimidated by the Zululand officials, but on 21 November the authorities clandestinely put Dinuzulu on a train and sent him on his way back to Zululand. There he and the other arrested uSuthu leaders went on trial in Eshowe.

To ensure that their trial was as impartial as conditions permitted, the uSuthu 'rebels' did not appear before Zululand officials but before a three-man Special Court of Commission. Proceedings opened on 15 November 1888, and cattle fines and prison sentences were imposed on the minor figures found guilty. The cases of the three ringleaders, Dinuzulu, Ndabuko and Shingana, who were accused of high treason and public violence, were heard between 13 February and 27 April 1889. Although energetically defended by a legal team led by Harry Escombe, the prominent Natal politician and barrister, all three were found guilty and were sentenced respectively to ten, fifteen and twelve years' imprisonment without hard labour. In passing sentence, Mr Justice Walter T Wragg (the senior Natal Supreme Court judge who was the President of the Special Court) had these words to say to the 20-year-old young man before him, whom many Zulu still regarded as their king, but whom the Court judged as a British subject:

> Dinuzulu, we find you guilty of high treason. After a patient hearing of your case we are justified in saying to you that we are convinced …
> you were endeavouring to regain that power to which the annexation of Her Majesty had put an end and that your intention was to overthrow the existing form of government in Zululand.[20]

✻

CHAPTER TWENTY

THE RULE OF ZULU
HAS DISAPPEARED

The Special Commissioners who sentenced Dinuzulu, Ndabuko and Shingana to imprisonment all strongly agreed, as did the Zululand officials, that they should serve their sentences neither in Zululand nor Natal since their presence would form a focus for Zulu disloyalty. The Colonial Office concurred, and directed that the three prisoners be held on the inaccessible, cliff-girt island of St Helena – once Napoleon's remote prison – far away in the mid-Atlantic.[1] The decision to imprison them on this remote rock was not as cruel as it might appear at first glance, and was in fact a mitigation of their sentence and a sop to their royal status. Since escape was impossible from St Helena, they would be far less closely confined than if detained in a southern African prison, and provision was made for a small Zulu retinue to keep them company. The three prisoners were allowed one male attendant each, and Dinuzulu's uncles, who were married, were both permitted the companionship of one of their wives. Dinuzulu, who was too young to have taken a wife, was allotted two of his *umndlunkulu*, both born of chiefly houses: Umkasilomo was the daughter of Ntuzwa of the Mdlalose; and Zihlazile's father was Qethuka of the Magwaza. An *inyanga*, Paul Mthimkhulu, accompanied them to look after their spiritual and physical health.

Dinuzulu and his uncles were kept in jail in Eshowe until their sentences were confirmed on 18 December 1889. Then, dressed in European clothing, they were taken under strict security to Durban and on 7 February 1890 were embarked on the mail steamer *Anglican*. The prisoners were understandably appalled that they were being taken so far away from the country where they had spent their entire lives, and the relatively comfortable conditions of their place of exile would never assuage their nagging homesickness.

When the prisoners and their companions landed on St Helena on 25 February they were taken to Rosemary Hall, a large house in spacious grounds six kilometres from Jamestown, the island's tiny capital squeezed into a gorge running down to the harbour. The house proved damp and was blamed for the bronchial complaints that afflicted the Zulu exiles, and they were later moved to a big house called 'Maldivia' on the outskirts of Jamestown. There they enjoyed considerable freedom of movement and Dinuzulu could spend hours riding his horse all over the island. The British government paid £1 000 a year for their maintenance.

Thanks in large measure to Harriette Colenso's untiring efforts, a relay of tutors (including Magema Fuze, the Zulu historian) was appointed for the exiles. Dinuzulu learned to speak, read and write English and, always a lover of music, took up the piano and American organ. He eagerly adopted the Western style of dress and wore his clothes with aplomb. Military dress intrigued him, and he took to wearing khaki uniforms and boots when not in his fashionable suits. Ndabuko, on the other hand, was never at ease in Western clothing and remained reclusive and obviously unhappy with his lot. Shingana, who was of a much more sociable and loquacious nature, was more adaptable. Dinuzulu, having become thoroughly comfortable with Western ways and being convivial by nature, enjoyed attending the social events arranged by the small circle of British notables on the island, and happily invited them back to the dinner parties he held in proper British style, with dancing afterwards.

Children were born to Dinuzulu while on St Helena. Umkasilomo gave birth to two sons: the future heir, Solomon Nkayishana Maphumuzana, who was born on 8 January 1894, and Arthur Edward Mshiyeni.[2] Zihlazile bore two sons: David Nyawana (Dinuzulu's eldest son, born on 24 March 1892) and Samuel Bhekelendada. On 25 May 1894 she also gave birth to a

Dinuzulu, in fashionable dress, poses shaking hands with the Governor of
St Helena, RA Sterndale. Behind them, from left to right, are Ndabuko, Paul
Mthimkhulu (the exiles' *inyanga*) and Shingana.

daughter, Victoria Helena Mphaphu. These children were all given a broad
but informal European education, and the Anglicans on the island were
vital in inculcating British attitudes and values, as well as the Christian
faith. All were baptised in St Paul's Anglican Church, and their names
were a suggestive blend of royal British and Old Testament names. In due
course, Solomon would become the first Zulu king formally to embrace
Christianity.

Isolated on St Helena, the Zulu prisoners played no part in the affairs
of distant Zululand although the indefatigable and devoted Harriette
Colenso never tired of lobbying on their behalf and did her best to keep
them informed of unfolding events. The British authorities, however, were
not even willing to consider Dinuzulu's return until they had devised a

Harriette Colenso (seated centre) photographed in February 1895 with the uSuthu exiles on St Helena. Dinuzulu is standing on the far right with Shingana sitting next to him, and Ndabuko is seated on the left. The two women in dark dresses sitting on the steps are the mothers of Dinuzulu's children: Zihlazile (left) holds Victoria Helena, with David next to her (at Harriette's feet); and Umkasilomo (right) holds her son Solomon, Dinuzulu's eventual successor.

(KILLIE CAMPBELL AFRICANA LIBRARY, UNIVERSITY OF KWAZULU-NATAL, DURBAN)

new settlement of Zululand calculated to keep the peace. Predictably, the fly in the ointment was Zibhebhu, the ally and cat's-paw of the Zululand officials. He had been permitted to return to his old district in August 1888 and had immediately taken his revenge on the uSuthu who had burned kwaBangonomo during his absence and ravaged his territory. Overriding his protectors in the Zululand administration, Havelock had him arrested to keep the peace. Finally, on 1 August 1889 the Colonial Secretary decreed that, in the interests of the future harmony of Zululand, Zibhebhu could not be allowed to return to his old district in Ndwandwe until new, uncontentious uSuthu and Mandlakazi locations had been laid out. Officials dragged their heels, and it was not until 26 August 1891 that a boundary commission was set up to demarcate the boundaries. It went about its task with thoroughness and impartiality and submitted its report on 23 September 1891. The commissioners set aside a main location each for the uSuthu and Mandlakazi and smaller subsidiary ones, and created others to accommodate irreconcilable interests. Thus Mnyamana (who died soon after on 29 July 1892) and Ziwedu were given their own locations, and because the latter's cut off a large body of uSuthu supporters from uSuthu Location No 1, uSuthu Location No 2 was created to accommodate them.

Then, as part of their policy of normalising the affairs of Zululand, in December 1891 the authorities commuted the sentences imposed on the coastal uSuthu chiefs and released them. Widespread speculation swept across the Zulu country, not only that would Dinuzulu be freed too, but also that he would return as a proper king. This agitation over Dinuzulu's return alarmed the authorities, who also feared that if Zibhebhu were allowed to return to his new, much diminished location, conflict between him and the uSuthu would erupt again. So the settlement of Zululand stalled and Dinuzulu and Zibhebhu continued to languish in their respective places of exile.

Yet a new initiative was made possible by the wiping clean of the political slate. In July 1892 a Liberal government was returned to power in Britain, while Osborn's retirement as Resident Commissioner opened the way for his replacement on 5 August 1893 by Sir Marshall Clarke, who had been the able and sensitive Administrator of Basutoland. Clarke was convinced that the root cause of persistent unrest in Zululand was the policy, first adopted by Wolseley in his settlement of 1879, of playing the Zulu factions against each other. He therefore advised that both Dinuzulu and Zibhebhu should be repatriated as a first step in healing divisions and restoring confidence in the British administration. However, he also counselled that, to placate his foes, Dinuzulu should not come back as a king or paramount chief, but merely as a Government Induna in the employ of the Zululand administration.

In January 1894 the Liberal government agreed to Dinuzulu's pardon and repatriation. But just as Cetshwayo's return to Zululand in 1883 had been delayed by the intervention of the Natal government, so too was Dinuzulu's. To make matters worse, this time the British government had to take more account of settler sentiment in Natal because the colony had been granted responsible government on 4 July 1893 and the objections of its parliament could not be brushed aside. Not only did the Natal settlers fear that Dinuzulu's return would ignite fresh strife, but also they were concerned that the placating of Zulu interests would hinder their desired opening-up of Zululand to mineral and agricultural exploitation and to white settlement.

Before anything could be decided, though, the Liberal government fell in June 1895. The Conservative administration that came in was more open to settler demands. Moreover, the new Colonial Secretary, Joseph Chamberlain, was reviving the plans for a British-ruled South African confederation that had been abandoned in 1881, and was keen to woo the Natal government. Once again, Zululand was to be sacrificed on the altar of imperial interests.

The upshot was that an agreement was reached whereby Dinuzulu's return would be coupled with the annexation of the Colony of Zululand by Natal. On 30 December 1897 the territory duly became Natal's Province of Zululand.[3] The Zulu chiefs received the news of their incorporation into Natal without any particular foreboding. As Mankulumana kaSoma-phunga, Dinuzulu's chief *induna*, put it with a shrug, the Zulu had in any case 'always considered Zululand and Natal to be one country'.[4] It would not be long, however, before they discovered the dire implications of annexation by settler Natal.

On St Helena the Governor informed Dinuzulu of the position he would occupy in the Province of Zululand. No longer a king, even in name, he was to be a Government Induna paid a salary of £500 per annum dependent on his good behaviour. He was required to live near Eshowe, and his duties involved giving the administration advice on Zulu customs. He would also be chief over uSuthu Locations Nos 1 and 2 and, like every other chief, be subject to the laws of Natal.

Dinuzulu and his uncles were naturally full of joy to be returning home, although they were concerned about the plight of those Zulu cut off in the Vryheid District of the ZAR (formerly the New Republic). As for the Province of Zululand, they informed Chamberlain that they were particularly anxious that their 'country should not be taken away from us by getting it distributed into farms, because we shall have no place for grazing our cattle or for ploughing'.[5] Chamberlain blandly reassured them that 'due provision will be made for the protection of the interests of the Zulus'.[6] However, he did not let on that, months before, he had already

Mankulumana kaSomaphunga, Dinuzulu's chief *induna*. He governed
the uSuthu while Dinuzulu was in exile.

(PIETERMARITZBURG ARCHIVES REPOSITORY, C. 667)

agreed with the Natal government that five years after the colony's annexation of Zululand a commission would be appointed to 'mark out sufficient
land reserves for native locations' preparatory to throwing the land open
to white settlement.[7]

Unaware that Zululand was destined to be carved up into African locations and white farms, just like the rest of Natal had been, on 5 January 1898
Dinuzulu and his uncles arrived in Durban harbour on board the steamship
Umbilo. Dinuzulu had set his heart on a triumphal entry, but the Natal officials were determined to thwart public demonstrations and bundled him
and his party ashore early the following morning. Stopping only to allow
Dinuzulu to have a short, private audience with Charles Saunders, the new

Resident Commissioner of Zululand, they pushed on to Eshowe, where the exiles arrived on 10 January. They did not travel light. Dinuzulu was accompanied by 40 tons of all the appurtenances of the Western lifestyle he had become accustomed to on St Helena: numerous suits of clothes, drawing-room furniture, books, pictures, ornaments and knickknacks, and his musical instruments.

Dinuzulu swiftly appealed against the requirement that he should live in Eshowe, and Saunders granted him permission to live among his adherents in uSuthu Location No 1 so long as he regularly performed his official duties in Eshowe, where a comfortable Western-style house was built for him. This time, Dinuzulu's journey north to the uSuthu heartland turned into the triumphal progress he had been denied in Durban, and thousands of loyalists thronged the route to acclaim their returning king. But there was the rub. In the eyes of both the Natal and British governments he was not – and never again could be – the Zulu king, but was only a salaried Government Induna and chief.

Zibhebhu was allowed back to the Mandlakazi location at the same time as Dinuzulu's return. In June 1898 Saunders staged a reconciliation in his office in Eshowe between Dinuzulu and the scourge of the royal house, and succeeded in extracting a promise that they would in future live harmoniously side by side. Unsurprisingly, not all the uSuthu and Mandlakazi were easily prepared to forgive and forget the blood that had been spilled between them and the ruin their fighting had brought down on the Zulu country. Zibhebhu died peacefully on 27 August 1904 at his kwaBangonomo *umuzi*, but memories of his betrayal of the royal house still linger.

As for Dinuzulu, he divided his time between his house in Eshowe and oSuthu, his *umuzi* in uSuthu Location No 1, built on a gentle slope between rocky outcrops below a wide, open plain close by the steep-banked Vuna River. It had been destroyed during the uSuthu Rebellion, but Dinuzulu rebuilt it in a combination of traditional huts and European-style dwellings. Indeed, as Pixley Seme put it, Dinuzulu 'stood in the place between the Zulu people and the white people', and could 'create a good impression' with white officials and Zulu notables alike, winning over both constituencies with his attractive style and manners.[8] But his position remained an anomalous one. Only a salaried African official and chief in the government's

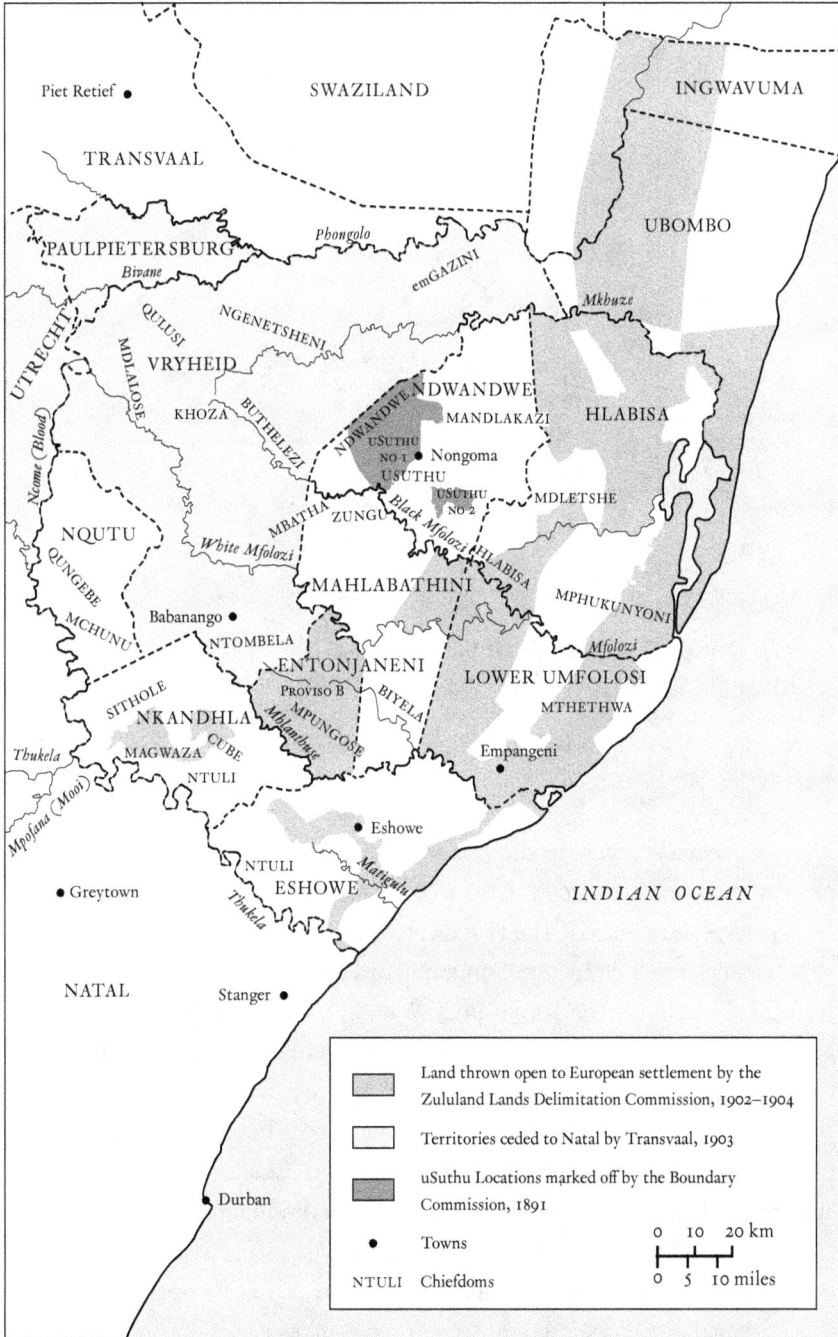

The Province of Zululand, 1904

A 1907 photograph of Dinuzulu's oSuthu homestead at the upper reaches of the Vuna
River, which he constructed in 1898 on his return from St Helena. It consisted of
traditional huts as well as European-style dwellings.

(PIETERMARITZBURG ARCHIVES REPOSITORY, (C. 556))

eyes, to the many *amakhosi* and *izinduna* who came from all over Zululand to
pay their respects to him at oSuthu he was still their king – but a king with
no actual powers outside the two locations over which he was chief.

Just how much influence Dinuzulu did in fact continue to wield was
tested by events in the Anglo-Boer War of 1899–1902. Zululand did not
become a main theatre of hostilities and remained a sideshow that saw a
few short-lived Boer incursions into British territory. Nevertheless, both
sides turned to Dinuzulu to influence how the Zulu responded to the conflict. The Boers in the Vryheid District of the ZAR, where many uSuthu
adherents lived, early called on him to use his influence to dissuade them
from taking part in the war. Then, when the war entered its guerrilla phase
in mid-1900, the British decided to sanction the active participation of
Zulu irregulars in their counterinsurgency operations. From Dinuzulu's
perspective, it was in his interests to cooperate fully with the obvious

future victors in the war. So, with his blessing, Zulu scouts and spies began from May 1900 to serve with the British forces.

Boer commandos continued to operate in northern Zululand. To regularise the arming and deployment of Zulu as combatants in support of the British forces, on 25 March 1901 the Province of Zululand was placed under martial law. On 4 April 1901 Colonel H Bottomley, who was in command of the Zululand operations, ordered Dinuzulu to ensure that 'all Zulu people' cooperated with the military.[9] Bottomley's assumption that Dinuzulu's authority extended beyond his location to encompass his former kingdom undermined the colonial officials' determined effort to restrain the latter's royal pretensions, but Bottomley was interested only in practical results. At oSuthu Dinuzulu raised the iNkomendala, a specially trained force of about 80 soldiers modelled on the Zululand Police, and several thousand traditionally armed Zulu levies responded to his call to muster under the command of Mankulumana, his chief *induna*. These forces remained in the field until operations in Zululand came to an end on 6 June 1902. Then, to the relief of the colonial officials who feared Dinuzulu would take advantage of the iNkomendala and Zulu levies to rebuild his power base, they were disbanded.

Nevertheless, the war had done much to enhance Dinuzulu's prestige among the Zulu who were in search of a leader who could bring them the rewards they believed were their due for loyally supporting their colonial rulers. And, like it or not, by calling on Dinuzulu to give the loyalist lead to other Zulu chiefs, the authorities had conceded that he was something far more than simply one chief among many. They were now left with diminishing as soon as practicable the superior status they had tacitly conceded him.

Developments in Zululand, both natural and political, swiftly worked to that end. A pattern of climatic deterioration and pestilence had begun in 1895, and these natural disasters hastened the dissolution of the Zulu pastoral economy and the disruption of the social relations and obligations of kingship upon which traditional chiefly power was based. Immense swarms of red locusts swept bare the fields in 1895–1896, 1898 and 1903–1904, and again in 1906. Between 1895 and 1907 there were six years of serious drought. In 1897 came the most devastating blow of all. Rinderpest, the contagious viral disease of ruminants, broke out among the cattle herds. Perhaps 85 per cent of the cattle, the Zulu people's chief form of storable wealth and the very foundation of their pastoral society, succumbed. And before the herds had time to recover, they were infected in 1904–1905 by the new and deadly tick-borne disease, East Coast Fever. Despite these hammer blows, the colonial government gave Africans no relief from the payment of the hut tax.

Nor was that all. No sooner had the Anglo-Boer War ended when, on 1 August 1902, the Zululand Lands Delimitation Commission was set up. It submitted its final report on 18 October 1904 when it demarcated 2 613 000 acres (or 40.2 per cent) of the Province of Zululand's potentially most productive land for white purchase and occupation, most of which was turned into privately owned sugar and wattle plantations once whites started moving in on 1 January 1906. The residue of 3 887 000 acres, land that the commissioners considered undesirable for commercial agriculture or white settlement, was set aside for African reserves.[10] Zulu who found themselves living on the new white farms were duly reduced to the status of squatters on land they had occupied since time immemorial, and were made subject to summary eviction to the reserves. In the Northern Districts (the Vryheid, Utrecht and Paulpietersburg districts), once part of the Zulu kingdom and which the ZAR had ceded to Natal on 27 January 1903 – thus ironically bringing all the constituent elements of the former Zulu kingdom under the administrative sway of Natal – there was no provision for reserves. Africans there possessed no land at all and rendered labour to the white landlords for their tenure. The prescient fears Dinuzulu had expressed to Chamberlain in 1897 that the Zulu would one day be dispossessed of their land had been fulfilled.

No wonder, then, considering all these accumulating disasters, that so many Zulu were forced onto the labour market outside Zululand in order for their families to survive. By 1904 17 000 Zulu had become migrant workers. The *ibutho* system established by Shaka as the main pillar of his rule, whereby the young men of the Zulu kingdom served their kings, was irrevocably a thing of the past. So too, it seemed, was the Zulu monarchy itself.

With his official status merely that of a chief subject to the authority of the Governor of Natal in his capacity of Supreme Chief,[11] Dinuzulu was in no position to ameliorate the sufferings of the Zulu people during this time of natural disaster, or to prevent the alienation of their land to white farmers. Moreover, despite his loyal and influential service during the Anglo-Boer War, settler and official hostility towards him continued unabated. Scurrilous, derogatory tales of his drunkenness and debauchery abounded, and there were repeated, inflammatory accusations that he intended to restore the Zulu monarchy and that (just as his father Cetshwayo was alleged to have done) he was plotting to overthrow white rule in the subcontinent.

Caught between white suspicion and hostility on one hand, and the support on the other of his adherents in Zululand and of many traditionalists in Natal, who regarded him as the legitimate head of the Zulu people and the embodiment of national pride, Dinuzulu was in an impossibly difficult position. It is hardly surprising, therefore, that when rebellion broke out in Natal in 1906 he should be fatally ensnared in the contradictions of his situation.

The Zulu Uprising of 1906, also known as the Bhambatha Rebellion, was sparked by the decision in 1905 by the Natal legislature, facing mounting deficits caused by the contraction of the colonial economy in the aftermath of the Anglo-Boer War, to relieve its financial embarrassment by imposing a capitation tax of £1 on every adult male, excepting heads of homesteads already liable for the hut tax. Hostility to this new 'poll tax' by a poverty-stricken people hammered by natural disasters, unemployment and poor wages became widespread. Its imposition focused their simmering resentment on a colonial government that interfered with chiefly authority and failed to accommodate the rising class of educated and commercially active Africans. On 8 February 1906 violence erupted when tax protesters clashed with police on a farm near Richmond in the Natal midlands. The authorities resolved on sharp retribution to uphold white rule, and 12 of those involved in killing two white policemen were executed by firing squad. British troops had been withdrawn from Natal after the Anglo-Boer War, leaving the colony to look after its own defence. The colonial government was in any case resistant to the slightest British interference in its affairs, and the ongoing containment of the uprising was conducted by over 5 000 colonial white militia and police and by over 4 500 African levies.

In late April 1906 the focus of operations moved to northern Natal, where Bhambatha kaMancinza, the minor *inkosi* of a section of the Zondi people, refused to pay the poll tax in Greytown and fled on 9 March to Dinuzulu. What transpired at oSuthu is unclear. Whether or not Mankulumana incited Bhambatha to rebel in Dinuzulu's presence remained unproven – and unlikely since Mankulumana was known to have attempted to keep the rebels at a distance from the royal house. But when Bhambatha then took refuge in the Nkandla forest he left his wife and two children behind at oSuthu in Dinuzulu's care. In Nkandla Bhambatha was taken in by Sigananda kaSokufa, the aged *inkosi* of the Cube and an ardent uSuthu loyalist, whom Dinuzulu apparently instructed to protect Bhambatha. Whether or not Dinuzulu meant Sigananda to join Bhambatha in fighting the Natal government is again obscure, but the fact is that the Cube *inkosi* joined Bhambatha's cause and took up arms.

A number of sharp encounters with the colonial troops – notably at Bhobhe on 5 May and at Mpukunyoni on 28 May – ensued over difficult terrain in which the colonial forces, with their considerably superior firepower and organisation, were successful. Between 24 and 26 May Bhambatha again visited Dinuzulu to request his support before returning to the Nkandla forest where Mehlokazulu kaSihayo, the *inkosi* of the Qungebe, was in command.[12] On 10 June their forces were surrounded and surprised in the remote Mome gorge by government troops, who remorselessly shot some 500 of them down. Both Bhambatha and Mehlokazulu were killed. With the consequent collapse of the rebellion in Zululand, the government troops withdrew by early July. However, in mid-June resistance flared up briefly in the Maphumulo Division of Natal, on the southern side of the lower Thukela, and further operations were required before the last embers of the rebellion were doused by late July 1906.

The official number of 'rebel' dead was 2 652 as compared to 36 government casualties (with 67 wounded). This was a considerable number of fatalities considering that, by official reckoning, there were 3 873 rebels in Natal and 2 031 in Zululand, and probably no more than 1 500 in the field at any one time. In the ensuing months of tough repression there were 4 368 convictions under martial law and 25 men were exiled to St Helena. All the death sentences imposed were commuted.

Dinuzulu did not escape the net. On 10 December 1907 he was formally arraigned for treason at the court house in Nongoma, close by oSuthu, for his alleged involvement in the 1906 uprising. The Natal authorities, who continued to fear Dinuzulu as a focus of resistance to white rule, were convinced that he must have played a leading role in inspiring and directing the uprising. Yet what role did Dinuzulu actually play? James Stuart, the first and still the most authoritative historian of the uprising of 1906, believed that while Dinuzulu was not 'whole-heartedly loyal' and was not above 'cautious wire-pulling from a distance', what characterised his conduct was his 'absolute fear of taking any step to start a rebellion in his own name'.[13] The titular Zulu king had been too badly burned in the past to dare to confront the colonial state openly and take up arms. He knew that the Zulu people were looking to him to take a stand against the poll tax, and that a large number of chiefs were expecting him to take the lead, that he was regarded as 'a high tree, upon which all the birds fed or congregated'.[14] But the risks of failure were paralysing, and Dinuzulu never openly offered himself as a rallying point for the rebels who hoped to harness his prestige to their cause and conjured with his name irrespective of his wishes. So his initial response in the crisis was to order the people in his own chiefdom to pay the poll tax at the earliest possible date and to be loud in his protestations of loyalty to the government, even offering to serve as an intermediary between it and the rebels. Yet under this smokescreen of cooperation he was probably by no means loath to see the 'rebels' succeed, although at the very most he should probably be regarded as no more than an accessory to their actions.

The government was nevertheless determined to prove that Dinuzulu had been behind the uprising from the start and that his relations with Bhambatha were incriminating. Harriette Colenso and her family saw the trial as the culmination of the lengthy persecution of the Zulu royal house by the Natal official establishment. They spared nothing to ensure that Dinuzulu received a fair trial and succeeded in securing WP Schreiner, the former Cape prime minister and a leading advocate, to head the legal team defending him. The trial before a Special Court, which was held in Greytown to avoid large crowds of African supporters, began on 19 November 1908. Dinuzulu was charged with 23 counts of high treason. The judgment of the

Dinuzulu and his defence team during his treason trial before the Special
Court in the Greytown Town Hall between November 1908 and March 1909.
From left: WP Schreiner (defence counsel), CE Renaud (advocate), Dinuzulu,
RCA Samuelson (attorney) and Harriette Colenso.
(KILLIE CAMPBELL AFRICANA LIBRARY, UNIVERSITY OF KWAZULU-NATAL, DURBAN)

court was delivered on 2 March 1909. Dinuzulu was found not guilty on the
major counts, but was found guilty on three lesser ones of assisting and harbouring rebels, permitting Bhambatha's family to stay at oSuthu, and not
reporting the visit of rebel leaders during the uprising. For these 'crimes' he
was fined £100 and sentenced to four years' imprisonment. He also forfeited
his annual stipend and position as chief of the two uSuthu locations, which
were abolished and their people parcelled out among four local chiefs.

In his remarkably fair and reasonable judgment, considering the animosity of settler opinion, the President of the Special Court, Sir William
Smith, the Chief Justice of the Transvaal, told Dinuzulu that in sentencing
him he had attached no weight to his previous conviction of high treason
20 years before since he 'must have been only a boy'. It was his opinion that
'at no time' did Dinuzulu 'attempt to take an active part in the rebellion'.
Nevertheless, Smith went on, 'people must understand that they cannot
touch pitch without being defiled, and that they cannot offer assistance to

the King's enemies and claim to be loyal. At the same time … I can understand that you were in conflict between your duty to the Government and
the position which you felt you held over the Zulu people.'[15]

The Natal government had suffered a moral defeat in not conclusively
proving their case against Dinuzulu, but his deposition and imprisonment
removed the last remaining symbol of African independence in the colony.
As Dinuzulu lamented to Schreiner during the trial: 'My sole crime is that
I am the son of Cetshwayo.'[16]

With Dinuzulu's conviction and imprisonment the Zulu monarchy fell
into abeyance. It was with bitter resignation that Magema Fuze wrote
in 1922: 'Today Zululand is no longer Zululand, it is Natal, ruled by the
English, the original government having passed away and a new one taking
its place. The rule of Zulu has disappeared.'[17]

Dinuzulu was initially imprisoned in Pietermaritzburg, although not for
long. On 31 May 1910 the Union of South Africa, made up of the four
former British colonies, came into being. Natal was reduced to a province
of the Union with limited local powers exercised by the Natal Provincial
Council (NPC). General Louis Botha became the Union's first prime minister. Remembering his friendship with Dinuzulu at the time of his alliance
with the Boers of the New Republic against Zibhebhu, one of Botha's first
acts in office was to release Dinuzulu from prison and restore his stipend of
£500 a year. However, Dinuzulu was not free to return home. Botha exiled
him from Zululand and Natal for the rest of his life and settled him on a
remote farm set aside for him in the Middelburg district of the eastern
Transvaal. A handful of wives and companions, including Mankulumana,
were permitted to join him there. Dinuzulu called his 5 000-acre farm
'kwaThengisangaye', or 'Barter with Him', meaning that the Zulu people
had bartered him to foreigners.[18]

Although only in middle age, Dinuzulu became progressively more ill
at kwaThengisangaye, probably with rheumatic gout and Bright's disease
(acute nephritis). He died there in great distress on 18 October 1913. The
Union government did not share Natal's paranoia about the Zulu royal
house, so without reference to the NPC it transported Dinuzulu's body
by train to Vryheid, where it was transferred to a wagon for interment
at kwaNobamba in the emaKhosini valley among his royal ancestors. The

funeral procession took three days to reach kwaNobamba and 7 000 people witnessed the burial on 27 October, including members of the royal house and most of the leading men of Zululand associated with the uSuthu cause. The circumstances of Dinuzulu's burial reflected just how much had changed in the Zulu country. His body was encased in a European-style coffin rather than wrapped in skins as those of his royal predecessors had been. Despite Dinuzulu's lack of enthusiasm for Christianity, an African cleric attended the funeral to give a Christian gloss to the traditional ceremony. Harriette Colenso, the untiring supporter of Dinuzulu's cause, was a prominent mourner, but she was accompanied by two white labour agents responsible for recruiting Zulu men for the gold mines. Local officials were present to keep an eye on the proceedings, even though it was official Natal policy to feign that the Zulu monarchy was strictly a thing of the past.

Mankulumana delivered the funeral oration and declared that Dinuzulu had died of a 'broken heart'.[19] In a sense that was true enough, for as Dinuzulu had despairingly said of his life and poisoned inheritance to Schreiner: 'My trouble is like that of no one else … Nkosi, what is grievous is to be killed and yet alive.'[20]

Nevertheless, Dinuzulu underestimated the inspiration his disappointments and sufferings proffered to his contemporaries and future generations. When the South African Native National Congress (SANNC) was formed on 8 January 1912 to fight for the rights of Africans, it elected him *in absentia* an honorary life president in recognition of what Sibusiso Ndebele, the future premier of the Province of KwaZulu-Natal, would refer to as his tireless struggle 'for the dignity of the people, their land and the royal house'.[21] On 20 September 2008 Ndebele unveiled a statue of Dinuzulu on Durban's King Dinuzulu Road (formerly Berea Road), facing an existing statue of Louis Botha – the prime minister whom Dinuzulu had considered his friend. Yet, true to the controversies that beset Dinuzulu's life, not even his statue could avoid becoming an object of discord. It became a victim of the fractious politics of modern KwaZulu-Natal and of complaints by the Zulu royal house that it was unseemly that Dinuzulu's statue was shorter than Botha's. So for two years it stood forlornly swathed in hessian before finally being unwrapped.

KING SOLOMON NKAYISHANA MAPHUMUZANA kaDINUZULU

꙰

CHAPTER TWENTY-ONE

THE HONEYBIRD THAT
DRINKS FROM DEEP POOLS

For two days Dinuzulu's body lay unburied in his hut at kwaNobamba because it was not yet decided who would succeed him as the
titular Zulu monarch, and it was the ritual duty of the recognised heir
to turn the first sod of the grave with the dead king's spear. The problem
was that Dinuzulu had two potential heirs, David Nyawana and Solomon
Nkayishana, and it seemed that he had not definitely named either one of
them as his successor. So Mankulumana (Dinuzulu's principal *induna* who
was in charge of the funeral ceremonies) consulted with the dead king's
izinceku since they were presumed to have been privy to his wishes. They
reported that Dinuzulu had favoured David as his heir. Mankulumana
thereupon announced to those assembled that David was their new king,
and the multitude acclaimed him with the royal salute, '*Bayede!*' But loud
dissenting voices, led by Mnyaiza kaNdabuko and Mkebeni kaDabulamanzi
(the influential sons of Dinuzulu's two prominent uncles), were raised at
Mankulumana's taking it upon himself to settle the royal succession without properly consulting all the leading men of the nation. The problem was
that although David was Dinuzulu's eldest son, the majority of those in the
inner royal circle did not want him as their king because they knew him to
be violent, morose and addicted to drink, and noted with abhorrence that
he was 'very free in using his sjambok on elderly men'.[1] They consequently

favoured Solomon, who was 'mild, kind and humble' and who possessed a commendable sense of social concern for his people.[2]

While acrimonious debate over the succession raged, Dinuzulu's corpse was fast decomposing in the summer heat and burial could no longer be delayed. With the matter still not settled, on 27 October 1913 Dinuzulu's daughter, Victoria Mpatshana, was authorised to ritually break the ground with her hoe so that the grave could be dug, cattle sacrificed to the royal *amadolozi* and the body at last lowered into the earth. But then the funeral ceremony came to a halt because it was for Dinuzulu's heir to place a stone ritually on his father's grave – and who was he? In desperation, Mankulumana turned to Harriette Colenso. She later averred that, during the previous night, Solomon had given her a letter from Dinuzulu nominating him as heir, although she never actually produced it. In any event, on her urging Solomon was led forward to lay the first stone on the grave, followed by David and then other members of the Zulu elite. At the end of the funeral rites Mankulumana thereupon announced that Solomon was the new king, and the assembly enthusiastically acclaimed him. It was then arranged that Solomon should have his father's Mahashini and oSutho *imizi*, while David, the dethroned king of a single day, was given the prestigious kwaNobamba in compensation – not that this was enough for him ever to forgive Solomon for displacing him.

The young man who was now the Zulu king – although unrecognised as such by the South African government – was modest and approachable. In recognition of his character, his *izibongo* proclaimed: 'Tuft of soft hair he speaks not, neither has heavy words.'[3] As a consequence of his upbringing, Solomon was thoroughly westernised. Always a dandy, he wore only meticulously tailored clothes and had a decided penchant for military-style uniforms. His most spectacular confection in this line was made of black cloth with cuffs, collar, epaulettes and sash of leopard skin, and was worn either with a plumed white sun helmet or a cap with gold-braided brim. He also exclusively favoured Western furniture and crockery, even inside traditional huts.

Soon after his succession, Solomon fell under the influence of the Anglican Church in Zululand, and was confirmed in February 1914.

Solomon Nkayishana Maphumuzana kaDinuzulu as a young man.

(CHARLES BALLARD, *THE HOUSE OF SHAKA: THE ZULU MONARCHY ILLUSTRATED*, 1988)

Now that he was in the Christian camp, the *amakholwa*, the mission-educated Africans like Pixley Seme (who was married to Solomon's sister, Phikisile Harriette), tirelessly worked on Solomon to transcend his traditionalist chiefly role in order to become a leader reflecting their Africanist cultural and political aspirations. Yet despite his reliance on *kholwa* advisers, Solomon simply could not afford to turn his back on his traditional royal position since it was the sole basis of his status and influence. He therefore surrounded himself with men of the Zulu hered-itary elite, all of whom were of the royal house or had served previous kings (or were descended from those who had). Mankulumana remained his chief *induna* until his death in 1926, when Solomon replaced him with

Matole kaThanibezwe, the Buthelezi chief and Mnyamana's grandson who in 1923 had married Solomon's sister, Magogo Sibilile Mantithi, as his tenth but senior wife.[4]

All was not clear sailing, however, even in the world of Zulu traditionalism. Those chiefs and headmen who were government appointees were unwilling to acclaim Solomon as their king lest they antagonise the government. And, for their part, many in the uSuthu camp were hostile to those they regarded as government collaborators, even if the old ill will towards the Mandlakazi and Ngenetsheni had largely healed, thanks in large part to Solomon's efforts to befriend Bokwe kaZibhebhu, the Mandlakazi *inkosi*. As Nicholas Cope, Solomon's biographer, has pointed out, the healing of the uSuthu-Mandlakazi feud after nearly 50 years of antagonism was considered among the Zulu as the most memorable achievement of his lifetime.[5]

Beset as he was by contradictory influences and by divisions in Zulu society, Solomon early decided on the direction he must take. As the embodiment of tradition, he would consolidate his hereditary right to lead and unify the Zulu people as their king, and he would strive to gain the Union government's recognition of his royal status.

A year after his father's death, Solomon held the traditional *ihlambo* ceremony to signal the end of the period of mourning. The aged Mkhosana, who had accompanied Cetshwayo into exile, was summoned to ensure that the ceremony adhered to all the traditional practices. Some 5 000 *amabutho* and people from all over Zululand attended, and Solomon led the great ritual hunt mounted on a horse and carrying a rifle. Before they dispersed, the *amabutho* confirmed him as the Zulu nation's undeniable king by tendering him their labour when they built a new cattle kraal at Zibindini, Solomon's *umuzi* in the emaKhosini valley, located uncomfortably close to the disgruntled David's kwaNobamba. Then, to unite people under him as the symbol of Zulu national unity, in 1916 – and again in 1918 – Solomon held an *ukubuthwa* ceremony when on each occasion he enrolled young men from all over Zululand in a new *ibutho*. This deliberate revival of the central institution of the Zulu monarchy was intended both to build up the personal loyalty of the *amabutho* to Solomon as their king and to inspire in them a sense of pride in their pre-colonial past. In all, about 6 000 young men were enrolled in the two *amabutho*, and they performed the traditional tasks of tending Solomon's livestock and crops and establishing a new royal homestead, called kwaDlamahlahla, very close to Mahashini, which he declared would in future be the *kwahlalakosi*, 'the place where kings dwell'.[6]

Dinuzulu had died in debt, and with no official stipend Solomon's resources were inadequate for the position he was attempting to uphold. Seme and Dinuzulu's uncle Mnyaiza were responsible for initiating a royal tribute-collecting campaign from Zulu migrant workers and urban residents and from peasants in the rural districts. The number of those willing to contribute gave the authorities unwelcome notice that a sense of Zulu solidarity was forming behind the figure of Solomon.

Like his royal ancestors, Solomon also employed marriage to cement social and political alliances across Zululand. In 1915 he took his first wife, Christina okaMathathela Sibiya, the daughter of *kholwa* parents, whom the Zulu formally addressed as 'Ntombeni'. But although Solomon preferred women who were Christian, educated, westernised and respectably bourgeois in their habits, he nevertheless contracted numerous other marriages with the more rumbustious, traditionalist daughters of the great chiefly houses of the old kingdom. Later, his growing influence among the Zulu-speakers of Natal proper required marriages with the daughters of prominent families there too. In all, Solomon (who was reputed to have been a decided Lothario) is believed to have married 58 women to consolidate his position as king. He also encouraged his many sisters to marry Zulu notables to tie them to the royal house – not that they necessarily complied.

Despite consolidating more and more Zulu sentiment about his person as their accepted king, Solomon was only too aware that he remained without any official status in the administrative structure of the Union. The Zulu people were under the direct administrative control of the Native Affairs Department (NAD), while a Chief Native Commissioner (CNC) presided over Zululand with his headquarters in Eshowe. That post had been filled since February 1913 by Dick Addison, Dinuzulu's old adversary at the time of the uSuthu Rebellion. Addison remained as doggedly opposed to the aspirations of the royal house as he ever had been, and on the eve his final retirement in 1916 he firmly stated in writing that 'Solomon ... holds no responsible position under the Government and I hope he never will. He is a menace to the peace of the country.'[7]

Addison's successor, Charles Wheelwright, was less abrasive but of essentially the same mould. He sternly warned Solomon to adopt a lower profile or face the government's displeasure, and would have nothing to do with his appeals for official recognition. To make the point, he studiously did not invite Solomon to an *indaba* to be held in Eshowe in July 1916 for the Zululand chiefs to meet their Supreme Chief, the Governor General, Viscount Buxton.[8] Solomon tried to crash the *indaba* regardless, but was humiliatingly turned away. The insult to the man many regarded as their king only served to rally Zulu sentiment behind him.

The counterproductive Eshowe *indaba* took place right in the middle of the First World War at a time when Louis Botha, still the prime minister of South Africa, decided to create the South African Native Labour Contingent (SANLC) to support the Allied armies in France in a non-combat role. Understandably, Botha anticipated that many of its recruits would come from Natal and Zululand. Solomon saw in this an opportunity to demonstrate his loyalty to the government, just as Dinuzulu had done during the Second Anglo-Boer War. Accordingly, he informed Wheelwright that he would assist in raising volunteers for the new labour battalion. But Wheelwright would have none of it. To accept Solomon's assistance in recruiting Zulu men would be to acknowledge his authority over the Zulu people, and the CNC turned him down flat.

Snubbed publicly once again, Solomon turned to Seme for advice, and under his tutelage began to play an astute political game. Defiantly ignoring Wheelwright's orders to keep out of the business, he issued a call forbidding any Zulu to enlist in the SANLC, and saw his authority triumphantly vindicated when the government's recruitment drive proved a dismal flop in Zululand. Botha and the NAD were consequently forced to admit that Solomon did indeed wield considerable clout with the Zulu people, even if he held no recognised official position. They therefore decided on a radical policy switch to secure his cooperation and to harness his influence over the Zulu for the war effort.

Solomon's house at kwaDlamahlahla, his chief residence, was built close to
the cluster of traditional huts at the Mahashini homestead.

On 25 November 1916 Solomon, Mnyaiza and other royal advisers met
Botha, Dinuzulu's old friend and patron, at the Union Buildings in Pretoria.
Botha announced that Solomon was to be recognised as a chief over the
reunited uSuthu locations, and that his domicile would be in the Nongoma
District. He would receive an annual stipend of £300. In return, Solomon
was to comport himself as a government official, raise no more *amabutho*
and maintain the peace. Otherwise, Botha warned, he would immediately
be banished. Then, tantalisingly, Botha hinted that if Solomon behaved
well his status might be elevated even further. Solomon saw the dazzling
prize of his recognition as the Zulu king within his grasp, and thereafter
would strain every sinew to secure it.

Solomon possessed a keen sense of what image a modern Zulu ruler
should present, even if it conflicted with the traditional customs and
practices he represented. As the newly restored uSuthu chief, Solomon
made his chief residence at kwaDlamahlahla next to the cluster of traditional huts at Mahashini. There he erected an imposing house in the

contemporary colonial style, with bay windows surrounded by a deep pil-
lared veranda reached by broad flights of steps. Long an enthusiastic and
athletic horseman, he would ride between his various *imizi* in Zululand
accompanied by the royal dogs and dressed in well-cut military-style
khaki riding clothes with a royal leopard-skin sash. On formal public
occasions he would appear in a silk top hat and frock coat or in his black
uniform with its leopard-skin trimmings, while his retinue incongruously
sported traditional skins and feathers. Unfortunately, Solomon's idea of
a modern royal style involved considerable expense, not only on clothes
and houses and many wives and children, but also on all types of alcohol.
European liquor was illegal for Africans, which had the effect of making
it the prestigious drink of kings and a favoured form of chiefly tribute.
The problem was that as early as 1918 Solomon was already drinking to
excess. In an act of perverse exhibitionism, he bordered the flower beds
surrounding his house at kwaDlamahlahla with rows of empty bottles of
spirits buried neck down.

Solomon understood that one way to secure government recognition
of the kingly status he so craved was to enhance his position nationally, and that meant moving outside the confines of a purely traditional
role and entering the modern political arena. The African population
of Natal and Zululand was beginning to recover by the 1920s from
the previous decades of drought and epidemics. It was also overcoming the initial shock of the 1913 Land Act, which prevented Africans
from purchasing land or remaining as squatters on white-owned land,
because the 1920 Native Affairs Act gave Africans greater flexibility in
purchasing land outside the reserves.[9] The consequent rise in African
prosperity encouraged the growth of an entrepreneurial African middle class with Christian and Western values. Quite naturally, this new
elite was beginning to strive for commensurately improved political
status. Its aspirations were first represented by the SANNC, founded
by Pixley Seme on 8 January 1912 with Dr John Langalibalele Dube as
its first president. The SANNC was a countrywide organisation, and
its regional arm was the Natal Native Congress (NNC) under Dr Dube.
However, in this volatile period, emerging trade union movements of
black industrial workers under militant leadership (notably the radical,

Edward, Prince of Wales, presenting Solomon with a gold-mounted
ceremonial stick on 6 June 1925 during the Eshowe *indaba*.
(DON AFRICANA LIBRARY, DURBAN)

syndicalist Industrial and Commercial Workers Union founded in 1920)
began to dismiss the SANNC leadership as too middle class and cautious. Confronted with this challenge, in 1917 the SANNC passed out
of the hands of moderates such as Dube, and in 1923 repositioned itself
as the more radical and activist African National Congress (ANC).

Dube nevertheless maintained his control over the NNC and looked
to gain fresh political momentum for its moderate economic and political goals from a new quarter, that is, from the members of the Zulu royal
house, whose lead the Zulu chiefs and their people could be counted on
to follow. Solomon had previously remained largely aloof from the turbulent pan-Africanist politics of the period, but Dube's opportunity to
win him over came in 1921 when the Revd Samuel D Simelane launched
a new organisation, the Zulu National Congress, with NNC support.
In October 1924, at a meeting held at kwaDlamahlahla, Solomon's

principal residence, the organisation became known as *Inkatha kaZulu*, thereby cannily associating itself with the mystical and unifying great coil of the nation that was also the symbol of the monarchy. Solomon became the official patron of this, the first Inkatha political movement. It usefully provided him with a platform to project himself as the symbol of African power and pride, and also gave him a modern political vehicle – along with its sources of revenue – to help further his ambition to be recognised as the Zulu king.

The official visit of Edward, Prince of Wales,[10] to South Africa in 1925 seemed to Solomon to be the moment, if properly grasped, when he could secure his claim to royal status.On 6 June 1925 Solomon greeted the prince in Eshowe at the head of many thousands of Zulu for a grand *indaba*. Both Solomon and the prince were in their gala ceremonial uniforms, the prince's laden with orders and decorations. In their encounter, the two seemed to interact as equals, one royal to another, and Solomon was repeatedly given the royal acclamation of '*Bayede!*' The Prince of Wales presented Solomon with a gold-mounted stick, but handed out only silver-mounted ones to nine other major chiefs, surely indicative that Solomon's status was recognised as being superior to theirs. The prince and Solomon later held a private discussion aboard the royal train, further stoking excited rumours that Solomon had been appointed king.

Yet the rumours were quite without foundation. Solomon did not know it then, but the Eshowe *indaba* was undoubtedly the apex of his political career. Far from all the promising talk and ceremonial at the *indaba* nudging the Union government into finally recognising him as king, it had the opposite effect. Alarmed by the royal honours paid Solomon at Eshowe, the NAD began to go out of its way to quash his royal pretensions, often in the pettiest ways. Solomon became ever more embittered with each new official snub, and in his frustration began to lose his sense of political judgement. His behaviour towards officialdom became ever more truculent and eventually self-defeating, never more so than at the *indaba* of 1930.

In that year the Governor General, the Earl of Athlone, went on an official tour of Zululand and called for an *indaba* at Eshowe with all the Zulu chiefs. Solomon petulantly slighted Athlone (who, to make it worse, was King George V's cousin and brother-in-law) by refusing to attend. Then, when the *indaba* did take place on 23 July, Solomon turned up unexpectedly and proceeded to embarrass the Governor General by publicly berating him for the poor treatment he and his people had received at the hands of the government. Solomon concluded his harangue by confrontationally proclaiming that as a king he recognised only the authority of the British Crown and not that of the South African government.

Afterwards, Athlone (who was, after all, the Crown's representative) severely reprimanded Solomon for his deplorable behaviour and fined him the equivalent of half his annual stipend. This demeaning debacle finally frustrated any hope Solomon might still have entertained of being recognised as the Zulu king. More than that, it diminished Solomon's already eroding political clout and took away his platform with Inkatha. In the early 1930s Inkatha was already beginning to disintegrate, battered by financial mismanagement and corruption, and by the loss of clear political direction.[11] Moreover, its base remained confined to the Zulu-speaking region and it failed to maintain its place in national African politics, where the ANC was making inroads. But, ironically, what materially helped finish it off was its close association with the Zulu royal house, since Solomon's erratic and embarrassing behaviour brought the organisation into disrepute.

Solomon was by then a frustrated and deeply despondent man. His mounting alcoholism was accompanied by appalling outbursts of temper and contributed to his reckless spending on luxury items that put him into serious debt. Even so, his people were inclined to forgive him his failings because they appreciated that he had striven as best he could to instil a new sense of unity and pride in the Zulu nation, hammered as it had been by decades of political and natural disasters, by the loss of its land and by the imposition of white rule. They could also understand that he desired so earnestly to elevate the status of the royal house precisely because it embodied the Zulu people and their proud history, and accepted how miserably thwarted he was in his failure to be recognised by the Union government as the Zulu king.

Solomon's health gave way as he relentless punished the bottle. Nevertheless, he continued to perform his duties. On 6 March 1933 he was visiting Kambi kaHamu, the Ngenetsheni *inkosi*, to settle a dispute – in itself an indication of how successful he had been in healing the festering rift between the antagonists of the Third Zulu Civil War. While there, Solomon collapsed and died. His grieving people came from far and wide to attend his funeral at Mahashini. He was interred in a great grave three metres deep and three metres square. Steps led down to a niche where a bed was prepared upon which his body was laid. *Ilanga lase Natal*, the Zulu newspaper John Dube had founded, lamented:

> We have died Zulu people! We have no place to hide! He is no more, the honeybird that drinks from deep pools! The giver of rest has gone! We are like sheep without a shepherd![12]

KING NYANGAYEZIZWE CYPRIAN BHEKUZULU kaSOLOMON

❀ ❀ ❀

CHAPTER TWENTY-TWO

THE HEALER OF NATIONS

A man and the meaning of his name are believed by the Zulu to be inseparable. Cyprian, who was born on 4 August 1924 at Solomon's Nsindeni *umuzi*, was the son of his first wife, Christina okaMathathela Sibiya, the daughter of a *kholwa* family settled at a Norwegian mission station near Nhlazatshe. It was she who named him Nyangayezizwe, 'the healer of nations', to signify that he had come to rescue the Zulu at a time of confusion, while Solomon chose Bhekuzulu, to proclaim that he would 'look after the Zulu nation'.[1] In naming him thus, Cyprian's parents were indicating their belief that he would resuscitate the Zulu monarchy.

When Cyprian was aged three, he and his mother, who has been described as 'regal almost to a fault',[2] moved to kwaDlamahlahla. There Cyprian enjoyed a traditional childhood herding the royal cattle with his half-brothers and cousins. He was then given a modern schooling. At the age of seven he was enrolled at Nhlophenkulu, the small palace school, where he passed standard six, and he completed his Junior Certificate at Umphumulo Training College near Vryheid.

Cyprian was not yet nine years old when Solomon died in 1933. He could not succeed to the uSuthu chieftainship until he came of age, so he was placed under the guardianship of his uncle, Arthur Edward Mshiyeni kaDinuzulu, Solomon's brother, who had been born on St Helena. Heavily moustached, with a penchant for British-style military uniforms complete with Sam Browne belt and shoulder strap, Mshiyeni was a stern and forbidding figure. In 1934 the government appointed him Acting Chief of the uSuthu. The officials of the NAD then kept a careful eye on how Mshiyeni comported himself as Acting Chief because they calculated that strengthening the tribal system would counteract the growing popularity of 'revolutionary' movements such as the ANC – so long as the chief in question was cooperative. Mshiyeni more than satisfied the NAD officials that, as a conservative traditionalist who was indignant at the embarrassing image of the royal house he had inherited, he would continue to work well with them. As his reward they made him Regent in 1939 and raised him to Acting Paramount Chief with a salary of £500 a year.

Until 1948 Cyprian was kept under Mshiyeni's strict thumb and was frequently punished, even for minor misdemeanours. Perhaps as a result of his stern upbringing, Cyprian grew up to be a subdued young man, lacking his father's flamboyance. In his photographs, his large, almond-shaped eyes, the windows to his reserved personality, always seem pensive and melancholy. In his youth he showed athletic promise and, like his father and Mshiyeni, was a keen horseman. He was adept at soccer, and was described in his *izibongo* as speedily disposing of his opponents:

> The hare with beautiful legs
> The chopper of small trees
> The big ones [trees] fall on their own.[3]

Cyprian matured into a heavily built man with a moustache, small beard and sideburns. Apparently, he was attractive to women. Like Solomon, he preferred the Western way of living and dressing, although he was always careful to revere the traditions and ceremonies of the Zulu people. On formal occasions, he favoured a version of his father Solomon's black uniform with leopard trimmings and white sun helmet (but without the plumes).

Cyprian's path to the throne was not straightforward. As with all his predecessors, he had to push rivals aside. At the time of his death in 1933, Solomon (just like Dinuzulu before him) had not proclaimed his successor. Some believed that Cyprian had been Solomon's favourite, and he was

Arthur Edward Mshiyeni kaDinuzulu, regent for his nephew,
Cyprian, and Acting Paramount Chief (1934–1948).
(KILLIE CAMPBELL AFRICANA LIBRARY, UNIVERSITY OF KWAZULU-NATAL, DURBAN)

after all the son of Solomon's first wife, Christina. But, unimpressed with
Cyprian's character, Mshiyeni and other influential chiefs initially favoured
Phikowaziwayo Victor, Solomon's eldest son by a junior wife. By 1939 they
had changed their minds, and informed the CNC that their choice was
now Absalom Thandayiphi, Solomon's son by Sokwenzeka, the daughter of
Mbulawa, the Buthelezi *inkosi*. To have done with the vexatious question of
the succession, the NAD thereupon ordered Mshiyeni to hold an *indaba* so
that the uSuthu elders could decide. Their choice fell upon Thandayiphi,
and the NAD duly recognised their decision.

Cyprian would not accept his exclusion from the succession, and protested with unexpected energy and vehemence. Since he could not be

ignored, the government took steps to decide the succession once and for all and appointed a Special Commission of Enquiry. Between February and April 1945 the commission took voluminous evidence from all the parties. Cyprian clinched the matter when he produced a letter from Solomon to Christina Sibiya, dated 26 March 1930, stating that she should produce it if need be 'so that it should be known that my heir is Cyprian Bhekuzulu'.[4] The commissioners acknowledged the authenticity of the letter and ruled in August 1945 that Cyprian would inherit the uSuthu chieftainship once he came of age. Mshiyeni and Thandayiphi thereupon rejected their ruling, and it seemed that violence between the two factions was about to erupt. To head that off, Major Piet van der Byl, the Minister for Native Affairs in Smuts' government, called an *indaba* at Nongoma for 15 September 1945. Before the large crowd of Zulu dignitaries and government officials gathered there, Van der Byl officially nominated Cyprian as Solomon's heir to the chieftainship of the uSuthu, and declared he would succeed once he turned 25 in four years' time. Van der Byl then used the occasion to spell out to Cyprian that any hope he might entertain of someday being officially recognised as the head of the Zulu people – and not simply as the uSuthu chief – depended on his not being 'headstrong' like Dinuzulu and Solomon, but rather following the obedient example set by Mshiyeni.[5] Cyprian duly took note that accommodation with the government was the only way forward for him, and henceforward this insight guided his actions.

Deeply offended at being publicly overruled, Mshiyeni immediately resigned as Regent, and his place was taken by Sifiya Sibiya, who had supported Cyprian's claim. To prevent any further discord, Cyprian's installation as chief of the uSuthu was hurried forward. Just after his 24th birthday, on 27 August 1948, the CNC formally installed him at a ceremony at kwaDlamahlahla before 5 000 Zulu who roared out the royal salute. Cyprian was awarded a stipend of £500 a year, plus another £250 for the maintenance of his father's dependants.

Before being installed as chief, Cyprian took two wives. The first was Priscilla ukaMasuku, who bore him only daughters, and the second was Jezangeni Thomo Ndwandwe (also known as ukaThayisa), who in July 1948 gave birth to his eldest son and future heir, Goodwill Zwelithini.[6] But then Cyprian breached all royal etiquette by falling in love with a

Paramount Chief Cyprian and his wife, Joyce Clementine Thoko Majali, at the
installation on 5 September 1957 of Mangosuthu Buthelezi (second from right, between
Cyprian and Isaiah Zulu kaMshiyeni) as Chief of the Buthelezi.

(SB BOURQUIN COLLECTION)

divorced schoolteacher and commoner twice his age: Joyce Clementine
Thoko Majali. A great scandal ensued and Cyprian was severely rebuked
by the Zulu elders led by Mshiyeni, but he ignored them and went on to
marry Joyce Thoko in church in August 1954. He moved out of kwaDlamahlahla, abandoning his other two estranged wives, and took up residence
in a new *umuzi* near Nongoma. This modest residence consisted of five
rondavels and a small Western-style cottage that Cyprian defiantly dubbed
kwaKhethomthandayo, or 'Choose Whom You Like'.[7] His wilful marital
woes caused Cyprian to fall into a deep depression, which he tried to allevi-
ate through frequent recourse to the bottle. In due course, like his father
before him, Cyprian became an irredeemable alcoholic.

As the uSuthu chief, Cyprian had graver problems to face than his
marital ones. Only months before his installation as chief, the right-wing
National Party won the general election of 26 May 1948. Under the pre-
miership of Dr DF Malan, the new government launched a far-reaching
legislative programme of social engineering to entrench white rule and

enforce the thoroughgoing segmentation between the races that rapidly developed into the notorious apartheid system. A major pillar of apartheid legislation was the Bantu Authorities Act 68 of 1951 (BAA).[8] The BAA gave substance to the racist government's ideology of separate develop-ment by creating a system of ethnic, 'tribal' authorities in the 'native' rural reserves and made traditional leaders part of the state's bureaucratic machinery. For this policy to succeed, it was essential to gain the support of traditional chiefs to administer the new 'Bantu homelands' in the inter-ests of the apartheid state. Inevitably, considering its size and coherence, the area of the old Zulu kingdom was earmarked as one such Bantustan.

It was Cyprian's ambition to achieve what his father had always been denied – official recognition as the Zulu Paramount Chief. But, as Anna Kolberg Buverud, Cyprian's biographer, has noted, the government made it clear from the outset that Cyprian first 'had to prove himself worthy and learn to obey'.[9] Cyprian indeed proved accommodating. The government consequently calculated that if it did elevate Cyprian to Paramount Chief it would strengthen those members of the Zulu royal family and the older *kholwa* establishment who favoured a moderate approach, and who were believed to be content with increased self-government in line with the BAA.

The government accordingly acted, but inexplicably without any prior announcement of its intentions. At a low-key meeting held at the Vuma Farm in the Eshowe District on 12 December 1951, and with few men of high status present to hear the announcement, the Secretary for Native Affairs, Dr WWM Eiselen, declared that the government conferred upon Cyprian the title Paramount Chief of the Zulu People, effective from 20 March 1952.

For the first time in the history of the Union of South Africa, the govern-ment had recognised the heir to the House of Senzangakhona as the Zulu monarch, but only with the lesser status of Paramount Chief. Many Zulu detested the title 'paramount chief', which they considered derogatory, and Cyprian himself felt insulted that, when it came down to it, his new title conferred only social prestige befitting his royal status, and gave him no new powers, leaving him subordinate to the local Native Commissioner. Furthermore, by increasing his stipend to only £600 per annum – less than that of the Mpondo Paramount Chief, for example – the government made it clear that Cyprian remained a lesser senior chief. However, there was a Machiavellian purpose behind confining him to this inferior status. Simultaneously with appointing him Paramount Chief, the government dangled the carrot of significantly enhanced powers before Cyprian's eyes – powers that depended entirely upon his acceptance of the implementation of the BAA and his own sensible cooperation generally.

The extent of Cyprian's obedience to the government was immediately tested. The ANC, the South African Indian Congress (SAIC) and various Coloured organisations all understood that the BAA and other discriminatory legislation were aimed at fracturing black political unity. On 26 July 1952 they called for a mass defiance campaign in protest, and the government responded with mass arrests. Cyprian was caught in a cleft stick. On the one hand, if he threw his weight behind the Defiance Campaign he risked alienating the government and being sent on the same path of exile and banishment trodden by Dinuzulu. On the other hand, he understood that if he aligned himself too closely with the government he was bound to lose popular African support for the royal house. He therefore avoided taking sides, adopting a cautious policy bordering on the evasive. So, while he drew back from openly joining the Defiance Campaign, he also refused to commit himself to accepting the BAA. Moreover, he did his best through good personal relations with the ANC leadership to ensure that the originally friendly bonds between the Zulu royal house and the ANC would not deteriorate beyond repair. Nevertheless, try as he might, Cyprian could not disguise that under his leadership the royal house was beginning to distance itself from the popular politics of African protest, and was instead tilting towards the politics of compromise and accommodation with the government.

Mshiyeni died in early 1953, and at his funeral on 18 March senior white government officials bore the coffin of the former Regent with whom they had worked so comfortably. With his death, Cyprian turned for guidance increasingly to Mangosuthu Buthelezi, his cousin who had herded cattle with him when a child. Born in 1928, Buthelezi came of royal lineage through his mother, Constance Magogo, a daughter of Dinuzulu. Acting since 1953 as the *inkosi* of the Buthelezi people, with Cyprian's support he was finally inaugurated as their chief on 5 September 1957. Although brought up to be proud of his high lineage and to value customary Zulu behaviour, like any other politically aware young African of his generation, Buthelezi responded to the rising calls for black liberation. Between 1948 and 1950 he attended the University College of Fort Hare, where African nationalism flourished, and he was expelled for his activism. But by the early 1950s his adherence to the vision of a revived Zulu nation based on ethnic pride and the illustrious history of the old kingdom motivated him to pursue a different political path. He perceived that the Zulu monarchy gave vital meaning to the idea of what it was to be Zulu, for (according to that way of thinking) the Zulu were defined by their loyalty to their hereditary monarch, as well as by their residence within the boundaries of the old Zulu kingdom – as they would be again if a Zulu Bantustan came into being. Buthelezi therefore began tirelessly to lay the foundations for a more stable base for the Zulu monarchy by linking it to Zulu nationalist sentiment.

The grand cultural festival Buthelezi arranged around the unveiling on 24 September 1954 of the Shaka memorial in Stanger must be understood in this light. In early 1930 Inkatha kaZulu (the Zulu cultural and nationalist movement inaugurated in 1924) had resolved to erect a stone monument topped by a carved funerary urn over the presumed site of Shaka's grave at kwaDukuza. The project had been bedevilled by poor financial management at Solomon's hands. Although the monument was ready by 1932, it waited in vain for an unveiling ceremony, and the sheeting covering it eventually rotted away. Now the moment had arrived.

The day before the main ceremony, the senior members of the Zulu royal family held a private one to appease Shaka's *idlozi* and to beg him 'to look with compassion upon his children, and drive away whatever "blackness" had followed his dying-hour prophecies'.[10] On the day itself, Cyprian and the Zulu chiefs wore traditional dress. Apparently, neither he nor most of the others had ever worn it before. But by donning it and by participating in the old rituals intended to secure the unity of the Zulu people, Cyprian paid his respects to the traditionalists and revived the nationalist sentiments of all present. Vitally, since only the king could address the royal ancestors, the people were reminded of Cyprian's unique, ritual link with the fathers of the nation.

Very soon after the Shaka celebration, on 2 November 1954, Dr Eiselen set up a meeting in Pretoria with Cyprian. The Defiance Campaign had only strengthened the government's resolve to implement the BAA as soon as possible to demonstrate that – despite appearances – it enjoyed the support of the majority of black people. Pressure and inducements were brought to bear on Cyprian at the meeting to accept the BAA and then to employ his prestige to make the other Zulu chiefs comply. The meeting failed because agreement could not be reached on precisely what sort of chieftainship was envisaged under the BAA. But the government did not give up. Dr Hendrik Verwoerd, the leading apartheid ideologue of the National Party, was then the Minister of Native Affairs. On 6 October 1955 he called a three-day meeting of some 300 Zulu chiefs at Mona, near Nongoma, with the intention of bulldozing them into accepting the BAA. But Verwoerd was stymied by Cyprian, abetted by Mangosuthu Buthelezi, his main adviser and now his chief *induna*, who was concerned to safeguard the status of the Zulu Paramount Chief as well as the rights of the chiefs, rural poor and traders. In the end, Cyprian refused to come to a final decision without discussing the matter far more widely with his people. Verwoerd was incensed at being rebuffed, and warned Cyprian: 'Do not throw honey on the honeybird!'[11] He was referring to the Zulu belief that the honeybird, which leads people to the hives of wild bees, will revenge itself if not rewarded for its efforts.

In the event, Cyprian did not hold out for too much longer against the government's plans for the Zulu people. The officers of the NAD continued to exert unremitting pressure, alternately tempting and threatening him. Cyprian eventually began to believe he saw the benefits of acceding to the BAA because it would give Zululand an institution that could express the views of the Zulu nation, bring administrative, educational and economic institutions more under Zulu control, and ultimately lead to greater autonomy. Cyprian and those chiefs who supported him did not mean this stance as an endorsement of apartheid policies, but they saw no future in joining the ANC and SAIC in what then appeared to be self-destructive and pointless resistance.

Consequently, in 1957 Cyprian decided to accept the BAA in principle, and on 31 October 1959 was present at the inauguration in Eshowe

THE EIGHT ZULU KINGS — CYPRIAN

Paramount Chief Cyprian and an official of the Department of Bantu
Administration and Developmen in Eshowe at the inauguration of the first
Zulu Regional Authority, 31 October 1959.

(*THE DAILY NEWS*, DURBAN)

of the first Zulu Regional Authority. By 1965, 12 regional authorities
had been established in Zululand, encompassing 102 tribal authorities. Not
all the Zulu *amakhosi* by any means were in favour of this development, and
some became openly insulting towards Cyprian for his perceived betrayal of
their interests. Following a whites-only referendum, South Africa had become
a republic on 31 May 1961. Under the new dispensation the Department of
Bantu Administration and Development took action against those *amakhosi*
rejecting the new regional authorities and deposed and banished many of them.

The next step in the protracted but measured drive by the government
of the Republic to establish a self-governing Bantustan in Zululand was the
creation of a Zululand Regional Authority. Cyprian's shoulder was accordingly set to the wheel, and in 1967 he called an *indaba* of chiefs at Nongoma
to discuss the matter, but (as so often before) no final decision was taken.
Undeterred, the authorities summoned Cyprian to Pretoria in mid-1968.
There they worked on him, and on his return Cyprian called another
indaba of the Zulu elite, who reluctantly approved the establishment of the

Sewn up in a white oxhide, the body of Paramount Chief Cyprian,
who died on 17 September 1968, is carried on a bier to his grave at his
kwaKhethomthandayo homestead for Christian burial.

Zululand Territorial Authority (ZTA) in principle. But long before they
could formally endorse it in 1970, and while discussions continued, Cyprian
died on 17 September 1968 in the Benedictine Hospital in Nongoma.

Cyprian's later life had been bedevilled by ill health and intensifying
depression that led to self-destructive behaviour. Not only did he suffer
from cirrhosis of the liver brought on by his incurable alcoholism, but he
was also a diabetic, and that condition was aggravated by his undimin-
ished intake of alcohol. Nevertheless, the Zulu people were forgiving of
his weaknesses, and recognised that, thanks to his efforts, a measure of
independence for the Zulu people was finally within reach. Some 15 000
mourners gathered to pay their last respects at Cyprian's funeral at his
kwaKhethomthandayo *umuzi*, where his coffin was covered by a royal leopard skin.

Cyprian had always followed a wary path between political extremes,
but despite his early sympathy for the popular African cause, he had
come to see that the obduracy of both Dinuzulu and Solomon would reap

no benefits. So, in the last resort, he followed the example of his uncle, Mshiyeni, and the wishes of many in the royal house, and cooperated with the apartheid state in the interests of Zulu self-government and the restoration of his people's ethnic and national pride. It was up to Buthelezi, who led Cyprian's obsequies and who would dominate Zulu politics for decades to come, to see what he could make of Cyprian's legacy.

KING GOODWILL ZWELITHINI
kaBHEKUZULU

✤ ✤ ✤

❧

CHAPTER TWENTY-THREE

CHASING THE KING
ALL OVER THE VELD

On 14 July 1948, Cyprian's second and chief wife, Thomo, who was descended from the Ndwandwe chiefly house on her father's side and from that of the Buthelezi on her mother's, gave birth to his eldest son and future heir. The boy was called Goodwill, and the second name he was given was Zwelithini, broadly meaning 'What does the country have to say about that?' That name not only signified Cyprian's pride in fathering an heir, but also implicitly referred to his succession dispute with Absalom Thandayiphi, who was being backed by the regent, Mshiyeni. Very soon afterward the answer was given when on 27 August 1948 Cyprian was installed as Paramount Chief.

Goodwill Zwelithini grew up at kwaDlamahlahla cared for by his grand-mother, Mpahleni Mtshali, one of Solomon's wives, since his mother died young, cast off by Cyprian when he married Joyce Thoko and moved to kwaKhethomthandayo. When his father died on 17 September 1968, Goodwill Zwelithini was studying at Bhekuzulu College of Chiefs, an educational institution built for members of the royal house. Since the young man was not yet of age to become Paramount Chief, his father's half-brother, Israel Mcwayizeni kaSolomon – a traditionalist who the authorities in Pretoria knew was willing to pursue a cooperative relationship with the apartheid government – was installed as Acting Paramount Chief in a great ceremony that included all the 280 chiefs of Zululand and some 8 000 spectators. Israel greatly relished his elevated position, and it soon became apparent through his deliberately insulting behaviour towards Goodwill Zwelithini that he was reluctant to step down. Thoroughly alarmed, Goodwill Zwelithini turned to Mangosuthu Buthelezi, his father's cousin and chief *induna*, for support. Buthelezi regarded Israel as a rival, if not an enemy, and took up the cudgels on Goodwill Zwelithini's behalf. He succeeded in pushing forward Goodwill Zwelithini's coronation as Paramount Chief to 4 December 1971 when he was still only 23 years old. As Goodwill Zwelithini's praises expressed it:

> Buthelezi was brave to keep up the spirit of the child
> Of Ndaba when they insulted
> and taunted him,
> Saying: 'Zwelithini will never rule,
> will never be king'[1]

Goodwill Zwelithini's traditional coronation ceremony was devised with the advice of the anthropologist Dr Peter Becker, and took place at the amphitheatre near Nongoma attended by nearly 20 000 Zulu.[2] For the occasion the *ukunqaka*, or bull-killing ceremony, was revived when Goodwill Zwelithini administered the final symbolic death blow with his axe. No one but the *ingonyama* could perform this ritual, which was associated exclusively with the monarchy. Having despatched the bull and affirmed his unique royal status, Goodwill Zwelithini then led his warriors in singing an ancient anthem, or *ibubo*.

Before his coronation, in 1969 Goodwill Zwelithini took his first wife, Sibongile Dlamini, whom he married in an unpretentious Western wedding ceremony in St Margaret's Anglican Church, Nongoma, followed by traditional dancing and feasting. Sibongile has since borne him five children. However, she is not Goodwill Zwelithini's only wife. He is a Christian, as were his father and grandfather, but like them he has also observed the Zulu custom of polygamy and his marriages (like theirs) have had the objective of creating a useful political and social network. Accordingly, after he had become Paramount Chief, in 1974 Goodwill Zwelithini married Buhle

Paramount Chief Goodwill Zwelithini, with Chief Buthelezi beside him, during his marriage to his third wife, Princess Mantfombi Dlamini, daughter of the late King Sobhuza II of Swaziland, on 24 June 1977.

(CHARLES BALLARD, *THE HOUSE OF SHAKA: THE ZULU MONARCHY ILLUSTRATED*, 1988)

MaMathe and had eight children with her. Next, in 1977 and with much traditional ceremony he married the Swazi princess Mantfombi Dlamini, daughter of the late King Sobhuza II, thus linking the two royal houses. They have eight children, and their son, Misuzulu, is rumoured to be a strong contender to succeed to the throne because his mother is the only one of Goodwill Zwelithini's wives with royal blood. (Some commentators believe that Lethukuthula, his only son by Sibongile, is his legitimate successor because she is Goodwill Zwelithini's first wife and they had a civil marriage.)[3] However, Goodwill Zwelithini has named no successor, any more than did his father or grandfather.

In 1988 Goodwill Zwelithini married Jane Thandekile Ndlovu in a spectacular 'blend of semi-western and Zulu traditional ceremonies',[4] and she has given him two sons and a daughter. His next marriage was to a Xhosa, Nompumelelo Mchiza, in a huge, five-hour traditional ceremony. Three children have been born of this union. Most recently, in 2014, he married Zola Mafu, who had been selected as his bride in 2003 when she was still 17. She gave birth to a daughter in 2005. Their traditional wedding ceremony was the most spectacular the king has ever held. Ten thousand guests attended, including President Jacob Zuma and Mrs Winnie Madikizela-Mandela, and 60 cows and untold numbers of sheep were slaughtered to feed them. Following tradition, Goodwill Zwelithini has put each of his wives in charge of one of his royal residences, where they preside in great comfort. Like his forebears, Goodwill Zwelithini has not confined his sexual proclivities to his six wives, and he has sired a plethora of children outside marriage. In all, he has about 40 children.

When Cyprian died in 1968, negotiations were still in progress regarding the establishment of the ZTA desired by the government. The Zulu chiefs officially agreed to it on 9 April 1970, and Proclamation 139 of 22 May 1970 set out its regulations. Following the precepts of apartheid, a territorial authority was intended to exert control over all the members of one particular (non-white) population group, such as the Zulu. Once a territorial authority was in place, its leadership could then request the foundation of an 'independent homeland', or what was dubbed a 'Bantustan'. At the launch of the ZTA, Buthelezi, whom it had elected as its chief executive officer, called for a transition to 'self-determination and self-realisation' for the 'Zulu nation', but he rejected the puppet role the leader of an independent Zulu homeland would have to assume, and the government realised he represented a serious obstacle to the full realisation of their Bantustan strategy.[5] So, they turned their attention to Goodwill Zwelithini, who, as they knew full well, chafed at having no prospect of real political power once he became Paramount Chief, even though he was the titular king of the Zulu nation. They also saw that he would be easy to manipulate because he was unversed in the realities of politics, and was presumed to be susceptible to blandishments that played on his jejune ambitions and elevated sense of hereditary status.

Accordingly, in 1971 Goodwill Zwelithini was summoned to Pretoria to meet Prime Minister BJ Vorster and the Minister of Bantu Administration and Development, MC Botha. Those two tough and experienced politicians found it easy enough to sweet-talk Goodwill Zwelithini into believing that the government supported his desire to revert somehow to the absolutism of Shaka's reign. They insisted that, as Paramount Chief, he would be no mere figurehead, and held out to him the possibility of his being given the executive power to appoint his own chief executive officer of the ZTA. In return, Goodwill Zwelithini would accept full independence from the government for the Zulu Bantustan, rather than the limited self-government Buthelezi was insisting upon.

Seeing the real danger that Goodwill Zwelithini would swallow the government's bait, and that he was strongly abetted in this by many of those close to him in the royal house who wanted him to exercise executive powers, Buthelezi knew he must attempt to restrain Goodwill Zwelithini by ensuring that he was restricted to a purely ceremonial, non-political role. Yet, at the same time, Buthelezi fully understood that the figure of the Zulu monarch gave meaning and coherence to Zulu politics, and that the subjects of the ZTA were in many ways defined by their loyalty to their hereditary ruler and by their associated historic sense of 'Zuluness'. As Buthelezi expressed it to his biographer, Ben Temkin, 'preserving the Zulu monarchy has as much to do with the restoration of the kingdom as it has to do with the preservation of traditional Zulu culture'.[6]

A delicate balancing act was therefore required, and Buthelezi set about dealing as carefully as he could with Goodwill Zwelithini in regard to his royal prerogatives. Nevertheless, he could not avoid generating much acrimony. Indeed, so angry did some members of the royal family become about Buthelezi's determination to circumscribe Goodwill Zwelithini's political role that they replaced him as the master of ceremonies at the coronation on 4 December 1971, and wild rumours flew about that Buthelezi would be assassinated during the ceremony. He was not, but Israel used the opportunity to announce that a royal council was being formed to assist Goodwill Zwelithini, and advised the young man to study how the Swazi king exercised his absolute powers.

Yet the insuperable obstacle for Goodwill Zwelithini was that power in a polity like KwaZulu was all about the control and distribution of patronage, and he did not command enough of it to attract sufficient people to his cause. It was Buthelezi who held all the patronage cards, and he played his hand deftly. In January 1972 the obedient ZTA unanimously supported

Buthelezi by voting to strip the freshly installed Paramount Chief of any executive powers, and to leave him with only the symbolic prerogatives of a constitutional monarch. On 24 September 1972, at the Shaka Day celebrations, Buthelezi spelled out in his harangue to the assembled throng that, as a constitutional monarch, Goodwill Zwelithini would in future stay above politics. Foiled and mutinous, Goodwill Zwelithini sat by in stony silence.

Thwarted for the time being by Buthelezi's victory over Goodwill Zwelithini, the government proceeded as far as it could with its Bantustan agenda for KwaZulu. On 1 April 1972 a government proclamation gave KwaZulu territorial expression and transferred the powers, functions and assets of all regional authorities in the territory to the KwaZulu Legislative Assembly (KLA), which was accorded limited delegated legislative and executive powers as well as control over its own civil service and police.[7] Problematically, though, KwaZulu did not consist of a single, coherent territory, and consolidation plans were released on 27 April 1972. Forty-four scattered African reserves and 144 'black spots' were to be brought together into ten areas.[8] The final step towards making KwaZulu a self-governing (but not independent) territory with enhanced status and powers within the Republic of South Africa was taken on 28 January 1977.[9] The former Executive Council was replaced by a cabinet that took over all matters except foreign affairs and defence. And the Chief Minister of KwaZulu, elected by the KLA, was Buthelezi, who was also President of the Inkatha National Cultural Liberation Movement he had formed on 21 March 1975, which exercised one-party dominance over the KLA.[10]

We have already seen how the first Inkatha, under the patronage of Solomon, gave organisational form to Zulu ethnic cultural nationalism. The new Inkatha represented not only the politicisation and mass mobilisation of Zulu identity, often framed in nostalgic terms laden with cultural and historical symbols, but also constituted one expression among others of mounting black resistance to white domination, and stood for a broadly based black rejection of apartheid. It was founded in the context of increasing government intolerance of radical opposition to its apartheid agenda, which reached a crisis in the Sharpeville Massacre on 21 March 1960. In Sharpeville's aftermath, the government banned the ANC and other liberation organisations on 8 April 1960, forcing their leaders into exile. In 1961 the ANC-in-exile formed its armed wing, Umkhonto we Sizwe, 'Spear of the Nation' (MK), and in response state repression continued to mount in South Africa. So, when Buthelezi launched the new Inkatha to fight apartheid in 1975, his initiative was welcomed by the exiled ANC as a new internal partner in the struggle.

However, Inkatha's relationship with other anti-apartheid organisations rapidly deteriorated. As the custodian and advocate of Zulu tradition, Inkatha's nationalism came to be regarded with deep suspicion by the ANC and others with their vision of a future non-racial society. Not only that, ethnic distinctiveness and segregation were basic to apartheid, and where did that position the KLA, dominated as it was by Inkatha under Buthelezi's leadership? How was it possible to resolve the contradiction between sustaining the avowed intention of dismantling apartheid from within and accumulating benefits from Pretoria, including armed support? Indeed, was a policy of 'loyal resistance', as Maré and Hamilton have termed it, ever sustainable?[11] It shortly proved not to be so. The Soweto student uprising of 16 June 1976 not only confirmed the ANC in its leadership role in the anti-apartheid struggle, but also led to the repudiation of Inkatha by Black Consciousness supporters. Inkatha broke with the ANC in 1979 over its support for international sanctions against apartheid because of the repercussions such measures would have on already disadvantaged people, and repudiated its commitment to the armed struggle. Thereafter, the ANC wrote Buthelezi and Inkatha off as apartheid stooges and labelled him an enemy of the people.

Where did this rapidly developing antagonism between Inkatha and the exiled liberation movements leave Goodwill Zwelithini, who remained unreconciled to his limited political role as a constitutional monarch? It seems that, while enjoying Inkatha's discomfiture, Goodwill Zwelithini saw no purpose in moving closer to the liberation movements since they were in no position to help him in achieving the status of executive head of state in KwaZulu he still so hankered after. Only the apartheid government had the necessary clout. Consequently, for the next few years he was linked to efforts by the Bureau for State Security and the Department of Information to set up new political parties in KwaZulu amenable to full independence and dedicated to undermining Buthelezi. They openly took Goodwill Zwelithini's part against his Chief Minister, and the *amakhosi* were urged not to permit Buthelezi to 'chase the king all over the veld'.[12] But these government-sponsored parties never got off the ground and Buthelezi prevailed. On 19 January 1976 Goodwill Zwelithini was induced to pledge his reluctant word to the Inkatha-dominated KLA that he would in future refrain 'from any participation in any form of politics and from any action or words which could possibly be interpreted as participation in politics'.[13] Goodwill Zwelithini's political ambitions had been effectively blocked.

As we have seen, KwaZulu was proclaimed a self-governing territory in January 1977, with Buthelezi as its Chief Minister. But Goodwill Zwelithini, thwarted in his ambitions and resolutely sulking, more often than not refused to undertake his ceremonial role as a constitutional monarch and attend sessions of the Legislative Assembly. Buthelezi decided he must tame Goodwill Zwelithini once and for all. Under his direction the KwaZulu government set up a commission in July 1979 to enquire into the king's neglect of constitutional duties. The crisis point was reached during the KLA's evening session on 8 August 1979 in Ulundi, the little capital of KwaZulu. The harried and mortified monarch burst tearfully out of the assembly building and disappeared into the darkness. He was spotted running along the road towards his home in Nongoma and his Swazi wife, Mantfombi, picked him up in her car. After this cathartic episode, relations were outwardly patched up, although Goodwill Zwelithini never found it in his heart to forgive Buthelezi and would later eat his revenge cold.

For the time being, though, the handsome, fully bearded Goodwill Zwelithini, who looked every inch a king, dutifully fulfilled his ceremonial role at Buthelezi's behest. It seemed that the bullied monarch had decided to make the best of it. Although still technically only a Paramount Chief, in KwaZulu he was officially referred to as 'His Majesty the King', and countrywide he was normally referred to as 'King Goodwill Zwelithini'. He followed the course Buthelezi had set for the royal house, making frequent joint appearances with the Chief Minister at cultural ceremonies and political rallies decked out (as occasion demanded) in smart suit and tie, in one of his array of splendid military-style uniforms, or in magnificent traditional dress.

Paramount Chief Goodwill Zwelithini and Chief Minister Mangosuthu Buthelezi
uncomfortably side by side outside the KwaZulu Legislative Assembly building in
August 1979 during the crisis over Goodwill Zwelithini's constitutional role.
(THE DAILY NEWS, DURBAN)

From Buthelezi's perspective, Goodwill Zwelithini was an essential figure in Inkatha mobilisation, the vital living cultural icon that personified
the continuity of the Zulu kingdom from Shaka to the present. Nor was
Goodwill Zwelithini loath to take on this particular role. In a speech on
9 September 1989 he declared: 'History has put me where I am and all Zulu
history demands that I make the unity of my people my first priority.'[14]
Deny it as he might, this public identification with Inkatha policies, along
with his heaping of personal honours on Buthelezi,[15] opened Goodwill
Zwelithini up to the charge that he had finally been absorbed into the
Inkatha fold, and that he had become nothing more than Buthelezi's obedient pawn. And, certainly, the material benefits of Goodwill Zwelithini's
compliance were far from insubstantial. He received not only the heady

KwaZulu self-governing territory, 1983

deference paid to him as monarch, but also the sundry royal residences, luxury cars, private schooling for his many children and other appurtenances of a lavish lifestyle paid for by the KwaZulu administration.

Meanwhile, events in South Africa were not standing still. Beset by internal and external opponents and foes, the apartheid government thrashed about seeking political solutions to its increasingly untenable situation, thereby increasing the dangerous volatility in the country. Following a whites-only referendum in 1983, the government created the Tricameral Parliament in which two chambers were added to the existing white one to give Coloureds and Indians a limited legislative voice, but not one to Africans who were technically catered for in their separate-development Bantustans.[16] But the Tricameral Parliament was not the solution. In fact, it was the reverse. The 1984 elections were widely boycotted, and internal rejection of the apartheid state in whatever form it took was stimulated, giving rise to the founding, on 20 August 1983, of the United Democratic Front (UDF). With its populist multi-class character and affiliations to youth organisations, the UDF commenced operating as the internal wing of the still-banned ANC and immediately raised the political heat in the country.

The creation of the Tricameral Parliament also had implications for the KwaZulu homeland, since one of its main administrative objectives was to overhaul provincial government. Buthelezi was already determined to achieve more than merely the territorial consolidation of the KwaZulu homeland. Earlier, in 1980 he had enlisted local academics who produced the Buthelezi Commission, which found that KwaZulu and the Province of Natal formed a single, integrated territory and that the Zulu kingdom was an unassailable feature of the region. This in turn led to the initiative known as the 'Indaba' of 1986. Its findings called for regional political unification to promote economic development, and advocated a high measure of regional autonomy for Natal and KwaZulu within a federal model of government in a post-apartheid South Africa. Inkatha's consequent espousal of the federal model would bring it into direct conflict with the ANC, which was wedded to the unitary model, and was destined to complicate future negotiations. Meanwhile, the Tricameral Parliament moved in sync with the 'Indaba', disbanding the

Natal Provincial Council on 30 June 1986 and establishing in its place the KwaZulu/Natal Joint Executive Authority, inaugurated on 3 November 1987.[17] Under this administrative umbrella KwaZulu continued its own existence, now operating from the elegant Legislative Assembly building in Ulundi, officially opened on 2 April 1984.

These constitutional developments occurred against the appalling backdrop of spiralling violence in KwaZulu-Natal between Inkatha and the UDF and their respective allies, although the Zulu heartland north of the Thukela remained relatively peaceful under Inkatha control, and official business in Ulundi carried on largely undisturbed, as did Goodwill Zwelithini's royal round.

Much is still made today of South Africa's extraordinarily peaceful transition from apartheid to democracy. Yet this upbeat narrative conveniently glosses over the vicious civil war that was centred in the province of KwaZulu-Natal from 1985 to 1995. It was at its most intense between 1986 and 1988, spreading from densely populated squatter settlements and townships around Durban and Pietermaritzburg and the corridor in between to the rural areas. Some 20 000 people died in the violence and a further 200 000 were driven out of their homes. Such casualties and the scale of suffering were far in excess of those inflicted in any specific previous conflict in the Zululand region, including the Anglo-Zulu War, and probably came close to being matched only during the period when Shaka was forging the Zulu kingdom.

When historians have turned their attention to investigating what this horrendous civil war in KwaZulu-Natal was about, it is the interpretation of the ultimately victorious side – the ANC-UDF alliance – that inevitably dominates. From this standpoint, the conflict is explained in terms of the deliberate mobilisation by the apartheid state of its traditionalist and predominantly rural surrogates in Inkatha against the 'progressive' and urban-based UDF. And certainly, since from the government perspective Inkatha was the legitimate authority in the region, it had to be supported against the UDF, which was officially characterised as a front for the revolutionary ANC and its ally the banned South African Communist Party (SACP), and was therefore part of the communist-inspired 'total onslaught' against white-ruled South Africa. So the government undoubtedly ignored

Inkatha-led violence, encouraged its vigilante action, and lent covert state police support and training.

Yet there was more to the civil war than that. Behind it were all the complex issues that bedevilled late-20th-century African communities in KwaZulu-Natal, such as the competition for land and scarce resources, and disputes over complex power and clientage relationships. Topping these was the matter of intergenerational conflict, in which Inkatha supporters attempted to maintain traditional patriarchal and hierarchical values against a militant youth who rejected the existing political and social order. Indeed, older people, 'respectable' householders, government servants, teachers, storekeepers and the like rallied to Inkatha to purge communities of malcontents and to foil their recruitment drives. And violent as Inkatha supporters undoubtedly were, and murderously nasty as local warlords could be – using the cover of the Inkatha banner to build their personal power bases – their opponents were equally wedded to violence to achieve their political ends, and threw up brutal warlords of their own, such as Harry Gwala, an unashamed devotee of Stalin.

The UDF and ANC's strategy was one of making the country ungovernable for the apartheid authorities, including the KwaZulu government. Integral to this approach was the deliberate fostering of a mentality of intransigent confrontation that forced people to choose between the heroes (them) and the apartheid sell-outs (Inkatha). At the forefront of this endeavour were the *amaqabane* – the Comrades – young people with an energising culture of revolt against the existing order. They embraced communism and the vision of a new society that they would create out of their violent and merciless destruction of the old.

Where did Goodwill Zwelithini stand throughout this turmoil and mayhem? He did play his part in pleading publicly for an end to violence and for a peaceful solution that would bring future investment, trade and prosperity to the ravaged region. Throughout the crisis he tried to maintain a neutral stance. But as a traditional monarch he could not help but feel threatened by what the *amaqabane* and *amakommunisti* stood for. At a meeting of *amakhosi* on 4 May 1990 he undiplomatically let his true sentiments slip when he flatly declared that communists would never rule the Zulu people. He then added provocatively (some might say presciently): 'I see the ANC as intent upon breaking down everything so that it can put the bits and pieces ... back together in such a way that South Africa becomes the ANC's property.'[18]

Doubtless, it was unwise for Goodwill Zwelithini to throw down the gauntlet in this way, but he had good cause to fear what would befall him and other traditional rulers should the ANC ever come to power. He only had to look north and contemplate the fate of other monarchs in post-colonial Africa. Where the former colonial powers had recognised a king as the head of state of an independent country, only a handful – the kings of Morocco, Swaziland and Lesotho – had hung on to their thrones. Otherwise, Farouk I, King of Egypt and the Sudan, had been overthrown by a military coup in 1952; King Mohammad I of Tunisia had been deposed by his prime minister in 1957; in 1964 Sultan Jamshid bin Abdullah al-Said of Zanzibar had been ousted in a popular, communist-inspired uprising; King Ntare V Ndiyeze of Burundi had been deposed in November 1966 in a military coup; and King Idris of Libya had likewise been sent packing by a military coup in 1969. In Ethiopia, the Soviet-backed *Derg* (military junta) had deposed the Emperor Haile Selassie I in 1974. In all these states, the monarchy was abolished and a republic proclaimed. The deposed rulers all fled into exile, with the exceptions of Haile Selassie, who died in 1975 while held in sordid captivity by the *Derg* (it is likely that he was executed along with most members of the imperial family), and of Ntare, who was probably executed by firing squad and his body thrown into a common grave when he foolhardily returned to Burundi in 1972.

The situation was only somewhat better for the lesser fry among traditional rulers of the newly independent states. In the period of constitution-making before independence, African politicians seemed not to be wholly committed to the elimination of royal or chiefly power. Nevertheless, there were strong demands for elective institutions to replace those based on heredity, and the emerging urban-based, educated African elite tended – often quite unjustifiably – to write traditional rulers off as illiterate bumpkins out of touch with modern developments. After independence, the new rulers soon found they could not tolerate any potential focus of opposition, and certainly not if it was based on claims of hereditary rule. In the case of Uganda, the five traditional monarchies of Buganda, Bunyoro, Busoga, Tooro and Ankole retained semi-autonomy under the constitution of the republic. The situation was not long allowed to continue, and in 1967 President Milton Obote abolished all the kingdoms and deposed their rulers.

If they were sensible, other traditional rulers grasped that their peers had always been the losers whenever they clashed with the new political elite, especially when military rulers displaced civilian administrations. So they prudently avoided banning, jail or deposition by settling for purely ceremonial roles as the custodians of the traditions of their people, and acquiesced in the severe curtailment of their previous political powers in return for state salaries and the incense of public deference. It was a lesson Goodwill Zwelithini did well to take to heart, for all his previous yearning for real executive power.

What saved the day for Goodwill Zwelithini and other traditional rulers in South Africa was the intervention of the Congress of Traditional Leaders of South Africa, or Contralesa. This extra-parliamentary opposition movement was launched on 24 September 1987 by 38 'progressive' chiefs and became an affiliate of the UDF. It grew rapidly, and by mid-1989 80 per cent of the chiefs in the Transkei were members, and 50 chiefs in KwaZulu had also joined. Buthelezi consequently saw in Contralesa a threat to his power base and disapproved of its political orientation, making sure that Goodwill Zwelithini held aloof.

In August 1989 a Contralesa deputation, led by its president, Mhlabunzima Joseph Maphumulo, the Maphumulo *inkosi* of Table Mountain (the Natal government had established his chiefdom in 1905), met with the ANC-in-exile in Lusaka, Zambia. The members of Maphumulo's delegation were no less concerned than Goodwill Zwelithini about their own positions in a country on the brink of political transformation, and suspected that the UDF intended to urge the abolition of chieftaincies under the new order. Their mission was to secure a guarantee from the ANC that when it came to power it would recognise the institution of traditional, hereditary authorities.

For a left-wing movement like the ANC, the perpetuation of traditional rulers in a modern, democratic South Africa was indeed a difficulty. But it had as a precedent those already independent African states that had prag-matically come to terms with traditional authorities because they exercised an irrefutable and age-old authority over their adherents, and had decided that in the long term it was more politic to work with them than to unleash chaos on the countryside by unseating them. In Ghana, for example, the Asante kingdom, which had entered a state of union in 1957 with the other territories that went on to form the Republic of Ghana, was a sub-national traditional state, and the Asantehene remained a constitutional monarch with a symbolic role. Likewise, in Nigeria, a federal republic since 1963, the constitution also recognised its own traditional rulers, of whom the Oba of Benin, the Emir of Kano and the Sultan of Sokoto were among the most respected. What was crucial in these cases (and in many others across Africa), and would have been carefully noted by the ANC, was that constitutionally the traditional rulers in question were forbidden to par-ticipate actively in party politics. Consequently, they posed no threat to the administrative machinery of a modern, parliamentary state, with its host of officials.

If that vital political exclusion were adhered to, it made sense for the ANC to draw the traditional leaders of South Africa in as allies and intermediaries. This would give the ANC access to the rural populations it would not otherwise have been able to engage to the same degree. Of course, a problem for the ANC leadership was that many in the movement spurned traditional leaders as the complicit collaborators of apartheid. Nevertheless, in Lusaka the ANC assured the Contralesa delegation that it recognised the role of traditional chiefs in forwarding the struggle against apartheid, and graciously conceded that chiefs had been forced into a false position by the apartheid regime that had manipulated and perverted the institution of chieftainship.

The final issue in Lusaka was the question of whether the institution of chieftainship was compatible with the secular democracy the ANC was striving for. There too the parties were able to come to an accord through their mutual recognition of the practice of *ukukhonza*. This term meant the paying of allegiance to a ruler that was essential if an individual were to be accepted as belonging to a chiefdom. In return for the acknowledgment of his authority, a chief allocated the individual land for his subsistence and provided leadership, protection and support. If either side in this relationship broke its terms, the arrangement was at an end. This meant that subjects and rulers were bound together in a mutually supportive relationship, and rulers were subject to criticism or rejection by their adherents. It was therefore possible to view traditional chiefs as the true representatives of their people, and to accept that their leadership and democracy were not in opposition and could coexist.

More than satisfied that they and ANC could work together, and assured that traditional leaders would not be eliminated in the new South Africa, the Contralesa delegation returned home. Henceforth Contralesa would be aligned with the ANC and would prove its most important rural ally.

Events in the apartheid endgame were now speeding up. The government legalised the ANC on 3 February 1990. In response, Inkatha transformed itself on 19 July 1990 from a cultural liberation movement into the Inkatha Freedom Party (IFP), a non-racial, less overtly ethnic political party ready to contest power in the expanding political arena. Over the next four years protracted negotiations were undertaken to effect a transition to democracy. In his determination to secure special status for KwaZulu-Natal in a federal structure, Buthelezi began to play an increasingly obstructionist role. In December 1991 he withdrew from the Convention for a Democratic South Africa (Codesa), where the Patriotic Front (formed on 25 October 1991 out of 92 anti-apartheid organisations) was negotiating a transition to democratic rule with the government and other parties at the World Trade Centre in Kempton Park. The reason Buthelezi walked out (some would say thereby cutting off his nose to spite his face) was that the ANC and SACP objected to Goodwill Zwelithini's delegation being included, along with those of other traditional leaders.

Multi-party negotiations continued, however, and on 7 December 1993 the Transitional Executive Council convened to manage the final stages of the transfer of power and to devise an interim constitution. This time, traditional leaders were successful in their demand to participate in the negotiations. After all, some 28 million people in South Africa lived as members of traditional communities, and it was recognised that an organ of state ought to be created through which their views could be expressed and their traditions and customs upheld. Consequently, on 11 December

1993 the political parties resolved to accommodate the concerns of the traditional leaders in the framework of the Interim Constitution through the creation of a National House of Traditional Leaders (NHTL) to advise the national government on matters of tradition and custom.[19] This meant that the future of traditional chiefs would be assured in the new democracy that was about to come into being.

❁

CHAPTER TWENTY-FOUR

THE MONARCH WHO REIGNS BUT DOES NOT GOVERN

On 2 February 1994 President FW de Klerk announced that the first democratic, non-racial elections in South Africa's history would be held on 27 April 1994.

Uneasy with the prospects for KwaZulu-Natal under a unitary government dominated by the ANC, but confident of the IFP's electoral majority in the province, Buthelezi now embarked on a dangerous game of brinkmanship. In one deadlocked meeting after another he threatened to boycott the elections, and went so far as to hold out the threat of civil war if Goodwill Zwelithini – who, at Buthelezi's urging, was now claiming his sovereignty over a Zululand defined by its 1834 boundaries during Dingane's reign, before the Voortrekker invasion – was not accommodated. On 8 April 1994 Goodwill Zwelithini and Buthelezi met President de Klerk and Nelson Mandela at the Skukuza rest camp in the Kruger National Park to thrash the matter out. There the ANC presented Goodwill Zwelithini with their draft agreement with the Zulu royal house, hoping to detach him from Buthelezi. They did not succeed, and with Buthelezi's advice Goodwill Zwelithini would not accept the draft until it had been amended to state that the ANC, National Party and IFP all agreed to

recognise and protect the institution, status and role of the King of
the Zulus and the Kingdom of KwaZulu, which institutions shall be
provided for in the Provincial Constitution of KwaZulu/Natal immediately after holding of the said elections. The 1993 Constitution shall
for this purpose be amended before 27 April.[1]

And indeed, as we have seen, the amended 1994 Constitution of the Republic
of South Africa duly provided for the recognition of the institution, role,
authority and status of the Zulu monarch in the Province of KwaZulu-Natal.[2]
With the IFP's eleventh-hour decision to participate, the general election of 1994 took place.[3] The IFP emerged as the third-largest party
nationally, after the ANC and National Party, and handily won the provincial election in KwaZulu-Natal. As a result, the IFP became a part of
the Government of National Unity on 11 May 1994, and Buthelezi was
appointed the Minister of Home Affairs. His national responsibilities took
him away from KwaZulu-Natal to Pretoria and Cape Town, and his absence
gave Goodwill Zwelithini the space to take stock of his future situation
in the new South Africa. In this he was closely guided by members of the
royal house such as Princes Zebulon, Clement and Israel – Buthelezi's old
foe – all of whom had long resented being subordinated to Buthelezi's dic-
tates. Two considerations seem to have occupied their thinking: the ANC
was now the dominant political power in South Africa; and Buthelezi (for
all the plastering over the cracks) could never be forgiven for his years of
bullying the monarch and manipulating the royal house to serve Inkatha's
political ends. Now was the moment for Goodwill Zwelithini to take his
revenge on Buthelezi by throwing him over and joining the ranks of the
new lords of the land. Nor were the ANC slow to scent the change of
atmosphere around Goodwill Zwelithini. Jacob Zuma, Jeff Radebe and
Sibusiso Ndebele, all hard-nosed political operators, veterans of the struggle and Zulu-speakers, wasted no time in making contact with Goodwill
Zwelithini to urge and facilitate his political realignment.[4]
    Buthelezi was quick to pick up on Goodwill Zwelithini's planned defec-
tion. At Nongoma on 10 September 1994 Buthelezi told the IFP election
victory rally that the royal house was trying to drive a wedge between
him and the king. He felt especially slighted that, as a gesture of goodwill,

Goodwill Zwelithini had invited Nelson Mandela to attend the upcoming Shaka Day without consulting him first. To defuse the issue, Goodwill Zwelithini arranged to meet Mandela and Buthelezi at his eNyokeni palace on 19 September 1994. But an IFP crowd led by Gideon kaMayayiza (Ndabuko's grandson) stoned Mandela's helicopter and damaged the palace. The next day, Goodwill Zwelithini's newly appointed spokesman, Prince Sifiso Zulu – who other members of the royal house disclaimed as a member, and whom Buthelezi believed was an ANC plant[5] – announced that the king would 'sever all ties' with Buthelezi as his traditional prime minister of the Zulu nation, or *undunankulu weSizwe samaZulu*. This was a hereditary office Buthelezi insisted he held, not as an elected politician in KwaZulu-Natal, but by virtue of his descent as the great-grandson of Mnyamana kaNqgengelele, King Cetshwayo's chief *induna*.[6]

Following the 1994 Shaka Day (which Buthelezi eventually celebrated without Goodwill Zwelithini or Mandela in attendance), Goodwill Zwelithini failed to attend Buthelezi's introduction of the KwaZulu-Natal provincial cabinet members to the royal house, and spent the weekend with ANC officials instead. To hammer home the point that he had definitely jumped ship, Goodwill Zwelithini replaced his KwaZulu Police security detail with former MK members who had been incorporated into the South African National Defence Force. The rift between Goodwill Zwelithini and Buthelezi was very public, and in 1996 Mandela warned the former that it was not serving his interests. Thereafter, Goodwill Zwelithini and Buthelezi did appear together at various ceremonies, but they did not interact and it was only too evident that no real rapprochement had taken place. Goodwill Zwelithini continued to submit Buthelezi to pointed slights that Zulu royal protocol made easy to administer, and their estrangement has never been entirely overcome.

Not that this rupture much mattered to Goodwill Zwelithini, since future political developments validated his wisdom in hitching his star to the rising fortunes of the ANC. Until 2004 the ANC and IFP were partners in the national and KwaZulu-Natal governments. But when that agreement was terminated, followed by the ANC's capture of the provincial government, the fortunes of Inkatha went into steep decline. As a party, it had always been rooted in the rural areas, and it is now largely confined to those northern parts of KwaZulu-Natal that once constituted the heart of the old kingdom. When Goodwill Zwelithini's fellow Zulu, Jacob Zuma, became the national president in 2009, the king's stock also rose, and for many years he enjoyed being deeply embedded in the ANC establishment.

Still, after 1994 Goodwill Zwelithini did not have it entirely his own way. For some time he still chafed at being no more than a constitutional monarch. It added almost nothing to his powers that he – or his nominee – was a statutory member of the five-person executive committee of the Provincial House of Traditional Leaders in KwaZulu-Natal, with its 76 elected members. Established in 1994, the KwaZulu-Natal House joined the other provinces (except for the Western Cape) in sending three members each to serve on the 23-member National House of Traditional Leaders.[7] But the sad truth is that, whether at the provincial or national level, these are toothless bodies, permitted to make recommendations concerning customary issues ranging from matters of law to indigenous land tenure, but with no means of forcing the politicians to accept their proposals.

Not therefore finding a political vehicle for his aspirations in the formal state organs for traditional leaders, Goodwill Zwelithini cast about for an alternative, and was encouraged in his search by a new royal council he had appointed under Prince Israel, and from which Buthelezi was deliberately excluded. However, a showdown in this regard occurred at a meeting on 19 February 1995 between the *amakhosi* and members of the royal house. The right of the new royal council to speak on the latter's behalf was summarily rejected. More than that, the gathering reaffirmed that their unconditional loyalty and allegiance was offered 'to the Monarch of the Kingdom of KwaZulu-Natal as the constitutional Monarch who reigns but does not govern'.[8]

And, with that, Goodwill Zwelithini's pretentions to wield real power finally came to naught. Nor should he feel hard done by. In Africa today, only four monarchs are still heads of state: Mswati III of Swaziland (which he renamed eSwatini in April 2018); Letsie III of Lesotho; Mohammed VI of Morocco; and Felipe VI of Spain (the Canary Islands off the coast of Morocco and the enclaves of Ceuta and Melilla in North Africa are Spanish possessions). Of these, Letsie and Felipe are constitutional monarchs carrying out purely ceremonial roles, while Mswati and Mohammed still retain extensive executive powers – although they have ceded some of them in the constitutions they granted, respectively, in 1998 and 2011. Even so, they are the two exceptions that prove the rule. Elsewhere in Africa, traditional rulers are fortunate if what status they still possess is based on more than customary law or practice. The lucky ones are those who enjoy constitutional or statutory recognition of their titles, status and role in the states that host them.[9] Such, as we have seen, is the position of traditional leaders in post-apartheid South Africa. On 29 July 2010 seven of them were formally recognised as kings by the state, the most senior of whom was Goodwill Zwelithini.[10] Thus, the title of king, forfeited under colonial rule by his great-grandfather, Dinuzulu, and never regained either by his grandfather, Solomon, or by his father, Cyprian, was at last Goodwill Zwelithini's in a South Africa under black majority rule.

King Goodwill Zwelithini might be only a constitutional monarch, but he is undoubtedly a very well-heeled one. As was pointed out in the Introduction, he receives more through government stipends and provincial allowances than does any of the other South African kings, and in the 2015/2016 financial year alone the Zulu Royal Household received R57.6 million. Nevertheless, this income still leaves him way out of the league of Africa's richest kings who have inherited great wealth from their forebears in the form of property, crown jewels and the like, and who have greatly added to their fortunes through sound investment and by starting successful enterprises and reinvesting profits into a diverse range of business, mining and shipping interests. The richest monarch in Africa today is the King of Morocco, and his family has one of the largest fortunes in the world, estimated to be several billion dollars. Swaziland (eSwatini) might be one of the poorest nations in Africa, but King Mswati's personal fortune is estimated to be $200 million, and in 2014 he increased his annual household budget to $61 million to pay for his several palaces, wives and lavish lifestyle.[11] Some constitutionally recognised traditional rulers within republics are also men of considerable means. One such is Otumfo Nana Osei II, the Asantehene of Asante in Ghana, whose wealth is estimated at $10 million. Another is the Kabaka of Buganda in Uganda, Muwenda Mutebi II, who owns the Nkuluze Trust that runs his properties in the kingdom and his business operations.[12]

Traditional rulers who don't possess their own large fortunes, and don't (unlike Goodwill Zwelithini and his peers in South Africa) receive generous stipends from their governments, have to depend for their income on the goodwill and generosity of their communities, who pay them what effectively amounts to tribute in the form of money, cars, land or houses. The arrangement is reciprocal, for such rulers are regarded as being the spiritual heads of their people – indeed, even godlike – and their blessings are sought. Such is the case of Ewuare II, the Oba of Benin in Nigeria. His people call upon him to mediate in family feuds, community disputes and land issues since, as a hereditary monarch, he stands above politics and is more trusted in such matters than salaried (and often corrupt) state officials.[13]

Until April 2015 the KwaZulu-Natal provincial government's Department of the Royal Household placed a budget vote for the maintenance of the king, his six wives and 28 legitimate children, for the running costs and upkeep of his seven palaces – kwaKhethomthandayo, kwaDlamahlala, eNoyekeni (the only one built of traditional materials), kwaKhangela, kwaLinduzulu, oNdini and eMachobeni[14] – for vehicles and drivers for his six queens who have outlays of their own, for the educational needs of his children, for medical expenses, and for salaries for staff such as courtiers, advisers, bodyguards and domestic workers. Since April 2015 the Office of the Premier of KwaZulu-Natal has been responsible for the Royal Household's affairs and has absorbed its staff and budget.

This budget is administered by the Royal Household Trust set up in 2007 to raise funds and generate income for the running costs of the royal family so that it would no longer have to depend on the public coffers. However, the Trust has signally failed in its objective and seems unable to operate as a going concern. In November 2015 its liabilities were reported to exceed its assets by R3.2 million, and it continues to depend on the stipend and allowance from the national and provincial governments.[15] (It should be mentioned here that despite the multi-million-rand state budget assigned to traditional leaders, Contralesa is dissatisfied, and is on record as calling for its members to receive the same salaries and benefits as elected politicians and office bearers, which, if implemented would cost the taxpayer over R3 billion a year.)[16]

Prince Mangosuthu Buthelezi and President Jacob Zuma with King Goodwill
Zwelithini during his wedding at Ondini Sports Complex in 2014 in Ulundi. Zola
Mafu was selected as the king's bride at the age of 18 while participating in the
2003 Swazi reed dance, and is the king's sixth wife.

(GALLO IMAGES/*SOWETAN*/THULANI MBELE)

In the 2014/2015 financial year the Department of the Royal Household
received R54.2 million and (as we have seen) in 2015/2016 R57.6 million,
but at the time the king requested an additional R18 million to build a
palace for his youngest and sixth wife, whom he had married in 2014. In
addition to these revenues, the king receives an average annual income
of R3.6 million from his farms. Even so, this is not sufficient for his lavish lifestyle. He consistently overspends on luxury vehicles (in 2016 six
Mercedes-Benz E-Class sedans were bought for the queens, another for the
queen mother and still another for the king),[17] on private jets and heli-
copters, on five-star hotel accommodation for himself and his entourage,[18]
on first-class international travel, on private schooling for his children, on
designer clothes for his wives, on spectacular ceremonies (such as the wedding in 2014 with its 10 000 guests), and on his seven palaces.

In the 2016/2017 financial year the Royal Household's budget was
reduced by more than 15 per cent (R9 million) to R48.8 million because, in

a time of financial hardship and drought, the Premier's Office had itself to take a cut of R95 million.[19] (Reductions were made to scholastic bursaries for the royal children, while royal grandchildren were no longer eligible for such benefits.) In the 2017/2018 financial year the Royal Household's budget was increased again and brought up to R58.8 million. Of this sum, amounts of R15.1 million in 2016/2017 and R16.5 million in 2017/2018 were transferred to the Royal Household Trust for the expenses of the royal family and the upkeep of their palaces. The remainder of the budget was allocated to staff salaries, royal ceremonies and traditional functions such as the revived *umKhosi woMhlanga* (Reed Dance) festival held at eNoyekeni, and to the Ingonyama Trust and its agricultural programmes, of which the king is the Trustee.

The Ingonyama Trust is central to Goodwill Zwelithini's continuing control over the land in KwaZulu-Natal and to his influence over the people who occupy it. Successive colonial and apartheid pieces of legislation were inimical to individual land ownership by Africans in the reserves set aside for them, so while Africans occupied such land, they did not own it, and it was held in trusteeship by the national government.[20] In KwaZulu, uniquely among the apartheid-era homeland states, the national government effectively loaned such land to the KLA to administer (along with its occupants) on its behalf. When the Abolition of Racially Based Land Measures Act 108 of 1991 repealed all previous land legislation it did not undo its consequences.consequently, in KwaZulu the land in the former reserves occupied by Africans was not given over to individual black ownership but remained under communal land tenure and continued to be administered by the KLA.

On the very eve of the first democratic, non-racial national elections (and in what some commentators have seen as part of a deal to encourage the IFP to participate) the KwaZulu government passed the KwaZulu Ingonyama Trust Act 3KZ of 1994, which came into effect on 24 April 1994. The Act ensured that the land occupied by Africans in the geographic area of the former homeland was not returned to the trusteeship of the national government. Instead, it established the Ingonyama Trust to be the custodian of all the land hitherto managed by the KwaZulu government.[21]

In terms of the Interim Constitution of 1993, the original Ingonyama

Act was comprehensively reviewed in order to meet all the constitutional requirements of both the Interim Constitution and the final Constitution of 1996. The result was the KwaZulu-Natal Ingonyama Trust Amendment Act 9 of 1997, which came into operation on 2 October 1998. A Board of Trustees administers the affairs of the Trust and is made up of the Ingonyama (the king) and eight members appointed by the Minister of Rural Development and Land Reform in the national government, after consultation with the king, the premier of KwaZulu-Natal, and the chairperson of the KwaZulu-Natal House of Traditional Leaders. At the time of writing, the chairperson of the Board was Judge Jerome Ngwenya.[22]

The land administered by the Trust is considerable, making up 26.9 per cent of KwaZulu-Natal, equivalent to 2.8 million hectares. Black people living on Trust land are issued with Permission to Occupy certificates, which grant them a form of tenure. In terms of section 2(3) of the Act the Ingonyama himself is the sole Trustee of the land, and the Ingonyama Trust Board understands this to mean that the Trust land vests in the king 'as trustee on behalf of the members of the communities defined by the Act'.[23]

Senzo Mchunu, the ANC premier of KwaZulu-Natal between 2013 and 2016, undertook to begin fundraising for the maintenance and renovation of the Zulu royal palaces, and to help realise their tourism potential with the aim of uplifting local communities. At the same time, he sternly insisted that the hitherto ineffective Royal Household Trust had to come up with aggressive revenue generation and fundraising to augment government funds. Indeed, the point has been vigorously made that it is high time that the royal house employed its status and exercised its influence to fundraise energetically. That way it would contribute positively to its livelihood and fund its lifestyle instead of asking for more and more out of the public coffers.

When in 2015 the king and the royal family grudgingly accepted that financial cuts in poor economic times were unavoidable, the IFP opposition in the province loudly complained that 'royalty in KwaZulu-Natal is being trampled upon by the Office of the Premier'.[24] That indeed seems to have been King Goodwill Zwelithini's fundamental attitude too. In July 2017 he publicly insisted with some vehemence that he was 'entitled' to the annual budget derived from tax revenue allocated to the Royal Household, and brusquely demanded: 'Don't Zulus pay taxes, am I not supposed to get this tax from my subjects?'[25] This is a deeply troubling statement, revealing that at times the king deludes himself into believing that he somehow exercises the sovereign powers of his pre-colonial royal ancestors, and conveniently forgets that he reigns as a ceremonial, constitutional monarch, and only because Parliament permits him to do so.[26] Nor in an objective sense is anyone his 'subject' since, in a modern parliamentary democracy such as South Africa, we are all citizens with our individual rights guaranteed by the Constitution. Of course, that does not prevent people from deciding to regard themselves as King Goodwill Zwelithini's 'subjects' as well as being South African citizens, but that is a subjective choice and cannot be imposed or enforced.

Taxpayers currently have no choice in funding the royal house because the central and provincial governments allocate some of the revenues they collect for that purpose. Yet, to what extent are these putative Zulu 'subjects' content to see their taxes spent in this way? No definitive answer is possible without a proper poll being conducted, but it is fair so say that support for the monarchy is strongest in conservative, rural areas, and is most firmly based in northern KwaZulu-Natal, in the territory that was once the Zulu kingdom. After all, Zulu-speakers south of the Thukela have not been ruled by a Zulu king since the Voortrekkers defeated Dingane 180 years ago. It is legitimate to speculate, therefore, how long taxpayers with no special attachment to the monarchy, but increasingly incensed by the royal house's profligate lifestyle and deep sense of entitlement, will tolerate their taxes being poured into King Goodwill Zwelithini's coffers. Never should it be forgotten that South Africa's sovereign Parliament could always amend the legislation that recognises Goodwill Zwelithini as a king and that allocates him taxpayers' money for his maintenance.

Until such time (and who knows if and when it will come to pass) it is fair to enquire what King Goodwill Zwelithini does in return for the millions he receives, and whether it is money well spent.

Despite his periodically resurfacing delusions of sovereign authority, as a constitutional monarch King Goodwill Zwelithini wields no formal political power. Yet, like those other African monarchs in his position, he owes spiritual and ceremonial obligations to the Zulu community that, in turn, reinforce his customary status as king. Such are his periodic formation of new *amabutho*, the resuscitation of the *umkhosi* (the annual 'first fruits' ceremony), and the great emphasis he has placed on the *umKhosi woMhlanga*, the annual three-day Reed Dance festival held in August or September at his traditionally-built eNoyekeni palace.

This festival calls for some consideration because, besides reviving and promoting the age-old Zulu cultural heritage, the king also perceives it as serving as a source of unity in contemporary society and as a proof of its common values.[27] At the *umKhosi woMhlanga* held in 2016, 200 years after Shaka seized the Zulu throne, the king vowed to protect the nation's inheritance, reminded the assembled throng of close to 30 000 participants and spectators of Shaka's legacy, and exhorted them to respect their elders and preserve Zulu culture.[28]

The festival originated during King Mpande's reign, when maidens from throughout the kingdom would assemble once a year at his *ikhanda* to celebrate their beauty, dignity and fertility. To symbolise their virginity and marriageability, they all carried long reeds in a joyous procession before the king and his court. This custom fell into abeyance with the destruction of the Zulu kingdom, but King Goodwill Zwelithini resuscitated it in 1984. During the 19th century, the festival was adopted by the neighbouring Swazi kingdom, and by his own account Goodwill Zwelithini was inspired to reintroduce it by Queen Mantfombi – his third wife and a Swazi princess.[29] Tens of thousands of maidens come each year to take part in the ceremony. Carrying a tall reed held high and upright, and led by a Zulu princess, they form a procession up the hill to eNoyekeni. As they approach Goodwill Zwelithini they lay their reeds down before him. They then dance bare-breasted for their king adorned in beadwork anklets, bracelets and necklaces, and attired in exiguous traditional attire.

A controversial aspect of the *umKhosi woMhlanga* is the virginity test all the girls are required to submit to before participating. The procedure is for the girls to 'line up, then lie in a row on their backs on grass mats … They part their legs while the the *umhloli* (inspector) peers briefly at each girl's exposed genitals before making her judgment.' She will sometimes 'use her hands to part a girl's labia'. The female elder 'who leads, directs and inspects' will also note 'the muscle tone' of the assembled girls and gauge their 'general demeanour' when 'determining virginity status'.[30] Leaving aside the problematical efficacy of such 'testing', the practice has come under much critical commentary, not least from the Commission for Gender Equality. But King Goodwill Zwelithini has been at pains to stress the contemporary value of the practice by explaining that, when he revived the festival, it was his hope that it would encourage young women to abstain from premarital sex and so arrest the spread of HIV/Aids. Yet he also hit out at critics, saying they 'did not understand the Zulu nation and its culture', and admitting to being 'baffled' as to why other cultures could not accept that Zulus had their own beliefs.[31]

It is inevitable, of course, that the king, who regards himself as the custodian of the timeless Zulu values of tradition, respect, wisdom and deference, will run up against those whose modern, secular outlook is at variance with his. Consequently, the king's fundamentally conservative cultural outlook, coupled with his belief that it is his duty to maintain the high moral ground and champion causes of lasting social value, has led him to make pronouncements that run contrary to the viewpoints held by many in contemporary civil society, and have involved him in subsequent damage control. Such was his condemnation in January 2012 of 'rotten' same-sex relations and the rampant sexual abuse of all kinds that motivates his defence of virginity testing.[32] And if homophobia were not bad enough, the king displayed what was roundly condemned as dangerous xenophobia when in March 2015 he called for foreign nationals to 'go back to their countries'.[33] His reasoning was that Zulu were being made to compete with foreigners for limited economic opportunities, and that as a monarch who deeply cared about his people and was attuned to their suffering, it was his obligation to come to their defence. Nevertheless, in response to criticism that his statement served to promote violence, the king had to retract it.

Cannily, King Goodwill Zwelithini has seen how royal ceremonies and festivals, whether truly ancient, recently revived or newly instituted, can both buttress his own position and serve the material interests of his people. Thus he has taken firm personal control of the Shaka Day celebrations, once Buthelezi's preserve and a manifestation of Inkatha's political dominance, and his prominent guests always include dignitaries of the ANC, with which he is now politically aligned. King Goodwill Zwelithini has also understood how the tourist industry provides employment and capital for betterment programmes, and, in the heartland of the old kingdom at any rate, has worked hard to open traditional Zulu spectacles to visitors and global markets.

Thus the annual *umKhosi woMhlanga* and the *umkhosi* 'first-fruits' ceremony held at eNoyekeni are magnets for tourists and spectators from all over, and local residents stand to benefit from the influx. But the king's recent plans to significantly enlarge the facilities at eNoyekeni, at exorbitant cost, with a cultural village, ablution facilities and sleeping accommodation have run into difficulties. The project has been put on hold by the Department of Arts and Culture 'and an auditing firm has been appointed to investigate potential wrongdoing'.[34] The multi-million-rand Heritage Precinct at the Isandlwana battlefield, which is very dear to the King's heart, has been in the planning stage since 1999 and has secured funding from the National Lotteries Board and the Department of Arts and Culture. Gugu Ngcobo, the CEO of KwaCulture, the non-profit organisation managing the project, has explained that the village 'is going to address who we were during the pre-colonial times', and that programmes there would run throughout the year and it would be a place where communities could hold traditional ceremonies.[35]

Far more controversial is the king's desire to build nine huts on the battlefield for the *amabutho* preparing for the annual commemoration of the Zulu victory at Isandlwana and a larger one for himself. Historians who are concerned that this particular project would destroy the integrity of the battle site have made formal objections, but have been overruled by an environmental impact assessment. Nevertheless, graves uncovered on the terrain – whether they are those of the British or of the Zulu is uncertain – make it an unsuitable place to build. Cynical observers have suggested that his determination to erect a royal homestead on the site is a means of his asserting a claim over the Isandlwana 'brand' and the funding it attracts, while at the same time establishing his 'struggle' credentials as a direct descendant of the Zulu kings who valiantly resisted colonialism.

᪥

CHAPTER TWENTY-FIVE

'THE LAND IS LIKE THE SOUL OF THE BODY OF TRADITIONAL LEADERSHIP'

In late 2017 the future of the Ingonyama Trust began to take precedence over the king's many other concerns. At the ANC's 54th National Conference, held at the Nasrec Expo Centre in Gauteng on 16–20 December 2017, various resolutions relating to 'economic transformation' were adopted and these were finally published on 26 March 2018. With reference to the ownership of the land, the key resolution read: 'Expropriation of land without compensation should be among the key mechanisms available to government to give effect to land reform and redistribution.'[1]

This resolution was strongly informed by the 600-page report released on 21 November 2017 by the High Level Panel on the Assessment of Key Legislation and Acceleration of Fundamental Change, headed by former president Kgalema Motlanthe. In its report, the Panel reviewed how legislation had impacted poverty, unemployment, equitable distribution of wealth, land reform, social cohesion and nation-building. Under the heading of Land Reform, the Panel identified the Ingonyama Trust as an obstacle to the security of land tenure for rural people in KwaZulu-Natal. It proposed repealing or amending the Ingonyama Trust Act and then transferring its assets to the Ministry of Rural Development and Land Reform, which should act as the custodian of those assets on behalf of the people living on Trust land.[2] And this can be effected without abrogating the Act governing the Trust since section 2(7) states that 'any national land reform programme established and implemented in terms of any law shall apply to the land … provided that the implementation of any such programme on the land … shall be undertaken after consultation with the Ingonyama'.

King Goodwill Zwelithini and the Ingonyama Trust Board naturally took these proposals and resolutions as a direct threat to the existence of the Trust. What made them worse in the eyes of the Ingonyama was the further resolution taken by at the ANC conference to 'democratise control and administration of areas under communal land tenure'.[3] This not only directly affected his status and power as king and as sole Trustee of the Trust, but also struck at the traditional powers of the *amakhosi* who administered the Trust and effectively governed the people. Goodwill Zwelithini most certainly would not agree with commentators such as Professor Musa Xulu, who has suggested that title deeds be given to those who occupy and use Trust land 'without intermediaries like *amakhosi* intercepting these rights'.[4]

But in leaping to the defence of the Trust as they were currently operating it, the king and the Board found themselves on shaky ground. Their mandate, as spelled out in section 2(2) of the Act, was to hold the land and administer the Trust for 'the benefit, material welfare and social well-being of the members of the tribes and communities' living on the land. Embarrassingly, Motlanthe's Panel had reported that the Board was far from operating in the best interests of those living on the Trust's land. Thus while the Trust was reported to have netted R96 million in the 2016/2017 financial year, the Panel concluded that there was little evidence that these funds were being fully used for the wider benefit of the community, and was scathing about the Trust's financial practices.[5]

Nor was that all. Section 2(5) of the Act states: 'The Ingonyama shall not encumber, pledge, lease, alienate or otherwise dispose of any of the said land or any interest or real right in the land, unless he has obtained the prior written consent of the traditional authority or community authority concerned.' However, the Panel found that the Board had regularly been authorising mining activities and leasing land to developers, commercial farmers and traditional leaders without proper community consultation, and that *amakhosi* had been asserting their sole authority to sign agreements with investors in respect of communal land. As a result, the benefits of such deals were not accruing to the ordinary users and occupiers of the land.[6] Furthermore, in November 2017 the Board had started calling on residents of Trust land to trade in their Permission to Occupy certificates for 40-year leases, thus converting the occupants of land inherited by families over generations into tenants who, if they default in paying their rent, could be forced to return their land and assets to the Trust. This, Parliament's portfolio committee subsequently decided on 7 March 2018, was a violation of existing rights protected by law, even if the law dated from the apartheid era. With such evidence before them, it is not surprising that the Panel charged that the people on Trust lands were justified in complaining that they were now more vulnerable to dispossession than they had been in the days of apartheid rule.[7]

All this has been welcome grist to the mill of the wittily ebullient, if deeply sinister, Julius Malema, the leader of the Economic Freedom Fighters (EFF), whose party has embraced the communist-inspired position that the state must be the sole owner or custodian of all the land in the country. 'If the land in the hands of the chiefs and the kings is indeed meant to benefit ordinary people,' Malema declared, 'the state can still do that. Unless,' he wickedly added, 'it's meant to benefit the elite found in those tribal arrangements.'[8]

And in KwaZulu-Natal members of this 'elite' have indeed been deeply riled by the threat to dissolve the Trust, and have warned strongly against attempting to do so. The 300 or so *amakhosi* who manage the Trust on the ground, along with the KwaZulu-Natal House of Traditional Leaders, were deeply angered that the Panel had made its recommendations without consulting them, let alone the king. As for the Zulu monarch, he was insulted that former President Motlanthe had not so much as paid him a courtesy visit about the matter. He has accused Motlanthe of trying to destroy the Zulu monarchy and the institutions of traditional leadership[9] – institutions, it should be remembered, that the ANC had embraced in 1989 when it met the Contralesa delegation in Lusaka and ensured that thereafter traditional leaders would be central to its support base.[10]

Indeed, in his dual capacities as the Zulu king and the Trustee of the Ingonyama Trust, Goodwill Zwelithini has vigorously taken the lead in opposing any interference by the government in the Trust. During the weekend of 20–21 January 2018 he seized his opportunity at the annual celebration of the great Zulu victory at Isandlwana to declare on that symbolic battlefield: 'I want to send a message once again to those who think they can do whatever they like about our soul, which is our land, that we should not be provoked. There is no need for Zulus to be abused for their inheritance.' He went on to insist that the land under the Trust 'which we hear that we don't deserve, was not a gift but a fraction of what was taken from us. This history makes us ask ourselves: what is the aim of the person who is brewing the war by saying that our land should be taken?'[11]

The king has no direct voice in the national Parliament that will decide on the future of the Trust, but Buthelezi, the leader of the IFP, certainly possesses one, and it was he who originally negotiated the Trust's inception in 1994. So Buthelezi, who is deeply imbued with a sense of Zulu history and who (despite his advancing years) has lost none of his fire, rose on 19 February 2018 to address a joint sitting of Parliament that was debating the newly elected President Cyril Ramaphosa's State of the Nation address.

The aim of the Trust, Buthelezi reminded the MPs, was 'to protect the few remaining pieces of land left to the Zulu Kingdom after colonial conquest and racial dispossessions'. He then enquired: 'Why has the Ingonyama Trust Act suddenly become public enemy number one? Why is the ANC determined to take the land away from our king, away from the custodianship of the *amakhosi* and away from traditional communities?' Referring to the ANC's land expropriation resolution taken in December 2017, he declared, '*Amakhosi* never expected that the first land to be taken would be the very land we placed in the hands of the people.' Thus, he argued, to repeal the Ingonyama Trust Act would amount to the 'dispossession of blacks by blacks'. And to attempt to do so, Buthelezi concluded, with many a threatening reference to the ancient military prowess of the Zulu nation, would be 'playing with fire' and would be a 'provocation against ourselves'.[12]

President Ramaphosa was very careful in his response to the debate and Buthelezi's inflammatory rhetoric, stating 'No one is saying that land must be taken away from our people. Rather it is how we can make sure that our people have equitable access to land security of tenure.' Rural Development and Land Reform deputy minister Mcebisi Skwatsha was even more cautious. 'There has been no decision by our government to take away land from the Ingonyama Trust,' he declared. 'We have to treat the matter with caution.'[13]

Nevertheless, Goodwill Zwelithini was not placated and kept up the pressure. At the opening on 27 February 2018 of the 5th KwaZulu-Natal Legislature at the Royal Showgrounds in Pietermaritzburg, he called on every Zulu to donate R5 for the fight against the government's proposed dissolution of the Trust, adding: 'Those who like their king or their land can donate even more. But what I am here to say as I announce this, is that "*Vuka Zulu*" (Rise Zulus).' He went on to vow that the Zulu would never allow their land to be taken from them and were prepared to die defending it: 'It's our fathers and mothers because that's where we are buried with our family members.' Moreover, the king explained that, from his perspective, 'Land cannot be removed from the traditional leadership. In fact, the land is like the soul of the body of traditional leadership. We will never allow, not for one day, that we be killed by taking our soul.'

Nonetheless, having beaten the war drum, Goodwill Zwelithini went on to remind his audience that he was 'the only one who steers the Zulu warship', and that the time had not yet come for the Zulu to fight for their land. This was because the issue had still to be debated in Parliament, and he had mandated the Board to assemble a team of retired judges to tackle the land issue on his behalf. 'For now,' the king ominously concluded, 'I am taking the legal route on this issue with the hope that those who want our land to be taken away follow the law.'[14]

The ANC took the matter a step further during its land summit held in Boksburg on 19–20 May 2018 when it firmly endorsed the policy of expropriation without compensation. During the debate, the issue of communal land and traditional leaders generated the most heat, with Motlanthe roundly declaring that the government must not be held to ransom by traditional leaders acting as 'village tinpot dictators' who laid claim to land that did not belong to them.[15] Others in the ANC were deeply upset by this standpoint, and President Ramaphosa tried to pour oil on the waters by insisting that the ANC were determined to work with traditional leaders on the matter, and that there would be a further summit dedicated entirely to the issue of communal land.

And this, at the time of writing, is where the matter stands. The Trust's fate is ultimately for Parliament to decide, and it seems that the king's strategy is to kick up enough of a row to dissuade the ANC from tampering with the Board's control of the land. Nor does Goodwill Zwelithini lack cards to play. Ironically, the resignation of his respected friend and ally, Jacob Zuma, has strengthened his hand. The political fallout from Zuma's disastrous presidency and the disarray of the ANC, smeared with well-substantiated charges of self-serving corruption, delivery failure and enervating factionalism, has rendered the ANC's victory at the national polls in 2019 less assured than ever before. Perhaps President Ramaphosa will succeed before then in restoring faith in the ANC. Meanwhile, the king holds the keys to electoral success in KwaZulu-Natal, and the leaders of the political parties all beat their several ways to Goodwill Zwelithini's doorstep to pay their respects.[16] For although KwaZulu-Natal has been an ANC bastion since 2004, and the king firmly in that camp, the furore over the Ingonyama Trust could undo that relationship. The *amakhosi* wield huge influence in swaying rural votes in the province, but they are as upset by the ANC's perceived betrayal over the Trust as is the king, whose lead they will follow. Most significantly, Willies Mchunu, the ANC premier of KwaZulu-Natal – a former chairman of the South African Communist Party in the province and a staunch ally of Zuma's – has also publicly expressed his displeasure and vowed that his province will never support any move to scrap the Trust or undermine the role of traditional leadership.[17]

It seems President Ramaphosa originally saw the logic of the Panel's recommendations concerning the Trust and endorsed them at the Boksburg summit, but with the 2019 elections looming, he has rethought the matter. His hand was apparently forced by an emotional and well-attended royal land *imbizo* held on 4 July 2018 at Ulundi in which the king lambasted the ANC's assault on the very nature of traditional leadership and on the Zulu nation itself. Only two days later the president urgently held a meeting with Goodwill Zwelithini and Buthelezi where he assured them that the government had 'no intention of touching that land or grabbing it from the Ingonyama Trust'.[18] Even if this presidential undertaking does not survive subsequent politicking (and in contemporary South Africa it seems almost anything might happen) the vexed matter of the Ingonyama Trust has brought King Goodwill Zwelithini to the forefront of the political landscape. In defending the Trust, the king is not only actively engaging with the greatest, most divisive issue of the day, namely, that of expropriation of the land without compensation, but also setting himself up as the champion of the institution of traditional leadership in South Africa, which he embodies more visibly than any other.

King Goodwill Zwelithini's determination to be associated with the deeds of his royal ancestors, to maintain their values, and to keep their and the Zulu people's culture alive and relevant in the present age represents a worthwhile set of goals. In that sense, the modern Zulu monarchy is much more than simply an institution for ceremonial occasions, and has a real part to play in the lives and self-respect of the Zulu people. King Goodwill Zwelithini might resent – and it certainly seems he does – that he is not an independent ruler as were the first four Zulu kings. But even as a constitutional monarch with no overtly political part to play – although, as his intervention in the debate over the Ingonyama Trust has proved, he still wields enormous influence in South African affairs – he should daily congratulate himself that, during his reign, the standing of the Zulu monarchy has recovered to an extent Dinuzulu, Solomon or Cyprian could never have envisaged, and that it receives the funds for him to live in a regal style beyond their imaginings. How successfully the House of Senzangakhona will withstand the inevitable storms of the tempestuous 21st century remains to be seen, however. Ideological foes such as Julius Malema might declare today that the EFF 'love the Zulu king', but will they still love him tomorrow and continue to bring him gifts of cattle in a ritual gesture of respect?[19]

King Goodwill Zwelithini's successors certainly face a perplexing future – but then, probably one no more uncertain than the prospect that he himself confronted, and all his royal ancestors before him.

GLOSSARY

In accordance with standard linguistic practice, Zulu words are entered under the stem and not under the prefix.

isAngoma (pl *izAngoma*) diviner inspired by ancestral spirits
iBandla (pl *amaBandla*) council of state
isiBaya (pl *iziBaya*) enclosure for livestock
imBongi (pl *izimBongi*) praise singer
iziBongo (pl only) praises
iButho (pl *amaButho*) age-grade regiment of men or women; warrior
ukuButhwa to enrol young men into an *ibutho*
ukuBuyisa to reconcile with the dead
isiCoco (pl *iziCoco*) headring
uDibi (pl *izinDibi*) baggage boy
inDlovukazi (pl *izinDlovukazi*) she-elephant; queen; queen mother
iDlozi (pl *amaDlozi*) ancestral spirit
inDlu (pl *izinDlu*) hut
inDuna (pl *izinDuna*) appointed officer of state, headman, councillor
umGando (pl *imiGando*) companions selected to accompany the deceased king into the spirit world
isiGodlo (pl *iziGodlo*) king's private enclosure at upper end of the *ikhanda*;

women of the king's establishment

isiGqila (pl *iziGqila*) maidservant, concubine

inGxotha (pl *izinGxotha*) brass armlet conferred by the king as a mark of distinction

iHlambo (pl *amaHlambo*) ritual cleansing ceremony

inHlangothi (pl *izinHlangothi*) wing of huts at *ikhanda*

ukuHlobonga to practise external sexual intercourse

iHubo (pl *amaHubo*) anthem

isiJula (pl *iziJula*) throwing-spear

iKhanda (pl *amaKhanda*) royal military homestead where *amabutho* were stationed

umKhandlu (pl *imiKhandlu*) council, assembly

iKholwa (pl *amaKholwa*) mission-educated Christian

ukuKhonza to pay allegiance to king or chief

umKhosi (pl *imiKhosi*) annual 'first-fruits' ceremony

umKhosi woMhlanga (pl *imiKhosi woMhlanga*) annual reed dance

isiKhulu (pl *iziKhulu*) great one of the realm, nobleman

iKlwa (pl *amaKlwa*) stabbing-spear (assegai)

inKosana (pl *amaKhosana*) king's heir by chief wife

inKosi (pl *amaKhosi*) chief, king

inKosikazi (pl *amaKhosikazi*) woman of status, principal wife of king

iLobolo (singular only) goods or cattle handed over by man's family to formalise marriage transaction

isiLomo (pl *iziLomo*) courtier, royal favourite

uMnyama (singular only) spiritual force of darkness or evil influence

iMpi (pl *iziMpi*) military force, army, battle, campaign

inNceku (pl *iziNceku*) king's personal domestic attendant and adviser

umNdlunkulu (singular only) maids-of-honour, girls of royal establishment

iNgonyama (pl *iziNgonyama*) Lion; His Majesty

iNkatha (pl *iziNkatha*) sacred grass coil, symbol of the nation

iNtelezi (pl *iziNtelezi*) ritual medicines to counteract evil influence or sorcery

iNtungwa (pl *amaNtungwa*) person of common Zulu ethnicity and identity; Zulu insider

umNtwana (pl *abaNtwana*) prince of the royal house

umNumzane (pl *abaNumzane*) married headman of a homestead
iNyanga (pl *iziNyanga*) traditional healer, herbalist
umQulu (pl *imiQulu*) rolled-up mat; throne
umShokobezi (pl *imiShokobezi*) cowtail decoration; sign of affiliation to uSuthu faction
inSila (pl *izinSila*) body dirt
ukuSisa to pasture livestock in the care of a subordinate
umThakathi (pl *abaThakathi*) witch or wizard
ukuThefula Zulu dialect spoken by Qwabe and other people of eastern seaboard
ukuThetha to go through the ceremony of giving praise to the ancestors
umuThi (pl *imiThi*) occult medicine
uTshwala (singular only) beer
ukuVuza to 'raise seed' for another man
iWisa (pl *amaWisa*) knobbed stick (knobkerrie)
isiXebe (pl *iziXebe*) concubine, lover
isiYendane (pl *iziYendane*) person with strange hairstyle; tributary from south of the Thukela River
umuZi (pl *imiZi*) homestead of huts under a headman

❀

TIMELINE

c 1781/1787   Birth of Shaka
1787   Portuguese fort and trading post established at Lourenço Marques
c 1788/1789   Birth of Dingane
c 1795/1798   Birth of Mpande

1814
13 August   Convention of London: Cape Colony affirmed a British possession

SHAKA (1816–1828)

c 1816   Shaka becomes the Zulu *inkosi* as Mthethwa tributary

Shaka's wars of conquest and consolidation (1816–1828)

1824
April   Shaka's first Mpondo campaign (*amabece impi*)
10 May   First party of hunter-traders from the Cape settle at Port Natal
August   Attempted assassination of Shaka at esiKlebheni

1826
October   Shaka and settlers crush Ndwandwe at battle of izinDolowane
              hills

1827
August   Death of Nandi

1828

4 May	First Zulu embassy arrives in Algoa Bay
May–June	Shaka's second Mpondo campaign (*ihlambo impi*)
June	Aborted plot by *abantwana* to assassinate Shaka at Mkhomazi River
June/July	Launch of campaign against Soshangane (*Bhalule impi*)
26 August	Failed embassy reports back to Shaka
6/7 September	Second Zulu embassy leaves overland for Cape
23 September	Assassination of Shaka at the kwaNyakamubi *umuzi* at kwaDukuza

DINGANE (1828–1840)

1828

December	Dingane acclaimed king

1829	Dingane purges *abantwana* and Shaka's leading men

1830

	Dingane's first campaign against the Bhaca
	Dingane's first campaign against the Ndebele
21 November	Dingane's unsuccessful embassy reaches the Cape

1831	Dingane's second campaign against the Bhaca

1832

	Dingane's second campaign against the Ndebele
	Birth of Cetshwayo

1836	Dingane's campaign against the Swazi

1837

June–September	Dingane's third campaign against the Ndebele
October	Boer invasion of Zululand

1838

4 February	Dingane cedes territory south of Thukela to Boers
6 February	Dingane executes Boer delegation at uMgungundlovu

Voortrekker-Zulu War (1838)

1839

25 March	Dingane recognises Boer Republiek Natalia south of Thukela
	Dingane unsuccessfully invades Swaziland
September	'Breaking of the Rope': Mpande flees to Republiek Natalia

First Zulu Civil War (1839–1840)

1840
February   Dingane killed at eSankoleni by the Swazi and the Nyawo

MPANDE (1840–1872)

1840
10 February   Boers recognise Mpande as Zulu king
14 February   Mpande makes further territorial concessions to Boers

1842
5 July   Republiek Natalia submits to British authority

1843
12 May   District of Port Natal annexed as a British dependency
June   Mpande kills half-brother Gqugqu and 'Crossing of Mawa'
5 October   British recognise Zulu kingdom north of Thukela River

1844
31 May   District of Port Natal annexed to Cape Colony

1845
30 April   District of Port Natal separated from Cape

1847   Mpande's first Swazi campaign

1848   Mpande's second Swazi campaign

1851   Mpande makes tributary of Mabhudu chiefdom

1851   Mpande raids Pedi

1852
17 January   British recognise independent South African Republic (ZAR)
                 Mpande's third campaign against the Swazi

1854
23 February   British recognise independent Orange Free State
September   Mpande cedes territory to Utrecht Republic

1856
15 July   Natal created as a separate colony of the British Crown

Second Zulu Civil War (1856)

1861   Cetshwayo attempts purge of surviving rivals

March	Treaty of Waaihoek
8 May	Shepstone recognises Cetshwayo as Mpande's co-ruler
June–August	Natal's 'Invasion Scare'
1868	Birth of Dinuzulu
1872	
September	Mpande dies at kwaNodwengu

CETSHWAYO (1872–1884)

1873	
August	Cetshwayo's Zulu coronation
1 September	Shepstone 'crowns' Cetshwayo

Langalibalele Rebellion in Natal (1873)

1875	
25 May	ZAR proclamations claiming the 'Disputed Territory'
	'Marriage of iNgcugce' crisis

Boer-Pedi War (1876–1877)

1877	
12 April	Shepstone annexes ZAR as Transvaal Territory
1877	
18 October	Failure of Anglo-Zulu negotiations at Conference Hill
December	uThulwane-Ngobamakhosi fracas

Ninth Cape Frontier War (1877–1878)

| 1878 | |
| 17 March | Boundary Commission convenes at Rorke's Drift |

Northern Border War (1878)

| 28 July | Mehlokazulu's raid into Natal |
| September | Partial mobilisation of Zulu army |

First Anglo-Pedi War (1878)

| 11 December | British ultimatum |
| 31 December | Dunn defects |

1879
January   Zulu army mobilises for war

Anglo-Zulu War (1879)

1879
4 July	Cetshwayo flees north
28 July	Cetshwayo captured in Ngome forest
1 September	Wolseley dictates peace terms, deposes Cetshwayo and breaks up Zulu kingdom (First Partition of Zululand)
4 September	Cetshwayo sent by sea to captivity in Cape Town

Second Anglo-Pedi War (1879)

1880
May   First uSuthu deputation to Natal

'Gun War' in Basutoland (1880–1881)

Transvaal Rebellion (1880–1881) (First Anglo-Boer War)

1881
February   Cetshwayo transferred to civilian custody

1882
April   Second uSuthu deputation to Natal

1882
5 August	Cetshwayo arrives in England
14 August	Cetshwayo meets Queen Victoria
11 December	Cetshwayo accepts terms of restoration to central Zululand (Second Partition of Zululand)

1883
| 10 January | Cetshwayo returns to Zululand |
| 29 January | Shepstone installs Cetshwayo as king of central Zululand |

Third Zulu Civil War (1883–1884)

TIMELINE

1883
21 July   Defeated Cetshwayo flees to the Reserve Territory
15 October   Cetshwayo accepts British protection at Eshowe

1884
8 February   Cetshwayo dies at Eshowe

DINUZULU (1884–1913)

1884
20 May   Zulu invest Dinuzulu as king
21 May   Boer Committee crowns Dinuzulu king
10 April   Cetshwayo interred in Nkandla forest
16 August   Dinuzulu cedes northwestern Zululand to Boers of New Republic
                 (Third Partition of Zululand)
7 September   Zibhebhu takes refuge in the Reserve Territory

1886
22 October   Britain recognises New Republic with reduced boundaries

1887
5 February   British protection extended over Eastern Zululand
19 May   Britain annexes Eastern Zululand, Proviso B and the Reserve Territory
                 as Colony of Zululand
25 November   British send Zibhebhu back to Ndwandwe District

1888
15 February   Dinuzulu seeks help from ZAR
26 April   Attempt to arrest uSuthu leaders fails

uSuthu Rebellion (1888)

1888
20 July   ZAR incorporates New Republic
6 August   Dinuzulu seeks refuge in ZAR
17 November   Dinuzulu surrenders in Pietermaritzburg

1889
February–April   Special Court of Commission in Eshowe finds uSuthu leaders guilty of
                 high treason
1 August   Zibhebhu forbidden to return to his location until its fresh
                 demarcation

1890
7 February   Dinuzulu and two uncles land as prisoners on St Helena

1893
8 January   Birth of Solomon
4 July   Colony of Natal granted responsible government

1897
30 December   Colony of Zululand incorporated into Natal as Province of Zululand

1898
5 January   Dinuzulu returns to Zululand as a Government Induna and Chief over
                 uSuthu Locations Nos 1 and 2
January   Zibhebhu returns to Mandlakazi location

Second Anglo-Boer (South African) War (1899–1902)

1903
27 January   Cession by former ZAR of districts of Vryheid, Utrecht and
                 Paulpietersburg (the Northern Districts) to Colony of Natal

1906
31 January   White occupation of Zululand commences in terms of the Zululand
                 Lands Delimitation Commission of 1902–1904

Zulu Uprising of 1906 (Bhambatha Rebellion)

1907
10 December   Dinuzulu arraigned for treason for role in the uprising

1908
19 November   Dinuzulu's trial for high treason commences

1909
2 March   Dinuzulu sentenced to prison

1910
31 May   Colony of Natal becomes a province of the Union of South Africa
                 Dinuzulu released from prison and exiled to eastern Transvaal

1912
8 January   Formation of South African Native National Congress (SANNC),
                 with Dinuzulu as honorary life president. Renamed African National
                 Congress (ANC) in 1923

1913

19 June	Natives Land Act
18 October	Death of Dinuzulu
27 October	Dinuzulu's burial at kwaNobamba

SOLOMON (1913–1933)

1913

27 October	Acclamation of Solomon as Dinuzulu's successor

First World War (1914–1918)

1916

25 November	Solomon recognised as chief over uSuthu locations

1924

October	Formal establishment of *Inkatha kaZulu*

1924

24 August	Birth of Cyprian

1925

6 June	Solomon meets Prince of Wales in Eshowe

1930

23 July	Eshowe *Indaba*

1933

6 March	Death of Solomon

CYPRIAN (1933–1968)

1934	Mshiyeni kaDinuzulu appointed Acting Chief of the uSuthu

1936

31 August	Native Trust and Land Act

1939	Mshiyeni appointed Regent and Acting Paramount Chief

Second World War (1939–1945)

1945

August	Special Commission of Enquiry rules that Cyprian will inherit uSuthu chieftainship

15 September	Cyprian officially named Solomon's heir at Nongoma *indaba*

1948
26 May	National Party wins South African general election
14 July	Birth of Goodwill Zwelithini
28 August	Cyprian installed as uSuthu chief

1950
30 March	Group Areas Act, 1950

1951
27 June	Royal assent to Bantu Authorities Act, 1951 (BAA)
12 December	Title of Paramount Chief of the Zulu People conferred on Cyprian, effective from 20 March 1952

1952
26 July	Defiance Campaign set in motion

1954
24 September	Unveiling of the Shaka monument in Stanger
2 November	Cyprian refuses to endorse the BAA

1955
6 October	Meeting at Mona rejects BAA

1957
1 November	Group Areas Act, 1957

1959
31 October	Inauguration in Eshowe of the first Zulu Regional Authority

1960
21 March	Sharpeville massacre
8 April	ANC banned and state of emergency declared

1961
31 May	South Africa becomes a republic
16 December	ANC launches Umkhonto we Sizwe as its armed wing

Border War (1966–1989)

1966
26 October	Group Areas Act, 1966

1968
17 September	Cyprian dies

GOODWILL ZWELITHINI (1968–)

1968   Israel Mcwayizeni kaSolomon appointed Acting Paramount Chief

1970
22 May   Proclamation of Zulu Territorial Authority

1971
4 December   Goodwill Zwelithini's coronation as Paramount Chief

1972
1 April   KwaZulu Legislative Assembly replaces Zulu Territorial Authority

1975
21 March   Formation of Inkatha National Cultural Liberation Movement

1976
16 June   Soweto uprising

1977
28 January   Proclamation of KwaZulu Self-Governing Territory

1979
8 August   Crisis reached in relations between Goodwill Zwelithini and Buthelezi

1983
20 August   Launch of United Democratic Front

1984
18 September   Tricameral Parliament commences

Civil War in KwaZulu-Natal (1985–1995)

1987
24 September   Launch of Congress of Traditional Leaders of South Africa (Contralesa)
3 November   Inauguration of KwaZulu/Natal Joint Executive Authority

1989
August   Contralesa delegation meets ANC-in-exile in Lusaka

1990
19 July   Launch of Inkatha Freedom Party

1991
30 June   Abolition of Racially Based Land Measures Act

25 October	Formation of Patriotic Front
1 December	Opening of Convention for a Democratic South Africa (Codesa) 1

1992
15 May	Opening of Codesa 2

1993
18 October	Presidential assent to Transitional Executive Council

1994
24 April	KwaZulu Ingonyama Trust Act comes into effect
25 April	Interim Constitution amended to recognise the traditional Zulu monarch in KwaZulu-Natal
27 April	Democratic elections
11 May	Government of National Unity
20 September	Goodwill Zwelithini severs ties with Buthelezi

1996
18 December	Promulgation of the Constitution of the Republic of South Africa recognising traditional leaders

1997
April	Establishment of National House of Traditional Leaders

1998
2 October	KwaZulu-Natal Ingonyama Trust Amendment Act

2003
11 December	Traditional Leadership and Governance Framework Act

2004
14 April	Elections sideline IFP nationally and provincially

2009
2 May	Jacob Zuma elected President of South Africa

2010
29 July	Official recognition of the Zulu 'kingship' in South Africa

2014
21 May	Re-election of President Zuma

2017
21 November	Release of the report by the High Level Panel on the Assessment of Key Legislation and Acceleration of Fundamental Change, which targets the Ingonyama Trust

16–20 December   ANC's 54th National Conference resolves to expropriate land without compensation

2018

14 February   President Zuma resigns

19–20 May   ANC Land Summit in Boksburg

NOTES

The following abbreviations are used in the Notes (for full details, see Select Reading List below):

JSA   C de B Webb and JB Wright (eds), *The James Stuart Archive of Recorded Oral Evidence Relating to the History of the Zulu and Neighbouring Peoples.*

RN   Dr BJT Leverton (ed), *Records of Natal.*

ZKS   C de B Webb and JB Wright (eds), *A Zulu King Speaks: Statements Made by Cetshwayo kaMpande on the History and Customs of His People.*

INTRODUCTION

1 For convenience, this book uses the 'English' prefix-less version of certain African proper nouns, for example Zulu (instead of amaZulu) and Swazi (instead of ama-Swazi). Other examples are Sotho (instead of Basotho) and Pedi (instead of Bapedi).

2 An alternative epithet for His Majesty is *Isilo*, or 'Wild Carnivorous Beast'.

3 The major axis of oNdini is 640 metres and the minor 507 metres.

4 Natal Law 107 of 1906 (5 August 1906).

5 In the 1850s King Mpande permitted the uThulwane *ibutho* (age-grade regiment) to wear crane feathers in their headdress because the regiment had so many princes enrolled in its ranks.

6 Native Administration Act 38 of 1927 of the Union of South Africa.

7 In terms of the Bantu Homelands Constitution Act 21 of 1971, the Constitution Proclamation R69 of 30 March 1972 created the KwaZulu Legislative Assembly. Proclamation R11 of 28 January 1977 declared KwaZulu a self-governing territory.

8 Constitution of the Republic of South Africa Second Amendment Act 3 of 1994: amendment of section 160 of the Interim Constitution, assented to on 25 April 1994.

9 The Constitution of the Republic of South Africa Act 108 of 1996, Chapter 12: Traditional Leaders.

10 Traditional Leadership and Governance Framework Act 41 of 2003, assented to on 11 December 2003. It has subsequently been amended (Act 23 of 2009). In KwaZulu-Natal in 2016 there was one king, with 296 senior traditional leaders and 3 100 headmen and headwomen.

11 Ministry for Cooperative Governance and Traditional Affairs, Republic of South Africa: The President's Announcement of the Findings and Recommendations of the Commission on Traditional Leadership Disputes and Claims (Nhlapo Commission), 29 July 2010; President Zuma's proclamation of the Rain Queen of the Balobedu (*Government Gazette*, 31 March 2016). The remaining six paramounts under investigation by the Nhlapo Commission did not qualify as kings, but they were nevertheless deemed to be kings until their deaths, upon which their successors would be recognised as senior (or principal) traditional leaders.

12 *News24*, 28 January 2013; *BusinessTech*, 12 February 2017.

13 *Sunday Independent*, 5 April 2015.

14 Zulu Royal Household Trust homepage (under construction). Available at Zuluroyaltrust.org/about, accessed 10 April 2017.

CHAPTER ONE

1 The Ethiopian succession was recorded in the Ethiopian Royal Chronicles, while written records were kept in all those parts of northern, western and eastern Africa that had converted to Islam.

2 It should be noted that oral history was always in danger of being distorted by the imbalance in power relations when being transmitted to a white recorder.

3 Kirby (ed), *Andrew Smith and Natal*, p 88.

4 *JSA 2*, p 210: Mangati; *JSA 3*, p 110: Mgidhlana; p 265: Mmemi.

5 Bryant, *Olden Times*, pp 32–3, 35

6 Shamase, *Zulu Potentates*, p 6.

7 *JSA 5*, p 270: Seme.

8 *JSA 4*, p 374: Ndukwana.

9 *Weekly Mail & Guardian*, 30 August–5 September 1991.

10 Nyembezi, 'Izibongo', Part I, p 114.

11 Wylie, 'White Myths of Shaka', p 82.

12 Wylie, *Myth of Iron*, pp 101–2.

13 Ntuli, '"Praises Will Remain"', pp 28, 32.

14 *ZKS*, p 4.

15 *JSA 5*, p 31: Ngidi.

16 *JSA 1*, p 179: Jantshi.

17 *JSA 1*, p 13: Baleka; Stuart and Malcolm (eds), *Diary of Fynn*, p 136, quoting her praises.

18 Cope, *Izibongo*, p 174; Ntuli, '"Praises Will Remain"', p 29.

19 *JSA 1*, p 189: Jantshi; *JSA 3*, p 105: Mgidhlana; *JSA 4*, pp 199–200: Mbekeni; Fuze, *Black People*, p 59.

20 *JSA 2*, p 247: Mayinga.

21 *JSA* 5, pp 29, 78: Ngidi.

22 Isaacs, *Travels*, p 219.

23 *JSA* 2, p 248: Mayinga.

24 Zibizendlela was said variously to have fled either to the Mpondo people to the south or to the Ndebele country to the northwest.

25 *JSA* 3, p 201: Mkebeni.

26 *ZKS*, p 4; *JSA* 2, p 51: Madikane; *JSA* 4, pp 201–5, 219–30: Ndhlovu.

27 Stuart and Malcolm (eds), *Diary of Fynn*, p 13; *JSA* 2, p 205: Mangati; *JSA* 3, pp 199, 200, 206: Mkebeni; *JSA* 5, pp 59, 76: Ngidi.

28 *ZKS*, p 4.

29 *JSA* 1, p 196: Jantshi; *JSA* 2, p 48: Madikane; p 162: Makewu; *JSA* 5, p 42, 66: Ngidi.

30 *JSA* 3, p 151: Mkando.

31 *ZKS*, p 4.

32 *JSA* 5, p 84: Ngidi.

33 *JSA* 2, p 92; Magidigidi; *JSA* 5, p 84: Ngidi.

34 Ntuli, '"Praises Will Remain"', p 29.

35 *JSA* 2, pp 47–8, 51: Madikane; *JSA* 4, pp 223–4: Ndhlovu.

36 *JSA* 4, pp 42, 59: Ngidi.

37 *JSA* 1, p 191: Jantshi.

CHAPTER TWO

1 *JSA* 1, pp 177, 183–4: Jantshi; *JSA* 2, pp 170–1: Makuza; pp 185–6: Mandhlakazi; Bryant, *Olden Times*, pp 163–6.

2 *JSA* 3, p 72: Melapi.

3 See Theal, *Progress of South Africa*, p 169.

4 *JSA* 3, p 158: Mkando.

5 Ntuli, '"Praises Will Remain"', p 31.

6 *JSA* 4, p 264: Ndukwana.

7 *JSA* 2, p 248: Mayinga. The shield was cut from the skin of an *ihwanqa* beast, black with white or grey markings.

8 See the sketch in *JSA* 1, p 326: Lunguza; and *JSA* 2, p 60: Madikane.

9 *JSA* 2, p 187: Mandhlakazi.

10 Maclean, 'John Ross', p 68.

11 *JSA* 3, p 87: Melapi.

12 *JSA* 5, p 60: Ngidi.

13 Cope, *Izibongo*, p 92.

14 Cope, *Izibongo*, p 94.

15 *JSA* 3, p 241: Mmemi.

16 *JSA* 4, p 226: Ndhlovu.

17 Fuze, *Black People*, p 54.

18 Bird, *Annals I*, pp 149–50: enclosure no 1 in Lt Governor Scott's despatch, 26 February 1864: 'Inhabitants of the Territory (now the Colony of Natal) ... before the

Extermination of Native Tribes by Chaka'.
19 *JSA 1*, p 183: Jantshi; *JSA 2*, pp 168–9: Makuza.
20 Wright, 'Reflections on Being "Zulu"', p 36.
21 Nyembezi, 'Izibongo', Part I, p 113.
22 Shamase, *Zulu Potentates*, p vi: Ndambi kaSikhakhane kaMlisa.
23 *JSA 5*, p 374: Sivivi.

CHAPTER THREE

1 In July 1879 King Cetshwayo took the spear with him in flight after his final defeat by the British, and on his death in February 1884 it was passed on to his son and heir, Dinuzulu.
2 Maclean, *'John Ross'*, pp 120–1.
3 *JSA 4*, p 219: Ndhlovu.
4 Ntuli, '"Praises Will Remain"', p 30.
5 *JSA 5*, p 75: Ngidi.
6 Ntuli, '"Praises Will Remain"', p 33; Cope, *Izibongo*, pp 88, 96.
7 Maclean, *'John Ross'*, p 135.
8 *JSA 2*, p 248: Mayinga.
9 Gibson, *Story of the Zulus*, p 37.
10 *JSA 1*, p 7: Baleka.
11 *JSA 4*, p 219: Ndhlovu.
12 *JSA 1*, p 7: Baleka. See also *JSA 3*, p 85: Melapi.
13 *JSA 3*, p 31: Mbovu; p 85: Melapi.
14 Kirby (ed), *Andrew Smith*, p 86.
15 *JSA 2*, p 163: Makewu.
16 Isaacs, *Travels*, pp 28–9.
17 *JSA 2*, p 51: Mayinga. See also *JSA 2*, p 162: Makewu.
18 Maclean, *'John Ross'*, p 76.
19 *JSA 3*, p 85: Melapi.
20 *JSA 4*, p 232: Ndhlovu.
21 *JSA 1*, p 8: Baleka.
22 *ZKS*, p 9.
23 Kirby (ed), *Andrew Smith*, p 86.
24 *JSA 6*, p 43: Socwatsha.
25 *JSA 6*, p 270: Tununu.
26 *JSA 5*, pp 53, 90: Ngidi.
27 Kirby (ed), *Andrew Smith*, p 84.
28 *JSA 6*, p 43: Socwatsha.
29 Maclean, *'John Ross'*, p 111.
30 Fuze, *Black People*, p 89.
31 Isaacs, *Travels*, p 28.
32 See, for example, *JSA 3*, p 72: Melapi.

33 See *JSA 1*, p 189: Jantshi; *JSA 2*, pp 60, 61: Madikane; *JSA 3*, p 31: Mbovu; *JSA 4*, p 205: Ndhlovu.

34 *JSA 3*, p 72: Melapi; *JSA 2*, p 248: Mayinga.

35 *JSA 2*, p 92: Magidigidi; *JSA 5*, p 40: Ngidi.

36 Nyembezi, 'Izibongo', Part II, p 161.

37 *JSA 2*, p 252: Mayinga.

38 *JSA 1*, p 8: Baleka.

39 *JSA 2*, p 247: Mayinga; *JSA 5*, p 40: Ngidi.

40 *JSA 2*, p 248: Mayinga.

41 *JSA 1*, p 57: William Bazley; *JSA 1*, p 8: Baleka; *JSA 5*, p 36: Ngidi.

42 *JSA 1*, p 195: Jantshi; *JSA 5*, p 62: Ngidi.

43 *JSA 3*, p 84: Melapi.

44 *JSA 4*, pp 158–9: Mtshebwe.

CHAPTER FOUR

1 *RN 1*, p 37: Farewell to Lord Charles Somerset, Governor of the Cape, 6 September 1824.

2 For this document, see *RN 1*, pp 38–40: Chaka's grant to FG Farewell, 8 August 1824.

3 The assassination attempt and Fynn's attendance on Shaka are described in Stuart and Malcolm (eds), *Diary of Fynn*, pp 83–6.

4 *JSA 5*, p 79: Ngidi.

5 *JSA 2*, p 253: Mayinga.

6 *JSA 6*, p 271: Tununu. The carver of Dingane's large chair was Cayana kaMaguya. See the black ivory or redbush willow chair in the collection of the Msunduzi (Voortrekker) Museum, Pietermaritzburg, which reputedly belonged to Dingane; the similar but simpler chair in the KwaZulu-Natal Museum, Pietermaritzburg, said to have been Cetshwayo's; and the three-legged chair of marula wood in Museum Africa (it also calls itself MuseuMAfricA), Johannesburg, which rather more dubiously is said to have belonged to Dingane.

7 A staff carved from the black ivory tree in the collection of the KwaZulu Cultural Museum, oNdini, is reputed to have belonged to Shaka and to have been used by Dingane, Mpande and Cetshwayo. The last-mentioned was carrying it when taken prisoner at the end of the Anglo-Zulu War, and took it with him into exile at the Cape.

8 A person would show similar respect to a chief, while a woman would employ avoidance speech with her in-laws.

9 *JSA 6*, p 96: Socwatsha.

10 *JSA 5*, p 378: Sivivi.

CHAPTER FIVE

1 Cope, *Izibongo*, p 100.

2 *JSA 5*, p 39: Ngidi.

3 Maclean, '*John Ross*', pp 118–20.

4 Isaacs, *Travels*, p 77.

5 Isaacs, *Travels*, p 106.

6 *JSA 5*, p 35: Ngidi.

7 *JSA 1*, p 42: Baleni.

8 *JSA 6*, p 101: Socwatsha. See also *JSA 4*, p 293: Ndukwana. See too *JSA 5*, p 72: Ngidi; and Fuze, *Black People*, p 64.

9 The site of Nandi's grave was refurbished in 2011 and a suitable monument erected.

10 *JSA 6*, p 272: Tununu.

11 Isaacs, *Travels*, p 113.

12 *RN 1*, pp 247–8: notarial deed signed by JA Chaboud on 29 July 1828 verifying the 'Scrawling fishbone signature of Shaka, Jacob's mark, and Isaac's signature as witness' on the document of February 1828.

13 Stuart and Malcolm (eds), *Diary of Fynn*, p 139.

14 *RN 1*, p 174: WJ Shrewsbury to Lt Col Somerset, 12 June 1828.

15 Mnkabi died there, and was carried back to Zululand to be buried.

CHAPTER SIX

1 *JSA 4*, p 219: Ndhlovu.

2 *ZKS*, pp 7–8.

3 *JSA 3*, p 83: Melapi.

4 *JSA 3*, p 55: Mcotoyi.

5 Cane claimed that Shaka had 1 000 women put to death (*RN 2*, p 52: Campbell to Bell, 19 December 1828), while Farewell put the total at 2 000 women killed at the rate of 300 a day (*RN 2*, p 60: Farewell's statement to Capt Aitchison, 19 December 1828).

6 *JSA 2*, p 295: Maziyana.

7 *RN 2*, p 74: Fynn to Lt Col Somerset, 28 November 1828. The English translation of the Zulu wording varies from one version to the next, but the meaning is the same. Essentially the same formulation can be found as an element in longer versions of Shaka's last words preserved in oral memory: 'Is it the sons of my father who are killing me?' (*JSA 1*, p 96: Dinya); 'Children of my father, are you killing me, I who am of your house and king of the Zulu?' (*JSA 1*, p 307: Lunguza); and, most dramatically of all, 'You stab me like this my father's sons, what have I done? You would strike and stab thus the wild beast of Mtetwa who shatters and destroys the nations he invades?' (Socwatsha's testimony, quoted in Eldredge, *Creation of the Zulu Kingdom*, p 272).

8 *JSA 3*, p 206: Mkebeni.

9 *JSA 1*, p 307: Lunguza.

10 *JSA 3*, p 155: Mkando.

11 Some accounts (primarily white ones, although note Fuze, *Black People*, p 71) suggest that Shaka's body was lowered into an empty grain-pit in the *isibaya* at kwaNyakamubi and his blanket laid over him without any further ceremony. See Bird, *Annals I*, p 97: Fynn's account; Stuart and Malcolm (eds), *Diary of Fynn*, p 157; Gibson, *Story of the Zulus*, p 41.

12 *JSA 6*, p 96: Socwatsha.
13 *JSA 6*, p 101: Socwatsha.

CHAPTER SEVEN

1 *RN 2*, p 49: Farewell to Lt Col Somerset, 15 December 1828.
2 *JSA 6*, p 97: Socwatsha.
3 Fuze, *Black People*, pp 89–90.
4 *JSA 1*, p 6: Baleka.
5 Rycroft and Ngcobo (eds), *Praises of Dingana*, p 71.
6 Isaacs, *Travels*, p 173.
7 *JSA 1*, p 6: Baleka.
8 Rycroft and Ngcobo (eds), *Praises of Dingana*, p 75.
9 *ZKS*, pp 97–8: Cetshwayo's evidence to the Cape Government Commission on Native Laws and Customs, 7 July 1881: Additions and Notes VII.
10 *JSA 6*, p 97: Socwatsha.
11 *JSA 6*, p 254: Tununu. Jantshi described Dingane as of 'a yellowish colour and tall' (*JSA 1*, p 197).
12 *JSA 1*, p 318: Lunguza.
13 Rycroft and Ngcobo (eds), *Praises of Dingana*, p 93.
14 Rycroft and Ngcobo (eds), *Praises of Dingana*, p 81.
15 Isaacs, *Travels*, pp 179, 289.
16 *JSA 5*, pp 368–9: Sivivi.
17 Archaeologists excavating in or near the *isigodlo* at uMgungundlovu have discovered large numbers of beads, the most common colour being white, followed by blue, and then green.
18 Isaacs, *Travels*, pp 179, 289.
19 *RN 2*, p 52: Campbell to Bell, 19 December 1828.
20 Fuze, *Black People*, pp 83–4.
21 Rycroft and Ngcobo (eds), *Praises of Dingana*, p 83.
22 Isaacs, *Travels*, p 219.
23 Isaacs, *Travels*, pp 177, 289.
24 Rycroft and Ngcobo (eds), *Praises of Dingana*, p 91.
25 Nyembezi, 'Izibongo', Part II, p 160.
26 Rycroft and Ngcobo (eds), *Praises of Dingana*, p 83.
27 *JSA 6*, p 254: Tununu.
28 Rycroft and Ngcobo (eds), *Praises of Dingana*, p 89.
29 Isaacs, *Travels*, p 177.
30 *JSA 5*, p 379: Sivivi.
31 *JSA 1*, p 196: Jantshi.
32 Rycroft and Ngcobo (eds), *Praises of Dingana*, p 75.
33 *ZKS*, p 10.
34 Rycroft and Ngcobo (eds), *Praises of Dingana*, p 95.

35 *JSA 1*, p 19: Baleni.

36 *JSA 4*, p 94: Mtshapi.

37 Rycroft and Ngcobo (eds), *Praises of Dingana*, pp 87, 175.

38 Bird, *Annals I*, p 289: Capt Gardiner, February 1835.

39 Nyembezi, 'Izibongo', Part II, p 162.

40 *JSA 4*, p 214: Ndhlovu.

41 *JSA 6*, p 10: Socwatsha.

42 For a list of henchmen executed, see *JSA 2*, p 272: Maziyana; and also those named in Dingane's praises, Rycroft and Ngcobo (eds), *Praises of Dingana*, pp 87, 89.

43 In 1830 the Mpondo and Bhaca defeated and scattered the Qwabe.

44 *JSA 6*, p 281: Tununu.

45 *JSA 1*, p 196: Jantshi.

46 *JSA 4*, p 7: Mqaikana.

47 Rycroft and Ngcobo (eds), *Praises of Dingana*, p 75.

48 Gardiner, *Narrative*, vol I, p 314; Bird, *Annals I*, p 314: Gardiner to Col Bell, 18 March 1837.

49 Bird, *Annals I*, pp 196–7: Campbell to Bell, 26 November 1830.

CHAPTER EIGHT

1 Etherington, *Great Treks*, pp xix–xxv, 1–9, 340–4.

2 Muzzle-loading muskets were tolerably accurate up to only 80 metres. The rate of fire was slow – no more than two to four shots a minute. But the Boers fired and loaded in rotation so that they could keep up a constant wall of fire.

3 *JSA 6*, p 174: Socwatsha.

4 *JSA 5*, pp 81–2, 88: Ngidi.

5 Mzilikazi's migrant kingdom would eventually come to rest in the Matopo hills, where he named his new capital kwaBulawayo in emulation of Shaka's *ikhanda*. His kingdom would endure until 1893 when it was conquered by the forces of Cecil Rhodes' British South Africa Company.

6 Bird, *Annals I*, pp 359–60: Retief to Dingaan, 19 October 1837.

7 Bird, *Annals I*, p 361: Dingaan to Retief (witnessed by Owen), 8 November 1837.

8 Bird, *Annals I*, pp 362, 364: Retief to Dingaan, 8 November 1837.

9 *JSA 3*, p 258: Mmemi.

10 Cory (ed), *Diary of Francis Owen*, p 117.

11 Ndlovu, 'Zulu Nationalist Representations of King Dingane', pp 98, 105–6. As early as the 1920s and 1930s intellectuals aligned to the ANC such as Selope Thema and Herbert Dhlomo, and African nationalists such as Petros Lamula and Isaiah Shembe, hailed Dingane as a patriot who defended the sovereign Zulu state in the face of relentless colonial assault and white oppression. See Ndlovu, 'Africans, Land and Images of Dingane', pp 112–41.

12 *JSA 6*, pp 284–5: Tununu.

13 Cory (ed), *Diary of Francis Owen*, p 89.

14 Bird, *Annals I*, p 366: Cession of Port Natal to the Boers by Dingaan, 4 February 1838 [certified copy of the original, found on 21 December 1838 in a leather hunting pouch with Retief's bones].

15 Called so because at dawn they would be staring (*gqaya*) at the moon (*inyanga*).

16 See Grobler, 'Retief Massacre', pp 123–4; for Zulu oral testimony affirming that the Boers were trying to surround the *ikhanda* with hostile intent, see *JSA* 5, p 118: Ngidi; p 201: Ntshelele; *JSA* 6, p 260: Tununu.

17 Cory (ed), *Diary of Francis Owen*, pp 110–11. By 'George', Dingane meant the British king, George IV, not realising that Queen Victoria had ascended the throne in 1837 following the death of her uncle, William IV.

18 *JSA* 5, p 374: Sivivi. Sivivi believed that 'Nkosinkhulu' was not the name of a king but was *isibhlonopho* for either Mpunga or Mageba.

19 See *JSA* 5, p 7: Nduna; and Delegorgue, *Travels*, vol 2, p 64. The reference to 'wizards' related to the Boers' nocturnal forays around the *ikhanda*.

20 The *herneutermes* was named after the Hernhutters, the Moravian Brethren, who manufactured these knives at their mission station at Genadendal in the western Cape.

21 *JSA* 5, p 81: Ngidi.

22 Bird, *Annals I*, p 381: William Wood.

23 Rycroft and Ngcobo (eds), *Praises of Dingana*, p 7.

24 See Sithole, 'Changing Meanings of the Battle of Ncome', pp 322–30.

CHAPTER NINE

1 He was nicknamed Hans Dons, 'Orphan Fluff', after his sparse beard

2 A few Zulu carried muskets, but for lack of training were completely ineffective.

3 *JSA* 6, p 268: Tununu.

4 *JSA* 6, p 268: Tununu.

5 Dingaan's Day underwent several name changes, representing the growing power of the apartheid government. In 1952 it was renamed the Day of the Covenant, and in 1979 the Day of the Vow.

6 The author participated in these proceedings in 1998 as a member of the Department of Arts, Culture, Science and Technology Battle of Blood River Reinterpretation Committee.

7 *JSA* 6, p 128: Socwatsha.

8 For the Governor of the Cape's reasons for finally intervening in the affairs of Port Natal, see *RN* 4, pp 46–49: Sir George Napier to Lord Glenelg, 16 October 1838.

9 For the treaty, see Bird, *Annals 1*, pp 516–19: Capt Jervis to Napier, 30 March 1839.

10 See *JSA* 4, p 276: Ndukwana.

11 *JSA* 5, pp 91–2: Ngidi.

NOTES

CHAPTER TEN

1 For a detailed account of Mpande's early career, see Kennedy, 'Mpande', pp 24–30.

2 *JSA 6*, p 45: Socwatsha.

3 Once he became king, Mpande would richly reward Mathunjana for risking his life to warn him of the danger in which he stood.

4 Fuze, *Black People*, p 81.

5 *JSA 5*, p 8: Nduna.

6 Fuze, *Black People*, p 80.

7 *JSA 4*, p 140: Mtshayankomo.

8 Bird, *Annals 1*, pp 538–40: Minutes of the Volksraad, 15 October 1839.

9 *JSA 2*, p 165: Makuza; *JSA 6*, p 31: Socwatsha.

10 For the Boer deputation to Mpande, see Bird, *Annals 1*, pp 540–4: Report of the Landdrost of Tugela, October 1839 (Embassy to Panda).

11 *JSA 6*, p 268: Tununu.

12 *JSA 4*, p 191: Ndabazezwe.

13 The Boers' grounds for repudiating the treaty were that Dingane had failed to deliver the cattle it had stipulated he should hand over.

14 *JSA 1*, p 172: Hoye. Nzobo had his quarters near the main gate at uMgungundlovu, and anyone coming in had to say whom they were visiting.

15 The Zulu widely believed that the Boers must have inflicted a far worse death on their great enemy than merely shooting him. The tale spread that Nzobo had been dragged to his death lashed face downwards from a wagon or, alternatively, had been tied to the spokes of a wagon wheel and left there until he died.

16 *JSA 6*, p 257: Tununu.

17 *JSA 6*, p 69: Socwatsha.

18 *JSA 3*, p 123: Mgundeni.

19 Mpande did not forget the part Ndlela had played in keeping him alive during Dingane's reign, and raised his sons Godide and Mavumengwana to be *izikhulu* in southern Zululand.

20 *JSA 6*, p 131: Socwatsha.

21 *JSA 3*, p 123: Mgundeni.

22 *JSA 6*, p 131: Socwatsha.

23 *JSA 5*, p 53: Ngidi.

24 *JSA 6*, p 44: Socwatsha.

25 *JSA 6*, p 13: Socwatsha

26 The vengeful Boers liked to believe lurid, invented tales that Dingane had been tortured to death by being pricked from head to toe by spears, bitten by dogs, blinded and starved.

27 *JSA 5*, p 53: Ngidi.

28 Fuze, *Black People*, p 85.

29 *JSA 6*, pp 44–5, 132: Socwatsha.

30 Rycroft and Ngcobo (eds), *Praises of Dingana*, p 87.

31 *JSA 6*, p 132: Socwatsha.

32 In 1947 HC Lugg succeeded in locating the grave and photographing it. The stones were still there but the site was thickly covered in trees and bush. See Lugg, *Historic Natal*, pp 162–8.

33 Fuze, *Black People*, p 89.

CHAPTER ELEVEN

1 *JSA 5*, p 346: Singcofela.

2 Fuze, *Black People*, p 89.

3 For the Boer proclamations of Mpande as king and the annexation of southern Zululand, see Bird, *Annals I*, pp 591–6: Journal of the Commando against Dingaan, 9–14 February 1840.

4 Fuze, *Black People*, pp 93, 146.

5 Delegorgue, *Travels I*, pp 85, 87–8.

6 *JSA 4*, p 74: Mtshapi.

7 *ZKS*, p 15.

8 By the Bloemfontein Convention of 23 February 1854, the British also recognised the independence of the Orange Free State, the Boer republic between the Orange and Vaal rivers.

9 See Bird, *Annals II*, pp 299–300: Articles of a Treaty between King Panda and Commissioner Cloete, 5 October 1843. Mpande made his own mark to the treaty, and Cloete signed.

10 In January 1847 Mpande 'sold' a triangle of territory between the Thukela and Mzinyathi rivers to Boers leaving British Natal and bent on setting up their own independent statelet. This territory was south of the Zululand-Natal border of 1843 and was not Mpande's to dispose of. The British brought the Klip River Insurrection, as it was known, to a close in January 1848 and admonished Mpande for the part he had played in it.

11 *ZKS*, pp 79–80, 93–4.

12 This is a hybrid name, derived from Xhosa, Zulu and Sesotho and essentially meaning 'pioneer'.

13 Lugg, *Historic Natal*, p 57.

14 *JSA 6*, p 258: Xaba.

15 *JSA 6*, p 102: Socwatsha.

16 *JSA 5*, p 299: John Shepstone.

17 Fuze, *Black People*, p 94.

18 *JSA 6*, p 375: Xubu. He was one of Theophilus Shepstone's African messengers.

19 Fuze, *Black People*, pp 94–5.

CHAPTER TWELVE

1 Fuze, *Black People*, p 89.

2 Mpande had either 28 or 29 sons. See the genealogical tables in *JSA 3*, p 110: Mgidhlana; and pp 266, 275: Mmemi.

3 *JSA 2*, p 165: Makuza.
4 Samuelson, *Long, Long Ago*, p 218.
5 *JSA 6*, p 30: Socwatsha.
6 *JSA 5*, p 41: Ngidi.
7 *JSA 4*, p 301: Ndukwana.
8 *JSA 6*, p 101: Socwatsha.
9 *JSA 2*, p 243: Maxibana.
10 *JSA 2*, p 244: Maxibana.
11 *JSA 3*, p 232: Mkungu.
12 *JSA 6*, p 282: Tununu.
13 *JSA 5*, p 136: Nkuku.
14 *JSA 6*, p 92: Socwatsha.
15 *JSA 4*, p 380: Ndukwana.
16 *JSA 6*, p 80: Socwatsha.
17 *JSA 2*, p 227: Manyonyana.
18 Cope, *Izibongo*, p 216.
19 Moodie (ed), *John Dunn*, p 7.
20 Cope, *Izibongo*, p 218.
21 *JSA 5*, p 303: John Shepstone.
22 *JSA 6*, p 102: Socwatsha.
23 *JSA 6*, p 14: Socwatsha.
24 Colenso's school was called Ekukhunyeni, the 'Place of Light'.
25 *JSA 3*, p 106: Mgidhlana
26 *JSA 6*, p 284: Tununu.
27 *JSA 2*, p 190: Mandhakazi.
28 *JSA 2*, p 207: Mangati.
29 *ZKS*, p 17.
30 *JSA 6*, p 155: Socwatsha.
31 In September 1854 Mpande had ceded the wedge of land between the Mzinyathi and Ncome rivers (technically part of the Zulu kingdom since the Anglo-Zulu boundary agreement of 1843) to the Boers who had been infiltrating the region. They set up the transient little Republic of Utrecht, but on 6 November 1859 it was absorbed into the ZAR, thus advancing the latter's southeastern border to the Ncome River.
32 *JSA 6*, p 114: Socwatsha.
33 Both Mpande and Cetshwayo were determined that missionaries should not disrupt the institutions of Zulu society and actively discouraged conversions – much to the missionaries' frustration.

CHAPTER THIRTEEN

1 See the testimony concerning Mpande's obsequies in *JSA 1*, pp 42–4: Baleni; and by Nomguqo Dlamini, a member of Cetshwayo's *isigodlo*: Filter and Bourquin (eds), *Paulina Dlamini*, pp 26–27.

2 *ZKS*, p 17.
3 See Colenso, *Digest*, series 1, part 2, p 672.
4 *JSA 4*, p 344.
5 *JSA 3*, p 312: Mpatshana.
6 Filter and Bourquin (eds), *Paulina Dlamini*, p 61.
7 Ndukwana recounted that when Mnyamana passed a pot of beer to Masiphula he did so with one hand only, whereas Zulu etiquette dictated that both hands be used when passing an object to a social superior (*JSA 4*, p 301: Ndukwana).
8 *ZKS*, p 18.
9 According to the British protocol of gun salutes at the time, 17 shots were reserved for second-tier Indian princes (top-ranking ones received 21).
10 *JSA 4*, p 127: Mthayankomo.
11 *ZKS*, pp 98–9.
12 *JSA 4*, p 338: Ndukwana.
13 *JSA 1*, p 199: Jantshi. See also *JSA 1*, p 32: Baleni.
14 *JSA 3*, pp 200–1: Mkebeni.
15 *JSA 5*, p 270: Seme; *JSA 6*, pp 150–1: Socwatsha.
16 *JSA 5*, p 265: CR Saunders.
17 Filter and Bourquin (eds), *Paulina Dlamini*, pp 45–6.
18 *ZKS*, p 72.
19 *JSA 4*, p 295: Ndukwana.
20 In February 1878 the British pressured the Portuguese to halt the sale of guns and ammunition to Africans through Delagoa Bay, although it took until August that year to make the ban effective.
21 *Natal Witness*, 22 August 1878: letter from 'Rufus'.
22 *JSA 3*, p 328: Mpatshana.

CHAPTER FOURTEEN

1 In 1867 Carnarvon had masterminded the creation of the self-governing federal Dominion of Canada out of three separate British colonies.
2 Basutoland and Griqualand East were administered by the Cape Colony, and Griqualand West would be from 1880.
3 Britain had recognised the independence of the Orange Free State in 1854, and that of the ZAR in 1852.
4 Shepstone to Herbert, 5 October 1877, quoted in Delius, *Pedi Polity*, p 229.
5 *BPP* C. 2242, appendix III, no 1: Shepstone to Carnarvon, 1 December 1877.
6 *ZKS*, p 49.
7 Theophilus Shepstone to Frere, 30 April 1878, quoted in Martineau, *Sir Bartle Frere*, vol II, p 235.
8 Frere was also drawn into an unanticipated small conflict between April and November 1878, the Northern Border War, in Griqualand West.
9 *BPP* C. 2222, no 5: Frere to Hicks Beach, 10 December 1878.

10 Frere to Hicks Beach, 28 October 1878; and notes by Frere, 3 February 1879, quoted in Laband, *Rope of Sand*, p 189.

11 Frere to Shepstone, 30 November 1878, quoted in Laband, *Kingdom in Crisis*, p 12.

12 *BPP* C. 2222, sub-enclosure 19 in enclosure 1 in no 6: message to Lt Governor from Cetywayo, 20 September 1878.

13 *BPP* C. 2308, enclosure 1 in no 7: message from Cetywayo to Lt Governor, 10 November 1878.

14 Frere to Hicks Beach, 8 December 1878, quoted in Martineau, *Sir Bartle Frere*, vol II, p 253.

15 It took five weeks for a despatch to travel between Frere and the Colonial Office, and between 15 and 21 days for a telegram because there was no direct cable link.

16 Frere to Hicks Beach, 28 October 1878, quoted in Martineau, *Sir Bartle Frere*, vol II, pp 259–60; *BPP* C. 2222, no 54: Frere to Hicks Beach, 14 December 1878.

17 Vijn, *Cetshwayo's Dutchman*, p 15: 24 November 1878.

18 Hamu to Landdrost of Utrecht (letter signed 'Home'), recd 6 November 1878, quoted in Laband, *Rope of Sand*, p 199.

19 Kumbeka Gwabe, 'Supplement', *Natal Mercury*, 22 January 1929.

20 *JSA* 3, pp 296–7: Mpatshana. On Cetshwayo's orders the same *isangoma* again doctored the army preparatory to the Khambula campaign in late March 1879. But when his magic failed to work then either, he set about poisoning the water the British must drink – with equally ineffective results (*JSA* 3, pp 312–13: Mpatshana).

21 *BPP* C. 2482, enclosure D in enclosure in no 32: statement by Ungungungunga taken by T Shepstone, Jnr, 4 July 1879.

22 *ZKS*, p 30.

23 Vijn, *Cetshwayo's Dutchman*, p 31. For a reiteration just before the battle of Ulundi, see p 48.

24 For Cetshwayo's strategic calculations, see *ZKS*, pp 30–32, 55.

25 Vijn, *Cetshwayo's Dutchman*, p 39.

26 Nzuzi, 'Supplement', *Natal Mercury*, 22 January 1929.

CHAPTER FIFTEEN

1 *JSA* 6, p 102: Socwatsha.

2 Swinney, *Zulu Boy's Recollections*, p 11.

3 Mitford, *The Zulu Country*, p 91.

4 Norris-Newman, *In Zululand*, p 81: Mehlokazulu kaSihayo's account.

5 Nzuzi, 'Supplement', *Natal Mercury*, 22 January 1929.

6 The eclipse reached its greatest phase at 2.29 pm.

7 Filter and Bourquin (eds), *Paulina Dlamini*, pp 69–70.

8 Vijn, *Cetshwayo's Dutchman*, p 28.

9 On 26 February 1879 Rowlands' No 5 Column was attached to Wood's command.

10 *Natal Colonist*, 20 September 1879; report by *Natal Mercury* correspondent on the march with the king to the coast.

11 Knight, 'Kill Me in the Shadows', p 12: statement of Mgelija Ngema.
12 Mehlokazulu, quoted in Norris-Newman, *In Zululand*, p 85.
13 *ZKS*, pp 33–4.
14 British infantryman quoted in Emery, *Red Soldier*, p 171.
15 *BPP* C. 2454, sub-enclosure in enclosure 1 in no 34: statement of Sihlahla taken by JW Shepstone, 3 June 1879.
16 *Natal Colonist*, 25 September 1879: Cetshwayo's comments taken from the *Cape Times*.
17 Mitford, *Zulu Country*, p 279: warrior of the uThulwana.

CHAPTER SIXTEEN

1 *BPP* C. 2454, sub-enclosure in enclosure 1 of no 32: statement of Sibalo taken by JW Shepstone, 1 June 1879.
2 *ZKS*, p 34.
3 Translation of a message from Cetywayo by Fynney, 25 June 1879, quoted in Laband, *Rope of Sand*, p 297.
4 *ZKS*, p 58.
5 Quoted in Iliffe, *Honour*, p 190.
6 Dawnay, *Campaigns*, p 65.
7 Mehlokazulu, quoted in Norris-Newman, *In Zululand*, p 85.
8 *BPP* C. 2482, enclosure D in enclosure in no 32: statement of Ungungungunga taken by T Shepstone, Jnr, 4 July 1879.
9 Magema Fuze, quoted in Vijn, *Cetshwayo's Dutchman*, p 143.
10 Vijn, *Cetshwayo's Dutchman*, p 54.
11 Mfunzi, quoted in Vijn, *Cetshwayo's Dutchman*, p 149.
12 Through the practice of *ukusisa* the king pastured his huge herds in the care of subordinate chiefs.
13 Wolseley to Lady Wolseley, 10 July 1879, quoted in Laband, *Rope of Sand*, p 327.
14 Preston (ed), *Journal of Sir Garnet Wolseley*, pp 97–8: 26 August 1879.
15 Laband and Knight (eds), *Archives of Zululand*, vol 4, pp 496–7: Oftebro, 'How We Captured Cetywayo'. Oftebro told his tale in 1927 to Carl Faye, who recorded it on an Ediphone wax cylinder and then transcribed it.
16 Special Reporter, *Cetywayo*, p 15.
17 Special Reporter, *Cetywayo*, p 15.
18 Laband and Knight (eds), *Archives of Zululand*, vol 4, p 504: Zungu, 'When the English Took Cetywayo', set down by Faye, no date.
19 Special Reporter, *Cetywayo*, p 30.

CHAPTER SEVENTEEN

1 Special Reporter, 'Cetywayo', p 17. Langalibalele and the Hlubi people had been settled in 1849 in the foothills of the Drakensberg after King Mpande had driven them

away in 1848. In 1887 Langalibalele was allowed to return to Natal, where he was confined to the Swartkop Location outside Pietermaritzburg.

2 Mwanga died in exile, but Prempeh was repatriated in 1924 and in 1926 restored to some of his former powers with the lesser title of *Kumasehene*.

3 *BPP* C. 2584, no 19: Wolseley to Hicks Beach, 13 September 1880.

4 In 1884 the Crown Colony of Basutoland became the first of the High Commission Territories, with considerable internal autonomy under its own chiefs.

5 After a spell on the notorious Robben Island, Langalibalele had been moved to Uitvlugt in 1875.

6 Ndabuko was very close to Cetshwayo in looks, and has often been mistaken for him in photographs.

7 Lord Kimberley to Gladstone, 2 September 1881, quoted in Guy, *Zulu Kingdom*, p 131.

8 Quoted in Laband, *Later Zulu Wars*, p 38.

9 Samuelson was dismissed for allegedly tampering with Cetshwayo's correspondence.

10 Samuelson, *Long, Long Ago*, p 150.

11 English Heritage affixed one of its blue plaques to the house on 25 October 2006. It reads: 'Cetshwayo, c 1832–1884 stayed here in 1882.'

12 They are now in Museum Africa, Johannesburg.

13 *Illustrated London News*, 12 and 19 August 1882.

14 *Illustrated London News*, 12 August 1882.

15 *JSA 6*, pp 352–3: Xaba.

16 Quoted in Theron, 'Cetshwayo in England', p 84.

17 The cup and Bible are in the KwaZulu Cultural Museum, Ulundi, and the ring is in the Adams Collection in the KwaZulu-Natal Museum, Pietermaritzburg.

18 The portrait was exhibited at the Royal Academy in 1883 and is currently on loan from HM The Queen to the Local History Museums, Durban.

19 The ZAR Boers eventually captured Mampuru and hanged him on 22 November 1883 for the murder.

CHAPTER EIGHTEEN

1 See *BPP* C. 3466, enclosure 2 in no 61: Terms, Conditions and Limitations of Cetywayo's Restoration.

2 The chiefdom of the deposed Mgojana to the north of Zibhebhu's chiefdom was incorporated into his new domain.

3 *BPP* C. 4366, no 72: Kimberley to Bulwer, 7 September 1882.

4 *JSA 6*, p 158: Socwatsha.

5 Pridmore, 'Diary of Fynn', vol 2, p 24: 20 February 1883.

6 *Natal Mercury*, 1 April 1883.

7 *BPP* C. 3864: enclosure 2 in no 51: testimony of Nomalhobodiya and Kukula, 4 August 1883.

8 Colenso, *Digest*, series 2, p 819.

9 Guy, *Zulu Kingdom*, p 204.

10 Pridmore, 'Diary of Fynn', vol 2, p 145: 24 July 1883.

11 *BPP* C. 3864, enclosure 12 in no 98: Zeize's message, 1 October 1883.

12 Also looted at oNdini and sold off in Durban and elsewhere were the bulk of the gifts Cetshwayo had received while in England, including the Churchills' cup and spoon, the Bible presented by the Queen and his gold ring. After heavy rains in 1938 a Zulu man called Gobi found the great silver loving cup protruding from the banks of a stream near the third oNdini. One of Cetshwayo's attendants must have secreted it there during the rout.

13 *JSA* 6, p 98: Socwatsha.

14 The pieces of the wagon have since been removed to the KwaZulu Cultural Museum at Ulundi for safekeeping.

15 *JSA* 6, p 210: Somciza, repeating the tale told by Tshonisile kaSiteku. For another version of the same, see *JSA* 5, p 201: Ntshelele.

CHAPTER NINETEEN

1 *JSA* 5, pp 272–3: Seme.

2 Fuze, *Black People*, p 123.

3 Manzonwandle, Cetshwayo's posthumous son, had not yet been born, but disquiet that the child in the womb (should it prove to be male) would have a better claim than Dinuzulu to be recognised as Cetshwayo's heir, on account of the superior status of his mother, also influenced the decision to move quickly.

4 *BPP* C. 4037: enclosure 1 in no 44: statement of Dabulamanzi, Ndabuko, Shingana and Ziwedu, brothers of Cetywayo, 11 February 1884.

5 *BPP* C. 4037: enclosure 1 in no 104: statement by Alfred Moore, 9 April 1884.

6 *BPP* C. 4214, no 4: Proclamation signed by Dinizulu (his mark) and A Schiel, 21 May 1884.

7 *BPP* C. 4625: enclosure 1 in no 21: Bulwer to Stanley, 18 August 1885.

8 *BPP* C. 4191, enclosure 3 in no 46: message relayed by John Eckersley, Jnr, 19 May 1884.

9 See *BPP* C. 4214, enclosure in no 44: Bulwer to Derby, 26 August 1884.

10 *BPP* C. 4913, no 60: Bulwer to Colonial Secretary, 6 January 1886.

11 See *BPP* C. 4214, enclosure in no 56: Proclamation of the New Republic, 16 August 1884.

12 The Ngenetsheni found themselves within the borders of the New Republic, but the Boers allowed Hamu to retain some authority over them. Hamu died in February 1887.

13 Dabulamanzi was prominent in his rejection of the Boer land grab, and on 21 September 1886 the Boers arrested him on a trumped-up charge of cattle theft and shot him in the ensuing fracas. He died the next day. The suggestion has been made that his brothers, jealous of his influence over Dinuzulu, were implicated in the affair.

14 *BPP* C. 4214, no 66: Colonial Office to Foreign Office, 10 October 1884.

15 *Natal Mercury*, 8 July 1887.

16 Siziba and Pagade kaNgonela, messengers to Havelock from Dinuzulu, Umnyamana, Undabuko and Heads of the Zulu People, 11 October 1887, quoted in Laband, *Rope of Sand*, p 387.

17 *BPP* C. 5331: enclosure 2 in no 37: Havelock to the uSuthu chiefs, 14 November 1887.
18 Samuelson, *Long, Long Ago*, p 285.
19 *BPP* C. 5892, enclosure 1 in no 70: Havelock to Osborn, 7 August 1888.
20 *BPP* C. 5892: enclosure 1 in no 170: Court of the Special Commissioners for Zululand, 27 April 1889.

CHAPTER TWENTY

1   It was only in November 2017 that an airport was opened on the island, and until then the sole way to reach St Helena was by sea.
2   The official records give the year of Solomon's birth as 1893, but Jeff Guy has suggested that photographic evidence indicates it was actually 1894. See Guy, *View across the River*, p 483. Umkasilomo's daughter, Magogo Sibilile Mantithi, was born in 1900 after the return to Zululand.
3   The new Province of Zululand included the Ingwavuma District to the northeast, which the British had annexed piecemeal in 1888, 1890 and 1895 to thwart the ZAR's attempts to reach the sea, and which had been incorporated into the Colony of Zululand on 15 July 1895. The Province also included Tongaland (Amaputoland), annexed as a British Protectorate on 30 May 1895 and incorporated into Zululand on 24 December 1895.
4   *BPP* C. 8782, no 45: Hely-Hutchinson to Chamberlain, 19 November 1897.
5   *BPP* C. 8782: enclosure in no 27: Dinuzulu, Ndabuko and Tshingana to Chamberlain, 4 September 1897.
6   *BPP* C. 8782, no 32: Chamberlain to Governor Sterndale, St Helena, 29 October 1897.
7   *BPP* C. 8782, no 19: Chamberlain to Hely-Hutchinson, 4 May 1879.
8   *JSA* 5, p 273: Seme.
9   Bottomley to Dinuzulu, 4 April 1901, quoted in Laband and Thompson, 'African Levies', p 71.
10 The areas cited were equivalent to 1 057 443 hectares and 1 573 013 hectares, respectively.
11 Natal Ordinance 3 of 1849 declared the Lieutenant Governor the 'Supreme chief' of the colony's African population with full powers to appoint or remove subordinate chiefs or other authorities among them.
12 This was the same Mehlokazulu whose incursion into Natal in 1878 to punish his father's unfaithful wives had been a *casus belli* in 1879.
13 Stuart, *Zulu Rebellion*, pp 501–2.
14 Stuart, *Zulu Rebellion*, pp 497–8.
15 *The Trial of Dinuzulu*, p xxii: The Judgement.
16 Quoted in Guy, *View across the River*, p 445.
17 Fuze, *Black People*, p 146.
18 Fuze, *Black People*, p 145.
19 Marks, *Reluctant Rebellion*, p 303.
20 Quoted in Guy, *View across the River*, pp 445–6.
21 Sibusiso Ndebele, 'Honoured at Last', *The Witness*, 19 September 2008.

CHAPTER TWENTY-ONE

1 *JSA 6*, p 149: Socwatsha.
2 Fuze, *Black People*, p 146.
3 Quoted in Cope, *To Bind the Nation*, p 47.
4 Their son, Mangosuthu Buthelezi, was born in August 1927.
5 Cope, *To Bind the Nation*, p 132.
6 Shamase, *Zulu Potentates*, p 115.
7 Addison to the Secretary for Native Affairs, 27 January 1916, quoted in Cope, *To Bind the Nation*, p 69.
8 The South Africa Act of 1909 designated the Governor General as the 'Supreme Chief', a position which gave him the power to create and divide 'tribes' and to appoint any person he chose as a chief or headman, and to depose such persons as he saw fit. The Native Administration Act 38 of 1927 consolidated these powers and all prior colonial legislation and vested them henceforth in the Minister of Native Affairs.
9 The Natives Land Act 27 of 1913 commenced on 19 June 1913. It was subsequently renamed the Bantu Land Act and then the Black Land Act. It was repealed on 30 June 1991.
10 He succeeded briefly to the throne in January 1936 as King Edward VIII before abdicating in December 1936.
11 Mshiyeni formally dissolved the first *Inkatha* in 1933 after Solomon's death.
12 *Ilanga lase Natal*, 10 March 1933, quoted in Ballard, *House of Shaka*, p 99. 'From deep pools' was taken from Solomon's *izibongo*, and the phrase suggests that Solomon's Zulu nationalism and his royal status derived from deep in the traditional Zulu past.

CHAPTER TWENTY-TWO

1 Buverud, *The King and the Honeybirds*, p 33.
2 Shamase, *Zulu Potentates*, p 104.
3 Shamase, *Zulu Potentates*, p 105.
4 *Natal Daily News*, 15 September 1945, quoted in Ballard, *House of Shaka*, p 104.
5 Buverud, *The King and the Honeybirds*, p 41.
6 Altogether, Cyprian had four sons and eight daughters.
7 Becker, *Trails and Tribes*, p 160.
8 Subsequently renamed the Black Authorities Act, the BAA was repealed on 31 December 2010.
9 Buverud, *The King and the Honeybirds*, p 45.
10 *Bantu World*, 25 September 1954, quoted in Buverud, *The King and the Honeybirds*, p 87.
11 *New Age*, 3 November 1955, quoted in Buverud, *The King and the Honeybirds*, p 8.

CHAPTER TWENTY-THREE

1 Shamase, *Zulu Potentates*, p 144.
2 For a description of the coronation, see Becker, *Trails and Tribes*, p 180ff.
3 *City Press*, 28 July 2013.
4 Ballard, *House of Shaka*, p 130.
5 Waetjen and Maré, 'Shaka's Aeroplane', p 356.
6 Temkin, *Buthelezi*, p 363.
7 In terms of the Bantu Homelands Constitution Act 21 of 1971, Constitution Proclamation R69 of 30 March 1972 created the KwaZulu Legislative Assembly to replace the ZTA on 1 April 1972.
8 The process was never fully completed. In 1983, at the end of its separate existence, KwaZulu still consisted of 29 non-contiguous areas.
9 Proclamation R11 of 28 January 1977.
10 The Legislative Assembly consisted of 141 members: the monarch and representatives nominated by him from the royal family; three chiefs from each of the 24 regional authorities, with one each from the two tribal authorities with direct representation; and 65 elected members.
11 Maré and Hamilton, *Appetite for Power*, p 195.
12 Circular by Lloyd Ndaba to the *amakhosi* of KwaZulu, quoted in Shamase, *Zulu Potentates*, p 125.
13 Shamase, *Zulu Potentates*, p 126.
14 Quoted in Waetjen and Maré, 'Shaka's Aeroplane', p 358.
15 Goodwill Zwelithini conferred on him the King's Cross Award and made him Prince of KwaPhindangene.
16 Republic of South Africa Constitution Act 111 of 1983 commencing on 3 September 1984. It was repealed on 27 April 1994 by the Constitution of the Republic of South Africa, Act 200 of 1993 (the Interim Constitution).
17 Proclamation No 119 of 7 August 1987.
18 Shamase, *Zulu Potentates*, p 135.
19 The NHTL was first established in April 1997 and is currently governed by the National House of Traditional Leaders Act 22 of 2009.

CHAPTER TWENTY-FOUR

1 Shamase, *Zulu Potentates*, p 136. President Mandela assented to the amendment on 25 April 1994.
2 Constitution of the Republic of South Africa Second Amendment Act 3 of 1994: amendment of section 160 of the Interim Constitution.
3 So late was the IFP's participation that the ballot papers had already been printed, and the IFP's slot had to be stuck on at the very end of the list of the 18 other parties contesting the election.
4 In 1998 Zuma would oust Buthelezi as national deputy president, and Ndebele would

become the first ANC premier of KwaZulu-Natal in 2004. In 1994 Radebe was Minister of Public Works.

5 Temkin, *Buthelezi*, p 312.

6 *New York Times*, 21 September 1994.

7 KwaZulu-Natal Act on the House of Traditional Leaders Act 7 of 1994.

8 Resolutions of meeting between *amakhosi* and members of the Zulu royal house, 19 February 1995, quoted in Shamase, *Zulu Potentates*, p 166.

9 In 1993 Yoweri Museveni, the President of Uganda, restored all the monarchies Milton Obote had abolished in 1967 (except for Ankole), and in 1995 the new Ugandan constitution granted these kingdoms a degree of autonomy under their constitutional monarchs.

10 Ministry for Cooperative Governance and Traditional Affairs, Republic of South Africa: The President's Announcement of the Findings and Recommendations of the Commission on Traditional Leadership Disputes and Claims (Nhlapo Commission), 29 July 2010.

11 *Guardian*, 14 May 2014.

12 For the sources of their wealth, see Mfonobong Nsehe, 'The 5 Richest Kings in Africa', *Forbes*, 3 June 2014.

13 See Femke van Zeijl, 'The Oba of Benin Kingdom: A History of the Monarchy', *Al Jazeera News*, 12 November 2016.

14 An eighth palace, kwaNobamba, which the King wished in 2014 to build in the ema-Khosini valley, has not materialised.

15 For the Royal Household Trust, see Zuluroyaltrust.org/about. For its financial difficulties, see *Witness*, 5 September 2012 and 18 November 2015.

16 BusinessTech, 'How much you pay for South Africa's royal families', 1 June 2015. Available at businesstech.co.za/news/government/88860/, accessed on 6 April 2018.

17 Nabeelah Shaikh, 'Seven Mercs for Zulu King's Wives', *Sunday Independent*, 5 April 2015.

18 Chris Ndaliso, 'King Zwelithini Does Not Use KwaMashu House', *Daily News*, 25 April 2016.

19 *Daily News*, 21 and 22 April 2016.

20 See the Natives Land Act 27 of 1913; Native Trust and Land Act 18 of 1936; Group Areas Act 41 of 1950; Group Areas Act 77 of 1957; and Group Areas Act 36 of 1966.

21 Professor Musa Xulu, *Daily Maverick*, 20 March 2018.

22 Ingonyama Trust Board homepage. Available at www.ingonyamatrust.org.za/, accessed on 15 February 2018.

23 Ingonyama Trust Board homepage.

24 Kaveel Singh, 'KZN Premier's Office Trampling on Zulu King', *News24*, 8 December 2015.

25 *Mercury*, 5 July 2017.

26 In June 2015 King Goodwill Zwelithini very publicly exposed his lack of understanding of the very limited powers possessed by a constitutional monarch when he declared that he wished the British royal family 'to compensate' the Zulu kingdom for the destruction of oNdini in the Anglo-Zulu War. The British Royal Household very correctly responded that it was 'not a matter' for it to comment on and that the issue was one for the British government since it was its predecessor in 1879 that went to war

with the Zulu kingdom (*The Mercury*, 24 June 2015; www.ibtimes.co.uk, 25 June 2015).

27 Zuluroyaltrust.org/about/.

28 Amanda Khoza, 'Zwelithini Vows to Protect Zulu Kingdom', *News24*, 12 September 2016.

29 Interview with King Goodwill Zwelithini on 1 July 1988, quoted in Ballard, *House of Shaka*, p 124.

30 Marcus, 'Virginity Testing', p 538.

31 Amanda Khoza, 'Zwelithini Vows to Protect Zulu Kingdom', *News24*, 12 September 2016.

32 *TimesLive*, 24 January 2012. The Human Rights Commission, the Commission for Gender Equality and gay and lesbian advocacy groups all demanded that Goodwill Zwelithini retract his criticism of same-sex relationships.

33 *Citizen*, 24 March 2015.

34 https://mybroadband.co.za/news/government/211584, 21 May 2017.

35 http://destinyconnect.com/2015/06/23, 23 June 2015.

CHAPTER TWENTY-FIVE

1 Stephen Grootes, *Daily Maverick*, 27 March 2018.

2 Paddy Harper, *Mail & Guardian*, 18 January 2018; Professor Musa Xulu, *Daily Maverick*, 20 March 2018.

3 Stephen Grootes, *Daily Maverick*, 27 March 2018.

4 Professor Musa Xulu, *Daily Maverick*, 20 March 2018.

5 Paddy Harper, *Mail & Guardian*, 18 January 2018.

6 It should be noted that former President Zuma's controversial R246 million Nkandla home is built on leased Trust land.

7 Paddy Harper, *Mail & Guardian*, 18 January 2018; Paul Herman, *Mail & Guardian*, 7 March 2018; Rebecca Davis, *Daily Maverick*, 8 March 2018.

8 Hlengiwe Nhlabathi, *City Press*, 8 March 2018.

9 Paddy Harper, *Mail & Guardian*, 18 January 2018. The *amakhosi* subsequently met on 24–25 January 2018 in the International Convention Centre in Durban to make known their opposition to the Panel's report.

10 Marianne Merten, *Daily Maverick* 19 March 2018.

11 Bongani Mthethwa, *Business Day*, 22 January 2018.

12 Carien du Plessis, *Daily Maverick*, 23 February 2018.

13 Carien du Plessis, *Daily Maverick*, 23 February 2018.

14 Bongani Mthethwa, *Sunday Times*, 27 Feb 2018.

15 Qaanitah Hunter, *Daily Maverick*, 20 May 2018.

16 Cyril Madlala, *Sunday Times*, 18 February 2018.

17 Hlengiwe Nhlabathi, *City Press*, 8 March 2018.

18 Siboniso Mngadi, *Sunday Tribune*, 8 July 2018.

19 Hlengiwe Nhlabathi, *City Press*, 8 March 2018.

SELECT READING LIST

The printed literature on the Zulu kingdom and its kings is extensive, especially when it deals with warfare, particularly the Anglo-Zulu War of 1879. This select reading list consequently does not pretend to be comprehensive, but is meant to provide a solid starting point for those intending to read further into the subject.

Individual chapters or articles contained in edited collections are not listed separately unless they have been specifically referred to in the Notes.

Aitchison, John. *Numbering the Dead: The Course and Pattern of Political Violence in the Natal Midlands, 1987–1989* (Pietermaritzburg: Natal Society Foundation, 2015).

Angas, George French. *The Kaffirs Illustrated in a Series of Drawings* (London: G Barclay for J Hogarth, 1849).

Ballard, Charles. 'Natal 1824–44: The Frontier Interregnum', *Journal of Natal and Zulu History*, IV (1982): 49–64.

Ballard, Charles. *John Dunn: The White Chief of Zululand* (Craighall: Ad Donker, 1985).

Ballard, Charles. 'Drought and Economic Distress: South Africa in the 1800s', *Journal of Interdisciplinary History*, 17, 2 (Autumn 1986): 359–378.

Ballard, Charles. *The House of Shaka: The Zulu Monarchy Illustrated* (Durban: Emoyeni Books, 1988).

Becker, Peter. *Rule of Fear: The Life and Times of Dingane, King of the Zulu* (London: Longmans, 1964).

Becker, Peter. *Trails and Tribes in Southern Africa* (London: Hart-Davis, 1975).

Berglund, Axel-Ivar. *Zulu Thought-Patterns and Symbolism* (Bloomington: Indiana University Press, 1989).

Binns, CT. *The Last Zulu King: The Life and Death of Cetshwayo* (London: Longmans, Green, 1963).

Binns, CT. *Dinuzulu: The Death of the House of Shaka* (London: Longmans, Green, 1968).

Bird, John. *The Annals of Natal 1495 to 1845.* 2 vols. (Pietermaritzburg: P Davis, 1888).

British Parliamentary Papers. C. 1342, C. 2000, C. 2079, C. 2100, C. 2144, C. 2220, C. 2222, C. 2234, C. 2242, C. 2252, C. 2260, C. 2269, C. 2308, C. 2316, C. 2318, C. 2367, C. 2374, C. 2454, C. 2482, C. 2505, C. 2584, C. 3174, C. 3182, C. 3247, C. 3270, C. 3293, C. 3466, C. 3616, C. 3705, C. 3864, C. 4037, C. 4191, C. 4214, C. 4274, C. 4587, C. 4643, C. 4645, C. 4864, C. 4913, C. 4980, C. 5143, C. 5331, C. 5522, C. 5892, C. 5893, C. 6070, C. 6684, C. 7780, C. 8782.

Brookes, Edgar H and Colin de B Webb. *A History of Natal* (Pietermaritzburg: University of Natal Press, 1965).

Bryant, the Rev AT. *Olden Times in Zululand and Natal Containing Earlier Political History of the Eastern-Nguni Clans* (London: Longmans, Green, 1929).

Bryant, AT. *The Zulu People as They Were before the White Man Came* (Pietermaritzburg: Shuter & Shooter, 1949).

Bulpin, TV. *Shaka's Country: A Book of Zululand.* 3rd edition (Cape Town: Howard Timmins, 1956).

Buverud, Anna Kolberg. 'The King and the Honeybirds: Cyprian Bhekuzulu kaSolomon, Zulu Nationalism and the Implementation of the Bantu Authorities System in Zululand, 1948–1957' (unpublished MA thesis, University of Oslo, 2007).

Callaway, Rev Canon Henry. *The Religious System of the Amazulu* (Springvale, Natal: John A Blair; London: Trübner, 1870).

Cameron, Trewhella and SB Spies (eds). *An Illustrated History of South Africa* (Johannesburg: Jonathan Ball Publishers, 1986).

Campbell, WY. *With Cetshwayo in the Inkandhla, & the Present State of the Zulu Question* (Durban: P Davis & Sons, 1883).

Carton, Benedict. *Blood from Your Children: The Colonial Origins of Generational Conflict in South Africa* (Pietermaritzburg: University of Natal Press, 2000).

Carton, Benedict, John Laband and Jabulani Sithole (eds). *Zulu Identities: Being Zulu, Past and Present* (Pietermaritzburg: University of KwaZulu-Natal Press, 2008; New York: Columbia University Press, 2009).

Chase, John Centlivres. *The Natal Papers: A Reprint of All Notices and Public Documents Connected with That Territory Including a Description of the Country and a History of Events from 1498 to 1843 in Two Parts*, facsimile reprint (Cape Town: C. Struik, 1968).

Clark, Nancy L and William H. Worger. *South Africa: The Rise and Fall of Apartheid* (Harlow: Pearson Longman, 2004).

Cloete, Dick. 'From Warriors to Wage Slaves: The Fate of the Zulu People since 1879', *Reality*, 11, 1 (January 1879): 20–23.

Colenso, FE. *The Ruin of Zululand: British Doings in Zululand since the Invasion of 1879.* 2 vols (London: William Ridgeway, 1884 and 1885).

Colenso, Bishop JW and HE Colenso. *Digest of Zulu Affairs Compiled by Bishop Colenso and Continued after his Death by His Daughter, Harriette Emily Colenso.* Series 1–9, 1878–1888 (Bishopstowe: privately printed, 1878–1888).

Cope, Nicholas. *To Bind the Nation: Solomon kaDinuzulu and Zulu Nationalism 1913–1933*

(Pietermaritzburg: University of Natal Press, 1993).

Cope, Richard. *Ploughshare of War: The Origins of the Anglo-Zulu War* (Pietermaritzburg: University of Natal Press, 1999).

Cope, Trevor. *Izibongo: Zulu Praise Poems* (Oxford: Oxford University Press, 1968).

Cory, Sir George E (ed). *The Diary of the Rev Francis Owen, MA, Missionary with Dingaan in 1837–38* (Cape Town: Van Riebeeck Society, 1926).

Crais, Clifton. *Poverty, War, and Violence in South Africa* (Cambridge: Cambridge University Press, 2011).

Cubbin, Anthony Edward. 'Origins of the British Settlement at Port Natal, May 1824–June 1842' (unpublished PhD thesis, University of the Orange Free State, 1983).

Davenport, Rodney and Christopher Saunders. *South Africa: A Modern History*. 5th edition (London: Macmillan, 2000).

Dawnay, Guy C. *Campaigns: Zulu 1879, Egypt 1882, Suakim 1885*, facsimile reprint (Cambridge: Ken Trotman, 1989)

Delegorgue, Adulphe. *Travels and Adventures in Southern Africa*, translated by Fleur Webb and edited by Stephanie J Alexander and C de B Webb. 2 vols (Durban: Killie Campbell Africana Library; Pietermaritzburg: University of Natal Press, 1990)

Delius, Peter. *The Land Belongs to Us: The Pedi Polity, the Boers and the British in the Nineteenth-Century Transvaal* (Berkeley: University of California Press, 1984).

Dixie, Lady Florence. *A Defence of Zululand and Its King: Echoes from the Blue-Books* (London: Chatto & Windus, 1882).

Dixie, Lady Florence. *In the Land of Misfortune* (London: Richard Bentley and Son, 1882).

Dominy, Graham. 'The New Republicans: A Centennial Reappraisal of the "Nieuwe Republiek", 1884–1888', *Natalia*, 14 (1984): 87–97.

Dominy, Graham. *Last Outpost on the Zulu Frontiers: Fort Napier and the British Imperial Garrison* (Urbana: University of Illinois Press, 2016).

Du Buisson, Louis. *The White Man Cometh* (Johannesburg: Jonathan Ball Publishers, 1987).

Dumat, Frank C and Harry Escombe. *A Remonstrance on behalf of the Zulu Chiefs, 1889* (Pietermaritzburg: City Printing Works, reprinted 1908).

Duminy, Andrew and Bill Guest (eds). *The Anglo-Zulu War: New Perspectives* (Pietermaritzburg: University of Natal Press and Shuter & Shooter, 1981).

Duminy, Andrew and Bill Guest (eds). *Natal and Zululand from Earliest Times to 1910: A New History* (Pietermaritzburg: University of Natal Press and Shuter & Shooter, 1989).

Eldredge, Elizabeth A. 'Delagoa Bay and the Hinterland in the Early Nineteenth Century: Politics, Trade, Slaves, and Slave Riding' in *Slavery in South Africa: Captive Labor on the Dutch Frontier*, edited by Elizabeth A. Eldredge and Fred Morton (Boulder: Westview Press; Pietermaritzburg: University of Natal Press, 1994).

Eldredge, Elizabeth A. *The Creation of the Zulu Kingdom, 1815–1828: War, Shaka and the Consolidation of Power* (Cambridge: Cambridge University Press, 2014).

Eldredge, Elizabeth A. *Kingdoms and Chiefdoms in Southeastern Africa* (Rochester, NY: University of Rochester Press, 2015).

Emery, Frank. *The Red Soldier: Letters from the Zulu War, 1879* (London: Hodder and Stoughton, 1977).

SELECT READING LIST

Etherington, Norman. *The Great Treks: The Transformation of Southern Africa, 1815–1854* (Harlow, Essex: Longman, 2001).

Filter, H (comp) and S Bourquin (tr and ed). *Paulina Dlamini: Servant of Two Kings* (Durban: Killie Campbell Africana Library; Pietermaritzburg: University of Natal Press, 1986).

Fuze, Magema M. *The Black People and Whence They Came: A Zulu View*, translated by HC Lugg and edited by AT Cope (Pietermaritzburg: University of Natal Press; Durban: Killie Campbell Africana Library, 1979).

Gardiner, Capt Allen Francis. *Narrative of a Journey to the Zooloo Country in South Africa, Undertaken in 1835* (London: Crofts, 1836).

Gibson, James Young. *The Story of the Zulus*, new edition (London: Longmans, Green, 1911).

Giliomee, Hermann and Bernard Mbenga. *New History of South Africa* (Cape Town: Tafelberg, 2007).

Gluckman, M. 'The Kingdom of the Zulus in South Africa' in *African Political Systems*, edited by M Fortes and E Evans-Pritchard (London: Oxford University Press, 1940): 25–55.

Gluckman, M. 'The Individual in a Social Framework: The Rise of King Shaka of Zululand', *Journal of African Studies*, 1, 2 (Summer 1974): 113–144.

Greaves, Adrian and Ian Knight. *Who's Who in the Zulu War 1879*. 2 vols. (Barnsley: Pen & Sword Military, 2007).

Grobler, Jackie. 'The Retief Massacre of 1838 Revisited', *Historia*, 56, 2 (November 2011): 113–132.

Grout, L. *Zululand; or, Life among the Zulu-Kafirs of Natal and Zulu-land* (London: Trübner, 1862).

Guy, Jeff. *The Destruction of the Zulu Kingdom: The Civil War in Zululand, 1879–1884* (London: Longman, 1979).

Guy, Jeff. 'Ecological Factors in the Rise of Shaka and the Zulu Kingdom' in *Economy and Society in Pre-Industrial South Africa*, edited by Shula Marks and Anthony Atmore (London: Longman, 1980): 102–119.

Guy, Jeff. *The Heretic: A Study of the Life of JW Colenso* (Johannesburg: Ravan Press; Pietermaritzburg: University of Natal Press, 1983).

Guy, Jeff. *The View across the River: Harriette Colenso and the Zulu Struggle against Imperialism* (Charlottesville: University Press of Virginia; Oxford: James Currey; Cape Town: David Philip, 2002).

Guy, Jeff. *Remembering the Rebellion: The Zulu Uprising of 1906* (Pietermaritzburg: University of KwaZulu-Natal Press, 2006).

Haggard, H Rider. *Cetywayo and His White Neighbours; or, Remarks on Recent Events in Zululand, Natal and the Transvaal* (London: Trübner, 1890).

Hamilton, Carolyn (ed). *The Mfecane Aftermath: Reconstructive Debates in Southern African History* (Johannesburg: Wits University Press; Pietermaritzburg: University of Natal Press, 1995).

Hamilton, Carolyn. *Terrific Majesty: The Powers of Shaka Zulu and the Limits of Historical Invention* (Cape Town: David Philip, 1998).

413

Hamilton, Carolyn, Bernard K Mbenga and Robert Ross (eds). *The Cambridge History of South Africa. Vol 1: From Early Times to 1885* (Cambridge: Cambridge University Press, 2010)

Hamilton, Carolyn and John Wright. 'The Making of the *Amalala*: Ethnicity, Ideology and Relations of Subordination in a Precolonial Context', *South African Historical Journal*, 22 (1990): 3–23.

Hammond-Tooke, David (ed). *The Bantu-speaking Peoples of Southern Africa* (London & Boston: Oxford University Press, 1974).

Hammond-Tooke, WD. 'Descent Groups, Chiefdoms and South African Historiography', *Journal of Southern African Studies*, 11, 2 (April 1985): 307–319.

Hammond-Tooke, David. *The Roots of Black South Africa* (Johannesburg: Jonathan Ball Publishers, 1993).

Hanretta, Shaun. 'Women, Marginality and the Zulu State: Women's Institutions and Power in the Early Nineteenth Century', *Journal of African History*, 39 (1998): 389–415.

Harries, Patrick. 'Ethnicity and the Ingwavuma Land Deal: The Zulu Northern Frontier in the Nineteenth Century', *Journal of Natal and Zulu History*, VI (1983): 1–27.

Hickel, Jason. *Democracy as Death: The Moral Order of Anti-Liberal Politics in South Africa* (Berkeley: University of California Press, 2015).

Holden, WC. *History of the Colony of Natal* (London: Heylin, 1855).

Iliffe, John. *Honour in African History* (Cambridge: Cambridge University Press, 2005).

Isaacs, Nathaniel. *Travels and Adventures in Eastern Africa Descriptive of the Zoolus, Their Manners, Customs with a Sketch of Natal*, edited by Louis Herman and Percival R Kirby (Cape Town: C Struik, 1970).

Jeffery, Anthea. *The Natal Story: 16 Years of Conflict* (Johannesburg: South African Institute of Race Relations, 1997).

Jenkinson, Thomas B. *Amazulu: The Zulus, Their Past History, Manners, Customs, and Language* (London: WH Allen, 1882).

Kelly, Jill E. *To Swim with Crocodiles: Land, Violence, and Belonging in South Africa, 1800–1996* (East Lansing: Michigan State University Press, 2018).

Kennedy, Philip A. 'Mpande and the Zulu Kingship', *Journal of Natal and Zulu History*, IV (1981): 21–38.

Kirby, Percival R (ed). *Andrew Smith and Natal: Documents Relating to the Early History of That Province* (Cape Town: Van Riebeeck Society, 1955).

Knight, Ian. 'Kill Me in the Shadows', *Soldiers of the Queen*, 74 (September 1993): 9–18.

Knight, Ian. *The Anatomy of the Zulu Army from Shaka to Cetshwayo 1818–1879* (London: Greenhill Books, 1995).

Knight, Ian. *Zulu Rising: The Epic Story of Isandlwana and Rorke's Drift* (London: Macmillan, 2010).

Koopman, A. 'Dingiswayo Rides Again', *Journal of Natal and Zulu History*, II (1979): 1–12.

Krige, Eileen Jensen. *The Social System of the Zulus*, 2nd edition (Pietermaritzburg: Shuter & Shooter, 1974).

Laband, John. *Rope of Sand: The Rise and Fall of the Zulu Kingdom* (Johannesburg: Jonathan Ball Publishers, 1995).

Laband, John. 'Zulus and the War' in *The Boer War: Direction, Experience and Image*, edited by John Gooch (London and Portland: Frank Cass, 2000).

Laband, John. *The Atlas of the Later Zulu Wars 1883–1888* (Pietermaritzburg: University of Natal Press, 2001).

Laband, John. *Kingdom in Crisis: The Zulu Response to the British Invasion of 1879* (Manchester: Manchester University Press, 1992; reprint Barnsley: Pen & Sword Military, 2007).

Laband, John (ed). 'Zulu Civilians during the Rise and Fall of the Zulu Kingdom, c. 1817–1879' in *Daily Lives of Civilians in Wartime Africa: From Slavery Days to Rwandan Genocide* (Westport: Greenwood Press, 2007).

Laband, John. *Historical Dictionary of the Zulu Wars* (Lanham: The Scarecrow Press, 2009).

Laband, John. '"Fighting Stick of Thunder": Firearms and the Zulu Kingdom: The Cultural Ambiguities of Transferring Weapons Technology', *War & Society*, 33, 4 (October 2014): 229–243.

Laband, John. *Zulu Warriors: The Battle for the South African Frontier* (New Haven and London: Yale University Press, 2014).

Laband, John. 'Zulu Wars' in *Oxford Bibliographies Online: Military History*, edited by Dennis Showalter (New York: Oxford University Press, 2015).

Laband, John. *The Assassination of King Shaka* (Johannesburg: Jonathan Ball Publishers, 2017).

Laband, John (series ed) and Ian Knight (volume ed). *Archives of Zululand: The Anglo-Zulu War*, 1879. 6 vols (London: Archival Publications International, 2000).

Laband, John and Paul Thompson. *Kingdom and Colony at War: Sixteen Studies on the Anglo-Zulu War of 1879* (Pietermaritzburg: University of Natal Press; Cape Town: N & S Press, 1990).

Laband, John and Paul Thompson. *The Illustrated Guide to the Anglo-Zulu War* (Pietermaritzburg: University of Natal Press, 2000).

Laband, John and Paul Thompson. 'African Levies in Natal and Zululand, 1838–1906' in *Soldiers and Settlers in Africa, 1850–1918*, edited by Stephen M Miller (Leiden and Boston: Brill, 2009.

Laband, John and John Wright. *King Cetshwayo kaMpande* (Pietermaritzburg: Shuter & Shooter; Ulundi: KwaZulu Monuments Council, 1983).

Lambert, John. *Betrayed Trust. Africans and the State in Colonial Natal* (Pietermaritzburg: University of Natal Press, 1995).

Leslie, D. *Among the Zulus & Amatongas* (Edinburgh: Edmunston & Douglas, 1875).

Leverton, Dr BJT (ed). *Records of Natal, Volume One 1823–August 1828* (Pretoria: Government Printer, 1984).

Leverton, Dr BJT (ed). *Records of Natal, Volume Two September 1828–July 1835* (Pretoria: Government Printer, 1989).

Leverton, Dr BJT (ed). *Records of Natal, Volume Three August 1835–June 1838* (Pretoria: Government Printer, 1990).

Leverton, Dr BJT (ed). *Records of Natal, Volume Four July 1838–September 1839* (Pretoria: Government Printer, 1992).

Logan, Carolyn. 'Traditional Leaders in Modern Africa: Can Democracy and the Chief

Co-Exist?' (Cape Town: The Institute for Democracy in South Africa; Legon-Accra: Ghana Centre for Democratic Development; East Lansing: Michigan State University; Afrobarometer Working Papers No 93, February 2008).

Lugg, HC. *Historic Natal and Zululand* (Pietermaritzburg: Shuter & Shooter, 1949).

Mackeurtan, Graham. *The Cradle Days of Natal (1497–1845)* (London: Longmans, Green, 1930).

Maclean, Charles Rawden. *The Natal Papers of 'John Ross'*, edited by Stephen Gray (Pietermaritzburg: University of Natal Press; Durban: Killie Campbell Africana Library, 1992).

Mahoney, Michael R. *The Other Zulus: The Spread of Zulu Ethnicity in Colonial South Africa* (Durham and London: Duke University Press, 2012).

Marcus, Tessa. 'Virginity Testing: A Backward-Looking Response to Sexual Regulation in the HIV/AIDS Crisis' in *Zulu Identities: Being Zulu, Past and Present*, edited by Benedict Carton, John Laband and Jabulani Sithole (Pietermaritzburg: University of KwaZulu-Natal Press, 2008).

Maré, Gerhard and Georgina Hamilton. *An Appetite for Power: Buthelezi's Inkatha and South Africa* (Bloomington: Indiana University Press, 1987).

Marks, Shula. *Reluctant Rebellion: The 1906–1908 Disturbances in Natal* (Oxford: Clarendon Press, 1970).

Marks, Shula. *The Ambiguities of Dependence in South Africa: Class, Nationalism, and the State in Twentieth-century Natal* (Johannesburg: Ravan Press, 1986).

Marks, Shula. 'Cetshwayo [Cetewayo] (c. 1826–1884), king of the Zulu' in *Oxford Dictionary of National Biography* (Oxford: Oxford University Press, online edition, 2004): article 39590.

Marks, Shula and R Rathbone (eds). *Industrialisation and Social Change in South Africa: African Class Formation, Culture and Consciousness, 1870–1930* (London: Longman, 1982).

Martineau, John. *The Life and Correspondence of the Right Hon Sir Bartle Frere, Bart.* 2 vols. (London: John Murray, 1895).

Maylam, Paul. *A History of the African People of South Africa: From the Early Iron Age to the 1970s* (London: Croom Helm, 1989).

Minnaar, Anthony (ed). *Conflict and Violence in Natal/KwaZulu: Historical Perspectives* Pretoria: Human Sciences Research Council, 1991).

Mitford, Bertram. *Through the Zulu Country: Its Battlefields and Its People* (London: Kegan, Paul Trench, 1883).

Moodie, DCF (ed). *John Dunn, Cetywayo, and the Three Generals* (Pietermaritzburg: Natal Printing & Publishing Company, 1886).

Moodie, DCF. *Southern Africa from the Time of the Pharaoh Necho to 1880* (London: Murray, 1888).

Morrell, Robert (ed). *Political Economy and Identities in KwaZulu-Natal: Historical and Social Perspectives* (Durban: Indicator Press, 1996).

Murray, Christina. *South Africa's Troubled Royalty: Traditional Leaders after Democracy* (Annandale: The Federation Press; Canberra: Centre for International and Public Law, Australian National University, 2004).

Ndlovu, Sifiso Mxolisi. '"He Did What Any Other Person in his Position Would Have Done to Fight the Forces of Invasion and Disruption": Africans, the Land and Contending Images of King Dingane ("the Patriot") in the Twentieth Century, 1916–1950s', *South African Historical Journal*, 38 (May 1998): 99–143.

Ndlovu, Sifiso. 'Zulu Nationalist Representations of King Dingane' in *Zulu Identities: Being Zulu, Past and Present*, edited by Benedict Carton, John Laband and Jabulani Sithole (Pietermaritzburg: University of KwaZulu-Natal Press, 2008).

Ndlovu, Sifiso Mxolisi (ed). *African Perspectives of King Dingane kaSenzangakhona, the Second Monarch of the Zulu Kingdom* (London: Palgrave Macmillan, 2017).

Ngubane, Harriet. *Body and Mind in Zulu Medicine: An Ethnography of Health and Disease in Nyuswa-Zulu Thought and Practice* (London: Academic Press, 1977).

Norris-Newman, Charles. *In Zululand with the British* (London: WH Allen, 1880).

Ntuli, Deuteronomy Bhekinkosi, '"Praises Will Remain"' in *Zulu Treasures: Of Kings and Commoners. A Celebration of the Material Culture of the Zulu People*, coordinated by Marilee Wood (Ulundi: KwaZulu Cultural Museum; Durban: The Local History Museums, 1996).

Nyembezi, CLS. 'The Historical Background to the Izibongo of the Zulu Military Age, Part I', *African Studies*, 7, 2–3 (June 1948): 110–125.

Nyembezi, CLS. 'The Historical Background to the Izibongo of the Zulu Military Age, Part II', *African Studies*, 7, 4 (June 1948): 157–174.

Okoye, Felix NC. 'Dingane: a Reappraisal', *Journal of African History*, X, 2 (1969): 221–235.

Omer-Cooper, John D. *The Zulu Aftermath: A Nineteenth-Century Revolution in Bantu Africa* (London: Longman, 1966).

Omer-Cooper, John D. 'Dinizulu [Dinuzulu] ka Cetshwayo (1868–1913), Zulu king', *Oxford Dictionary of National Biography* (Oxford: Oxford University Press, online edition, 2004): article 53757.

Omer-Cooper, John D. 'Shaka (c. 1783–1828), king of the Zulu' (*Oxford Dictionary of National Biography* (Oxford: Oxford University Press, online edition, 2004): article 54934.

Peires, Jeff (ed). *Before and After Shaka: Papers in Nguni History* (Grahamstown: Rhodes University, Institute of Social and Economic Research, 1981).

Plant, Robert. *The Zulu in Three Tenses: Being a Forecast of the Zulu's Future in the Light of his Past* (Pietermaritzburg: P Davis & Sons, 1905).

Poland, Marguerite, David Hammond-Tooke and Leigh Voigt. *The Abundant Herds: A Celebration of the Nguni Cattle of the Zulu People* (Vlaeberg: Fernwood Press, 2003).

Preston, Adrian (ed). *The South African Journal of Sir Garnet Wolseley 1879–1880* (Cape Town: AA Balkema, 1973).

Pridmore, Julie. 'The Diary of Henry Francis Fynn, Jnr: 1883' (unpublished MA thesis, University of Natal, 1987).

Raum, OF. 'Aspects of Zulu Diplomacy in the 19th Century', *Afrika und Übersee*, 66 (1983): 25–42.

Ritter, EA. *Shaka Zulu* (Harmondsworth: Penguin Books, 1985).

Roberts, B. *The Zulu Kings* (London: Sphere Books, 1974).

Ross, Robert, Anne Kelk Mager and Bill Nasson (eds). *The Cambridge History of South Africa. Vol 2, 1885–1994* (Cambridge: Cambridge University Press, 2011).

Rycroft, DK and AB Ngcobo (eds). *The Praises of Dingana (Izibongo zikaDingana)* (Pietermaritzburg: University of Natal Press; Durban: Killie Campbell Africana Library, 1988).

Samuelson, RCA. *Long, Long Ago* (Durban: Knox Printing and Publishing, 1929).

Saunders, Christopher (ed). *Black Leaders in Southern Africa* (London: Heinemann, 1979).

Saunders, Christopher (ed). *Illustrated History of South Africa: The Real Story*, 3rd edition (Cape Town: The Reader's Digest Association South Africa, 1994).

Shamase, MZ. *Zulu Potentates from Earliest to Zwelithini kaBhekuzulu* (Durban: SM Publications, 1996).

Shooter, Rev Joseph. *The Kaffirs of the Natal and Zulu Country* (London: E Stanford, 1857).

Sithole, Jabulani. 'Changing Meanings of the Battle of Ncome and Images of King Dingane in Twentieth-Century South Africa' in *Zulu Identities: Being Zulu, Past and Present*, edited by Benedict Carton, John Laband and Jabulani Sithole (Pietermaritzburg: University of KwaZulu-Natal Press, 2008).

Smail, JL. *From the Land of the Zulu Kings* (Durban: AJ Pope, 1979).

Soga, John Henderson. *The South-Eastern Bantu* (Johannesburg: Witwatersrand University Press, 1930).

Special Reporter of the 'Cape Times' [RW Murray]. *Cetywayo, from the Battle of Ulundi to the Cape of Good Hope* (Cape Town: Murray & St Leger, 1879).

Stapleton, Timothy J. *Encyclopedia of African Colonial Conflicts*. 2 vols (Santa Barbara and Denver: ABC-CLIO, 2017).

Storey, William Kelleher. *Guns, Race, and Power in Colonial South Africa* (Cambridge: Cambridge University Press, 2008).

Stuart, James. *A History of the Zulu Rebellion 1906 and of Dinuzulu's Arrest, Trial and Expatriation* (London: Macmillan, 1913).

Stuart, James and D McK Malcolm (eds). *The Diary of Henry Francis Fynn* (Pietermaritzburg: Shuter & Shooter, 1969).

Swinney, GH. *A Zulu Boy's Recollections of the Zulu War*, edited by C de B Webb, *Natalia*, 8 (December 1978): 8–21.

Tabler, Edward C. *Pioneers of Natal and South-Eastern Africa 1552–1878* (Cape Town and Rotterdam: AA Balkema, 1977).

Taylor, Stephen. *Shaka's Children: A History of the Zulu People* (London: HarperCollins, 1994).

Temkin, Ben. *Buthelezi: A Biography* (London and Portland, OR: Frank Cass, 2003).

The Trial of Dinuzulu on Charges of High Treason, at Greyton, Natal, 1980–09 (Pietermaritzburg: 'Times' Printing and Publishing, 1910).

Theal, DG McC, *Progress of South Africa* (London: Linscott, 1900).

Theron, Bridget. 'King Cetshwayo and Victorian England: A Cameo of Imperial Interaction', *South African Historical Journal*, 56 (2006): 60–87.

Thompson, Leonard (ed). *African Societies in Southern Africa* (London: Heinemann, 1969).

Thompson, Paul. *The Zulu Rebellion of 1906 in Maps* (Howick: Brevitas, 2001).

Van Wyk, AJ. *Dinuzulu en die Usutu-Opstand van 1888* (Pretoria: Staatsdrukker, 1983).

Vijn, Cornelius. *Cetshwayo's Dutchman. Being the Private Journal of a White Trader in*

Zululand during the British Invasion, translated and edited by the Right Rev J W Colenso, Bishop of Natal (London: Longmans, Green, 1880).

Von Sicard, H. 'Shaka and the North', *African Studies*, 14, 4 (January 1955): 145–153.

Waetjen, Thembisa and Gerhard Maré. 'Shaka's Aeroplane: The Take-off and Landing of Inkatha, Modern Zulu Nationalism and Royal Politics' in *Zulu Identities: Being Zulu, Past and Present*, edited by Benedict Carton, John Laband and Jabulani Sithole (Pietermaritzburg: University of KwaZulu-Natal Press, 2008).

Walker, Eric A. *A History of Southern Africa*, 3rd edition (London: Longmans, Green, 1968).

War Office: Intelligence Division. *Précis of Information Concerning Zululand with a Map. Corrected to December, 1894* (London: Her Majesty's Stationery Office, 1894).

Webb, C de B and JB Wright (eds and translators). *The James Stuart Archive of Recorded Oral Evidence Relating to the History of the Zulu and Neighbouring Peoples*. 6 vols (Pietermaritzburg: University of Natal Press; Durban: Killie Campbell Africana Library, 1976, 1979, 1982, 1986, 2001, 2014).

Webb, C de B and JB Wright (eds). *A Zulu King Speaks: Statements Made by Cetshwayo kaMpande on the History and Customs of His People* (Pietermaritzburg: University of Natal Press; Durban: Killie Campbell Africana Library, 1978).

Welsh, David. *The Roots of Segregation: Native Policy in Natal 1845–1910* (Cape Town: Oxford University Press, 1971).

Williams, J Michael. *Chieftaincy, the State, and Democracy: Political Legitimacy in Post-Apartheid South Africa* (Bloomington: Indiana University Press, 2010).

Wilson, Monica and Leonard Thompson (eds). *The Oxford History of South Africa*. 2 vols (Oxford: Oxford University Press, 1969 and 1971).

Wood, Marilee (ed). *Zulu Treasures: Of Kings and Commoners. A Celebration of the Material Culture of the Zulu People* (Ulundi: KwaZulu Cultural Museum; Durban: The Local History Museums, 1996).

Worden, Nigel. *The Making of Modern South Africa: Conquest, Apartheid, Democracy*, 4th edition (Oxford: Wiley-Blackwell, 2007).

Wright, John. 'Pre-Shakan Age-Group Formations among the Northern Nguni', *Natalia*, 8 (1978): 22–30.

Wright, John. 'The Dynamics of Power and Conflict in Late 18th and Early 19th Centuries: A Critical Reconstruction' (unpublished PhD thesis, University of the Witwatersrand, 1989).

Wright, John. 'AT Bryant and the "Wars of Shaka"', *History in Africa*, 18 (1991): 409–425.

Wright, John. 'Reflections on the Politics of Being "Zulu"' in *Zulu Identities: Being Zulu, Past and Present*, edited by Benedict Carton, John Laband and Jabulani Sithole (Pietermaritzburg: University of KwaZulu-Natal Press, 2008).

Wylie, Dan. 'Textual Incest: Nathaniel Isaacs and the Development of the Shaka Myth', *History in Africa*, 19 (1992): 411–433.

Wylie, Dan. *Savage Delight: White Myths of Shaka* (Pietermaritzburg: University of Natal Press, 2000).

Wylie, Dan. *Myth of Iron: Shaka in History* (Pietermaritzburg: University of KwaZulu-Natal Press, 2006.)

Wylie, Dan. 'White Myths of Shaka' in *Zulu Identities: Being Zulu, Past and Present*, edited by Benedict Carton, John Laband and Jabulani Sithole (Pietermaritzburg: University of KwaZulu-Natal Press, 2008).
Wylie, Dan. *Shaka: A Pocket Biography* (Johannesburg: Jacana, 2011).

ACKNOWLEDGEMENTS

This is the second book I have written since Jonathan Ball, now the Editor-at-Large at the publishing house he founded, brought me back into the fold. His keen enthusiasm for this project, which he initially proposed, has braced me at every stage of research and writing. At Jonathan Ball Publishers I have been fortunate to have been taken in hand once again by an admirably proficient team. Ester Levinrad, the publisher, and Ceri Prenter, the editorial manager, have kept their fingers on the pulse of this endeavour. Alfred LeMaitre, the freelance editor and project manager, has for a second time guided a book of mine to completion with infinite professionalism, tact and patience. Kevin Shenton, and his assistant, Danel van Jaarsveld, were responsible for the elegant design and typesetting, and also for the complex maps. The expert proofreader, Paul Wise, rooted out my remaining textual lapses. And last (because that is where the index always is in a book) my thanks are due to Sanet le Roux, who compiled this one. I am also very grateful to those generous individuals and to the unfailingly helpful staff of the institutions who gave their permission for the illustrations that appear in this book.

Greyton, a pretty village in the Overberg nestled in the lee of the Riviersonderend Mountains, has proved the perfect place to amble, ponder

and then write. Even so, idyllic surroundings are not in themselves sufficient, and without Fenella to sustain me this book would have been a far
more arduous undertaking than it has proved.

INDEX

INDEX

427

INDEX

www.ingramcontent.com/pod-product-compliance
Lightning Source LLC
Chambersburg PA
CBHW071728270326

41928CB00013B/2595